45 $\frac{00}{1}$

CONSCRIPTS
AND
DESERTERS

CONSCRIPTS

—— AND ——

DESERTERS

THE ARMY AND FRENCH SOCIETY
DURING THE REVOLUTION
AND EMPIRE

Alan Forrest

New York   Oxford
OXFORD UNIVERSITY PRESS
1989

Oxford University Press

Oxford   New York   Toronto
Delhi   Bombay   Calcutta   Madras   Karachi
Petaling Jaya   Singapore   Hong Kong   Tokyo
Nairobi   Dar es Salaam   Cape Town
Melbourne   Auckland

and associated companies in
Berlin   Ibadan

Original title of French Edition
Déserteurs et Insoumis sous la Révolution et l'Empire

Published by Oxford University Press, Inc.,
200 Madison Avenue, New York, New York 10016

Oxford is a registered trademark of Oxford University Press

Library of Congress Cataloging-in-Publication Data
Forrest, Alan I.
Conscripts and deserters.
Translation of: Déserteurs et insoumis sous
la Révolution et l'Empire.
Bibliography: p.
Includes index.
1. France—History, Military—1789–1815.
2. France. Armée—History—Revolution, 1789–1799.
3. France. Armée—History—Napoleonic Wars, 1800–1815.
4. Napoleonic Wars, 1800–1814—Desertions—France.
5. France. Armée—Recruiting, enlistment, etc.
6. France—History—Napoleonic Wars, 1800–1815—
Draft resisters.   I. Title.
DC151.F6713   1989   944.04   88-34568
ISBN 0-19-505937-9

2 4 6 8 9 7 5 3 1

Printed in the United States of America
on acid-free paper

Acknowledgments

I CAME to the study of desertion and draft-dodging by a somewhat oblique route, almost as a by-product of work on charity and Revolutionary social policy. That it has now grown into a full-length study is due in no small measure to the insights and encouragement of others. Financial assistance with archival research was provided by the British Academy, by the Sir Ernest Cassell Educational Trust, and by the University of Manchester. Academic assistance came from many different sources. I owe much to the help unstintingly given by archivists in whose *dépôts* I worked, both at the Archives Nationales and in the cluster of departmental archives whose holdings form the basis of this study—in Aurillac, Bordeaux, Epinal, Foix, Lille, Valence, Vannes, and Versailles. In my "home" department of the Hauts-de-Seine, the archive staff were generous in bringing much-needed documentation from far-flung corners of the country. Their interest and assistance is greatly appreciated. So, too, is the constructive criticism offered by colleagues at various seminars and colloquia where I have had the opportunity to present some of the ideas contained in the present book. In particular I should like to thank Roger Dupuy and François Lebrun at Rennes, Jean Nicholas at Paris-VII, Alison Patrick at Melbourne, Steve Kaplan at Cornell, and John Merriman at Yale.

Fellow historians have rallied round with ideas and inspiration. Clive Emsley of the Open University advised me on the eighteenth-century police; Colin Jones of Exeter University and Peter Jones of Birmingham passed me valuable references to military sources. In France, Louis Bergès let me read his excellent thesis on conscription problems in the Southwest, and Frédéric Rousseau, at the University of Montpellier, entered into a lengthy and illuminating correspondence on his work on the Hérault. Jonathan Dalby on the Cantal and Michael Broers on Piedmont provided insights into the problem of recruitment in a local context, and helped convince me that there really was a subject there worth studying at all. Jean-Paul Bertaud of the Sorbonne and Isser Woloch of Columbia shared with me their vast experience of the Revolutionary and Napoleonic armies. Back in Manchester I have benefited from the comparative insights shed by various of my colleagues in Modern History, and have been fortunate in the succession of research students—Godfrey Rogers, Simon Reeve, Martin Stocker, Piers Willson, and Jon Skinner—with whom I have had the opportunity to work. Historical research is in so many ways a collaborative enterprise, and their contribution to the writing of this book has been considerable.

On the publishing side, my warmest thanks are due to Nancy Lane and her colleagues at Oxford University Press in New York who have seen the English version of this book through the press.

Three final words of thanks are due. To Richard Cobb, for ideas and inspiration over two decades of research in Revolutionary history: the very subject matter of this book owes much to his influence and to his unwavering belief that history belongs as much to those who suffer from it as to the politicians and policy-makers. To Mireille Marchant, whose kindness, hospitality and unfailing cheerfulness have been a source of support on repeated visits to Paris. And, most of all, to my wife, Rosemary Morris, who must rather too often have felt herself the victim of desertion and *insoumission* during the ingestion period of the present work.

Preface

THIS BOOK is not about military history, at least not in the conventional sense of that term. Rather it is an examination of the varied responses to the massive militarization that France underwent in the revolutionary and Napoleonic years—responses that divided Frenchmen against Frenchmen and often created conflict between local communities and the ambitions of the centralist state. The scale of that militarization had no precedent in France's previous history; nor was there to be anything remotely comparable during the remainder of the nineteenth century, when the numbers forcibly recruited for the armies remained generally modest and when disaffection was in consequence contained. Between 1791 and 1814 the government's appetite for recruits seemed insatiable, especially in the last years of the Empire when no sacrifice seemed too great in the quest for military glory. In all some two to three million men were incorporated into the revolutionary and Napoleonic battalions, many of them against their will and without regard to the long-established traditions of their local communities. With the introduction of annual conscriptions under the Loi Jourdan in Year VI, the draft became for nineteen- and twenty-year-old peasant boys a part of the routine of growing up, a sort of *rite de passage* that marked their adolescence. For many the routine quality of conscription was to end their resistance and guarantee their smooth incorporation in the ranks. For others, however, it merely added to the difficulties they incurred in avoiding the recruiting-sergeant and remaining with their families in their native villages. Their resentment directed against the army, the Emperor, or the village mayor was to remain a fact of political life throughout the long years of war.

This resentment was demonstrated in a number of different ways, but especially in consistently high rates of desertion and in the deliberate and stubborn avoidance of service by hundreds of thousands of young men for whom the military lifestyle held few charms. This book is about these unwilling soldiers and the lengths to which they were forced to go to escape the clutches of their regiments. It is also about the many side-effects of their defiance—their impact on the military and the morale of the armies, on political opinion at home, the social fabric of local villages, and the Napoleonic dream of bringing about a coherent and centralist state. The arrival on French soil of a whole army of fugitives could only add to the problem of crime and lawlessness and threaten the judicial order on which the government was so dependent. Their presence in villages where royalists and *chouans* were actively recruiting for their counterrevolutionary crusades necessarily added further strains to political loyalties. More generally, the fact that thousands of young men were in hiding in or near to their native communities supplied so many others with an immediate problem of conscience and of loyalty—parents and younger brothers, their peergroup in the community, local farmers in desperate need of casual labor, mayors and other officials who were charged with law enforcement in the countryside. Indirectly as well as directly, the refractory conscript soon threw down a formidable challenge to the pretensions of the state.

The state responded increasingly by turning the full panoply of its powers against deserters and *insoumis* and the communities that offered them protection. Policing was increased; garrisons were imposed on the homes of anyone suspected of harboring fugitives; fines were levied on entire villages in an attempt to break local loyalties; and mobile columns of soldiers swept across the countryside in a search for the young and able-bodied. Over conscription, as over no other single issue, the interests of the state and the local community were seen to come into open conflict, and the state had no other recourse but to repression. Ordinary Frenchmen were increasingly forced to face up to their responsibilities and to take sides in a conflict of loyalties that pitted the interests of the nation against those of the community. Desertion, in other words, soon ceased to be solely or even primarily a military issue, and it is its wider ramifications that are the principal concern of this study. The conscriptions of the Imperial years were imposed with increasing success on a demoralized population, but the cost—in ill-will, resentment, and covert defiance—was there for all to see. The demands of the state were not accepted without protest, and the military demands were those that were most sullenly contested. For conscription threatened the rural economy, the integrity of the family, the traditional autarchy of the village. It created an open clash between the archaic and the modern, and though in the long term the modern undoubtedly triumphed, in the short term it antagonized public opinion and put the governability of the state at risk. In a recent article the American historian Isser Woloch depicts conscription as a battleground between "individual and local communities on the one hand and a distant impersonal state on the other," and he calls for a substantial examination of the problem to throw light on the essential nature of the Napoleonic regime and its relationship with those it administered. (1) This gap in current historiography seems a serious one, and one that is as puzzling for the revolutionary period as for the Empire. It is hoped that this text will provide an answer.

Manchester, U.K.   A. F.
October 1988

Contents

CONSCRIPTS
AND
DESERTERS

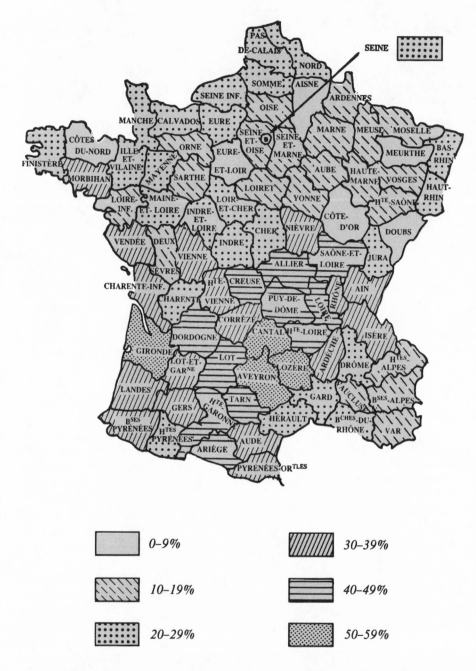

SEINE

Legend	
0–9%	30–39%
10–19%	40–49%
20–29%	50–59%

Deserters and *insoumis* as a percentage of persons conscripted from
Year VII to Year XIII (according to Hargenvilliers's figures).

Labels on map: PAS-DE-CALAIS, NORD, SOMME, AISNE, SEINE INF., OISE, ARDENNES, MANCHE, CALVADOS, EURE, SEINE-ET-MARNE, MARNE, MEUSE, MOSELLE, CÔTES-DU-NORD, ILLE-ET-VILAINE, ORNE, EURE-ET-LOIR, SEINE-ET-OISE, MEURTHE, BAS-RHIN, FINISTÈRE, MORBIHAN, MAYENNE, SARTHE, LOIRET, AUBE, HAUTE-MARNE, VOSGES, HAUT-RHIN, LOIRE-INF., MAINE-ET-LOIRE, INDRE-ET-LOIRE, LOIR-ET-CHER, YONNE, H^TE-SAÔNE, CÔTE-D'OR, DOUBS, VENDÉE, DEUX-SÈVRES, VIENNE, INDRE, CHER, NIÈVRE, ALLIER, SAÔNE-ET-LOIRE, JURA, CHARENTE-INF., H^TE-VIENNE, CREUSE, PUY-DE-DÔME, LOIRE, RHÔNE, AIN, ISÈRE, CHARENTE, CORRÈZE, CANTAL, H^TE-LOIRE, ARDÈCHE, DRÔME, H^TES-ALPES, DORDOGNE, LOT, LOZÈRE, GARD, VAUCLUSE, B^SES-ALPES, GIRONDE, LOT-ET-GAR^NE, AVEYRON, LANDES, H^TE-GARONNE, TARN, HÉRAULT, B^CHES-DU-RHÔNE, VAR, GERS, B^SES-PYRÉNÉES, H^TES-PYRÉNÉES, ARIÈGE, AUDE, PYRÉNÉES-OR^TLES

1

The Problem and Its Context

BETWEEN THE DECLARATION of hostilities against Austria in 1792 and Napoleon's final debacle in 1814 France remained almost continuously at war, frequently standing alone against coalitions of the other great powers of Europe. Nor were these ordinary wars to be compared with those of the eighteenth century. For the French in this period were impelled not merely by the desire for limited conquest but by new and more ideological impulses. Nationalism and revolutionary zeal mingled in the 1790s to form a heady and dangerous cocktail. France believed, and her leaders preached in the incessant propaganda of the Revolutionary years, that this war was about absolutes of good and evil, that the people were fighting a war for liberty and against tyranny, for their revolution against the reimposition of monarchical absolutism. The conflict was not just between two armies but between two political systems, and such a war could not be settled amicably by the agreed exchange of plots of territory or by the cession of colonial possessions. It was widely believed that it could end only in the defeat of one political system by its enemies, in the spread of revolution across the whole of Europe, or in the forcible reimposition of the Bourbons on the French people by the victorious monarchies. The evidence of contemporaries makes it very clear that this vision of an ideological war between two irreconcilable systems is not the invention of historians and political scientists looking back on the period from the vantage point of the twentieth century. Brissot was perhaps the most voluble of the many members of the Convention who believed that the Revolution had the choice between being expansionist and being destroyed. The Declaration of Pillnitz and the Brunswick Manifesto left little doubt that the Austrians would push home the advantage of any victory by reimposing the absolute rule of Louis XVI on a defeated France. The carnage of the September Massacres bears tragic witness to the level of fear in Paris that such threats were on the point of being implemented. Under Napoleon the messianic idealism of the early years of the Revolution had certainly faded, and the thirst for liberty had given way to more traditional, imperialistic ambition; how-

3

ever, the extent of that ambition posed a threat to the stability and security of the rest of Europe, and the Allied powers were unlikely to be satisfied by a victory that did not also overthrow France's internal political institutions. Napoleon's prestige, too, was so tightly bound up in the successes of French arms abroad that foreign conquest became the consuming goal of his reign. However awesome the cost in men and materials, winning the war remained the principal aim of the state throughout the Revolutionary and Napoleonic years.

It also demanded the build-up of state power and pretension to a degree unparalleled in the previous history of modern Europe. The scale of the war had the ineluctable effect of increasing the role that the state had to play in the lives of the French people: organizing billets, policing the passage of troops, requisitioning foodstuffs, ordering carters and wheelwrights into the service of the armies, organizing the collection of saltpetre and the manufacture of guns, finding uniforms to clothe the troops, directing the distribution of supplies, and persuading farmers to part with mules and horses. All these tasks were essential to the success of the military effort, yet all required innovation and change in the traditional role of the state and the traditional expectations of the people. All were liable to be resented as unwarranted intrusions into the accepted balance of local society. Yet they all paled into relative insignificance compared to the problems implicit in recruiting millions of young Frenchmen for military service—a level of recruitment unknown to previous generations and widely resented as an attack on the liberties of local communities. Military demands on this scale brought with them a sharp increase in the policing and regimentation of civilian society. They also brought to a head the opposition of local people to the demands of the center, sparking off revolts and resistance on an unprecedented scale. Especially after the introduction of annual conscription in Year VII, the issue of recruitment divided French opinion like no other, moulding attitudes and mentalities in provincial France and going far to explain the reaction of Frenchmen to the new order of the Napoleonic regime.

For this reason, the scope of this book is not limited to the relatively narrow field of military recruitment and of the resistance that it caused, but looks at the implications of that resistance for government and administration, especially in the villages and hamlets of rural France where opposition to the draft was often most intense. It was not just the success of the armies that was at stake, but the credibility of the nation-state. Reports from government *commissaires* and prefects expressed constant anxiety that the entire fabric of French society would be eroded and saw in the recruitment issue a dangerous lever by which enemies of France might hope to destroy confidence and undermine public order. The majority of the population was in no sense counterrevolutionary by instinct; rather they were portrayed as being easily swayed by temptation and seduction, poorly educated and politically naive, a ready prey to the cunning insinuations of men better informed and more ruthless than themselves. But the military question exposed them to such approaches, since for many Frenchmen the service demanded by the government quickly assumed the guise of a new and unwelcome *corvée,* a tax in blood to a distant and impersonal master, imposed in the name of a national cause that they understood only in the dimmest terms (1). In Year IV the Directory's *commissaire* in Pau summed up the feelings of many of his colleagues when he reported that the main danger facing the government lay in the apathy and the lack of political concern that was widespread in the countryside of the Southwest. It was this which made the majority such easy game for extremists:

> L'esprit public se compose de quatre parties plus ou moins opposés. Le plus nombreux et le moins puissant est formé de ces hommes faibles de moyens, faibles de caractère, toujours irrésolus, toujours tremblants. Ils aiment la Constitution mais ne peuvent encore croire à leur bonheur: ils ne peuvent croire à la stabilité et au maintien de cette liberté douce et aimable qu'elle leur procure, et leur imagination pusillanime leur fait sans cesse redouter la sanglante réaction de la royauté ou de l'anarchie. (2)

In rural France especially, public opinion often consisted of such people, confused by politics, reassured by their traditional ways, fearful that these traditions would be disrupted by the ambitions of the government in Paris. And for many nothing in those tumultuous years seemed as unsettling and disruptive as the fear that they would be removed from their communities by government order and forced to serve as soldiers in the revolutionary or Napoleonic armies.

Such was the context that most commonly produced a problem of resistance, which would in turn lead to conflict between civil and military society and between the local community and the state. Of course it could be pointed out, and with some justice, that there was much in this context that was in no way novel, that was taken for granted by the state and the citizenry alike. Michel Auvray, in his book on desertion and conscientious objection, is right to stress that the refusal of military service is an age-old problem that affected the Roman Empire as it did the European armies of the two world wars. In World War I, indeed, the French army was more prone than its neighbors to shoot deserters as an example to others. Faced with mutinies and mass desertions, especially in 1917, the military turned to repression to reimpose the authority of the officers and, through them, the authority of the state (3). Where Auvray's interpretation is less relevant for the eighteenth century is in the importance he attaches to the role of *objecteurs,* of those who, through a commitment to pacifism or a principled rejection of killing, refused to become soldiers and accepted whatever consequences the state might reserve for them with apparent equanimity. The *objecteur,* the man of conscience, emerged in the nineteenth rather than the eighteenth century, in the English armies of the Boer War and throughout the continent between 1914 and 1918 (4). In the period that concerns us, those rejecting military obligation would seem to have acted from more prosaic motives, for there is no evidence that pacifism had taken a hold on the French peasant mind of the Ancien Regime or had been inculcated by the belligerent nationalism of the Revolution. In the hundreds of depositions made to tribunals and the numerous interrogations that accompanied the trials of deserters and *insoumis,* there is nothing to suggest a resistance rooted in a principled opposition to war. Rather the eighteenth-century deserter acted out of traditionalism, from a well-founded suspicison of the effects of the war on his conservative rural lifestyle. In no sense can he be called a radical for his act of rebellion or defiance.

To this extent the role of the refractory after 1790 was little different from that of his counterpart under the Ancien Regime. Eighteenth-century generals complained continually of the losses of manpower that they suffered as a result of desertion, and not even the threat of the most savage punishments, including running the gauntlet and lengthy terms in the galleys, provided a real deterrent (5). In periods of war the death sentence had been imposed as a routine penalty, and even in peacetime anxious governments had resorted to capital sentences. As recently as 1716 a royal *ordonnance* had attempted to stave off a crisis in the army by reinstituting the death penalty, generally by hanging, for men convicted of desertion. In accordance with the terms of this ordinance, those found guilty of deserting in foreign countries were to be *pendus et étranglés,* while men deserting inside France who had not, in consequence, placed their fellows at risk were to be given some hope of survival. Where one soldier had deserted on his own, the court had the discretion to impose a death sentence or not, as it might elect; where several men were involved in the same incident, they were made to draw lots in groups of three to determine which of the three must die (6). If such measures were intended to deter, there is little evidence that they bore fruit. Indeed, it is arguable that the very severity of army life in the Ancien Regime and the callous disregard shown by officers for the welfare of their men contributed significantly to the desertion rate. Soldiering was poorly esteemed by the population at large, and enlightened opinion treated the individual *fantassin,* infantryman, with open contempt. In *Candide* Voltaire drew a picture of the massed armies of Europe as being composed of the dregs of their respective societies, of "un million d'assassins enrégimentés courant d'un bout à l'autre de l'Europe," assuaging their appetite for pillage and banditry. In the pages of the *Encyclopédie* the infantryman of the French royal armies is similarly maligned—an object of scorn and pity to be compared only to the lowest rabble, "la canaille, parce qu'elle est à meilleur marché" (7). This is overharsh, and André Corvisier concludes that whereas the bourgeoisie and the intelligentsia increasingly held this view, the popular classes of society held on longer to the feudal vision that respected those offering protection to the rest of society through "le métier des armes" (8). Examining Parisian recruitment in the years after 1763, Jean Chagniot notes that many of the recruits lied about their origins and their profession, implying that they were joining the armies in an attempt to conceal their past and to seek anonymity elsewhere. Only 14 percent of the men in his sample were born in Paris, and the majority he classes as "de pauvres provinciaux venus à Paris, parfois avec leurs parents, mais plus souvent isolés, et dont l'activité déclarée ne révèle aucune qualification" (9). Often the eighteenth-century soldier would seem to have drifted into soldiering through boredom or misfortune rather than to have chosen the army in any positive sense as a career. Poverty was more likely to have driven him to volunteer than any burning military zeal. The occasional glimpse into army life that we can glean from the memoirs of serving soldiers tends to confirm this rather dejected and fatalistic impression. Army life *was* hard and often brutal. One diarist, describing the pestilential conditions that reigned in a French field-hospital during the War of the Austrian Succession, tells of the horror he felt when he looked at his wounded comrades, three-quarters of whom died within three days of admission. It is the everyday banality of his words, the brutal and matter-of-fact style of his presentation that make his account of death and dying so moving and so deeply harrowing (10).

Degrading conditions of service and long years of physical suffering undoubtedly played their part in stimulating desertion during the Ancien Regime, even among men who had signed on voluntarily. Exact statistics for desertion are difficult to determine, in part because there was still a substantial element of seasonal campaigning in the eighteenth century, with soldiers slipping off home to their farms and villages at the end of each campaign, but in part also because generals did not want to draw attention to the extent of the problem in their own ranks. During the 1780s Jean-Paul Bertaud suggests that in an average year there were approximately 3,000 desertions from the French armies, though in times of war these figures would increase dramatically (11). By the end of the Hundred Years' War, for instance, the figure for desertion had increased to more than 10,000 annually, a reflection both of the size of the armies compared to peacetime and of the degree of demoralization in the ranks (12). Despondency could spread rapidly in a force in which there was little bond of sympathy or camaraderie between officers and infantrymen, and in which the physical contact between them was deliberately kept to the very minimum. The fact that France had what was effectively a peasant army only added to the problem of indiscipline, as men were lured home by simple homesickness or by the call of the harvest. Many had lived on the margin of civilian society, earning the barest subsistence as seasonal harvesters or migrant workers; the extent of seasonal migration in the population at large provided protection for soldiers on the run or seeking refuge from the *maréchaussée* or constabulary. Eighteenth-century generals were well-briefed on the favored refuges of soldiers under their command: the Comtat Venaissin in the early part of the century, until the French government reached an understanding with the Pope; Catalonia and the Spanish side of the Pyrénées, especially favored by the men of the Southwest who knew every inch of the smugglers' trails across the mountains; the Dutch coastline, a natural hiding-place for deserters from the northern regiments of Artois and Picardy because of its marshy topography; and, above all, the territory of the Holy Roman Empire, where they could breathe freely without fear of capture or extradition to France (13). To contemporaries desertion seemed more a necessary corollary to an army than a form of independent criminal activity; officials talked of deserters without any marked rancor. Desertion was seen as being timeless and even inevitable, as constituting a natural and necessary part of French rural life (14).

This casualness of approach was, of course, deceptive, although even the army was not blind to the seasonal needs of agriculture and the short-term demand for labor in a peasant economy. During the Ancien Regime the apparently casual attitude to service was further exaggerated by the widespread practice of *billardage,* whereby men would leave their regiment with the express aim of joining another either to be with their friends or, more commonly, to pocket a second signing-on bounty (15). Desertion was so common that amnesties had to be used at regular intervals to lure former soldiers back into uniform; yet, with no guarantee that he would be released from service after the fixed term for which he had enlisted, the deserter would require a considerable inducement if he were to be attracted back voluntarily (16). It is perhaps indicative of the scale of the problem that the *maréchaussée,* whose responsibility was otherwise restricted to patrolling highways and chasing vagabonds, was also periodically given the task of recapturing men on the run from their regiment. Choiseul's definition of the work of the force was quite explicit. They were constituted "for the capture of deserters, the safety of travellers, and the transport of the tax receipts," but as Iain Cameron has shown in his study of the Auvergne and the Guyenne, these were not functions that necessarily endeared the *maréchaussée* to the local community (17). There is little evidence that villagers viewed deserters with any particular fear or hatred. Occasional denunciations were reserved for those who passed from simple desertion to brigandage or banditry, crimes that harmed local people and posed a threat to their domestic well-being. The military, of course, saw things very differently. The eighteenth-century army laid great store by the standard and the thoroughness of its training, and every man who deserted represented a considerable loss of investment. Generals therefore went to great lengths to lure deserters back to their posts and to secure the prompt release of any who were taken prisoner by the enemy in time of war. In 1758 Belle-Isle was more than happy to pay the Prussians a ransom of eleven *livres* for every additional French soldier in Prussian hands after an exchange of prisoners had been concluded; their battle experience was too valuable to be lightly cast aside (18).

If there were continuities between the pattern of the Ancien Regime and that imposed by the Revolution, there were also substantial differences. Most importantly, the majority of young Frenchmen were not threatened with the reality of military service as they would be in the later years of the Napoleonic campaigns. The scale of soldiering was much more discreet. Whereas the Revolution would set out to create an army of three-quarters of a million men, the entire period from 1700 to 1763, encompassing the great European wars of the eighteenth century, used only 2 million, and they included a substantial force of around 300,000 foreign mercenaries (19). At the time of the Seven Years' War the total numbers incorporated in the regular army amounted to 200,000; yet France at that time had 3,800,000 men between sixteen and forty years old on whose energies she could have called (20). So in all, not more than 1 in 20 of those eligible was actually called on to make the very real sacrifice of serving in person in the regiments of Louis XV. Just as important was the fact that service was different in kind from the national recruitment of the Revolution or the annual conscriptions of the Empire. Men were recruited locally to serve in regiments commanded by local nobles. The recruiting-officers would in many cases be personally known to them, and the whole aspect of recruitment seemed more acceptable because of a personal contract between seigneur and commoner. As Corvisier has observed, such recruitment, once account is taken of the seigneurial nature of Ancien Regime society, made sense to local people in a way that the national appeals after 1792 could not hope to do. For "ce recrutement direct par les recruteurs naturels du régiment, eu égard à son caractère de recrutement local, voire seigneurial, donne à chaque régiment un aspect bien particulier, principalement en temps de paix" (21). It is true that in times of war and national emergency this rather gentlemanly way of proceeding proved inadequate to the King's needs, and they often resorted to the use of professional *racoleurs,* to *embaucheurs* and recruitment agencies, to the hated and feared *marchands d'hommes* who would set up their stalls at the local fair or market or *battre la caisse* in village squares, lying, cheating, and bribing until the requisite number of recruits had been assembled (22). But the normal peacetime methods of recruitment would have aroused little sustained complaint.

What did arouse widespread anger in the eighteenth-century countryside was the complementary force to the regular battalions, the *milice royale.* This was intended to be a reserve force that could be raised at short notice to protect the local community or to help cope with some national emergency; it had been first introduced in 1688 by Louvois to fill gaps in regular recruitment (23). As originally conceived, its military role was not to include active fighting, which was the preserve of the line army, but was confined to ancillary duties such as the guarding of baggage, the garrison of frontier towns, or the defense of the rear of fighting columns (24). Unlike the regular regiments, the militia's recruitment involved elements of both chance and compulsion. It was highly unequal in its demands on the population, and this perceived unfairness lay at the root of its unpopularity. In coastal regions, for instance, the inhabitants were often totally exempt from service with the armies; instead, they would be called upon to act as coastguards and give warning of enemy attack from the sea (25). Individual towns might enjoy total exemptions—like Saint-Ybars near Pamiers, which was never called on to supply a single militiaman in the course of the century, to the visible anger of other towns and villages in the surrounding area (26). Or again, whole provinces might at one time or another be exempted or specially favored—the pays de Gex, for instance, was privileged in this way until 1726, when it was suddenly ordered to provide fifteen men; and the province of Roussillon was allowed in the early years to raise its own militia and opt out of the national scheme (27). But for those who did have to serve, that service could be time-consuming and onerous. In peacetime there was generally little reason for grievance. The militiaman might be expected to undergo training for two weeks each year—at Pézenas this program was reduced to nine days—and he might have to perform some services in the community. In return he could expect to enjoy a rather privileged position if he were seeking employment (28). In times of crisis, however, *miliciens* were used in active combat in lieu of volunteer regiments, and the period of incorporation was often arbitrarily extended to suit the convenience of the military (29). The extent of militia service was in any case becoming more grueling as the century progressed. Claude Achard has shown that between 1740 and 1788 the period of service in Pézenas was doubled from three to six years. And the numbers demanded increased threateningly in wartime. Pézenas was a community of approximately 8,000 persons, which in normal circumstances was called on to provide 7 *miliciens* each year. But war or national panic increased these demands to 15 men in 1745, 33 in 1743, and 50 in 1689 (30). For this reason militia service posed a real and unpredictable threat to the young males in the community, and they would go to considerable lengths to extricate themselves from any possibility of having to perform service in person. Replacements were allowed for those with the necessary funds to provide an able-bodied villager to serve in their stead—an economic criterion that caused widespread anger among the poor—with the result that few bourgeois or notables ever ran the risk of being incorporated. Intendants were generally left with considerable latitude in determining how widely exemptions should run, but there was no thought that the wealthy should be expected to submit themselves to ballot. In 1743, for instance, "il y eut exemption pour les gros laboureurs, les gros fermiers, leurs fils ou valets, les garçons ayant charrue ou exploitant une ferme de 300 livres, les bergers d'au moins cent bêtes, les marchands et artisans payant au moins 30 livres de capitation, les procureurs, greffiers, notaires, commis, employés, médecins, chirurgiens, apothicaires, les propriétaires d'un office d'au moins 4000 livres . . ." (31). The fact that servants and lackeys did not have to serve explains the desperate scramble for posts as "domestique, garde-chasse ou maître-valet" in the service of a local noble or public official whenever recruitment was imminent (32). In their bid to escape the *milice,* some young men went much further, and we hear regular reports in the 1760s and 1770s of voluntary self-mutilation among countrymen fearful that they would be chosen to serve. In 1766 the *subdélégué* at Remiremont complained that in his area such abuses were widespread, that peasants frequently tried to destroy their health by rubbing herbs into their eyes to induce blindness or by injecting open wounds with "mouches cantarides" to help turn them septic (33). Fear of the *milice* was capable of driving French peasant boys to the most extreme measures.

Statistically their fears appear grossly exaggerated, since an average of only about 100,000 men (or 1 in 40 of those eligible to serve) were called on to perform militia duty at any one time (34); however, for those incorporated the burden only seemed the greater. Their anger and resentment became focused on the recruitment process itself, the ceremony of the *tirage à sort* that determined which villagers were taken and which were allowed to go calmly about their everyday lives. This process was relatively simple to administer and would form the prototype of the recruitment principle adopted by the revolutionaries in 1793: all the young men of the commune between eighteen and forty years old, unmarried or married without children, would assemble on the village green and draw tickets from a hat—the *billet blanc* which gave them their liberty, or the *billet noir* which condemned them to serve. The intendant had overall charge of the operation. It was he who received from the *bureau de guerre* the demand for a fixed number of men from his area and who divided that number among the parishes he administered. It was a highly unpopular role, as was witnessed by the riots and outbreaks of popular violence that frequently accompanied the *tirage* (35). Around Lille, indeed, the government came to accept that such was the hatred of the militia in the local community that there was little point in insisting on the drawing of lots, since the unlucky men who drew the *mauvais numéros* would simply slip across the frontier and be lost to the French economy as well as to French arms (36). Public anger only increased as the century passed, for, although the numbers demanded oscillated wildly from year to year, it was clear that the *milice* was becoming a permanent part of the King's army, not a reserve arm in moments of crisis, and that the burden imposed on the people was increasing. Only for two brief periods was the force wholly disbanded—between 1715 and 1719 and again from 1721 to 1726 (37)—and over the century the proportion of the army that was composed of militiamen increased rapidly, until by 1789 there were five militiamen for every eight soldiers of the line (38).

The extent of popular outcry against militia service is faithfully reflected in the *cahiers de doléances* of 1789, especially in the parish *cahiers* that came closest to recording the true voice of local anger. Village communities throughout France seemed united in the belief that the raising of the *milice* was at best an unacceptable burden, at worst an outrage that ran counter to natural law and justice. One village, Saint-Vincent-Rive-d'Olt in the Quercy, suggested that the fundamental freedoms of the French peasant were at issue because "la milice à laquelle le cultivateur est assujetti est une servitude entièrement contraire aux lois constitutionnelles de l'Etat" (39). Agriculture suffered unnecessary deprivations and the whole balance of the local economy was put at risk, as those liable to be incorporated took every available precaution to avoid service. Again and again we hear the claim that the most common implication of the *tirage* was the lemminglike rush of youngsters seeking an escape through marriage or emigration. The parish *cahier* of Nouans was one of many that emphasized the damage that this could cause both to the lives of the individuals involved and to the communities to which they belonged. Precipitate marriages, it warned, led irreparably to misery and impoverishment, to families reduced to charity and to meager expedients if they were to avoid sinking into rootlessness and vagabondage. The *milice* compounded the problem by forcing the hand of the young; it "détermine à se marier des garçons qui n'ont pas seulement gagné de quoi s'habiller; de là naît une famille de pauvres, à qui les parents montrent à mendier, sitôt qu'ils sont en état de marcher" (40). Or again, the impending threat of military service might suffice to drive young men to leave their villages altogether, with the consequent risk of rural decay. Generally they drifted to the towns in search of work, often, as we have seen, as valets and footmen. As the *cahier* of the *tiers état de Troyes* noted, it was scarcely satisfactory, either from the point of view of agricultural production or from that of human dignity, that

> un garçon robuste, d'une taille riche et avantageuse, approche-t-il de l'âge fixé pour subir le sort, sa famille s'empresse pour l'y soustraire de découvrir dans la ville voisine, dans la capitale, la condition de quelque riche privilégié qui croit rehausser son éclat en s'escortant de la livrée fastueuse dont il couvre ces hommes de la plus riche taille, hommes robustes, dont les forces sont perdues à jamais pour la terre qu'ils deśertent. (41)

This last cry was repeated in one form or another all over the countryside, fearful lest the loss of vigorous young workers result in the undercultivation and even the premature abandonment of the land. The parishioners of Drugeac in the southern Massif regretted that rural depopulation would surely follow in the wake of the *tirage.* It was, they insisted, the King's job to provide for the defense of the realm with the regular soldiers who were recruited in the normal fashion to serve in his regiments:

> La nation payant au Roy un subside pour entretenir, soulager, et recruter ses troupes, les milices ne doivent point avoir lieu, cette levée de miliciens qui sont presque toujours sans fonction et sans presque aucune solde ni entretien

désolent les familles des laboureurs, causent l'émigration et en conséquence l'inculture des biens. (42)

Driven by such considerations, some rural *cahiers* went so far as to suggest that those engaged in agriculture should be exempted from service, and that the *tirage* should be restricted to "la classe des artistes et des domestiques non occupés à la culture des terres." (43)

Of course, even in bad years, not all those whose numbers were drawn at the *tirage* actually served in the militia. Money counted for a great deal, and the right to buy oneself out by providing another man to serve in one's stead effectively guaranteed, as it would for much of the Revolution, that the richer farmers, the bourgeois in the towns, and the astute and the *nantis,* were never to be found wasting years of their lives in the force. In many local communities the obligation of local boys to serve was effectively removed by the simple device of raising a *bourse,* levying an agreed sum of money from every household in the village. Those who contributed would be exempted from participating in the *tirage* and the money used to pay an indemnity to those unlucky enough to be designated. In practice, however, this kind of arrangement was regarded with intense dislike as an unjustified supplementary tax on local families, especially on those families with adolescent boys. The parish of Tassé protested in its *cahier* in 1789 that the scheme constituted a serious and unnecessary drain on limited resources:

> On a toléré cet usage et on ne pourrait avec justice l'empêcher; chacun est libre de faire de son argent l'emploi qu'il juge à propos. Cependant cet usage coûte à chaque paroisse, chaque année, environ 300 livres.... Ce n'est pas trop que de porter à 20 millions par an la somme de cet impôt indirect. (44)

Furthermore, with the coming of the Revolution and the encouragement of ideas of liberty and equality, the whole imposition that the militia had come to represent was intensely resented, especially in the rural areas. Even in peacetime, when the men chosen would not have to leave their villages or don their uniforms for war, their civil liberties were being infringed and a deep shadow was cast across their lives for a six-year period. This sentiment is admirably expressed by the *tiers état de Troyes:*

> Nous savons que celui que le sort de la milice a frappé ne quitte pas pour cela ses foyers en temps de paix, et qu'il continue, presque sans interruption, à vaquer aux travaux de l'agriculture. Mais est-il libre? Espèce de serf attaché à la glèbe, il ne peut plus s'absenter sans permission, soumis à des inspections, à des revues; il est privé, pendant six ans, du plus précieux de tous ses droits, celui de s'associer une compagne de son choix. (45)

Opposition to the *milice* was soon caught up in the generalized claim of Frenchmen for the restitution of their civil liberties.

That opposition expressed itself as much through desertion and draft dodging as it did through protest and petition. In particular, the distaste of local people for militia service was demonstrated in the high rates of absenteeism with which communities responded to the *tirage*. At Pézenas, Claude Achard relates, the normal rate of *insoumission* expressed by absence on the day of the *tirage* was between 2 and 8 percent; but when the local community was angered by the extent of the army's demands, peasant boys would stay away in droves—32 percent in 1752, for example, and 41 percent in 1755 (46). In many parts of France the idea of performing an act of personal military service was still very foreign to the peasant mentality, which continued to believe that only voluntary enlistment was acceptable as the basis for a national army. The concept of personal service, as Corvisier notes, found approval with none outside the ranks of the bourgeoisie and the Enlightened reformers. In the countryside it proved especially unpopular, because there "il rencontre aussi bien l'opposition de ce qui reste de l'esprit féodal, que de la nouvelle conception de la vie fondée sur l'économie et l'utilité publique" (47).

The rejection of militia service was just part of a growing dissatisfaction in the last decades of the Ancien Regime. Generals were concerned about the extent of desertions, intendants anxious about the incidence of disturbance and riot at recruitment meetings. But this dissatisfaction was not uniformly spread across France, with the consequence that it is difficult to generalize at national level on matters of attitude and mentality. France in the eighteenth century was still in many ways little more than a political unity, in which regional traditions and regional loyalties remained deeply entrenched. In part differences of response may be ascribed to geography, differences of mentality between town and country, pasture and agricultural land, agglomerated bourgs and dispersed habitation (48). In part they also reflect the kind of rural autarky that exists where market networks and administrative practice have had little impact. It is no accident that much of the most deeply rooted opposition to the military was to be found in remote and mountainous areas where modern government and the assumptions on which it is based had had little opportunity to penetrate. Describing Haute-Provence in the sixteenth century, Fernand Braudel remarked that there was neither powerful noble nor affluent cleric to impose order on the local population; furthermore,

> there was no tight urban network, so no administration, no towns in the proper sense of the word, and no gendarmes either, we might add. It is only in the lowlands that one finds closely knit, stifling society, a prebendal clergy, a haughty aristocracy, and an efficient system of justice. The hills were the refuge of liberty, democracy, and peasant "republics." (49)

These remarks were just as true in 1800, or in 1851. Recruitment laws that were respected in Paris Basin and that were devised for a single nation could easily incur opposition in the village communities of the South. It is not unexpected, therefore, that the highest desertion rates in the eighteenth-century armies were recorded in areas of difficult terrain far removed from the influence of central government: the peripheral areas of the country like the Pyrénées, the Alpine foothills in the Southeast, and the Flemish-speaking regions along the northern frontier (50).

These regional diversities were well-known to contemporaries, including the deputies of the National Assembly who addressed themselves to the problem of how best to reform the army that they had inherited. The chevalier des Pommelles, who wrote about the subject in 1789, noted that the taste for soldiering was a concept that was hard to define but one which should not for that reason be dismissed from consideration by the legislators. "Le goût," he warned, "tient à l'éducation, à l'habitude, aux circonstances et aux préjugés de chaque pays, au séjour des troupes; mais surtout il paraît subordonné d'une manière constante à l'influence du climat" (51). His explanation was principally a climatic one, with extremes of hot and cold apparently making the South of France exceptionally unpromising country for the recruiting-officer. He noted the evidence of the widely divergent figures for military service in the various provinces of the country: whereas in Alsace there was 1 soldier for every 61 members of the population, in Lorraine 1 for every 72, and in the Franche-Comté 1 for every 76, refractory areas of the Southwest produced relatively few volunteers—in the *généralité* of Auch a miserable 1 for each 628 of the population (52). Corvisier, analyzing the regimental records for 1716 in an attempt to construct a map of regional recruitment patterns, provides statistical corroboration for Pommelles' claims. The manpower provided by different regions was glaringly unequal, with Midi generally the least forthcoming part of the country, but Corvisier's detailed evidence suggests a much more subtle analysis than a simple north–south division. Using as his source the intendants' *enquête* of 1700, he shows that the three most willing areas of recruitment were indeed in the north and east—the *généralités* of Besançon, Châlons-sur-Marne, and Flandre-Artois-Cambraisis—but the region around Grenoble also came high on the list, and, even more surprisingly, the *généralité* of Montpellier was the fourth most cooperative in the entire country. In contrast *généralités* like Pau and Perpignan provided only a fraction of the men asked of them, while Rennes produced the lowest return of all, emphasizing Corvisier's conclusion that recruitment problems were in no sense a southern monopoly (53). Interestingly, the distaste of Bretons would seem to have been directed at service with regular battalions, since their response to militia service was noticeably more enthusiastic (54). The *milice* cannot, however, be seen as a general means of equalizing regional burdens, because here again the numbers of men demanded of local communities would appear to have borne only the slightest relationship to their population or their ability to answer the state's appeal. Pommelles, campaigning vigorously for some reform of the existing system, produced figures to demonstrate how absurd the levies often were. In Poitou, for instance, the *milice* in an average year took 1 young man in 11, whereas in neighboring Aunis it contented itself with 1 in every 48 (55). Even neighboring communes might be treated with outrageous inequity. In the province of Aunis he showed how the village of Jonsac had to produce 1 *milicien* of 11 possible candidates, while Saint-Amand-de-Noéré, just down the road, escaped with 1 man in a population of 126. The Ancien Regime recruiting system worked in the sense that sufficient men were found to fill the battalions, but Pommelles was not alone in seeing the methods used as constituting an affront to the ideal of equality in the new era that was dawning in 1789.

The early years of the Revolution brought entirely new changes, not just to recruitment practices, but to the nature and structure of the French armies. A government that claimed to act in the name of the people of France could not but listen to the expressed grievances that made up the *cahiers*. A government that legislated for equality of all its citizens before the law could not continue to depend on an army in which all the officers were nobles and where office was venal. A government that fought wars against the monarchies of Europe in the name of liberty could scarcely use as its instrument of liberation an army in which morale was low, discipline was imposed by savage corporal penalties, and the ordinary soldier was himself deprived of all his civil rights and privileges. More practically, once the Revolution turned its attentions to reforming the monarchy and to ending feudal privilege, it faced a major challenge from large sections of the aristocracy, who shut up their *châteaux* and chose to emigrate rather than accept the new political and social order in France. Since, under the terms of the Ségur Ordinance of 1781, all army officers had to boast four quarterings of nobility, the line army was commanded by men whose sympathies with the new political order could not be relied on, and relations between the politicians and the military in the early months of the Revolution were understandably strained. Many high-ranking officers were among the first Frenchmen to emigrate, abandoning their posts and their responsibilities rather than betray their king or their church. And the flood of emigration did not stop in 1789. Sam Scott has calculated that in the months between September 1791 and December 1792 the line army may have lost one-third or more of its officers through resignation, illegal absence, or political emigration (56). The yawning gaps in the officer ranks were just one reason why the Revolutionaries had to turn with some urgency to the problem of reforming the military and of moulding the Ancien Regime army into a force capable of beating off the attacks of the Austrians and their monarchist allies.

Army reforms were also the result of pressure from the soldiers themselves. The libertarian message that the Revolution encapsulated inevitably excited those of its citizens who served the government most directly, those who bore arms in the service of the revolutionary state. In 1788 and 1789 units returning to France from abroad had already shown a marked tendency to support the peasantry against the government, sympathize with complaints about shortages and riots over food prices, and fraternize with the people when they drew up their *cahiers de doléances* (57). The policing of the popular demonstrations in Paris in the summer of 1789 placed another strain on the loyalty of the troops, and when they were ordered to defend the Bastille against popular attack and turn their arms on the angry Parisian crowd, the crisis in the ranks became glaringly obvious. Some 760 soldiers deserted in the days around 14 July, some joined the new National Guard and fought for the rights of the populace, while the majority played a vitally significant passive role by their refusal to take any part in the repression of the people. The result was an endemic crisis of confidence in the French army, with soldiers deserting on a large scale and joining in civilian demonstrations. Disobedience and insubordination generally followed the use of troops to perform a policing role that brought them into confrontation with ordinary Frenchmen and forced them to establish their principal loyalties (58). It was here that the essence of the problem lay. Were they, first and foremost, soldiers whose duty was to obey the orders of their officers—the *armée de métier* of Ancien Regime France—or a new kind of army composed of men who saw themselves primarily as citizens, enjoying the privileges that citizenship conferred and proud to exercise their authority in the defence of the rights and privileges of their fellows? By 1790 it was clear that their new self-awareness and consciousness of what citizenship meant, was undermining traditional army discipline, and the demands of the troops were felt in a series of risings and mutinies against their superiors—at Perpignan, Saint-Servan, Epinal, Brest, Longwy, Sarrelouis, Hesdin, Compiègne, and elsewhere (59)—before the movement culminated in a major act of mutiny at Nancy. Three regiments of troops were involved in the "affaire de Nancy," two French and one Swiss, and the main aim of the mutineers was to put right wrongs within the army itself, to obtain satisfaction on pay and a series of grievances concerning political rights and disciplinary arrangements in the battalions. The men confidently claimed what they saw as the ordinary rights of Frenchmen, locking up their officers until these rights were granted to them, and preventing any correspondence between Nancy and the National Assembly, a move that was seen as a threat to essential lines of military communication and to the very security of the state (60). The mutiny was savagely repressed by 4,500 loyal troops led by the Marquis de Bouillé. The two French regiments involved were disbanded, the Nancy Jacobin Club, held responsible for the spread of egalitarian sentiments among the soldiers, was closed, and all troops were moved out of the city. The most brutal punishment was reserved for the Swiss. One soldier was condemned to be broken on the wheel, 22 were hanged, and 41 others condemned to 30 years in the galleys (61). The extent of the repression reflected the anxiety of those in power that the entire army could be a prey to egalitarian political ideals and to the perils of anarchy. But equally, they realized that the old established structures of the Ancien Regime army were increasingly untenable and that reform was a practical as well as a political necessity.

The extent of the reform that was introduced was without precedent in French history and shocked European military opinion. The officer corps, based on rank and privilege, had to be dismantled and replaced by a system of promotion that respected military and strategic ability. Some system of recruitment had to be found that would end the humiliation of press-ganging and would restore a measure of dignity and honor to the individual infrantryman. Given the intense nationalism of the revolutionary cause, France had to end its high dependence on foreign mercenaries, an obligation that became even more pressing after the King's Swiss Guards fired on the Paris crowd at the Tuileries in 1792. The army, in short, had to be transformed into an instrument of the state; it was, of necessity, politicized by the very experience of revolution. By 1793 the main elements of the new military strategy were largely in place, culminating in the *amalgame* of the old line regiments with new volunteer units in Dubois-Crancé's *demi-brigades* of February of that year (62). The *milice* was, predictably, abandoned in response to public opinion, and it was decreed that France should have an army of volunteers, of men burning with patriotic fervor who would willingly sacrifice themselves for liberty and the defense of the *patrie*. Officers whose loyalty was suspect were dismissed or retired, and new principles were adopted for the selection of their successors. For *sous-officiers* or NCOs the principle of election was enthusiastically adopted. In a revolutionary army it was the men, the soldiers in the ranks, who would choose their own petty officers for their patriotic commitment and their powers of leadership. As for the generals and commanding officers, they would henceforth be directly chosen by the government, so that the Revolution could be assured that it was defended by men who shared its ideals and who would be prepared to give their all in an ideological war against the monarchies of Europe. Politics, indeed, was assumed to be an important element in the creation of military enthusiasm, a contribution to the success of French arms in the early years of the revolutionary period. Soldiers were encouraged to discuss revolutionary strategy and to join revolutionary clubs; such was their right as free men. It was deemed that involvement in the activity of clubs or popular sections would also contribute to the creation of a determination and pride in their calling that had been noticeably lacking in the regiments of the Ancien Regime. Political idealism could take over where traditional discipline had been abandoned, for the cruel physical punishments that had characterized the eighteenth-century army were also early casualties of the reformers' attentions. The soldier of the Revolution enjoyed status and political freedoms denied to his Ancien Regime predecessor. He could hope to be rewarded with a higher rate of pay and in return the state assumed that it could depend on his loyalty in the difficult times that lay ahead.

These early reforms reflected the optimistic mood of France in 1792 and 1793, the zeal and legislative idealism of the early years of the Revolution. It was an impressive achievement, and one which, it was hoped, would sweep away the demoralized image of soldiering under the monarchy. For, idealism aside, the principal aim of these measures was to create a dependable and effective army, to end the crisis of military discipline that had greeted the Revolution in 1789, and to restore the country's faith in its soldiers. In 1791 the government even agreed to grant amnesty to all those indicted for military offences since 1789—a measure that was seen as necessary if army morale were to be restored and the damaging drain of desertion ended. In the words of Sam Scott,

> Despite the problems of implementation, the National Assembly had legislated an impressive array of military reforms in the first two years of the Revolution. It had established full constitutional control over the Army. It had dramatically improved conditions by increasing pay, reforming military justice, and changing the bases for promotion. It had carried out a major transformation of the organisational framework and tactics of the line army. (63)

In doing so, it should be added, whatever the derogatory responses that it attracted from politicians and army officers in London and Vienna, it had laid the foundations of the great victories of revolutionary arms at Valmy, Jemmapes, and beyond, and had changed the nature of European warfare irreversibly. The defense of France was now assigned not to the small, well-trained units of the Ancien Regime regiments, but to massed armies that necessarily lacked the skill of their predecessors in precise tactics and military formations. For this reason the armies of 1793 and the Year II talked much of the value of patriotism and *élan* (64). They could scarcely have done otherwise. The courage and bravura of the young volunteers were as much a product of ignorance in the ways of war as they were a reflection of their patriotic fervor.

In the short term, in the heady days of 1792 and 1793 when they were fighting to defend *la patrie en danger,* there is little doubt that the soldiers were inspired by the promise of new freedoms and encouraged by the heroic rhetoric of the *commissaires* and deputies-on-mission sent to motivate them on the eve of battle. *Fêtes civiques* and patriotic ceremonials helped give visual substance to the words of ministers and generals as the government made strenuous efforts to politicize the military to create in the French battalions what Jean-Paul Bertaud has termed an "école du jacobinisme" (65). Enthusiasm in short staccato bursts could provide a substitute for training and discipline. But as the war dragged on and extended into new fronts and new campaigns, in particular when it became clear to all that its purpose was aggressive and expansionist, that *la patrie* was no longer *en danger,* patriotic enthusiasm began to wane and the need for traditional military qualities became evident once more. The new officers promoted through the ranks of the armies of 1793 and Year II combined political commitment with technical expertise: they were literate, skilled in military tactics and maneuvers, and capable of detecting merit in others. In other words, there was already a move away from the amateurish elitism of the old officer corps, based on birth and status rather than on ability, and the beginning of a drive to achieve professional excellence (66). Under the Directory professionalism was the clear winner, as the government relaxed its political control over the armies and left effective decision making to its generals. For officers the army was once more a source of status and profit, where promotion could be very rapid, talent quickly rewarded, and the pickings very considerable. The soldiers of Year VII were no longer the "défenseurs de la patrie et de la République" to whom the Jacobins had appealed in the summer of Year II; instead they had assumed a much more straightforward, professional role. The French army had changed markedly since the time of the first *volontaires* and the *nation en armes;* and in Albert Meynier's terse and diplomatic judgment, the difference was in kind rather than in military effectiveness. Comparing the army that Napoleon inherited with the battalions of the Year II, he notes that "elle ne lui était pas inférieure en qualité, mais elle était autre" (67).

This is not to say that the army became wholly apolitical, or that youthful patriotism ceased to play a part in the success of the Directorial or Napoleonic campaigns. In fact, political cells remained active inside the armies long after their civilian counterparts had been rooted out in France itself, and various former Jacobins made new careers for themselves in the service of the Emperor. Marc-Antoine Jullien, for instance, who had carried out missions on Robespierre's behalf to Nantes and to Bordeaux during the Terror, followed Bonaparte's army to Italy in 1796 when anti-Jacobin repression made it inadvisable for him to remain in metropolitan France, and he continued his radical career in journalism by editing the *Courrier de l'Armée d'Italie* from the relative safety of Milan (68). But if political activism of this kind was tolerated in the armies, it no longer played any part in promotion or in military strategy; these matters were left increasingly to professional soldiers, whose influence and status increased as the wars became ever more extended. In the same way political idealism played relatively little part in the motivation of the ordinary infantry-man who served in Russia or the Peninsula. They saw themselves with increas-ing resignation in the role of mercenaries doing a job in return for pay. Nation-alism, the dream of "la grande nation" so dear to historians of the First Empire, had little appeal to those who were called on to fight in its name, and Jean Tulard has remarked that this loss of faith and commitment on the part of the French occurred at almost exactly the time (the opening up of the Spanish front) when the war was beginning to excite popular nationalism elsewhere in Europe (69). Military service in the Imperial armies was widely regarded as a *corvée* to be endured, only rarely as an honor or a privilege, and Napoleon's apparently insatiable appetite for conquest did nothing to dispel traditional distrust of the recruiting-sergeant. The selfless idealism of Year II was soon squandered in the long years of attrition that followed.

By the last years of the Empire there were few illusions. Even Napoleon him-self seemed to realize the full extent of the change in attitude that had taken place, and despite the quite remarkable rapport that he was able to establish with those serving in his name, he seemed almost to share it. Manpower, after all, was a commodity like any other, especially in wartime, and Napoleon's com-ments on his needs and his losses can seem shockingly callous. In 1805, after annexing Liguria, he wrote in outraged tones to the new governor, rebuking him for thinking of delaying or reducing the incidence of recruitment in his territory. Without the bonus of extra bodies for the army and navy, he declared, there would have been no point in moving into Liguria in the first place: "Je n'ai réuni Gênes que pour avoir des marins" (70). The need for additional troops became one of the key driving forces behind Napoleon's expansionist policies as an increasing proportion of the men serving in the armies were recruited from the states he had already conquered. And soldiers were always replaceable. "J'ai cent mille hommes de rente," boasted the Emperor after a costly reverse. Even more chillingly, in a letter to Metternich in 1813, he expressed in a famous passage his contempt for the detail of warfare, for the inevitable accompaniment of human losses. "Un homme comme moi," he wrote, "ne regarde pas à un million de morts" (71).

2

The Weight of Military Recruitment

IF FIGHTING a revolutionary war implied a new approach to army organization, the sheer scale of the conflict demanded the recruitment of vast numbers of soldiers. The new tactics adopted, the use of massed infantry battalions on a grand scale, and the rejection of foreign mercenaries as a means of pursuing a national crusade all had the effect of creating an unparalleled demand for manpower. The revolutionaries deliberately set out to create an army that represented the whole people of France, an army that would more clearly mirror the idealism and egalitarian spirit of the revolutionary state. They believed that citizenship carried with it duties and obligations as well as palpable benefits, and that the bearing of arms for France was just such a duty, incumbent on every young Frenchman whose service the state might require. In consequence the demands of the recruiting-officer were represented not as an intolerable burden (as they had been in the aristocratic atmosphere of the Ancien Regime) but as an opportunity for the young to play their part in establishing the revolution and in defending the *patrie* from its ideological enemies. The result was a quite astonishing level of militarization. During the revolutionary decade itself nearly one and one quarter million Frenchmen were incorporated in the battalions. The *levée en masse* of Year II created an army three-quarters of a million strong, and it was to restore this strength that Jourdan recommended the systematic institution of conscription in Year VI (1). During the Empire the state's demands for soldiers became more insatiable as Napoleon's armies stretched across Europe. Though exact statistics are unavailable, it is clear that between the introduction of conscription in Year VII and the last desperate levies in November 1813 more than 2 million men were recruited into the armies. Roger Darquenne has suggested a figure of 2,150,000; Jacques Houdaille more cautiously estimates it at 2,025,000. Of young men born between 1790 and 1795, Houdaille calculates that 42.5 percent, a staggeringly high figure, served in the rapacious armies of Napoleon's last years (2). Over the whole period of the Revolution and Empire we must conclude that between 3 and 3.5 million Frenchmen were incorporated in the military, and that first-hand experience of soldiering became familiar to every family in France.

The genuine idealism that lay behind the reforms to the army structure was reflected in the insistence of the early years that all forms of compulsion were unnecessary and a betrayal of revolutionary principle. There was general agreement that only voluntary inscription could produce the national army that France required, and it was assumed that volunteers would be found to defend France's frontiers just as volunteers had rushed to present themselves for service in the National Guard in response to the various decrees passed in 1790 (3). This assumption was rapidly put to the test. Both 1791 and 1792 saw appeals to the young to volunteer to save the country from the threat that faced her, and not surprisingly it was in 1791 that the response was more convincing, with department after department reporting that its battalions had been filled without difficulty and that its *jeunes gens* were burning with patriotic zeal. This was the period when enthusiasm ran highest, especially in the weeks after the King's flight to Varennes when popular anxiety was at its peak. But even Albert Soboul, the most enthusiastic believer in the power of such political commitment, rightly counsels caution. It was no accident that, at the very moment when the new volunteer battalions were full to overflowing, the recruiting-officers for the line regiments were complaining of a shortfall of 50,000 men, or that the volunteers knew, or thought they knew, that their period of service was limited to a single compaigning season, after which they fully expected to be restored to the routine of village life (4). The rush to arms could just as easily be explained by hunger as by patriotism (5). For many there was still a sort of innocence about volunteering that would soon vanish once hostilities were declared. There was still something unreal about the idea of fighting, and few of the new recruits had any notion of the realities of warfare. Like young Philippe-René Girault, who volunteered as a musician in 1791, the inspiration to leave home and offer himself to the armies might have had little to do with politics or with soldiering. As he explains in his campaign memoirs, chance and boredom played the largest part in his decision:

> Entré au chapitre de Sainte-Radégonde de Poitiers, comme enfant de choeur, à l'age de quatre ans et demi, j'y restai pendant plus de dix ans. La révolution vint, et comme les chapitres étaient supprimés, on me renvoya. Mon père, qui était tailleur de pierre, me fit travailler avec lui. Le métier ne me plut pas, et je résolus bientôt de quitter ma famille et de me faire soldat. Mais, ayant communiqué mon dessein à mes parents, ils me décidèrent à rester encore quelque temps au milieu d'eux. Cependant, au bout de quelques jours, comme je m'ennuyais beaucoup, je pris la résolution de partir sans rien dire. Un matin, me trouvant seul, je prends mon paquet, quelque argent, et je me mets en route pour La Rochelle. (6)

Others again rushed to embark on what they assumed would be a brief and glorious adventure, and their inscription, offered in the first flush of revolutionary liberty, was not a little tinged with the spirit of a village *fête*.

The volunteer battalions that were recruited in 1791 represent the clearest instance of enthusiasm and popular involvement in the military effort. In some areas officials were themselves surprised by the large numbers of recruits who presented themselves and by the patriotism that they demonstrated. The ideal of a citizen army seemed to be in the process of taking a practical shape. As yet enthusiasm was not confined to any single class or section of the population, although it was in the towns that the response was most gratifying and among the peasantry that resistance was most prevalent. In general, the recruits came from the artisan groups in society rather than from the ranks of the farmers and farm laborers, from what Bertaud terms "le monde de l'échoppe et de la boutique" (7). But urban France was still widely represented with bourgeois and professional men figuring among the new recruits as well as tradesmen and shopkeepers. At Aurillac, for instance, among the *tailleurs, cordonniers,* and *chaudronniers,* trades that had a fairly consistent patriotic record, were a sprinkling of recruits from commerce and the liberal professions: an *homme de loi,* a *bourgeois,* a *chirurgien,* and four of the clerks working at the Palais de Justice (8). Mayors were entitled to feel encouraged by the names they found inscribed once the lists were opened in town halls and sectional offices up and down France. Yet even in 1791 there were already certain unhappy signs that even in the first flush of revolutionary enthusiasm the voluntary principle was not proving quite equal to the country's military needs. The response was far from being evenly spread across the country, and the old distinctions between areas of military tradition and areas of *insoumission* were making themselves felt. Paris, always the most patriotic of cities, responded with predictable conviction as did the frontier departments of the East, like the Meurthe and the Marne. But elsewhere the response was less encouraging. If the Meurthe provided five battalions, the Indre-et-Loire and the Vienne managed only one each; certain inland departments of the Massif Central and Aquitaine were exempted altogether; and a few areas of which there were high expectations, especially in Alsace and in the Breton departments of Finistère and the Côtes-du-Nord, failed to come close to their agreed targets (9). Even parts of the traditionally militarized Ile-de-France could prove intractable. Annie Crépin, in her study of the Seine-et-Marne, notes that enthusiasm tended to fade in cantons farther removed from the great urban centers where regular contact with Paris was assured. Hamlets like Lizy-sur-Ourcq and La Ferté-Gaucher, for example, were already showing in 1791 a marked reluctance to volunteer, their inscription lists remaining open for several weeks before names could be found. And in many cantons the concept of volunteers was already somewhat imprecise, with mayors eagerly accepting the names of men who had only recently moved into the area, vagrants and petty criminals, and men who did not enjoy sound health or who had physical disabilities, or those who could not hope to meet the basic height requirements (10). More significantly, not all the volunteers showed any disposition to march with the army; some of the municipal councils were themselves still under the impression that the young men who came forward were volunteering not for real soldiering but for service in the community with the National Guard (11).

When the government tried to repeat the process in the spring of 1792 and called on men's patriotism a second time, the shortcomings of the voluntary principle became sadly evident. The reported rush of young men toward their *mairies* or town halls in 1791 was seldom repeated. In part this may be explained by a greater professionalism among the recruiters, by a refusal to accept boys of fifteen or old men of sixty five years of age for military service, as had occurred in the Meurthe the previous year (12). In general, however, it reflected a decline in enthusiasm and a drying-up of the supply of politically committed men who could be relied on to respond. This should have surprised nobody since the majority of those eligible to serve in 1792 had been equally eligible a year earlier and the patriots among them were already on the frontiers. Areas with strong military traditions, like Versailles, were still able to find men willing to serve, among them former professional soldiers from the Ancien Regime regiments and Swiss Guards anxious to continue in the only profession they knew. But even here it was remarkable how many of the new volunteers were outsiders to the area, men who had drifted to the Seine-et-Oise in the recent past in search of work and who were now drifting rather aimlessly into service with the armies. Among the 286 volunteers who signed on in the district of Versailles, for instance, were men from more than half the departments of the *hexagone,* besides a handful of immigrants from abroad (13). Need rather than patriotism may be assumed to lie at the root of many decisions to serve, and regions of the country where there was no established tradition of soldiering might not even be able to rely on the force of need. The Cantal was one department where by 1792 the opening of a communal register for volunteers provided no guarantee that anyone would step forward, and in village after village mayors were forced to admit that they had failed to find a single soldier. This was the case in Lascelles and Laroquevieille, Salers and Saignes, Apchon and Les Arbres (14). Where men were found, a high proportion came from the main town and relatively few from the outlying hamlets. Of the 600 volunteers who were formed into the First Battalion of the Cantal in July, well over half were provided by the towns, a curious record for one of the most rural areas of the country. The pattern was remarkably consistent. In the district of Aurillac, 170 of the 250 volunteers came from Aurillac itself and a further 43 from the town of Maurs; in the district of Mauriac 28 of the 58 recruits were from the *chef-lieu;* and in the district of Saint-Flour 97 of 156 came from Saint-Flour (15). At Montsalvy in March of 1792 the demand for volunteers was already creating the sort of response that would become familiar later in the Revolution, with rioting by the local population and the seizure of communal papers relating to the previous year's recruitment. As a result, the mayor could only report rather weakly that not a single volunteer had been found, and that, in the circumstances, he thought it extremely unlikely that any would. In his own words, "nous voyons avec peine que notre ville soit hors d'état de donner des plus grandes marques de patriotisme, surtout dans le moment qui semble l'exiger le plus" (16). It would be hard to imagine a response more unlike the enthusiasm shown by the people of Paris when the *patrie* was declared to be "en danger" and when the recruiting-officers in the capital were deluged with passionate and determined volunteers.

In general, the men who came forward in 1792 were younger than the volunteers of the previous year. As might be expected, the band of eighteen year olds, men who were technically ineligible in 1791, was particularly prominent. Jean-Paul Bertaud has demonstrated that of the new recruits three-quarters were twenty-five years old or younger and that of these some 15 percent were underage, being fifteen, sixteen or seventeen years old when they enrolled (17). They were often very raw recruits especially in rural France where they were generally lacking in the most basic education or literacy. At Cayrols in the Massif, not a single one of the new volunteers could sign his name, the communal register sporting only the crude crosses of the illiterate (18). Many were there for the signing-on bounties that were frequently held out as bait. Sums of 80 *livres* for infantrymen and 120 *livres* for the cavalry were quite customary as towns and villages encourgaed their young men to fill the local quotas. With admirable pragmatism the department of the Aude noted in February 1792 that "l'intérêt fut toujours le mobile des actions des hommes," that *primes* should therefore be paid as a matter of course, and that they would have much greater impact on men's minds if they could be paid in hard currency rather than in the distrusted and seriously devalued *assignats* (19). In communes where it proved impossible to find volunteers by any other means some form of balloting was used to designate those who should serve, a technique that was to become universal in later recruitments but which clashed jarringly with the rhetoric about the freedom of each citizen to choose for himself, especially where it became evident that the richer inhabitants were hiding behind the *tirage* to designate others for the honor of representing their community in the armies (20). Even in 1792 many of the problems that would dog military recruitment throughout the Revolution and the Empire were becoming apparent. Men who volunteered in a fit of enthusiasm began to have second thoughts when the implications of their decision became clear. One volunteer from Saint-Flour, Chazal, grew sufficiently disenchanted with the idea of service in the weeks that followed his inscription and he lost patience and accepted a post as *commis* to the *receveur du district* (21). Another, from Mauriac, asked to be excused on the grounds that he had signed on in a flush of patriotic excess, overlooking the fact that he was only fourteen years old and therefore ineligible (22). A third, and he was typical of many in the villages of the southern Massif, complained that he had never signed the register of volunteers, that he had found his name added to the list without his knowing by an "ennemi personnel" whose uncle fortuitously worked in the *mairie* and had access to the document (23). This loss of enthusiasm, associated in some instances with charges of forgery and corruption, had the inevitable effect of draining the resources on which the armies were dependent, and cynicism spread among the volunteers with damaging rapidity. By May the volunteers from Aurillac and Murat were sufficiently alarmed by the trend they observed to request that the department put aside funds to finance a propaganda campaign to fill the gaps in the First Battalion and to "rechauffer et revifier le patriotisme qui semble expirant" (24). Just as serious for the government was the widespread belief among the young men who volunteered in the spring of 1792 that French victories at Valmy and Jemmapes had dispersed the foreign threat, so that they could, in the time-honored fashion, return to their homes once the campaigning season was over. Because volunteers signed on for one year only, they were technically in the right, and the Convention could only appeal to their patriotism to break with custom and remain at their posts (25). The appeal had little effect. At the end of the 1791 campaigning season there had been between 400,000 and 460,000 men under arms; by the beginning of 1793 fewer than 350,000 remained. For many of the volunteers, their sense of duy was appeased, their soldiering over, and they returned with ill-concealed relief to life on the farm or in the *atelier* (26).

The ideal of a volunteer army had therefore to be abandoned, but with the greatest reluctance. Faced with the reality of war and with the likelihood that that war would both persist indefinitely and be extended in scope, the government could not allow France to stand undefended. The internal troubles of the spring and summer of 1793, from counterrevolution in Brittany to the threat of open revolt from the federalist towns of the South and West, merely added to the sense of military urgency. If they refused to step forward voluntarily, then young men would have to be persuaded to serve by other means if the Republic were to be secured. The summer of 1792 was already witnessing a move towards some form of compulsion as more and more communes failed to fill their levies by voluntary means. Somewhat plaintively, the district of Saint-Flour expressed the ambiguity that many felt when it asked in August whether those nominated as volunteers had the right to refuse that nomination, "si les volontaires nommés aux assemblées du 30 août pourront refuser d'accepter purement et simplement ou seront obligés de motiver leur refus, dont sera juge chacune des assemblées" (27). The question was neatly turned, for the government continued to use the term "volontaire" long after inscription into the armies had ceased to be in any sense voluntary. The Republic shared the dislike felt by many of its citizens for any form of recruitment that smacked of compulsion, of bureaucratic selection, of the abuses associated in the public mind with the old *milice*. Communes expressed deep shock when they learned that they were obliged to fill their quotas even when volunteers failed to materialize, that they might have to resort to some form of direct nomination or election, for the belief was widespread that the introduction of any form of compulsion would turn public opinion against soldiering and kill such patriotic feeling as remained. The idea of drawing lots, protested the Breton town of Ploërmel, aroused a particular sense of repugnance among people who had only recently thrown off the chains of the Ancien Regime (28). So the fiction was meticulously cultivated that Revolutionary soldiers were indeed volunteers, and throughout the 1790s communes were first asked to encourage voluntary enlistment before any form of compulsion was used. In practice, however, this was little more than fiction, since after 1792 the numbers coming forward voluntarily seldom rose above derisory levels. Only the most dedicated or the most militaristic would still volunteer rather than simply submit to some form of chance or selection with the rest of their peers, or those so poor and desperate that they wanted to escape from their present lot and saw in the army a form of shelter and a source of nourishment. Even in the district of Versailles, despite centuries of tradition, the numbers decreased dramatically once compulsory levies were introduced. If the district produced 286 volunteers in 1792, there were only 15 in 1793, 25 in 1794 (when Jacobin nationalism did win a few hearts), 11 in 1795, 7 in 1796, 11 in 1797, and 7 again in 1798 (29). Individual volunteers often told poignant tales of the circumstances that had led them to sign on. Jean Constant from Jouy-en-Josas claimed that he had volunteered only because he had been drunk at the time of the *appel* and had been "séduit par un de ses camarades" (30). Joseph Langlois from Courgent in the Seine-et-Oise protested that only the fact that he was momentarily "pris de vin" could have induced him to offer to abandon his wife and child by volunteering for the army. His commune supported his plea, adding for good measure that "comme il n'est pas accoutumé à boire, nous savons qu'une bouteille de vin lui met la tête au champ, lui fait oublier toutes ses affaires domestiques, et ne le fait penser qu'à la guerre" (31). Family quarrels, like drink, could lead unhappy youngsters to volunteer in moments of despair. Such was the case of two lads from Saint-Prain in Year V, who agreed that they had volunteered knowingly, without the false courage supplied by alcohol, but less through a sense of military vocation than as a result of "quelques désagréments qu'ils avaient essuyés de leurs parents" (32). By the end of the decade genuine volunteers had become so rare that individual inscriptions were sometimes notified to Paris as local events worthy of remark; when one eighteen year old from Fours in the Nièvre presented himself for the army in Year VII his grateful fellow citizens signed a public statement of their appreciation for his patriotism and selflessness (33).

Only very locally did recruiting-officers have the satisfaction of finding that men continued to come forward voluntarily in worthwhile numbers. The national register of *enrôlés volontaires* for Year XI indicates the full extent to which first the revolutionary *levées* and then full-blooded measures of conscription had drained away any desire for service that might previously have existed in the population, and it underlines the degree to which Saint-Just's much vaunted *élan* had been dissipated in the course of a decade of war. The cities of Paris and Lyon, it is true, still made more than a token effort. The departments of the Seine and the Rhône still responded to the nation's call to arms with, respectively, 620 and 277 volunteers. But only one other department, the Calvados, provided more than 100 volunteers, and only a handful of areas, generally the stalwarts of the eastern frontier, exceeded 50. In striking contrast were the thirty-six departments that offered 4 or fewer volunteers to the nation, including sixteen that did not produce a single soldier. They provide a fitting epitaph to the original dream of an army composed of patriots throwing themselves into battle for nation and liberty (34).

In the spring of 1793 the government's answer to its urgent need for manpower was the *levée des 300,000*. Three hundred thousand additional troops were required for the summer campaign season, and each department was held responsible for raising a portion of the total allocated to it by central government. In principle, the *levée* was fixed in accordance with population, although areas that had proved recalcitrant in the raising of volunteers were more heavily assessed. All men between eighteen and forty years of age who were unmarried or widowers without children were placed in a state of permanent requisition; replacement was permitted and certain professional categories were expressly exempted. Each department had its assigned quota, which was then subdivided according to population among its component districts; the districts in turn assigned quotas to their various cantons. Beyond this, however, the decree was deliberately vague. The government still encouraged voluntary enrollment, but insisted that any deficit be made good by the recruitment of those requisitioned, without giving any instruction as to how this might be achieved. In the words of the decree, "les citoyens seront tenus de le compléter sans désemparer, et pour cet effet ils employeront le mode qu'ils trouveront le plus convenable, à la pluralité des voix" (35). In other words, the government wanted only to fill its regiments, and beyond a shallow continuing commitment to the ideal of voluntarism it was not prepared to lay down any binding guidelines. The first major exercise in compulsion was left to local opinion and to local elected officers; and inevitably the complaints soon came flowing in from all over France. They stemmed partly from incomprehension, confusion, and lack of experience; more generally, they alleged unfairness and inequality of sacrifice.

The administrative problems were enormous. In fact it is surprising that the *levée* raised as many soldiers as it did for the service of the Republic. For mayors, especially in rural areas, were often themselves semiliterate and unschooled in matters of this kind. They were being asked to force members of their village communities to march off to the army generally against their will, and they had neither the bureaucratic information nor the coercive power with which to accomplish the task. Even regions where enthusiasm ran relatively high experienced considerable problems because they did not know exactly who was available to serve. As the District of Cambrai complained in March 1793, there were no *tableaux* of recruits, and therefore no accurate records that could act as the basis for an efficient recruitment (36). Just as serious was the fact that the military failed to keep their civilian colleagues abreast of their movements and requirements, which made the policing of recruitment unnecessarily difficult. Mayors frequently did not even know to which battalions to send their men, such was the general administrative chaos of these early months. The district of Lille expressed understandable frustration in August 1792 that although its recruitment seemed to be progressing well, disorder and confusion were threatening the entire enterprise: "C'est qu'on ignore absolument quels sont les régiments complets et quels sont ceux qui ne le sont pas; un homme s'engage pour un régiment et on le renvoie sous prétexte que ce régiment est plus qu'au complet" (37). The Ministry of War accused mayors and civilian officials of a lack of determination in the field of recruitment, but the fault was not theirs alone. The habit of regular and thorough communication between different levels of administration had not yet had an opportunity to develop. And local authorities were often left without instructions and uncertain of the powers at their disposal. In the Gironde, for example, the district of Bazas was already complaining that it could employ only the weakest armory of measures, "les exhortations, la persuasion," to force men to leave for the armies (38). And the army itself was criticized for neglecting its part of the process. How could local administrators get men into uniform when *commissaires* were turning them away from their battalions and *chirurgiens* were failing to turn up for medical examinations (39)?

Just as serious was the widespread suspicion that the *levée* was inequitable and that others were escaping scot-free. Rural France was only too prone to believe that the entire burden of recruitment was falling on the peasantry while the inhabitants of towns and *gros bourgs* stood back from the recruitment proceedings and watched the countrymen march off to die. At Tassé in the Sarthe it was whispered that "dans les gros endroits on ne satisfaisait plus," and in nearby Vernie the local people refused to take any part in the recruitment until others had demonstrated their good will; "il faut attendre," they reasoned, "à voir comment les autres communes feront et ne pas se presser" (40). The power of the rich to buy their way out was deeply resented by ordinary Frenchmen, and in many communities there remained a profound suspicion, well expressed in a letter from Saint-Flour in May 1793, that "les municipalités se coalisent avec les riches propriétaires et se concertent pour désigner ou les pauvres ou leurs ennemis personnels" with the result that "en général le recrutement ne se porte que sur les pauvres" (41). For some the answer was obvious: the richer citizens should take the lead in offering themselves for the army and those who had benefited most from the Revolution should make the greatest sacrifice for its survival. In the villages of the Sarthe in 1793 popular animosity focused especially on those wealthy peasants who had further enriched themselves by the purchase of *biens nationaux*. The young men of the area, for fear that they be forced to leave for the front, tended to see in the local *acquéreurs* a class of men who had gained everything and given nothing for the Revolution, and their seditious mutterings spread through the country inns of the department. "Il vaudrait beaucoup mieux," Jean Livache told the *juge de paix* at Fresnay," que ceux qui ont acheté des biens nationaux, ainsi que tout le monde de la campagne le dit, aillent les défendre; ceux qui n'en ont point acheté n'iraient qu'après les autres" (42). On frequent occasions recruitment officials came into conflict with village sentiment and solidarity, and rioting often ensued. At Ploërmel the first attempt at a recruitment meeting ended in uproar, with the officials jeered by an angry crowd that insisted that everyone be treated alike. The young men of the town declared that they would march to the front and were as patriotic as the youth of other parts of France, but they would do so only when their administrators and those favored by exemptions marched at their side (43). At Hesdin in the Pas-de-Calais, where again the sense of popular egalitarianism was strong, the recruitment procedures had to be hastily abandoned because of the danger that the military *commissaire,* Darthé, might be lynched by an infuriated mob (44). In many towns and villages the local people felt that they had right on their side, and that the new recruitment laws were an outrage to the precious ideals of *égalité* that the Revolution had promised them. In consequence the law was frequently flouted, generally with impunity. At Marcolès in the Cantal, where again rioting forced the abandonment of the recruitment meeting, the municipal council felt obliged to recommend a pardon for the young men involved on the grounds that public opinion in the community was so unanimous in their support (45).

Popular suspicion of the new recruitment was increased by the fear that it was being unfairly implemented by corrupt officials. In particular, the extensive powers conferred on local mayors gave rise to lengthy recriminations from villagers who believed that the *notables* of the local community were again taking advantage of their status to turn the law to their own profit. The mayor was, after all, one of them, in most cases a peasant or small landowner who would be more prosperous than the average villager, owning perhaps a few acres of farm or small vineyard. He would have been chosen by his peers back in 1790 for what all assumed to be a largely honorific post as representative of the village community. Yet for both the *levée des 300,000* and the *levée en masse* that followed, the government placed on the mayor's shoulders all the onus of responsibility for ensuring that the communal quotas were filled. Inevitably jealousies and internecine tensions became unleashed, especially because it was the mayor who had to decide on the method of selection that was to be used, which could not but be the most unpopular of tasks (46). The choice before him was usually between some form of ballot *(tirage au sort)* and selection by nomination or *scrutin,* whereby the entire community was invited to assemble on the village green or in front of the church to choose patriotic young soldiers who would represent them in the national cause. Neither method was popular. Left to themselves, many communes would have preferred to raise money to buy recruits to serve in their stead. At Bollène in the Drôme, for instance, the local people opened a *registre civique* and tried to buy the services of volunteers by means of a public subscription. When this failed to raise sufficient funds, they talked of imposing a local tax to meet the costs incurred (47). At Saint-Mamet in the Cantal volunteers obviated the need for balloting, but to encourage them to come forward the commune had promised payments equal to one quarter of the entire land tax paid by the village (48). And at Thiézac in the same department, when the possibility of holding a ballot was mooted, angry, murmuring, threats and menaces persuaded the mayor to abandon the meeting. The local people made no secret of their preference:

> Ils ont d'une unanime voix répondu qu'ils ne voulaient point tirer, mais qu'ils voulaient que tous les paysans de la paroisse contribuassent au marc la livre pour acheter les vingt hommes qu'ils devaient fournir, et après leur avoir représenté qu'ils agiraient contre la loi de se comporter ainsi et qu'ils se compromettraient, les murmures et menaces qui ont été faites dans ladite assemblée ont obligé le maire et officiers municipaux de dire qu'ils allaient se retirer pour la sûreté de leurs jours. (49)

This may have been an extreme response, but it illustrates the hostility which the very idea of recruitment evoked in many parts of rural France.

Both *tirage* and *scrutin* were frequently cited as causes of disaffection and riot. *Tirage* was widely recognized to be the fairer of the two methods, the one less open to fraud and abuse, and by the time of the *levée en masse* it was insisted on by central government. Yet it was widely disliked in rural areas where the very concept of a ballot was controversial and seemed to resurrect the practice of the old *milice* which they had believed to be buried along with the rest of the Ancien Regime (50). At Oust in the Pyrenean foothills there was serious trouble as soon as the villagers were asked to draw lots, and the meeting disintegrated into an angry wrangle over whether or not the curé should be obliged to submit himself to the *tirage* with the other young men of the village (51). In the Morbihan, too, it was the procedure of the *tirage* that was most hotly contested. In the commune of Tréal, for example, ten of the young men of the locality replied to their summons with a blank refusal to take part in the ceremony to decide which of them must serve as a *cavalier* in the army, taking refuge instead in a series of bloodcurdling threats against the members of the local council (52). Although the government might try to insist that all ten be made to serve as an example to the rest of the villagers, that scarcely resolved the problem for the local mayor. To effect the *tirage* he was obliged to call a mass meeting of all the *jeunes gens* of the commune, and that in turn raised a problem of public order and police. "Comment l'effectuer," he demanded, "comment nous exposer à rassembler des hommes indisposés et récalcitrans dans notre ville sans force répressive, sans moyens actifs de police?" (53). Faced with such difficulties, communes were sorely tempted to resort to tricks and subterfuges to prevent the danger and public humiliation that the *tirage* might easily incur. In Chaudesaigues they adopted the expedient of nominating men who were conveniently absent from the commune when the ballot was to be held (54); Le Quesnoy (Nord) chose to avoid a ballot altogether by signing on volunteers of 60 years or older (55). Guesnain, in the same department, asked six of its veterans to continue serving for three extra months so that balloting could be avoided, a procedure that was totally illegal but which had the virtue of delaying a decision that was likely to cause rioting in the village (56).

The other method, that of *scrutin,* led to endless quarrels and complaints by those who felt, often rightly, that they had been abusively treated by their fellow villagers. For it was naive to believe that villagers would select the most able-bodied or the most patriotic to serve in the armies; much more plausible explanations were the interests of their families and friends, or the economic loss if their cowman or *métayer* were selected. It should be no surprise that *cabales* quickly formed, or that self-interest was paramount. In fact, it is significant that many of the most refractory communes in the mountain regions of the Ariège figure among those that stated a preference for *scrutin,* presumably on the grounds that they could manipulate it to their own advantage (57). Social envy and personal rancor could be satisfyingly assuaged, and the government rightly concluded that the system constituted an outrage to the reputation of the army and to the ideal of equality. There were numerous instances of blatant discrimination. The farming community of La Bastide-de-Besplas insisted on nominating a lawyer to march on its behalf, despite the fact that the man involved, Jean-Paul-Antoine Trinqué, had not lived in the village for over two years and had already submitted to a ballot in his adoptive commune (58). Another village to choose *scrutin* was Coudequerque, near Bergues, which had first tried to raise a subscription to buy soldiers for its quota but had failed to find men of sufficient height. Forced to look to its own people, Coudequerque nominated a local farmer, Landschoote, and ordered him to leave; yet Landschoote protested that he was the victim of jealousy and personal hatred, a wealthy farmer who had already found himself "en butte à quelques individus de la commune" to the extent that both he and his brother had been compelled by public harassment to leave the village and take up residence in a nearby town. Unpopularity, he alleged, not patriotism or physical strength, was the basis of his designation for service (59). In the Cantal villagers often conspired to send recruits from outlying hamlets and isolated farmsteads to avoid serving themselves. At Junhac ten young men from the farthest corners of the commune complained that the isolation of their homes had prevented them from attending the recruitment meeting, and for that reason they had been unfairly chosen by the others (60). Cowherds leading solitary lives on remote hillsides would seem to have been particularly highly regarded by village meetings anxious to protect their own interests. In March 1793 thirteen *bouviers* from La Besserette petitioned that the village boys had conspired to send only outsiders like themselves, that "il s'est formé une coalition entre les garçons natifs de laditte paroisse pour nommer tous les garçons étrangers" (61). Such examples tell a poignant story of pettiness and interfamily feuding. It is not difficult to see why the system was so unpopular among sharecroppers and farmworkers (62), or why so many communes rejected it as a method of recruitment. The district of Cambrai noted pertinently that "le scrutin dont on a usé dans un certain nombre de municipalités nous a démontré tant de cabales et tant d'inconvénients que nous n'avons pas cru pouvoir hésiter de prescrire un autre mode d'élection" (63). And in a reply to the commune of Laroquebrou about its intended *scrutin* the department of Cantal went so far as to question the fairness of the whole system. Designation, especially where all the citizens were not expressly consulted, constituted a breach of the spirit, if not of the letter, of the law (64).

Though bitterly contested, the *levée des 300,000* served its primary purpose of getting a large number of men into uniform in a very short period of time. It had broken with the voluntary principle without returning to the professional army of the Ancien Regime. It had made use of the new departmental and district divisions and the different layers of civilian administration to recruit for the military. It had reestablished the practice of *remplacement* in the recruitment process. What it had not done was to introduce conscription in the full sense of the term, because there was not as yet any obligation placed methodically on the *jeunes gens* of a particular *classe* to present themselves for service. The army recruited in 1793 contained men of all ages from eighteen to forty years old, exactly as the recruitment law stated that it should, even if there was a marked tendency to take those at the younger end of that spectrum. The district of Romans (Drôme) provides as good a case study as any. The district provided a total of 330 recruits for the army, ranging in age from forty to sixteen years old, the last named being a young *tailleur d'habits* from Le Péage-lès-Pisançon whose youthful high spirits had induced him to sign on as a volunteer even though he was substantially underage. Of the 330 men, 185 fell into the age range between eighteen and twenty-two years old, 250 into that between eighteen and twenty-six. Yet as many as 39 of them were aged thirty years and older (65). The recruitment had produced problems of noncooperation, but these tended to be regionalized; more generally the difficulties encountered stemmed from administrative confusion, inexperience, and the failure of the government to explain the law to its officials. In the Vosges, for instance, where there was scarcely a flicker of revolt, legal exemptions took a heavy toll of the manpower due to the armies, since many of those recruited worked in arms factories, foundries, forges, and ironworks (66). The law on exemptions, as the district of Crest discovered, could be utterly bewildering for those called on to enforce it:

> Les vicaires, les ex-chanoines, les assesseurs des juges de paix, les chefs de manufacture exempts par une loi du mois d'août dernier, notre archiviste, les chefs at commis de nos bureaux, les curés enfin qui ne sont plus envisagés comme fonctionnaires publics, les notables qui par une décision du départe-

ment furent reconnus exempts lors du tirage des grenadiers et qui pourraient se prétendre tels à cause de la permanence, tous ces personnages sont-ils dans le cas ou non? Nous ne partageons pas tous ces doutes; mais il en est dont la décision préalable est nécessaire. (67)

Nor were the results of the *levée* always what the government had intended. In the Drôme, Kellermann noted sourly, undersized soldiers were being sent to the battalions without scruples, and on inspecting new recruits at Briançon in March 1793 he found that they included both "beaucoup de vieillards" and at least eighty children no more than thirteen or fourteen years old (68). In some areas of recruitment law ambiguities still remained that cried out for clearer definition.

There would be ample opportunity to provide that definition, since 1793 was to witness a heavy succession of recruitment drives by an increasingly harassed government. Following the *levée des 300,000* in February and March, there was a supplementary levy, then another for the Vendée, before the major recruitment of the autumn of that year, the *levée en masse.* This time there was to be no *remplacement,* one of only two occasions throughout the entire period of the Revolution and Empire when the rich were unable to buy themselves out of military service, and personal sacrifice was demanded from all young Frenchmen in the cause of the Republic. The *levée* was proclaimed in a nationalistic tone of high moral fervor, demanding equality of sacrifice from all. The spirit of Jacobin democracy ran through the text of the new law, and deputies-on-mission in the departments were instructed to ensure that its terms were fully understood in village *mairies,* since Paris was determined to learn from the troubles of the previous February. What the Jacobins envisaged was a national crusade against the forces of reaction that were threatening the Republic from all sides: the decree of 23 August established that:

Dès ce moment jusqu'à celui où les ennemis auront été chassés du territoire de la République, tous les Français sont en réquisition permanente pour le service des armées. Les jeunes gens iront au combat; les hommes mariés forgeront les armes et transporteront les subsistances; les femmes feront des tentes, des habits, et serviront dans les hôpitaux; les enfants mettront le vieux linge en charpie; les vieillards se feront porter sur les places publiques pour exciter le courage des guerriers, prêcher la haine des rois et l'unité de la République. (69)

In practice military recruitment was confined to those between eighteen and twenty-five years of age who were bachelors or widowers without family responsibilities. But it was also by far the most equitable draft of the Revolutionary years, and it is significant that it gave rise to fewer protests and caused less hostility than either the *levées* that preceded it or the conscription to which it gave way. The underlying sense of injustice that was present in previous recruitments had been largely alleviated.

The *levée en masse* aimed to create a massive army three quarters of a million strong to defeat France's enemies abroad and to guarantee the internal security of the Republic. The recruitment process was supervised closely in the departments by the local Jacobin clubs and by deputies-on-mission sent out from the Convention. Democratic rhetoric mingled with the early manifestations of Terror to ensure that this levy was much more successful than its predecessors. The government had learned from the administrative mistakes of February, and the filling of the army quotas assumed the very highest priority among the affairs of state. The rhetoric was valuable in that it made the recruitment and the *tirage* seem more palatable, although Jean-Paul Bertaud rightly comments that the Jacobins were not really interested in democracy and that what really occurred in August 1793 was the subtle transformation of the *levée en masse* into a straightforward requisition (70). The East of France was, as usual, especially responsive. The department of the Marne, for example, obediently sent eight full battalions complete with arms and equipment before the end of September (71). But even areas not noted for their patriotic fervor often responded with surprising alacrity. In the Morbihan, where the *levée des 300,000* a few months before had been fraught with problems, district after district reported after only a few days that their contingents were ready to depart. In this part of France, the only real problem arose from the attempt to requisition horses and *cavaliers* because horses played a minimal role in the local economy and were in scarce supply (72). In large measure this enthusiasm did reflect the new element of politicization that had been injected into the recruitment process. Ruamps and Milhaud, on mission to the Alsatian departments, noted with some wonderment that the peasants of Wissembourg responded to the ringing of the tocsin by arming themselves with whatever implements were at hand, pikes and scythes and hunting rifles, and launching themselves fearlessly against the enemy (73). But it was also a tribute to honest and painstaking administration, and it would be wise not to be carried along too willingly on the billowing clouds of Republican rhetoric. At La Bastide-de-Besplas there was little sign of the unbounded zeal that had impressed Ruamps and Milhaud. Rather, their battalions were composed of *laboureurs* and *gens de travail* from the surrounding hamlets whose hearts were still on their farms and who were likely to desert at any moment (74). In the Seine-et-Marne, far from the most troublesome region of the country, the designated recruits had left their communes obediently enough, though showing every sign of reluctance, accepting their lot only because of the strict and public egalitarianism that provided some justification for the levy (75). And although they were far less frequent than before, there were still instances of rioting in August and September 1793 that indicated that not everyone was appeased by the language of equality. The village of Montréal in the Aude saw its most bitter insurrection in August when the *tirage* was announced. The young men of the village shouted down their elected officials, sang the *carmagnole* in a rousing act of collective defiance, and threatened the mayor with physical violence. Far from submitting to the recruitment, they showed the utmost defiance for the government and its policies, "se jetèrent sur le bureau, se saisirent de la plupart des lois et arrêtés relatifs au recrutement, les foulèrent sous leurs pieds après les avoir déchirés en mille morceaux" (76). After another riot, at Saint-Dié in the Vosges, the prosecutor talked in alarmist tones of 5,000 or 6,000 rioters who had come from all over the surrounding countryside to break up the recruitment meeting. His figure is certainly exaggerated, but it remains true that when they dispersed, 2 people were dead and 75 were charged with public order offenses (77).

The army created by the *levée en masse* remained the principal fighting strength of the Republic throughout the 1790s. By a curious anomaly no provision was made in the law for the young men recruited in 1793 to be released from service after a fixed period of years, and no further systematic recruitment took place until the very end of the decade. Those drafted in the *levée des 300,000* and the *levée en masse* were to serve until the end of hostilities. As Gustave Vallée remarks in his study of the Charente, it was the greatest of injustices that one generation, those unlucky enough to be between eighteen and twenty-five years of age in 1793, should thus have been "chargée à elle seule d'acquitter intégralement l'impôt du sang" (78). Such perfunctory attempts as there were to organize additional levies during the intervening years achieved little, and the numbers of volunteers continued to decrease. *Levées extraordinaires* were especially resented and seldom produced worthwhile results. In Year III in the Ariège municipal councils were so disheartened that they scarcely dared to summon the young to village meetings (79). Popular fear of sudden calls to arms resulted in damaging and unfounded rumors sweeping the countryside, sending young men into hiding and arousing the anger of their parents against the state. In the region around Quimper in Year IV it was widely believed that the local *commissaire*, without any legal authority, was about to conscript any young man he found between fifteen and thirty years of age during his *tournée* of local villages (80). Such incidents served only to increase fear and resentment at a time when the actual strength of the armies continued to decline at an alarming pace. For if there were 750,000 men in arms in September of 1794, that number had decreased to less than half a million by *fructidor* III, to 401,749 in *thermidor* IV, and to only 326,729 by the end of Year VI (81). Through losses in battle and decimation by disease, but also because of large-scale desertion, the much vaunted army of three quarters of a million launched by the *levée en masse* progressively wasted away until its strength fell to only half its initial complement. The continuing state of war meant that new recruits were urgently needed to swell the ranks, though the fact that those already in uniform were mostly experienced soldiers with at least four years' service behind them guaranteed a solid framework of veteran units into which new blood could be quickly integrated (82). The time was ripe for a new initiative to provide the basis for a permanent, more professional army, consistent with the needs of a prolonged war yet loyal to the overall principles of Year II.

That initiative was the loi Jourdan of 19 *fructidor* VI, which introduced conscription on a systematic basis for the first time. The law aimed at providing for a regular, smooth regeneration of the army, with new recruits available every year as and when they were required. Those affected were young men twenty to twenty-five years old on the first day of *vendémiaire* each year, who had to sign on one of the five *tableaux* corresponding to their age. The maximum length of service prescribed was five years, which meant that the young were no longer deterred by the awesome prospect of unlimited military service that had hung over their elders. And since the youngest would in principle march first, the

twenty year olds who formed the *première classe,* this also implied that any conscript who reached his twenty-fifth birthday, who had worked his way through
to the fifth *classe* without being mobilized, would automatically receive his
congé absolu and enjoy total peace of mind. If all young men in that age range
had to present themselves, not all had to serve. The exact numbers required by
the army would vary with the fortunes of war, and Jourdan himself was convinced that relatively few would actually see service: "Beaucoup sont destinés à
servir, vraisemblablement peu serviront ... La classe des citoyens de 22 ans
marchera rarement, et celle d'un age au-dessus ne marcheront jamais" (83). In
fact, in Jourdan's eyes, that was precisely the beauty and the originality of his
reform, that a distinction could be made between obligatory conscription and
possible incorporation in the armies (84). Not only was Jourdan's proposal
accepted, but his concept of conscription, of a *roulement* between *classes* as and
when the needs of war dictated it, remained the basis of French recruitment
throughout the rest of the Revolutionary and Napoleonic Wars. What did vary
dramatically from year to year was the degree to which the government called
up the young men on the *tableaux;* again, some generations were much less
lucky than others. After the first conscription in Year VII *remplacement* was
again allowed, thus terminating the brief experiment with democratization; and
the order of service within each *classe* was, as with the recruitments of 1793, to
be decided by balloting. From Year XI any vestige of municipal autonomy in
selecting the means of determining who would march first was abolished by law;
tirage au sort became, for the first time, mandatory for all (85).

The extension of centralized control and the erosion of local discretion were
the guiding principles that underlay most of the subsequent legislation on conscription. Control was taken out of the hands of municipal councils and passed
first to *conseils de recrutement* (in Year X), then to the *sous-préfets,* who from
Year XIII had overall responsibility for drawing up the recruitment lists (86).
Sailors and river workers in maritime departments were conscripted for active
service from Year IX and placed at the disposal of the navy. In *floréal* X further
legislation placed reservists in the army in a state of readiness should the minister wish to avail himself of their services. From 1806 *gardes nationales* in turn
found themselves drafted into the army, first on coastguard duty, later to defend
France's frontiers against invasion. Each successive measure played its part in
the government's campaign to organize manpower in such a way that it could
at short notice send as many men as possible to fight a war that was extending
into an increasing number of fresh theaters. Napoleon's regime was increasingly
geared to achieving military success whatever the social cost, and the priorities
of the state are well reflected in the steady stream of legislation amending and
tightening the government's control of the conscription process.

The needs of that state oscillated wildly from year to year, but from the outset it became apparent that Jourdan's optimistic prediction would rarely be ful-
filled. Given the enervating rundown of the battalions in the previous years and
the demands of war in Year VII itself, the first levies were particularly heavy
and deeply shocking to French public opinion. Yet the conscription of Year VII
was soon overtaken by the deteriorating fortunes of the armies, with the result
that it was rapidly followed by a supplementary levy of 200,000 men and by a

further *levée générale* from all five *classes*. It was one of the harshest conscriptions of the entire period, and men from all five classes were called on to march. At Bélesta in the Ariège, for instance, of the four twenty-four year olds listed, all unskilled agricultural laborers *(brassiers),* three left to join the army (87). In contrast, if the conscription of Year VII reached maximal proportions, that of Year VIII was light, and no men at all were taken in Year IX, the year when peace was beckoning and Napoleon could even afford to demobilize approximately one-eighth of those currently in uniform. From Year X, however, with campaigning resumed in earnest, there was again a wholesale commitment to conscription; Year XII saw reservists called up for the campaign against England; and Year XIV heralded the exhaustive *levées* that were to follow with the proclamation of a *mobilisation générale.* In that year the reserve was called up as well as the *armée active.* Reporting on the demands being made of his department, the prefect of the Rhône pointed out that he now had no reservists for the previous five years, since all were on active service, while the reserve was composed of men from the *dépôt,* those whose family responsibilities would normally have ensured that they could remain in their homes. The economy of the region would be threatened if this practice continued, but already it was clear that the use of the reserve was becoming just another implication of Napoleon's total dedication to the pursuit of victory (88). The government's insistence that men who died or deserted be replaced by their fellows in the reserve further stretched the resources of communities, and must have sown bitter dissensions within local society (89). Between 1806 and 1813 the government demanded *levée* after *levée* with monotonous regularity, the weight of the demands reflecting fairly accurately the desperation of the generals and the fortunes of the war. When, as in 1809 to 1810, prospects for peace seemed bright, the conscription machine was allowed to run down, but once the defeats in the Peninsula began to pose a threat to the Pyrenean frontier, Napoleon again instituted exhaustive levels of recruitment. From 1811 conscription was universally heavy, reflecting the increasing desperation of France's military situation. By 1813 the former *classes* were arbitrarily forgotten in the quest for able-bodied recruits, and the rules governing conscription were cavalierly ignored, with conscripts of four feet eight inches being sent to the battalions and men of thirty-eight years of age included in the reserve. Desperation seemed to justify any illegality on the part of the government (90). In the words of Roger Darquenne, commenting on the situation in the department of Jemmapes, conscription had progressively been transformed into "une institution inhumaine, centralisée à l'excès, draconienne jusqu'à l'illégalité" (91).

The success of conscription cannot be called into question because it was by this means that soldiers were found, year after year, to replenish the battalions of Napoleon's *Grande Armée.* But the Loi Jourdan did not achieve overnight acceptance, nor did it instantly remove the feelings of grievance that had been aroused by the various initiatives of the 1790s. French society was still unaccustomed to compulsory service in Year VII, and in some parts of the country the new conscription law was greeted with angry rioting. In the Jura a spirit of rebelliousness spread from village to village when the law was promulgated, causing particular alarm in view of the proximity of the Swiss frontier (92).

There is considerable evidence, moreover, that towns and villages that had been noted for the level of their resistance to the *levées* of 1793 often greeted the new conscription with undisguised hostility. The total level of violence in Year VII came nowhere close to that of 1793, but there was still violence. At Quinsac in the Gironde, which had earned a certain local notoriety by its previous conduct, the young men of the canton banded together and defied the government *commissaire* to force them to leave. They took oaths among themselves, vowing that not one of them would serve, and promising that they would add strength to their cause by seeking support from neighboring communes (93). More seriously, the troublesome village of Escalquens in the Haute-Garonne staged a major clash between villagers and *gendarmes* over the new conscription laws, a clash that saw some 400 or 500 young men (if police estimates are to be believed) united by a common determination to resist the new law and prepared to go to any lengths to protect their liberty. In the ensuing battle the lieutenant in charge of the *gendarmes* was shot dead and five of his men were seriously wounded, leading to an intensive police search of the surrounding woodlands and to the forcible disarming of the villagers (94). Trouble on this scale was exceptional, but Escalquens was one of a number of communes that gave evidence in Year VII of a deeply engrained tradition of insubordination over matters of military recruitment, a tradition that was not to be dissipated by the alleged virtues of the system of conscription.

These virtues were not, in any case, immediately evident. The implementation of the Loi Jourdan depended essentially on the drawing-up of accurate, up-to-date *tableaux* of those liable for service, which was a new and daunting task for an administration still understaffed and uncertain of its responsibilities. In the Hérault, for instance, ten months passed between the date of the promulgation of the decree and that when the last of the fifty-eight cantons had sent in its returns; in the following year, when the process was more familiar, there were still long and damaging delays (95). Throughout the Empire there were continued reports of administrative failure and bureaucratic incompetence, often caused by overlapping jurisdictions and inadequate records. The correction of errors in the conscription lists remained an important part of the recruitment process, and one which caused local officials hours of research and formfilling. Simple mistakes had to be corrected and changes of address notified before the conscription could proceed. At Salers in the Cantal, the *tableau* for the *classe* of 1806 was found to contain twenty-eight errors of various kinds, and the canton was obliged to provide as much information as it could obtain from both official sources and local gossip. Four of the twenty-eight were dead—one, unsurprisingly for a lad from this part of the Auvergne, while doing seasonal work in Madrid six years previously; an illegitimate boy had disappeared from the commune and no one knew anything of his whereabouts; three had moved away from the area after the death of their parents; one had spent four years in the dragoons, and another worked for the naval administration in Brest; twenty had moved with their families to other villages and were no longer liable to conscription in Salers (96). These cases were highly typical and illustrate the Pandora's box of confusion that was opened up for local officials by the new law. There were clear instances of mistaken identity that passed unnoticed, like Guillaume

Toueillès from Penne in the Lot-et-Garonne, condemned for being refractory though he had already drawn the previous year; or poor Antoine Martinet, arrested for desertion in 1806 when he had not been drafted in the first place. In this case the prefect was forced to admit that such confusions did arise from time to time, given that so many people in local villages had the same names (97). The sources of potential confusion were manifold. Men absent from their homes to find work would have two possible addresses and faced the possibility of being called up twice (98). Careless spelling on death certificates or the noting of the wrong Christian name on marriage records provided mayors and *commissaires* with added problems in identifying those liable to serve (99). The constant movement of the sick and wounded from one hospital to another behind the war fronts made administrative errors the more likely (100). Men sometimes changed regiment (101) and less frequently went through the legal procedure of changing their name (102). The inevitable result was confusion, wrongful arrest, and considerable frustration both on the part of the hapless officials and of the public at large. Their frustration was only increased by the fact that in several areas civilian and military officials were using very different figures as the basis of their calculations, and departments found their honest efforts rewarded by stinging rebukes from the generals and the Minister of War (103).

If conscription did not solve the considerable administrative problems of earlier recruitments, nor did it dissolve fears of discriminatory treatment and allegations of unfairness. Throughout the period there were few more powerful stimuli to popular anger than the belief that the burden of service was not equally shared. Resentment of conscription could be so easily confused with envy of others on whom the demands of the state fell more lightly. And though the conscription law was devised to reduce to the minimum the element of favor in the selection of the troops, exemptions and replacement remained major sources of grievance. A poor conscript who could not contemplate the purchase of a *remplaçant,* Bernard Coton wrote angrily in Year VII about an abuse that he saw as a betrayal of the entire principle of the revolutionary army. He was, he said, proud to serve his country, so much so that he intended to enroll voluntarily rather than submit to the ballot, and yet he was bitter about those who quite legally hid in the safety of their homes:

> Je vais verser mon sang pour la liberté et l'égalité: rentrant vainquant dans mes foyers, avec quel plaisir verrai-je en place cette classe privilégiée de conscrits auxquels il a été permis de se faire remplacer avec de l'argent. Dans un état républicain il ne doit pas y avoir deux poids et deux mesures . . . (104)

Similarly those enjoying exemptions because of the offices they held were often envied by their fellow villagers, especially those who had deliberately sought the safety of reserved occupations to avoid being conscripted. The number of these positions itself occasioned anger, and in isolated instances that anger turned into popular protest. Such was the opportunity for the well-to-do, those able to read and write and those with influential connections to gain employment in local government service, that the poor could still be persuaded that only they were being expected to serve. In the rural canton of Feignies in the Nord, for instance, the *commissaire* noted that conscription was being hampered and good will lost because "les citoyens aisés restent dans leurs foyers sans être inquiétés ni même portés sur aucun état de réquisition ni de conscription" (105). In the Haute-Garonne a minor conscription riot in Year VII was blamed on the favors showered on the wealthier conscripts, on the discouragement of the others by "tant de préférences accordées à de plus fortunés qu'eux, qui ont su se soustraire aux coups en se plaçant dans les bureaux et en faisant la service auprès d'un bon feu et de la bonne chair" (106). In the first year of the new law there were even occasional hints from far-flung rural communes that they were being penalized to the advantage of more urban areas. Gif in the Seine-et-Oise felt especially aggrieved when several of its young men were denounced by the canton of Jouy for failing to sign on when they were called and were subsequently placed "en tête du tableau." The mayor pointed out that it was hardly their fault, as they had turned up on the alloted day and declared their names at the *mairie,* before returning home thinking that they had done all that was required of them (107). But Jouy was pressing home its advantage in the hope of filling its conscription obligations with ignorant and ill-informed countrymen, and to the people of Gif this was a clear instance of the local town pulling rank and insisting on a high level of sacrifice from those less educated than themselves. Suspicions of those with money, with influence, close to administrative channels and in towns, these were not just anachronistic throwbacks to the early recruitment experiments of 1793 but were ineradicable elements in village psychology. It is a tribute to the men who enforced the Loi Jourdan in the districts and cantons that these complaints were few and that they tended to die out as the conscription procedures became better known and understood.

What did remain a source of grievance throughout the Empire was the belief that conscription was geographically unequal and that some communities were expected to provide a disproportionately large number of men. In theory, of course, the weight of conscription was equally distributed across the country, divided by department in accordance with official population statistics; nothing could have been more equitable. For the conscription of Year VIII, for instance, when the needs of the government were light, the quota from each department was found by dividing its population by 805 to provide the number of conscripts; in other years the number would be much higher (108). But in practice the levels of sacrifice seemed very different, and there were constant complaints that these aggregate population statistics were much too crude an instrument for the calculations being built on them. Two prefects, in Bordeaux and in Vannes, explained in some detail why their departments were especially resentful. The prefect of the Gironde believed that the population base applied to his department was about one-third higher than it ought to be; while his colleague in the Morbihan claimed that the assessment of 425,485 used by the ministry should be reduced to 393,665 for conscription purposes. Their reasoning was clear and convincing. Until Year XIII no allowance was made in the calculations for the fact that coastal departments and those with substantial river trade were also providing men for the navy. Yet the numbers involved could be considerable. In the Gironde in Year XII 30,000 men were reserved for naval service, many of them signing on before their twentieth birthday, directly reducing the pool from which the department's military conscription was drawn. Even after Year XIII, when account was taken of this naval contribution, the prefect of the Morbihan could complain that the Minister of War was underestimating the numbers savagely, by merely taking the naval *classement* and multiplying it by four to obtain the quota for the army. The population of the Morbihan, he protested, did not conform to such a crassly mechanistic law. Given the large size of rural families in the Basse-Bretagne, a factor of six would be more accurate, while in time of war the manning of warships consumed almost all the men *classés* in the area and made coastguard service onerous and time-consuming (109). This was only one variable among many of which no account seemed to be taken in Paris. There were, claimed the prefect of the Gironde, 145 (of 583) communes in his department where men were congenitally small and feeble, "une race d'hommes si chétive, si abâtardie que la taille ordinaire n'y excède point quatre pieds dix pouces," and where conscription was virtually excluded in consequence. Nor did the government take into consideration the fact that many of the names included on the *tableaux* were those of foreign or migrant workers who came to the Bordelais for the *vendange* but moved on before the conscription was held. Paris, he protested, had promised justice and equity, but when he put a reasoned case he was being fobbed off with generalizations and irrelevancies (110).

The extent of the inequality between one department and another was recognized at the time by Hargenvilliers in his careful statistical reports (111) to the Minister of War. In 1808, discussing the impact of the five previous *classes,* he pointed out that the theoretical basis of these levies was an equitable distribution between all departments in a proportion of 1 conscript for every 138 inhabitants. But if the *tableaux* were drawn up with that norm fixedly in mind, the numbers of men incorporated, a much more real index of sacrifice, told a very different story. There were in fact wide variations between departments. The highest contribution came from departments like the Puy-de-Dôme (1 for every 114 inhabitants), the Haute-Loire (1 in 108), the Alpes-maritimes (1 in 105), and the Yonne (the worst afflicted, with a ratio of 1 in 97). At the other extreme the Hautes-Pyrénées provided 1 for every 171 inhabitants, the Basses-Pyrénées 1 in 179, the Seine 1 in 209, and the Rhône 1 in 212. The lack of precise statistics, even at this period when Napoleonic administration had become relatively sophisticated, makes reliable calculation difficult. But Hargenvilliers' estimates do allow for an appreciation of the relative weight of conscription in different areas of France and help to put the prefects' complaints into some perspective.

Such discrepancies were not entirely a matter of chance. As the government became more and more desperate in its quest for able-bodied men for the battalions, it showed less concern for equity and geographical spread. By 1807 the tone of ministerial correspondence on the subject was visibly changing, as the perceived problem became the simple one of finding enough soldiers at any price. Lacuée realized the constraints of height and health that the law placed on him, but beyond that he was no longer interested in explaining the particular problems of recruitment in individual regions or departments. Instead, his letters were increasingly addressed to the companies and battalions of the army and directed to the immediate requirements of individual commanders (112). There was even an advantage in turning to those areas of the country where recruitment was traditionally easy, where military enthusiasm and a sense of duty ran high. Fairness and social justice were concepts that could be sacrificed to victory and military efficiency. Jean-Pierre Bois, analyzing the figures for recruitment in the Maine-et-Loire, shows how the years that demanded the greatest sacrifice were 1808 and 1813, especially the latter, when the *classe de 1814* was supplemented by several exceptional levies. And even within that one department he finds glaring discrepancies in the numbers demanded, from town to town, from region to region (113). The *Directeur-général de la Conscription* admitted as much when he told the prefect in Foix that the ability of an area to produce soldiers and past records of recruitment were being used as much as simple population statistics as the basis for this last, desperate levy (114). There was, of course, a price to be paid, even if by the end of the Empire there were few flickers of open revolt. The cost was measured in less dramatic terms, in the dreadful demoralization that was setting in and the continuous drain on manpower and resources. In September 1813 the prefect of the Ariège protested at the weight of yet another *levée* announced in his department, not because of any threat to order, for there was none, but because of the permanent harm that he saw being perpetrated around him:

> J'enlève tout. Il ne restera des années 1813 et 1814 personne capable de pro-créer si je puis le dire. Cette mesure est désastreuse. Elle s'exécute, mais il est de mon devoir de vous le dire, ces deux années sont privées par ce moyen de tous les hommes capables de travailler ou de se marier. (115)

His is a chilling epitaph on the social and demographic effects of twenty-five years of virtually unbroken war.

There was, it is worth repeating, little threat to public order by the last years of the Napoleonic era. French public opinion was too exhausted and French resources too battered for violence to erupt on any major scale. The army desperately took anyone who was capable of bearing arms and the economic effects of conscription on local communities were increasingly ignored as the war fronts closed in on France's own territory. Even social distinction so dear to the Emperor in happier days was firmly cast aside in the national emergency. The *gardes d'honneur* who had been raised in 1808 to perform ceremonial functions and to provide escorts for the Emperor were suddenly reduced to the ordinary tasks of soldiering as the need for manpower became ever more pressing. As has recently been demonstrated in the case of Béziers these *gardes* were drawn from the cream of local society; they had volunteered for what was seen as a privileged and honorific role:

> C'était pour les jeunes gens de la classe aisée de la société bitteroise l'occasion de montrer leur supériorité, leur fortune, leur bonne éducation; en même temps, peut-être, espéraient-ils être remarqués par Napoléon, qui pouvait tou-jours les protéger dans leur carrière. (116)

Yet by 1813 they were being prepared for the battlefields of Leipzig, a contribution to filling the yawning gaps left in the French cavalry regiments after the disasters of the Moscow campaign. Like the millions before them, they accepted their destiny and left for the front without protest. Unlike the 1790s and the early years of conscription, the later years were relatively untroubled by violence. There were, of course, exceptions, like the series of village riots that broke out in the Landes in 1814 when the *levée* was held for the *garde nationale,* or the more serious rioting involving 1,200 to 1,500 conscripts that resulted in looting and pillaging, attacks on the subprefect, and the burning of official records at Hazebrouck in the Nord in 1813 (117). But generally recruitment remained calm. Effective policing, a more professional approach to bureaucracy, and the sheer habit of annual conscription helped ensure that the vast majority of twenty year olds turned up for medical inspection and submitted to the *supplice* of the ballot. Even in formerly troubled departments reports on these later conscriptions were often surprisingly bland, assuring Paris in self-satisfied terms that the conscripts were proving to be docile and obedient. By 1811 the prefect of the Cantal could boast that his department was now "entièrement régénéré" to the degree that it was now one of the departments filling its annual quota with the greatest exactitude (118). The casual reader, skimming such reports in the Ministry of the Interior, could have been forgiven for concluding that there was no longer a recruitment problem in France, that Napoleon's wars had succeeded in altering the habits of generations, and that for the young of the First Empire military service had come to be part of an accepted and largely unquestioned lifestyle.

3

The Extent of Evasion

THE TRUTH was rather less flattering to the government, less gratifying to those who believed that France had at last rediscovered her military instincts. For though the armies were consistently renewed and expanded through the period of the Revolutionary and Napoleonic Wars, though new recruits continued to be conjured out of the most unlikely milieux, these successes barely concealed the great underbelly of resentment and evasion stimulated by such regular levies. Patriotic fervor could be whipped up by the onset of crisis, the fall of a vital frontier, or an insult to national pride such as the murder of the French deputies sent as plenipotentiaries to Rastadt in Year VII (1). The effect of such incidents, however, was inevitably short-lived. To maintain any impetus of enthusiasm the government required an atmosphere of constant crisis, endless outrages, and an unstauched flow of adrenolin. The normal pace of war was considerably less heady, and if the generals could take pride in those heroes who stepped forward to share in the Emperor's glory, equally they were somewhat sobered by the degree of animosity that their recruiters encountered, and by the extent of fear, incomprehension, and popular resistance. The extension of the scale of the war brought little rejoicing, especially in rural France where war weariness was well-established by the end of the 1790s. In the Gironde it was noted that men and women sickened by years of war "ne sont pas les chaleureux amis de la Révolution" (2); in the Vosges the impatience of the people for peace had combined with the new ideas of liberty to create a dangerously subversive spirit because "la fausse idée que les gens sans éducation se sont faite de l'égalité" had helped turn them against the state (3). For many families the only consolation was that for much of the period the majority of youngsters could still hope to escape the clutches of the armies or at worst to be placed in the reserve. But with the Peninsula and the Russian campaign Napoleon's demands became ever more taxing, until by 1814 the entire *classe* of those eligible was being sent off to fight. Those seeking to avoid the army at almost any price could no longer realistically count on the fortune of the ballot.

43

In desperation, the young sought refuge in any means that presented itself whether within the law or in defiance of it. They were not innovators nor endowed with particular resources of imagination, and the ruses they turned to—like the measures employed against them by the recruiting-officers—were largely those that had been tried and tested throughout the long wars of the Ancien Regime. Ironically, one of the principal routes for escape lay in the framing of the recruitment law itself, since at no time in these years were all young males equally liable to service. A certain height, for instance, was a prerequisite for incorporation throughout the period, though the requirements became looser and more flexible with the passage of time. From an insistence that all troops should be at least five feet tall in the 1790s, the law was progressively changed until, during the last levies of the Empire, Napoleon was eagerly snatching men of four feet eight inches for active service (4). What made the height restriction so galling for the government was that it had such contrasting effects in different areas of the country, given the widely varied physiques of Flemings and Auvergnats, Bretons and Catalans. In their computer analysis of the extent of *défaut de taille* during the Restoration period, Emmanuel Le Roy Ladurie and Paul Dumont found wide divergences between one department and another, with the numbers of men rejected because of their small stature oscillating between only 6.5 percent in the Doubs and nearly 30 percent in the Haute-Vienne (5). Yet no allowance for height was made in the quotas demanded of each department for the annual conscription and prefects were apt to plead, not unreasonably, that the chance factor of the physique of their people merited some adjustment to quotas if lasting damage were not to be done to the local economy. In the Landes the prefect was sufficiently alarmed by the numbers pleading height as a reason for a *congé* that he ordered all those excused service on these grounds to present themselves at their town halls to be officially measured in the presence of those of their fellows who had been designated to march (6). In the Vosges, consistently among the most obedient of areas, there was little difficulty in finding men for the ordinary foot regiments during the Empire, but height was increasingly a stumbling block to recruitment into the artillery, where the stipulations were more severe: in 1808, of 122 men called, only 17 were accepted (7). Confusion reigned as to whether those below the minimal height should take part in the ballot. Undersized soldiers were dispatched to the front by well-intentioned and bamboozled mayors; country lads prayed that they would not grow too quickly before their nineteenth birthday. They were helped by Napoleon's impatience for cannonfodder that resulted in their being examined at this younger age, for the effect was the granting of larger numbers of *réformes*. The prefect of the Vendée spelled this out to the Minister in 1807 when he commented on the larger numbers being sent away by the *conseils de révision*. No fraud was involved nor yet were young men becoming more stunted in their growth. It was simply that many of them were not fully developed physically by the time they presented themselves for their medical "de sorte qu'il en est, j'en suis persuadé, qui ont été renvoyés par défaut de taille et pour faible constitution qui trés certainement auront à l'expiration de leur vingtième année toutes les conditions exigées pour le service militaire" (8).

The law further stipulated that a conscript had to be of a certain standard of physical strength and fitness if he was to be of any use to the army. Given the general poverty and the unhealthy conditions in which so many Frenchmen lived, it is hardly surprising that their health was frequently poor and that large numbers failed even the most basic medical examination. For the majority of peasant boys farming was not a healthy way of life, and it was country areas that consistently reported the highest numbers of exemptions on grounds of health and disability. Scrofula and hernias were very numerous in agricultural regions like the Aisne, and ulcers were being continually diagnosed (9). The state of physical condition varied with lifestyle and topography even within very localized areas so that recognizable patterns could be discerned in the kinds of *réformes* granted. In the Seine-et-Oise, for example, the prefect categorized the various cantons under his jurisdiction according to the prevalence of their ailments, for there was nothing homogeneous about his department. At Mantes, he reported, men were very strong and hardy, but because they worked from early childhood on steep escarpments they tended to suffer from severe curviture of the spine. In Etampes and Corbeil they were often of very weak constitution. Near Versailles there were frequent cases of shortsightedness and at Pontoise a large number were infected with ringworm (10). Often local patterns of disability were connected with a particular trade, as in the Oise, where the prefect had no hesitation in linking the high incidence of hernias and constitutional diseases to the occupational structure of his department, "pays des éventails, lunetiers et frotteurs de verre à Songeons et dans les communes voisines, faiseurs de bas, fileurs de laine" (11). The variety of ailments diagnosed and accepted as the basis for exemption gives a frightening insight into the standards of health at the time. At Vic-sur-Cère in the Cantal, for instance, fifty-seven young men underwent a basic medical in Year VII and only three were considered fit for military service. And however cynically one may view the judgments of the jury in an area not renowned for its enthusiasm for soldiering, many of those examined were seriously ill. Deafness, epilepsy, wounds that had turned septic, respiratory troubles and the spitting of blood, ulcers, tumors, unexplained lumps, and untreated fractures were all present. Some had deformities that made walking difficult and painful, several suffered from chest diseases and lung failure, in a few cases the ailments were hereditary, and one man had apparently been bitten by a rabid dog (12). In mountainous areas like Vic *faiblesse de constitution* complemented *défaut de taille* as a major impediment to efficient recruitment.

As with exemptions for height, so exemptions on health grounds were very unevenly spread across France. In the five *classes* up to and including Year XIII, some 35 percent of all conscripts were exempted following their appearance before a *conseil de révision*. Yet in two departments, the Meurthe and the Puy-de-Dôme, only 10 percent of recruits were excused, whereas in twenty-seven others the figure was 40 percent or higher, and in a few it exceeded half of the youngsters on the *tableaux*. The Charente and the Creuse both exempted 51 percent of their conscripts, the Cher 54 percent, and the Eure an astonishing 63 percent (13). The prefect of the Seine-Inférieure was himself sufficiently shocked by the high number of men in the conscription of 1813 who were physically weak or deformed that he offered the Minister the explanation that he had been given by local doctors—that the poor state of health of the conscripts resulted from the conditions in which they had grown up and the deprivations they had suffered; "Les médecins s'accordent à croire que la faiblesse de leur constitution peut tenir à l'époque à laquelle ils sont nés, et ne doutent pas que la disette et les doutes politiques de 1793 n'aient influé d'une manière très puissante sur leur organisation physique" (14). While this might seem politically acceptable, it scarcely justified the enormous variations from town to town. In 1811, noting these discrepancies, the Minister complained that far too many *réformes* were being handed out and implied that very high proportions (the deparment of Mont-Blanc exempted 58 percent of its conscripts) could only mean feeble or even corrupt local administration (15). The government put increasing pressure on local officials to use medical exemptions sparingly and took a detailed interest in the workings of the *conseils* that granted them.

The mechanism for granting these exemptions was always likely to be fraught with suspicion because local people were involved and interest and influence never far away. In the 1790s, when municipal councils still retained a large measure of discretion in determining who was fit for service, allegations of malpractice were especially prevalent, with Paris tending to interpret large numbers of exemptions as further evidence of lax administration and poor *esprit public.* Men with relatively minor ailments, it was claimed, were getting themselves exempted by benevolent councils, and even those who had obviously inflicted their wounds themselves were being excused service without as much as a rebuke. Throughout the period, it was a constant theme of ministerial correspondence that local men were necessarily venal and open to pressure, and that the sons of the rich and influential were always the most likely to receive the coveted *réforme.* From the Sarthe came the forthright statement that equality was being outraged, that those with money could always succeed in being exempted leaving the poor to fight: "Il n'y a que les pauvres à soutenir la République, ceux-là seuls sont contraints de rejoindre les armées, parce qu'ils ne peuvent, faute d'argent, se procurer des exemptions" (16). Even in 1813 the general in charge of recruitment in the Gironde wrote angrily to the prefect that the sons of rich Bordeaux families were still managing to secure the most improbable exemptions on medical grounds. Latour, of the paper firm, had been excused "quoiqu'il soit un des plus beaux hommes de la ville". The son of another merchant, Graves *aîné,* had been rejected on the spurious grounds that he had one arm shorter than the other, although this had never before been noticed in the town. "Le Juif Gradis," found fit at his first medical, had mysteriously developed a hernia by the time of his second, "quoique l'infirmité alléguée n'existe pas" (17). The general added that it might not be entirely coincidental that these rich families offered handsome presents to the captain in charge of recruitment, who had amassed a sizable fortune through his display of discreet generosity. Such instances made a laughingstock of the principles on which conscription was constructed and constituted a dangerous example to others. The large number of exemptions granted in the Nord was seen as a direct incentive to desert (18). The social imbalance often evident in the dispensing of *réformes* also added to the intensity of feeling against conscription in many areas of the country (19).

That is not to suggest that all mayors were corrupt or to impugn the workings of the system as a whole. But there were enough cases of graft and favor in the course of the decade to make ministers seek to tighten up the procedures for granting *réformes,* and the introduction of conscription was accompanied by the establishment of departmental juries to perform this delicate task. Their composition was fixed by law, each jury consisting of three military officers, assisted by three doctors who could offer expert opinion (20). As conscription became more and more pressing, so the control of the *conseil de révision* grew more centralized, under the chairmanship of the subprefect and finally of the prefect himself. The guidelines issued were equally restrictive, laying down precisely what kinds of disability should be regarded as grounds for exemption. Some the jury could determine on the spot. They were to look, said the prefect of the Seine-et-Oise, for the loss of an eye, the atrophying of a limb, the mutilation of some essential organ, the curviture of the vertical column, or the total loss of teeth. Others might be less immediately apparent, but in the interests of public order they should assure themselves that the grounds for a *réforme* were always such as were generally accepted in the community and unlikely to cause uproar among the other conscripts (21). These criteria are interesting, for they throw light on the more fundamental interests of the government, both in maintaining public order and in guaranteeing a general sense of fairness in the conscription process.

Evidence from the registers of the *conseils de révision* bears witness to the painstaking thoroughness that was usually displayed in coming to a decision. Conscripts would appear before the jury and ask for some ailment to be considered or some deformity to exclude them from the ballot. Solemnly they shuffled forward, parading their bent left toe, their lameness, their "cuisse beaucoup plus courte," their limp and useless right arm, and the jury would pass judgment. If the conscript still felt he had a grievance he had the right to represent himself and provide new evidence with some prospect that his appeal would be successful (22). Sometimes the appearance would involve a detailed and intimate medical examination, as in the case of Laurent Chol who declared to the *conseil* at Bordeaux in Year VII that an axe had sliced through his left testicle. The jury noted solemnly that Chol had indeed suffered this terrible accident,

> que cette position du testicule doit faire éprouver des douleurs vives qui se propagent dans la région lombaire lorsque cette partie éprouve la plus légère pression dès que le malade fait quelque exercice un peu pénible ou qu'il se tient longtemps debout, que cette affection ne présente point de grands moyens curatifs à moins une opération qui serait très douloureuse et douteuse, que ce citoyen serait plus onéreux qu'utile à la République dans les armées. (23)

But there were other disabilities that were less easy to detect with any confidence in the course of a short medical, blindness, and epilepsy being two of the most common examples. Doctors asked to make rapid diagnoses found it impossible to rule with any certainty, and in such cases the testimony of other villagers and a sworn statement by the mayor were still accepted as binding evidence (24). This was not done without considerable misgiving because there was little confidence in the truthfulness of friends and neighbors when asked to provide evidence that would allow one of their own to escape the draft. By 1806 even doctors' notes were being treated with open scorn. The prefect of the Gironde reported maliciously in that year that all but 200 or 300 of his conscripts had turned up with the regulation medical note, adding that if they were to be believed "tout le département ne serait qu'un immense hôpital" (25). Even less receptive was the prefect of the Somme, who informed his mayors that conscripts seeking a *réforme* should not bother to collect petitions or medical certificates before coming to Amiens, since the *conseil* had clear instructions to ignore all of them; only official letters from mayors would have any effect. The *conseil*, he added flamboyantly, was there to examine men's bodies not their papers (26). But the success of the *conseils* in avoiding abuse varied considerably, not least because some of them were accepting bribes and according favors to their friends. Some 7,000 or 8,000 exemptions were handed out by the *conseil de révision* in Aurillac between 1806 and 1810, the majority of them purchased for approximately 1,000 francs apiece, a scandal that implicated the prefect himself and which led to his dismissal (27). The young Cantalien might view the medical examination as a proper moment to buy his freedom, whereas for his counterpart in the Seine-et-Oise, faced with a steely integrity and a reluctance to exempt any but the most glaring cases, no such opportunity existed (28). By the end of the war the law on the composition and conduct of the councils had been tightened to such a degree that they offered little hope of honest escape from the regiment. The able-bodied recruit could expect little of them composed as they were of army men and propertied *notables* who had already seen their own sons incorporated into the battalions. The odds were so stacked against the conscript that in the Ariège, an area where few young men were eager to sacrifice themselves in the nation's service, only those whose disabilities were quite patent and who were therefore confident of obtaining a *réforme* were presenting themselves for examination (29).

Since for the greater part of the war it was single men who were subjected to military service, another legal route to freedom lay in timely matrimony. All the recruitment laws of the 1790s and the early years of conscription specifically exempted or placed *en fin de dépôt* those young men who had married before twenty years of age, and no government could make marriage illegal in the interests of its military. Nevertheless, successive ministers viewed with a jaundiced eye the lines of young men presenting themselves for marriage during the spring months, the months that also marked the recruiting season before the new campaigns began. Progressively the government tried to prevent any last minute rush to the *mairie* by designating in the recruitment law a precise date, usually some weeks earlier, by which a conscript must have been married if he were to benefit from military exemption (30). Further restrictions were added in 1809 when the demands of the army reached a new peak. From that year it became necessary in practice to have children as well as a wife to be sure of exemption; such was the weight of that year's conscription that married men without dependents were being taken, while the death of his wife would render a conscript immediately liable to service unless he had taken the precaution of starting a family (31). This was merely the last turn of the screw since the marriages of potential conscripts had been increasingly circumscribed by regulations and prohibitions since the first conscription law in Year VII. The effect was, of course, an increase in policing in an area that most villagers regarded as intensely private and in which state meddling was bitterly resented. For mayors and prefects the application of such a law was fraught with difficulties and ambiguities. When the department of the Rhône asked for a ruling in Year VII on the circumstances in which marriage could actually be refused, the Minister of the Interior was suitably cautious. It was not the government's wish to discourage matrimony, far less procreation, he explained, and *agents municipaux* should not refuse to marry those conscripts who had legal exemptions or who were not called for active service. But too many of those presenting themselves were using their married status to avoid their obligations, and in these cases their requests must be refused. Any officials marrying conscripts who had no exemption from service would, indeed, be commiting a criminal offense by becoming the accomplices of soldiers intent on defrauding the state, and they risked being punished accordingly (32).

Though the aim of this legislation was universally understood, its effects were not always welcomed by the administrators who had to enforce it. The prefect of the Gironde was particularly outspoken in Year IX in condemning what he saw as the damaging implications of a law that had seriously reduced the number of marriages in many villages in his department. The region was already suffering from a shortage of labor that was putting agriculture at risk, and any decrease in the number of marriages could only lead to a subsequent decrease in the birthrate at a time when it was imperative to expand the population to aid the nation's recovery from a long and costly war. The implications, he added, extended beyond the demographic field because the effect on morals was a corrupting one with a new casualness in attitudes to cohabitation and illegitimacy (33). But more galling for the army were the many marriages that *were* celebrated and which, even when within the letter of the law, showed incontrovertibly the degree of hostility to soldiering that was prevalent in the community. Small villages in the Basses-Pyrénées were deluged with "une foule de mariages," some legal, others fraudulent, as young men rushed to cover themselves with the most accessible alibi (34). Desperate conscripts on finding themselves drafted tried to escape by rushing into marriage. We learn, for instance, that following the publication of the conscription lists on 11 January 1813 in the canton of Meulan, one of the lads affected got married on 13 January and a second on the following day (35). Public opinion would generally seem to have favored fugitives, especially if their conduct could be portrayed as "honorable." Grellier, a conscript of the Year IX from Lausun in the Lot-et-Garonne, is a case in point. He was a refractory and therefore ineligible for marriage, but he succeeded in persuading the mayor of La Réole to marry him to a local girl whom he had got pregnant. It is difficult not to sympathize with the hapless mayor in such a case. Grellier was a plausible enough young man, a *coutelier* by trade who would have every reason to travel to other towns in search of work, who had lived in La Réole for only a few months. Had the mayor undertaken the checks that the law demanded, a local family would have been unnecessarily embarrassed. He therefore married the young couple and betrayed his trust as a magistrate (36).

What particularly worried the authorities was the growing number of marriages of the kind that they termed "abusifs" or "disproportionnés," those of twenty- or twenty-one-year old conscripts to women very much older than themselves. The cases are legion, especially in rural villages where marriageable young girls were at a premium and lads found themselves in need of wives at a few days' notice. In such circumstances a young man could not always afford to be selective. The village of Maucourt in Picardy produced in 1808 a galaxy of rare matches, with young conscripts selecting brides of 72, 74, 77, even 87 years old to win the privilege of staying on their farms, undisturbed by the recruiting-officer (37). Similarly in the Drôme in 1813, the prefect was angered by a rash of rather curious weddings, uniting conscripts to women of 75, 77, and 82 years old, widows from farming communities who had accepted to save young, able-bodied men from the battalions. One of the four conscripts involved had even gone to see the *sous-préfet* in Valence to convince himself that his intended marriage was valid in the eyes of the law. Another, the son of the mayor of Larnage who had married a woman of 55 years old, could point out that the marriage was not conceived of as a means of draft dodging but as a step, in no way unusual in a peasant village, aimed at the accumulation of wealth. His father added that he saw nothing reprehensible in the union because at 55 years of age "une femme n'est point encore une pièce de débris, elle est encore bien en état de gouverner une maison, elle peut se promettre encore plusieurs années de travail" (38). The mayor of Erôme, defending his decision to conduct two of the offending ceremonies, added that mayors were not appointed to investigate whether marriages were devised "par aisance" or "par amitié" (39). It is, perhaps, significant that the *sous-préfet* of Nyons rushed to their defenses, adding that the mayors who had permitted these marriages had nothing to answer for because they had acted in good faith and had not broken any law or ministerial instruction (40).

If the subprefect was right in believing that the strict letter of the law was being respected, its spirit was being broken on a disturbing scale. Even the oldest of village women could be escorted to the *mairie* by young men suddenly alerted to the benefits of matrimony. Paul Viard, in his discussion of the abuse in the Nord, has unearthed one improbable marriage between a lad of eighteen years and a widow of ninety-nine years, and the case may not be unique (41). Recruiting-officers were understandably irate that no action could be taken against the conscripts involved, for, as the prefect of the Aisne pointed out, there was little moral difference between a recruit who mutilated himself to avoid service and his counterpart who by entering a solemn marriage ceremony with an octogenarian "répugne à la fois aux bonnes moeurs et outrage la nature" (42). The Revolution had even facilitated the process by instituting divorce since the young recruit who married for reasons of short-term convenience was not committed to his bride for longer than was strictly necessary and she would generally be discarded once the threat of conscription receded. For the women the attraction was usually financial. They were suddenly in desperate demand and were able to profit accordingly. In the Calvados, the *jeunes gens* entering into such contracts were almost always from reasonably comfortable homes and the women were predictably the impoverished inmates of the local poorhouse. The arrangement could be portrayed as a kind of rescue operation for them as well:

C'est parmi des septuagénaires, des octogénaires que ces insensés choisissent des compagnes qu'ils abandonnent ensuite en leur accordant quelques secours journaliers. Ces jours-ci un jeune homme de l'arrondissement de Pont l'Evê-que, riche de 1500 francs de rentes, a donné son nom à une misérable femme d'un age trés avancé, vivant d'aumônes et à qui il se contente de faire une trés modique pension. De plusieurs côtés il m'arrive des avis d'alliances de cette nature. (43)

Some women could even aspire after the role of professional wives for village boys facing the draft, marrying conscripts on two or even three separate occasions, the marriages punctuated by timely divorces (44). The authorities were understandably anxious that such marriages would reach epidemic proportions, since already there were marriage brokers established in business seeking out wives for reluctant soldiers. Information on their activities was often rather shadowy given that they operated in bars and cafés in the proximity of large towns where peasant boys had to come to present themselves to the *conseil*. One suspect from Avesnes in the Nord was denounced as a "grand fabricateur de mariages" between conscripts and "vieilles femmes," but there was insufficient evidence to mount a charge (45). Generally such men operated just within the bounds of legality, to the great frustration of local officials who were powerless to halt their enterprise. Prefects were often reluctant to give too much publicity to their activities in case word spread to other villages and recruitment suffered still more damage. The prefect of the Calvados, for instance, refused to issue a decree on the matter and preferred to work indirectly through the Church authorities by asking the bishop of Bayeux to discourage his parish clergy from condoning this abuse of the marriage vows (46).

Contemporary opinion was that military recruitment was being seriously impeded by a suspiciously high rate of marriage and by a tendency to marry young. The municipal council of Gorze in the Moselle found the trend very alarming. Youngsters of seventeen and eighteen years of age, knowing that early marriage would dispense them from service, were rushing headlong into wed-lock with results that the council stigmatized as "rien moins que l'abâtardisse-ment de l'espèce et la destruction prochaine de nos armées" (47). The bride-grooms, it adjudged, were too young to accept the responsibilities of marriage having neither the maturity of temperament nor the physical strength of grown men. They were innocents deprived of their youth in a lemminglike quest for security. The language used by Gorze was exaggerated and alarmist, but there is no doubt that the fear that conscripts were marrying in increasing numbers to escape the draft was widely held. Letters home from older brothers on the frontiers urged matrimony in preference to service. There was little ambiguity in the advice of men like Louis Goddos, from Larchamp in the Mayenne, when he wrote in 1813: "Je vous dirais à notre frère qu'il se maris pour son mieux" (48). Nor was there any doubt in the minds of the young men of Mantes who, at the time of the *levée des 300,000,* seized the board posted outside the town hall announcing forthcoming marriages and paraded through the town streets mockingly bearing it aloft. They did so, said the mayor, with good patriotic intent "pour empêcher les mariages de leurs concitoyens qu'ils supposent prendre ce parti pour se dispenser de voler à la défense de leur patrie" (49). By 1809 the seriousness of the issue was being discussed at the very highest level, with the Minister of War reporting to the Emperor that the scale of "mariages disproportionnés," in particular, made it desirable to re-examine the blanket exemptions that had previously been granted to married conscripts (50). Two years later Duplantier, the prefect in Douai, went further, issuing a decree on his own initiative demanding that all marriages of conscripts to women aged fifty years and older should be carefully scrutinized before an exemption was issued (51). In the Loir-et-Cher the authorities could cite human tragedy in support of their plea for greater controls after a conscript of 1810, Pierre Labbé was found hanged from a beam in his loft in the village of Vineuil. Village gossip was unanimous; the unfortunate Pierre, whose parents had arranged a civil marriage for him with the express aim of preserving him from the armies had committed suicide which stemmed directly from his ill-advised marriage. Pierre had not previously seemed blighted by depression, yet "depuis ce mariage ce malheureux jeune homme a été constamment plongé dans une sombre rêverie, il a refusé pendant plusieurs jours à prendre aucun aliment, et avait même tenté de se noyer" (52). The lesson was clear that forced marriages of this kind could be as damaging to the individual as they were to the interests of the state.

Demographers and local historians, while acknowledging that matrimony did provide a loophole that was seized on by reluctant recruits, are rather less impressed than were contemporaries by its global impact on the Revolutionary and Imperial armies. Roger Darquenne, writing on the annexed Belgian department of Jemmapes, observes that marriage rates oscillated considerably, with marked increases in 1801 to 1803 but also with a significant retrenchment in 1805 and 1806. Economic as well as political and military considerations were affecting the propensity of people in his area to rush into marriage. But there were two exceptional upsurges in the marriage rate that did relate directly to the progress of the war. In 1796 the increase reflected the number of marriages that had been deferred as a result of the Belgian Campaign and the near famine conditions of the previous two years, and what he terms a wedding fever or *"fièvre"* swept the department in 1813, the year of the most massive levies for Napoleon's armies (53). Even more telling is the evidence by Gustave Vallée from his exhaustive research on the Charente. Like Darquenne, he is cautious about making any generalization for the earlier period when there were regular complaints about the implications of individual marriages but no huge increase that would suggest a coherent trend. A discernible increase did occur from 1807, however, when heavier conscription levels for the Peninsular War began to cause panic, and in these later years the relationship between war and marriage rates was both consistent and logical. In 1810 a year of relative peace and optimism, the level of marriages decreased. Thereafter it increased steadily from 1811 through to the peak year of 1813 when the demands of the recruiting-officers were so great that even the sons of rich families found themselves pressed into service.

The result, say Vallée, was a staggering increase in the number of marriages among the sons of economically secure families seeking an outlet from the Grande Armée. He isolates the figures for young men of conscription age from *familles aisées* in one provincial town, Angoulême, and finds that the rate of marriage in this group increased from 5 percent in 1811 to 12.6 percent in 1812 and a remarkable 19 percent in the crisis year of 1813. In the following year, once the danger was seen to have passed, the rate resumed its normal moderate tenor. The exceptionally high rates were always short-lived with three significant peaks—in Year XII, 1809, and especially 1813—and with equally high birth rates following in Year XIII, 1810, and 1814 (54). For this reason, Vallée concludes, the *crise de population* in the Empire was perhaps less extreme than one might have expected; and the losses to the armies resulting from early or arranged marriages, though a perpetual irritant to the authorities, had serious implications for recruitment only in short staccato bursts.

Exemptions from active service were granted on other grounds too, especially before the Loi Jourdan and the introduction of conscription. Throughout the 1790s certain occupations deemed essential for the furtherance of the war effort were systematically reserved, with the result that certain categories of "citoyens utiles" were exempted from service. From March 1793 the Convention specifically exempted for the duration of the war all bakers, carters and drivers who could provide evidence that they were engaged in servicing or provisioning the armies. And in the following month the same privilege was extended to various categories of munitions workers—to those "attachés à la fabrication des armes, aux fonderies de canons, aux grandes forges et aux mines de fer"—whose skills were needed if the army was to have the wherewithall to continue fighting (55). In the Year II such was the fear of famine and grain shortage that the government offered exemptions to peasants and farmworkers with a generosity that was denied those living and working in the towns (56). Discretion was generally left to the municipal authorities in these early years, and they were predictably deluged with petitions from soldiers and parents anxious to bend the regulations to their own advantage. Education was frequently used as a justification for seeking favored treatment: *notaires* were apt to claim exemptions for themselves and their clerks (57); continuing study might be used as a welcome escape hatch (58); and several cases where local school teachers obtained the *congés* they sought (59). From Year IV, however, the level of discretion left to local authorities was drastically reduced as the government ruled that exemptions should be restricted to agricultural occupations and to *artistes,* to specialist artisan crafts that were sorely needed by the community if food production and the servicing of the armies were to proceed apace. Paris felt obliged to intervene in the interests of equity in an area where local practice varied widely and where the rather arbitrary treatment of individual claimants could cause outrage and a sense of searing injustice.

Defining the categories for which exemptions could be given was difficult enough. Persuading semiliterate villagers of these distinctions proved a hard and thankless task, especially in the early years of the Revolutionary *levées* when the vagueness of the law encouraged a rash of optimism. Petitions flooded in to district officials mostly from farmers or peasants asking on grounds of personal misfortune or agricultural efficiency that their son or brother or farmservant be granted a special dispensation. Where piles of these petitions still exist, for example for the Morbihan at the time of the *levée des 300,000,* the extent of the confusion becomes apparent. The majority of them have no real grounds for preferential treatment. Most come from the wealthier members of the farming community who seem to believe that they have some grounds for exemption on the basis of their wealth. They tend to list their land holdings and their head of livestock as though in these figures might lie their or their sons' salvation. Marie Horau, a widow from near Ploërmel, in pleading that her only son be left to work the farm, lists his responsibilities in support of her case: "Je vous demande que mon dit fils me soit accordé, ayant deux boeufs, deux chevaux, trois vaches, une genisse, cinquante-huit moutons et brebis, ce sera justice . . ." (60). Mathurin Morice, a *laboureur* at Taupon, again listed his livestock, this time to protect his only farmservant from the army. Without him, said Morice, he would be forced to give up the holding with a serious consequent loss to the nation (61). After Year IV, in contrast, the law was so precise in its definition of those eligible that the swarm of petitioners receded. The lists of men exempted in that year illustrate the kinds of circumstances that the authorities deemed deserving of exemption, and it is clear that there is a moral element as well as a purely functional one in their decisions. The canton of Hellimer in the Moselle restricted exemptions almost entirely to those who were carters and *voituriers* engaged in provisioning the armies, who used their engineering skills in the *parc d'artillerie,* or who could provide overwhelming social reasons for their indispensibility at home on the farm (62). The lists for various communes in the rural Cantal in Year VI confirm this impression. The men exempted at Pleaux, for example, were artisans adjudged to be needed by local agriculture: "charpentier et très utile au public," "maréchal et nécessaire au public," "charron et utile au public." Or their work and income were recognized as being necessary to the welfare of a large and vulnerable family, to the continued independence of elderly parents, or, exceptionally, to the culture of a smallholding. In this final case it was noted that the young man's parents had both been killed by lightning and that there was no one else in the family to keep the land under cultivation (63). In nearby Pierrefort, though some were simple tradesmen and artisans, the majority again had already proved their worth to the Republic: one looking after his blind father; another the son of a widow who had already been with the army as a carter; a third, again responsible for his elderly father's welfare, had lost a brother on the frontiers and had taken the precaution of providing another man in his stead (64).

The policy of granting exemptions of this kind did have the serious defect that it quickly led to allegations of unfair discrimination and of favoritism. Certain religious groups, most notably the Anabaptists, had a conscientious objection to war that was recognized by both their deputy to the Convention and by the district of Colmar where they were particularly numerous. The district, accepting that their "caractère doux et paisible" made them unsuitable for bearing arms, ordered that they be used for military convoys and that they and their animals be requisitioned for that purpose (65). But it was more difficult to persuade their fellow villagers of the justice of their case when the communes were forced to conscript others in their place, and local disturbances were reported.

At Sembach in Mont-Tonnerre the refusal of Jewish parents to let their sons march with the other conscripts—a refusal that was quite illegal but which had been left unpunished by the very sensitive administration—led to anger among the Catholic population who viewed their behavior as "un luxe insultant pour leurs concitoyens," and matters reached a head when the other villagers arrested the two Jewish fathers who were giving protection to their sons (66). The anger caused by localized religious groups and by the *de facto* exemptions that they were granted was nothing compared to the fury aroused by the exemption of officials and clerks serving in municipal and departmental bureaucracies. For such instances were not confined to limited areas nor did they cease with the introduction of conscription. In law there was no justification for them, but municipalities found themselves under pressure from friends and business associates to employ their sons in office jobs, and in many parts of France, especially in country areas where literacy rates were low, intelligent young men were at a premium for the rapidly mushrooming tasks that fell to the councils to perform. The department of the Indre-et-Loire attempted to intercede with the Minister of War in Year IV to maintain five *réquisitionnaires* at their posts, arguing that their loss would lead to damaging chaos in its operations (67). In German-speaking areas of Alsace the fact that much of the day-to-day work had to be conducted in German added further conviction to municipal appeals for the exemptions they desired (68). In the Meurthe the *commissaire du Directoire* in one of the districts was himself liable to be requisitioned (69). The fact that young men were finding refuge from the armies in the offices of the government itself was a particular source of embarrassment. Often the administrations would use as an excuse the fact that in 1793 such exemptions had been allowed, if only briefly, to provide infant organizations with a certain aptitude. But by Year IV such excuses were tame and smacked of corruption. How could the government persuade other young men to join their regiments without trouble when their comrades were being offered protection in the offices of the navy or the *Armée des Alpes* and in the service of the *commissaire-ordonnateur* for military supplies (70)? Resentment was soon fanned by rumor and disruption followed. In the Nièvre, where the district authorities were experiencing considerable difficulty in enforcing the law, popular anger focused on the fact that all levels of government still seemed to be employing young men of the requisition in their own administrations (71). At Sabarat in the Ariège the local youth turned out in force to the *tirage* in Year III but adamantly refused to draw unless all public officials were included in the ballot. Not even the news that Puycerda had been taken by the Spanish and the implied threat to their homes could change their minds (72). Behind such protests was, once again, a sense of injustice, a feeling that while peasants and working men were being sent to the front, the sons of the rich and the educated were finding comfortable niches in civilian life. This feeling was well expressed by five self-styled *"Républicains de Dijon"* who petitioned the Cinq-Cents in Year VII about the exemptions that allowed the sons of the bourgeoisie to spend their war behind office desks or in hospital wards:

> Par quelle fatalité se fait-il que le sang de nos enfants coule abandamment pendant que celui des riches est ménagé? Pourquoi, malgré toutes les lois, ces petits messieurs trouvent-ils toujours le moyen d'encombrer les bureaux et

les hôpitaux et de tenir la plume ou le bistouri tandis que leurs camarades
font le coup de fusil? (73)

The sense of class outrage was never far removed.

If these forms of exemption were seen as being damaging to recruitment and
to the morale of the armies, there was another category of exemption that was
specifically devised to improve France's fighting strength—the exemption of
men from maritime areas to serve in the navy. Those eligible for naval *classement* were strictly defined by law because it was not the intention of the government to starve the army of recruits or to cause unnecessary confusion in the
departments. The "loi sur les classes des gens de mer" passed in January 1791
restricted naval service to regions with a coastline or a tradition of river navi-
gation and to those men who had experience of relevant trades and skills—officers and men on naval and merchant shipping, of course, but also fishermen,
bargers, ferrymen, and a limited number of maritime crafts like ropemaking,
sailmaking, barrelmaking, and carpentry. The attraction was that once a man
had been *classé,* he could be called up only for service at sea, but the government
insisted that all those applying for naval service must be fully apprenticed or
able to pass an examination in their trade or skill (74). Under the Empire the
departments defined as "littoraux" and therefore liable to naval levies were limited to thirty, twenty-three of them in metropolitan France with the heaviest
levies imposed on the Seine-Inférieure, Finistère, Gironde, and Manche (75).
Even departments with poor records of recruitment for the army could sometimes point to a robust recruitment of sailors and port workers; because the law
encouraged them to opt for naval *classement* before their nineteenth birthday,
the result was a correspondingly high number of *réformes* when the military levies came to be held (76). In some coastal areas where the seafaring tradition was
strong, the numbers taking advantage of naval *classement* during their teens
were so high that their communes became drained of manpower and the military conscription failed miserably to produce the necessary quotas of men. Such
was the case in Lorient in Year XI when the municipal council noted rather
plaintively that along the Morbihan coast "dans les ports de mer tout est à peu
près marin" (77); and in the maritime regions of the Nord around Dunkerque
and Gravelines where persistent conscription and service on corsairs in the
Channel had by 1812 drained the local community of both sailors and craftsmen
(78). In a region where coastal and river traffic was vital to the economy, over-
conscription of seamen and bargers also put trade and industry at risk; the mines
at Anzin were among the enterprises affected when they could no longer find
commercial shipping to transport their coal stocks (79).

Although the practice of exempting *gens de mer* from military recruitment
had a long and honorable pedigree (80), the system of *classement* attracted a
great deal of criticism. On the one hand, it was alleged that the practice did nothing to improve the caliber of the navy, especially as the conscription included
ouvriers marins who had never previously set foot on board a ship. At Dunkerque the *sous-commissaire de la marine* was believed to be incorporating anyone with the least nautical background in his bid to fill the required quotas,
regardless of the effect that this might have on morale (81). Indeed, the minister

for the navy became convinced by Year XII that artisanal skills had little relevance to the quality of young sailors, for their craft always remained their primary interest and seafaring took a poor second place. He complained to the Emperor that the *ouvriers marins* whom he was being forced to accept made the worst of seamen, lacking both experience and commitment, and made an impassioned plea for unsophisticated ignorance for men with experience of life at sea without any pretensions to craft status:

> Les bons matelots sont ceux qui sont les plus ignorants, ceux qui n'ayant point de métier qui leur donne à vivre pendant qu'ils sont à terre sont obligés de se rembarquer continuellement, ceux enfin qui n'ayant pas à tirer vanité d'une industrie étrangère au gréement et à la manoeuvre placent la leur à l'avance dans cette partie. (82)

On the other hand, the critics could point to the fact that naval *classement* was increasingly seen as a way by which able-bodied conscripts could escape the rigors of the armies, especially during the Empire when the navy was little used by comparison with the military. In the Pyrénées-Orientales it was observed that naval inscription was almost the equivalent of total evasion of military responsibilities (83). In the Landes there was little question of really competent boatmen serving in the navy, because they were receiving open protection from local officials who were in most cases themselves the captains of merchant ships desperate for experienced crews (84). Hence local recruitment offices were forced to twist the rules and accept men for the navy who had no right to be *classés,* men who should in law have been balloted for the armies. Such a man was Pierre-François Loton, one of many ill-qualified sailors signed on in hard-pressed Lorient. Whereas in theory all candidates for *classement* in his age group had to prove their prowess by two years' apprenticeship, eighteen months at sea, or experience of two long voyages or two seasons of fishing, Loton seems never to have been on a ship but to have spent his youth in study at the *collège* in Vendôme and the law school at Rennes. It could only follow that he, along with many of his fellows, had obtained his certificate of competence by fraudulent means to escape from the regiments. This suspicion was futher strengthened when Loton's younger brother followed his example and produced a false certificate attesting to his naval *classement.* It was finally revealed that the boys' father was employed as a *commis de marine* in Lorient (85).

Similar criticism was leveled against that other form of legalized inequality, the system of *remplacement* whereby those unlucky enough to draw a *mauvais numéro* in the ballot could purchase the services of others to serve in their stead. Again there was nothing new about this practice which dated from 1758, but it seemed to many Jacobins in particular to constitute a dangerous breach of the most fundamental principles of citizenship. Carnot, for instance, on mission to the Nord in 1793, argued cogently against it on the grounds that it encouraged a squalid "commerce d'hommes" and that it had "décomposé, décomplété les bataillons" and put the safety of the Republic at risk (86). Yet the practice was accepted with only a brief intermission at the time of the *levée en masse* throughout the revolutionary decade, with the proviso that replacements were allowed on an individual basis only and for those who provided them before the *tirage*. The Loi Jourdan made no provision for replacement with the result that the first recruits of Year VII were denied this option, but the omission did not last for more than a few months and some form of replacement was available for conscripts throughout virtually the entire Napoleonic period. From Year VII men of the second and third *classes* of the conscription were allowed to offer replacements; from the following year the practice was again generalized. Subsequent legislation alternated between a liberal system of replacement whereby anyone with the money could buy himself out by finding a man to serve in his place, without restriction beyond the requirement that he be of sound health and military age and a much more restrictive system known as *substitution,* which insisted that the man hired to serve had to come from the same commune and even from the same *classe.* The government was groping toward a compromise formula that would allow the rich to buy their sons out of active service while protecting the army from the ill effects of a vulgar trafficking in men (87). The Law of 8 *fructidor* XIII finally offered a definitive ruling on the matter, laying down the principle that replacement was a right and not a personal favor. It was enshrined in a highly bureaucratized legal framework, however. The *suppléant* had to be found locally and from within the department, and had to provide evidence of physical fitness, conform to the army's height qualification, and be the bearer of a *congé absolu,* since the administration had to be assured that replacement did not involve the double service of men already conscripted (88). Once these conditions were satisfied, the government saw no reason to interfere in a simple commercial arrangement between two of its citizens. From Year VIII the form of the contract was standardized, with the two parties obliged to draw up an *acte devant notaire* in front of the local lawyer (89). In addition, after 1809 the scope of replacements was extended further when men posted to the reserve were allowed to sell their services to those of their comrades marked down for active service (90).

The most persistent criticism leveled against the whole system of replacements was that it was, yet again, a device that favored the rich. By the later Empire the moneyed classes were more and more desperate to buy their sons out of the army, and there was bitter resentment that the poor were increasingly denied this option, that their fate was determined by the number they drew at the ballot, and by the sums of money dangled before them as inducements to serve. The cost of a replacement was, of course, fixed by the market, and Jean Vidalenc suggests that it represented the equivalent of between eighteen months' and ten years' income for a poor peasant or agricultural laborer (91). The extent of price fluctuations from one year to another is well illustrated by the figures that Alain Maureau has extracted from the notarial records of one provincial city, Avignon (92). The widespread belief that the end of fighting was in sight was clearly the major factor explaining the exceptional decrease in prices between Year VIII and Year X, while the pessimism that accompanied the massive extension of the war effort is reflected in the spiraling cost of *remplacement* after Year XIV. Against that backcloth the demand for *remplaçants* proved insatiable, and if the rich could buy themselves out almost as a matter of course, even families of more modest means were sometimes prepared to make massive sacrifices to keep their sons on the farm. In some country regions, indeed, it was

Cost of *Remplaçants* in Avignon from Year VIII to 1814

Year	Average Price	Highest Price	Lowest Price
Year VIII	548 francs	800 francs	432 francs
Year IX	416	650	100
Year X	192	–	–
Year XI	541	800	380
Year XII	1,074	1,920	336
Year XIII	2,050	2,200	1,800
Year XIV	2,100	2,500	1,450
1806	2,880	4,000	1,500
1807	3,110	3,950	1,000
1808	4,100	6,300	3,000
1809	5,167	10,000	3,800
1810	(two contracts only, at 5,600 francs and 600 francs)		
1811	4,437	6,500	1,200
1812	4,181	6,100	1,200
1813	4,900	8,000	2,400
1814	4,509	6,500	2,000

not always possible to detect a wide divergence of income between the man seek-ing a replacement and the man he equipped for service. In Avignon Maureau found 115 *cultivateurs* among those buying replacements and 146 among the replacements they bought; he also cites one man who bought a replacement in 1811 for 1,400 francs, then after some difficult economic setbacks allowed him-self to be bought in his turn in 1813 for the inflated sum of 5,550 francs (93). In the Drôme the pregnant wife of a conscript from the village of Lens-Lestang, afraid that the loss of her husband would reduce her to penury, signed away her entire property to a young man from the Isère who was willing to leave for the regiment (94). Police records show how often traveling artisans found the money needed to buy themselves out of the army before they set out on their seasonal circuit; and such was the desire of parents to secure the freedom of their children that even the very young might be encouraged to make prudent provision for their future:

C'est ainsi que dans la Mayenne les enfants mettaient dès leur jeune age les menus profits que leur rapportait la cueillette des fruits sauvages, des fleurs ou des champignons, pour se constituer les filles une dot, les garçons de quoi payer un remplaçant. (95)

The degree of dependence on *remplacement* naturally varied dramatically from one part of France to another, reflecting both the enthusiasm for soldiering among potential mercenaries and the level of prosperity in the area. A depart-ment like the Moselle or the Pas-de-Calais, where the economy was relatively robust and the habit of soldiering solidly engrained, predictably produced a siz-able quota of *remplaçants*. In Year VIII when the practice was again officially condoned, the army's lists of soldiers sent out from Arras to join their regiments show that there was often a majority of *remplaçants* among them (96). In such areas the appetite for liberal legislation was considerable, and replacement on the most untrammeled basis was seen to be in the interests of the community. Thus the subprefect of Saint-Jean-d'Angély arguing against any narrow definition of a *substitut* painted a bleak picture of its likely social effects. Affluent farmers useful to their communities would be forced to abandon the land, whereas the law would maintain in their villages "des oisifs, des gens sans ressources et sans famille qui chercheront des moyens de subsistance dans l'escroquerie, le bringandage" (97); however, such an image of *remplacement* could apply only in relatively wealthy towns and villages. In poorer areas there was little opportunity to seek replacements and for many peasants, especially in remote mountain communes, desertion might seem a more obvious course. It is significant that two of the most troublesome departments for the recruiting-officer, the Cantal and the Ariège, produced two of the lowest rates of replacement, even compared with relatively dutiful areas like the Seine-et-Oise or the Vosges. Where deserters were left relatively undisturbed in their villages, there was little incentive to pay for a *remplaçant*. At Crest in the Drôme, another conscription blackspot, the issue of replacement was not even mentioned when the recruitment meetings were held (98).

What sort of men agreed to sell themselves to the army as replacements for their more fortunate compatriots? It might seem likely that they would be among the most vulnerable members of society, drawn from the ranks of the unemployed and the more marginal peasants, but this was not always the case. In fact, where we know the occupations of these men it is striking how accurately they reflected the occupational range of the community as a whole. In the Vosges during 1813, the only year for which the register is complete, we discover that of 109 *remplaçants* figuring in notarial contracts, 35 were laborers *(manoeuvres)* and 19, rather imprecisely, *cultivateurs;* along with 6 *vignerons* they were the only ones to be specifically engaged in farming activity. On the other hand, the list includes a rich mixture of artisanal jobs from tailors and shoemakers to sawyers and stonemasons. Two were former soldiers, 2 blacksmiths, weavers and locksmiths and clockmakers, and, adding a touch of local color, 2 *luthiers* from the violin-making capital of Mirecourt (99). Between October 1813 and March 1814 the 82 replacements provided in the district of Aurillac also included a wide range of craftsmen as well as peasants and laborers. Again nonagricultural occupations were in the majority, but it is the breadth of occupational range not its narrowness that is striking—the *poëllier* and *verrier, chaudronnier* and *vinaigrier* who offered their services alongside the more predictable *cultivateurs, journaliers,* and *tisserands.* Former soldiers who had not settled easily into civilian life seemed keen to rejoin. In this sample, 6 retired soldiers and 1 who had been granted his *réforme* came forward a second time. Just as noteworthy is the geographical range on which Aurillac could draw, for the insistence on local origins had long been abandoned. Of the 82 men in the sample, 35 came from outside the Cantal, 15 from the Lot, 7 from the Puy-de-Dôme, 6 from the Corrèze, and 1 each from the Aveyron, Lozère, Rhône, Saône-et-Loire, and, remarkably, the Côtes-du-Nord (100). While the lure of very substantial sums of money provided their primary motive, adventurism and the desire to escape from the boredom of village life would also seem to have driven some of these young men to offer themselves to the army. By 1812 and 1813 so many of their friends were in uniform that for many youngsters there seemed little point in staying behind. After twenty years all they knew was war, and the annual conscription had become part of the routine of growing up. For them, even after the horrors of the Moscow campaign or of the Peninsula, the armies would seem to have lost their terror; soldiering, for some at least of that generation born in 1793 and Year II, must have seemed a natural outlet for the enthusiasms of adolescence. Therefore even in these most tragic last years of the war, some young Frenchmen could still be found as *remplaçants,* at a price.

In a country where so many people were weary of war and where large numbers of conscripts marched unwillingly to their battalions, the enthusiasm of some at least of the *remplaçants* could only be welcome to the government. The acceptance of *remplacement* and its subsequent extension was a pragmatic step to improving the caliber of an army in which any pretence of voluntarism had long since died. Many communes, fearful of the effects of continuing conscription on public opinion, had argued in favor of replacement either as a small step back towards an army of volunteers or as a means of exempting citizens ill-suited to the military life and valuable to the economy of the local community. The village of Fontaine-au-Bois near Landrecies made exactly this point when petitioning for greater freedom in arranging replacements, urging the government to accept that there was such a thing as "dégoût" for military service and suggesting that too much energy was being devoted to policing those who did not cooperate. They insisted that unwilling soldiers would not be effective soldiers: "il y a très peu à prétendre de ceux qu'il faut conduire enchaînés aux bataillons" (101). Seen in this light, replacement assumes the role of the most important of the outlets available to those eager to escape, outlets that include medicals and reserved occupations and naval *classement*. It had the supreme advantage of being within the law at least during the Empire and relatively unambivalent; once the expense of finding another man to fight had been incurred, the conscript could feel secure in his civilian role. Only if the *remplaçant* failed to perform the service demanded of him, if he deserted the ranks or was absent without leave, only then was there a danger that the original conscript would be called on to make another sacrifice. For this reason it was always a popular option with the richer members of the community, many of whom preferred to pay their contribution to the war in francs than to pay their *impôt de sang*. But it was also divisive. It drew the attention of others to the legalized evasion that was available to those with wealth, and government ministers were not alone in fearing that if it became too pervasive the loyalty of the mass of conscripts might be sorely strained. And that in turn could open the floodgates to the alternative, illegal forms of evasion that were open to them.

In essence, these illegal forms of resistance can be summarized in two words: *désertion* and *insoumission*. To the modern legal mind they may seem to be quite distinct offenses. The deserter was a soldier. He had taken the apparently positive step of allowing himself to be recruited, of joining his unit, or at least of setting out with his fellows with the express intention of joining it armed with his *feuille de route* and, in all likelihood, with traveling expenses and a bounty from his grateful village. In contrast the *insoumis* was a draft dodger. He was not and had never been a soldier. He had failed to respond to the call to arms, had refused to take part in the *tirage,* or had gone into hiding as soon as he had drawn the fateful number that condemned him to serve. His crime in that sense was more one of omission than of commission, of failing to carry out the duties prescribed for him by law. But to contemporaries that distinction was anything but clear, especially because so many deserters chose to desert in the first days or even hours of their life in uniform. Desertion in battle or to the enemy was, of course, recognized as the serious military offense it was and it was generally punished by death; however, this was a remarkably rare crime when compared with the more innocuous *désertion à l'intérieur,* which by Year II was so endemic that it was accepted almost fatalistically by the authorities as an inevitable by-product of foreign war (102). The law itself remained unclear on the distinction between this sort of desertion and draft dodging. The decreee of 19 *fructidor* VI, for instance, talked of the need to pursue "les conscrits réfractaires ... comme des déserteurs," and only in Year XII did the law try to draw an official distinction between the two categories of offense (103). As late as 1806, when Hargenvilliers collected statistics for the Emperor on the problems besetting his armies, his calculations were marred by the same confusion, and he was forced to note, rather weakly, that "les mots déserteur et réfractaire se prennent ici dans le même sens" (104). Even prefects and Imperial administrators admitted to uncertainty on the question, and in 1809 the prefect in Aurillac felt bound to ask for official guidance. The reply he received from Paris reveals the full degree of legal complexity and confusion that had grown around the definition in law. *Réfractaires,* explained the Minister, included those who were late in presenting themselves for service or who failed to come forward within the prescribed period; excluded were those who had left their department and who subsequently detached themselves from their units, those who were captured with their arms and equipment, and those who committed some other criminal offense while on the run. Deserters included not only those who abandoned their battalions, but men who had received *congés* to undergo medical treatment and who had not returned once their *congés* expired, those arrested as refractories who subsequently escaped from custody, and those volunteers and *remplaçants* who failed to join their units as instructed (105). Not surprisingly, such niceties were only imperfectly understood by the young and by the public at large.

The *insoumis* were for the most part the ordinary young men of the locality, subject to the same pressures as the community as a whole. Where their occupations are known to us, they represent a cross section of local people: of the seventy-four *conscrits réfractaires* in the Charente-Inférieure in Year XIV, for instance, exactly half were agricultural workers or peasants, and the other half belonged to associated trades integral to the economic well-being of the countryside as day laborers or vineyard workers, servants or millers, carpenters, coopers, tailors (106). As local lads belonging to local families, they presented no immediate threat to the community, and enjoyed a large measure of protection and support from their fellow villagers, who would warn them of the approach of the *gendarmes,* prime them on the movements of local garrisons, supply them with food when they were on the run, and welcome them back into the community when the danger was past. The young men were, after all, able to make a substantial contribution to the local economy, whether as peasants on their own account or, more probably given their youth, in the service of others. It was not in the interests of the villagers as a whole to see their lifeblood drained away into the ranks of the Armée du Nord. In any case, not all those officially listed were necessarily hiding in the village. Some were ill or wounded, others were artisans working for the armies in an ancillary capacity. Two of the men from the Seine-et-Oise in Year XIII were already doing work as a *garçon boucher* and a *conducteur de guimbarde* (107); others again had left the area in search of work. The local reality was rarely as clearcut as the clinical lists of *insoumis* sternly posted at the local *mairies* would suggest. And where the authorities had been so rash as to distribute money and items of clothing—their "petit équipe-ment"—to conscripts in advance, there need be little surprise that some at least among them chose to stay in their village and profit from their unexpected wind-fall. In the Drôme in Year VII this would seem to have been standard practice. A sum of thirty-five francs was handed over to the conscripts so that they could buy their own clothing before marching off to their units. They turned up eagerly for the money, but at Valdrome only nine of nineteen subsequently presented themselves for service, and at Saint-Nazaire-le-Désert only six of twenty (108). The local cantons through their inexperience were creating a problem of *insoumission* by placing before their young soldiers an almost irresistible tempta-tion.

That *insoumission* remained a problem even under the Empire is a reflection of the wide gamut of personal experience that the term could embrace and the loopholes that still existed in the policing system. Occupations, places of resi-dence, even names could change in a conscript's quest for freedom, and the *gen-darmerie* never attained that degree of sophistication that would have been required if determined draft dodgers were to be successfully tracked down. In the Gironde in 1806, for instance, few draft dodgers were even brought to justice, such was the confused state of police records and the lack of help forthcoming from the local population. Suspects were lost between different communes where they were reported to have lived at some time or another. Arnaud Durand was sought in his native Barsac, where all that the mayor could provide was a vague story that he had moved to Bordeaux twenty years previously to an address in the Chartrons. Philippe Reynaud from Bordeaux was recorded as having taken a passport to Périgueux, where his brother lived. There the trail petered out, and the police were left empty-handed, the more so in that both his parents were now dead. Others had taken advantage of Bordeaux's position as a major colonial port to make a more permanent getaway. Guillaume Nion had left for the colonies and a new life overseas. He had died in Santo-Domingo even as the authorities in Bordeaux were hunting him as a refractory. Another Bor-delais, Nicholas Lelorin, had received a passport for Philadelphia, settled in the United States, and married a girl from New Jersey. Tracing the whereabouts of such men was frequently a lengthy and fruitless task that only served to under-line the inadequacy of the information on which the prefecture and the *gendar-merie* were working. Of the refractories listed, several had died in the interven-ing years, several had actually served in some other capacity, and a number were seamen who had slipped out of the official records when they embarked on their first voyage. Jean Coche from Caudéran was listed as a refractory when he was serving in the naval artillery under the assumed name of Jean Cazeau. Etienne Bojat from Bordeaux was condemned to a fine of 1,500 francs when in fact he had been captured by the British navy on board a French corsair and was languishing in an English jail. Seven years after their *classement,* the bulk of these men remained suspects, often condemned in their absence for crimes that they might or might not have committed. Their personal case histories, typical of many, are a pertinent reminder of the imprecision of official statistics on *insoumission;* for the state bureaucracy it was a category of offense that remained irritatingly elusive (109).

In contrast to the *insoumis,* the deserter was a serving soldier at the moment when he took the decisive step of resisting military service. His might therefore appear the more conscious act of rebellion, the more specific rejection of the obligations imposed on him by the state. Yet there is little evidence that public opinion made any such distinction, preferring as in so many different circumstances, to judge people by their character and utility to local society than by the technical nature of the offense they were supposed to have committed. The individual act of desertion often seemed to be quite remarkably casual, totally lacking in any element of guile or premeditation. In Year IV, for instance, several soldiers deserted from their unit in the outskirts of Sarrelibre and set out for their homes in the Paris Basin. They made no attempt to disguise their uniforms or conceal their identity, had neither *congés* nor valid papers, and walked quite openly along the highways, yet they got within ten miles of Melun before being stopped or questioned (110). Even more blatant was the behavior of a deserter at Bourg-de-Péage in the Drôme, who wandered the streets of the town trying to sell stolen goods still dressed in his army uniform and accompanied by the girl with whom he was living. Both were strangers to the local community, they were staying in a house known locally for its criminal associations, yet it was the suspect merchandise and not the sight of the uniform that led to his arrest (111). Deserters were not so rare or so threatening that they aroused much interest in the villages through which they passed. They were taken very much for granted by local people, a fact that did much to undermine the entire recruitment exercise.

The lure of home was, of course, especially strong on the first days of military service when the young conscript had just left the bosom of his family and was setting out to join his regiment. It was then that the doubts and the regrets took over and the careful indoctrination of the recruitment officer might so easily be brushed aside. It was in these first days, too, that desertion was most feared, while home remained an attainable goal and before the army had the opportunity to impose its own values and discipline. The problem for the government often lay not in the recruitment process itself but in relaying the new conscripts to their units. Like the prefect of the Nord in Year IX, they managed to find their full quota or even numbers in excess of that quota but then lost hundreds of men on their journey to join their regiments in Douai, Metz, or Valenciennes (112). In the Rhône, it was desertion *en route* that placed in jeopardy the entire conscription exercise with the result that the reserves from previous years were being consumed to fill the department's obligations. Between Year IX and Year XII, the prefect's records showed that 1,100 men had duly left for the army; but subsequent returns from the army indicated that of these 1,100 only half, 550 men, had ever been incorporated into their units (113). Where a long and arduous journey lay ahead of them, even the most resolute of recruits were liable to be discouraged, as happened in northern Italy, where the conscripts, Italians dragooned into the cause of France, had set out with every appearance of enthusiasm in 1811, only to desert as they faced the long, unending march across Tuscany (114). Enthusiasm was often short-lived. Faced with the prospect of a long trudge to Lille to join their regiment, two young soldiers from Libourne in the Gironde got as far as Angoulême before making the decision to desert. They were heading for the anonymity of Bordeaux when they were arrested on the high road at Saint-André-de-Cubzac in April 1793 (115). The route itself was a deterrent. In similar circumstances in 1807 twenty conscripts from the Seine-et-Oise were dispatched with their comrades to join their units at Bayonne. They made an overnight stop at Arpajon, abandoned their equipment, and disappeared into the reassuring countryside of the Ile-de-France (116). Theirs was a typical case of desertion, effected before new habits could be formed or new loyalities moulded. The prefect of the Drôme went so far as to claim that desertion generally took place at the very outset of a man's service, "avant le départ" (117); more commonly it was agreed that the first nights of the march constituted the period of maximal danger. In the Morbihan desertion was concentrated in "les premiers jours" of service, while the deserters could slip off easily to their homes (118). More specifically, a report from the Cantal suggested that most desertions took place on the first night of the march, once the conscripts had been issued with their uniforms (119); another, from the Tarn, was convinced that the temptation was even greater "au second logement" once the novelty and the initial fear had worn off (120).

The military were prone to blame the new liberalism of the Revolution toward its soldiers for the scale of desertion that followed, and there is a degree of truth in their claims. In particular, the signing-on bounties that were paid to recruits in the revolutionary years were open to the grossest forms of abuse because half the money had to be paid in advance along with an allowance to cover the cost of the journey to the battalions. It was an open invitation to those who sought to take advantage by signing on, taking the money, and deserting at the first convenient opportunity. In the Somme, the *commissaire* angrily denounced the frequency of such frauds, often perpetrated on two or three different municipal authorities across a wide geographical area (121). And until policing was stepped up under the Empire, many *fraudeurs* enjoyed rich pickings. Officials expressed their anxiety that the revolutionary authorities were so eager to sign volunteers that they were easily duped by those unlikely recruits who presented themselves for service, asked to leave immediately for the frontiers, and disappeared without a trace clutching the precious bounty that the local community had painstakingly assembled (122). François Vergnes from Monteau in the Aveyron was such a man. He presented himself to the authorities in the village of Pauliac near Saint-Flour who paid him a bounty of 695 *livres* on the understanding that he would form part of the village quota; however, he never turned up at his regiment. Instead, he was arrested on the public highway as a deserter, vainly claiming that he was traveling to Villefranche to inquire about his military obligations and complaining that the sum he had received was insufficient to justify personal service in the armies (123). Or take the case of

François Vergoin from Saint-Loup in the Rhône who collected his bounty but before traveling to his regiment he made a short detour to the village of Tarare to bid farewell to his parents. On the way, he claimed, he was attacked and robbed, a misfortune that made it impossible for him to continue on his journey (124). There was no way in which such a story could be checked, although fraud was obviously suspected. Some were caught and brought to justice and the extent of their deviousness became apparent. Joseph Boussard from Mont Saint-Pierre in the Aisne was technically a deserter several times over. He had by the time of his arrest in 1810 wandered the Midi defrauding local communes who were eager to use his services. He had been condemned for desertion twice, in the Aisne and the Seine-et-Marne, but his frauds were concentrated in southern departments where he was less likely to be discovered (125). Whole families were prone to such corruption. In Year III conscripts from several villages near Valenciennes deserted their regiments and took refuge on Belgian soil, yet "les pères et mères de ces lâches fuyards se font comprendre dans le tableau des secours que la bienfaisance nationale accorde aux parents des défenseurs de la Patrie" (126).

Desertion *en route* to the regiments enjoyed such overall popularity precisely because of the opportunities that were offered. For most of the Revolutionary decade new recruits were generally expected to make their own way to their units, often spending long weeks on the road with little policing or supervision. They were issued with their *feuille de route,* outlining the roads they should follow and the towns where they should make overnight stops and they were paid a fixed allowance per mile to cover their basic expenses. Technically, these should have been issued only by *commissaires des guerres* or by the hospitals that had treated injured or fevered soldiers, which would have provided some guarantee of supervision, but by Year IV districts and municipal councils were cavalierly issuing *feuilles* on a lavish scale (127). Two years later the Minister of War reproached local officials for the general terms in which many of these *feuilles* were worded, often lacking even the name of the town where the unit was stationed, which resulted in men setting out on vague and unsupervised wanderings around the countryside armed with papers that could be valid more or less anywhere (128). The *feuille de route,* in short, could rapidly become a passport to desertion, and recruits were not slow to take advantage of the bureaucratic deficiencies of the system. Soldiers with a proven record of desertion were issued with simple papers instructing them to find their way to their new regiment (129). Others were provided with a blank printed sheet that could be easily stolen or transferred, and widespread abuse followed. In the Gironde *feuilles* were forged by the troops themselves (130). In the Ariège they were persistently reissued to the same conscripts even after it had become clear that they were hardened deserters (131). Everywhere, complained one *officier de santé,* would-be deserters knew exactly how to turn the system to their own advantage. They obtained printed *feuilles* from complaisant officials or had them printed in their local town, feigning that they had lost their papers and needed temporary documents until their *congé* arrived. Thereafter it was all too easy:

> Ils remplissent les dites routes et se donnent la destination que bon leur semble, avec laquelle ils passent à la commune dont ils connaissent les officiers

municipaux pour être peu scrupuleux sur l'écriture et la signature empruntée du commissaire. Ils feignent la perdre, et ils obtiennent leur attestation, comme quoi elle a été enregistrée avec la destination, avec laquelle ils en obtiennent une bonne au commissariat le plus voisin. (132)

For the *gendarmerie* such men became a problem of nightmarish proportions and an added source of anxiety for the local population.

Attempts by the military authorities to force their recruits to keep to agreed routes were doomed to failure, and both conscripts on their way to join their units and those bearing the coveted *congé d'hôpital* were liable to stray far from their approved itineraries. The temptations that beset them were legion, and their carefully allotted allowances soon spent, usually on drink in the many roadside inns that they passed. It is surely no accident that the *gendarmerie* when instructed to trace deserters unfailingly began by ordering a thorough search of local hostelries. The law, indeed, became increasingly specific in the controls it imposed on *cafetiers* and *aubergistes* in the course of the 1790s. They were obliged to keep a register of all travelers who spent a night on their premises; they were forbidden to entertain anyone armed with a gun who was not known to them and resident in the commune; and they were prevented from receiving into their inn any stranger, armed or unarmed, after nightfall without first making a report to the local mayor (133). Once they had spent their money, conscripts were invariably reduced to begging or to crime to stay alive with the result that many soldiers came to be seen as part of the wider problem of begging and *mendicité,* wandering from village to village along their route, demanding alms, issuing threats, and posing a particular problem because they were in almost every case armed with their army-issue rifle (134). Desertion, in short, rapidly assumed the guise of a major social malaise as well as that of a purely military problem, though it was seriously aggravated by the lack of strict policing and by the habit of sending new recruits unescorted over extraordinarily long distances. Of the men of the *classe* of 1809 in the Morbihan who left Vannes in groups for their regiments, not one faced a short journey: 100 were bound for Lille, 13 for Bruges, and the rest for various destinations in the Southwest (Toulouse, Auch, and Bayonne), ready to begin campaigning against the Spaniards (135). Even more astonishing is the evidence of the register of *militaires voyageant isolément* from Valence in Year IX, of those men who were simply handed the fixed allowance of 15 centimes per *lieue* and ordered to find their own way to their destination. All were on their way to join or rejoin their regiment, or were traveling from home or from hospital to the next military administration post for more papers and further instructions. Generally, therefore, they were journeying not to nearby towns but to important military centers like Lyon or Grenoble or Nîmes, distances that ranged from seventy to more than 100 miles (136). Furnished with quite substantial sums of drinking money, they could not all be expected to reach their assigned destinations.

The army was further hampered by the fact that there was as yet no clear realization in the community of what soldiering entailed. In 1792 the law on military service was still phrased in terms of duty and of individual honor. One department, the Calvados, expressed itself "surpris et affligé" to learn that its youth was deserting in large numbers and reminded mayors that what was at stake was the honor and reputation of their communities (137). There was a marked tendency to equate service with virtue, desertion with a lack of moral commitment. Yet the population at large still thought of soldiering in terms of short, staccato campaigns at the end of which those involved would quite naturally return home to their normal agricultural pursuits. Several municipal councils passed resolutions in Year III urging their men to come home for the harvest. There were many deserters that autumn who, told of their communes' plight and anxious to help their families, wandered off from their units without any form of *congé,* yet fully convinced that they were entitled to take an unofficial leave (138). Military campaigning remained largely seasonal, and many recruits preferred to believe that their personal commitment was likewise seasonal and that they had a perfect right to return home once the year's activity was over (139). In some of the armies they were assisted by the attitude of generals and commanders who took a very liberal stance once the campaigning was over to the granting of *congés* both on health grounds and for humanitarian reasons. Looking after aged parents was frequently regarded as an adequate basis for a period of weeks or even months at home. In Year V *congés* were granted both to serving soldiers and to returned prisoners of war so that they could help bring in the harvest (140). All sorts of family turmoil and catastrophe might serve as the basis for compassionate leave in this early period; for example, Pierre Guillemot from Caudéran was allowed home in Year III when his father attempted suicide (141). In addition a prolonged period of service might be rewarded with an automatic *congé,* like that granted to soldiers returning from the Italian front in Year VI. When it became clear that the men from the Drôme almost all took advantage of this liberation to desert, the army, rather surprisingly, took their side, pointing out that some of the soldiers had been in the army for six long years and that the very shortness of the *permission* could have explained their reluctance to return to the ranks (142). And yet the damage inflicted on military strength by such desertion was clear to all. In the Bataillon de La Réole in Year III, men with expired *congés* constituted the largest single category of deserters (143); and General Michaud wrote angrily in the same year from the Army of the Rhine that the wholesale distribution of hospital passes was creating habitual desertion and draining the strength of his battalions (144).

The question of desertion during the 1790s may therefore be seen as enshrouded in a certain official confusion. Military *permissions* were easily confused with exemptions granted to certain categories of recruit, and the conditions under which *congés* applied were constantly changing. The government might wish to institute the concept of a revolutionary army dedicated to the cause of victory, yet the generals themselves showed indulgence to those slipping home during the winter lull in the campaign, and official correspondence implies that desertion during the winter months did not truly constitute a criminal offense (145). The law might appear increasingly specific in its definition of desertion, but local opinion remained thoroughly confused both by rapid changes in the legal requirements and by the contradictory dictates of custom and tradition. From Montivilliers in the Seine-Inférieure Clément could report to the Directory in Year IV that a month after the promulgation of the new law on desertion nothing had been done by local officials and the population remained in total ignorance (146). In Year VII the Seine-et-Oise was still happily granting permissions to entire categories of conscripts who had ceased to benefit from exemption more than a year before (147). Legal distinctions were still blurred in the minds of local people, both because of the sheer weight of legislation and because of the unfamiliarity of the distinctions that the law was attempting to create. For many of those who technically deserted were not clear-cut cases, easily identified and diagnosed by local officials. The highly subjective return made by the commune of La Bassée in the Nord in Year VI illustrates the sorts of problem cases that faced rural mayors. Philippe Leleux had been "dragon du 6e régiment, employé ensuite dans les charrois, il a un congé de trois mois pour cause des infirmités, il est marié depuis le 1er germinal." Desmazières confused them even more since "il a fixé son domicile dans le Pas-de-Calais, a quitté son corps depuis environ deux ans, et s'est engagé avant la réquisition dont il a dépassé l'age." Louis Laloi who had come home from the Sixth Dragoons to have treatment for his wounds but who had long overstayed his permission, was justified in the commune's eyes inasfar as "sa mère infirme est hors d'état de conduire sa labour et son moulin" (148). The ambiguities of revolutionary recruitment provided a wealth of loopholes and communal officials usually connived at their exploitation.

These ambiguities largely disappeared with the institution of conscription in Year VI and the much tighter system of annual *classes militaires.* Traditions of desertion and evasion had, of course, developed during the 1790s, but it is from the Loi Jourdan onward that deserters came to be perceived as a major problem on a national scale. The new anxiety is clear in the tone of the quarterly reports sent to Paris from the departments under the Directory and the early years of the Consulate. Until Year VI, for instance, reports from the Drôme retained a generally optimistic approach, implying that the only cause for alarm was the failure to implement the forest laws in some parts of the region because of a shortage of *gardes-champêtres.* Desertion was not mentioned as a problem before *thermidor* of Year VII when the *compte décadaire* on public opinion suddenly became more cautious. Rumors had spread about defeats abroad and about the shortages suffered by the armies, men were being discouraged from serving, and banditry was assuming antimilitary and even royalist connotations in the mountains around Saint-Paul-Trois-Châteaux in the South (149). In the Lot-et-Garonne the *commissaire* became almost fatalistic in his comments in Year VII, seeing desertion as part of a continuous and insoluble problem. Soldiers from his department, he reported, viewed desertion almost as a part of their everyday routine, "ils partent, désertent, rentrent, et repartent de nouveau" (150). Neither their desertion nor their reappearance seemed to cause any scandal or outrage in the community. It was the view of the prefect of the Landes three years later that the system of annual conscriptions itself was responsible for this attitude because it united all the twenty year olds in the local community in their common defense and common hatred of the recruitment law that threatened them. The prefect was blunt in his criticisms:

Appeler une classe entière, c'est former de tous ceux qui la composent une coalition dont tous les membres sont prêts sans cesse à se secourir et à se protéger mutuellement. C'est frapper toutes les familles et les intéresser à la même cause. De là la facilité donnée à la désertion à l'intérieur; de là les nombreuses retraites qui lui sont offertes. (151)

Desertion statistics would appear to offer him some support since, as with *insoumission,* it is in Year VII and succeeding years that desertion reached its peak.

The Revolution and Empire drove hundreds of thousands of Frenchmen to seek their salvation from the armies in either desertion or *insoumission.* Of that we can be sure, although any detailed statistical breakdown is fraught with problems. There are figures in abundance such was the alarm that the problem caused to contemporaries; it is their accuracy that is highly debatable. Thus Hargenvilliers produced detailed statistics in 1808, outlining the number of deserters still at large from the various conscriptions between Year VII and 1806 and showing that over a quarter of a million men had successfully evaded capture (152). Six years earlier the Minister of War had reported to the Consuls on the success of the amnesty of 1800. There were, he had said, some 175,000 men seeking to benefit from the generous terms offered, 175,000 who would otherwise continue to live in hiding and defiance of the law (153). In January 1813, after determined police campaigns and selective amnesties, the government admitted to some 50,000 rebels, mostly army deserters, in France and the *départements réunis,* the hard core of resistance after years of systematic persecution (154). But even the administrators warned that figures like these had to be treated with caution. Many prefects accepted that exact numbers were impossible to obtain and stressed that amnesty laws merely made the collection of accurate statistics more difficult. The Drôme suggested that men of the annual *classe* were being widely confused with those for supplementary levies; the Aude confessed that its figure was something of a guess and that amnesties might have the effect of halving it; and the Isère advised the Minister that the statistics collected from the *mairies* and those provided by the *conseils de guerre* were contradictory (155). What every department could provide was a list of condemnations, but some at least were honest enough to recognize that such a list was more valuable as a guide to police activity than as a measure of public opinion. The distinction between desertion and *insoumission* was similarly imprecise, and if to a harassed administration it often seemed that desertion was the more pressing problem, this may have been because desertion had a more immediate and harmful effect on army morale. Numerically it is likely that it was *insoumission* that posed the greater threat. In his study of conscription in the Maine-et-Loire, Jean-Pierre Bois concludes that the number of refractories remained stubbornly high throughout the war, and that the percentage of *insoumis* always exceeded that of deserters (156). All would agree that though police raids and military campaigns under the Empire did succeed in breaking the back of the problem of resistance, Napoleon never totally succeeded in stamping out this form of opposition to his rule. Desertion and *insoumission* ebbed and flowed with government policy, especially with the weight of repression. Hence the last years of the war were marked by relative quiescence and submission, broken only in the confusion of defeat in the scenes of anarchic abandon that scattered defeated regiments on their return to French soil in 1814.

If the rate of desertion varied sharply over time, so it oscillated wildly between one part of France and another. There was no unitary response to the national call to arms; rather the response was a regional one tied in with the traditions and the opportunities that each region of the country jealously maintained. The differences could be quite startlingly wide. In Hargenvilliers' carefully assembled report on the first conscriptions between Year VII and Year XIII, he supplied a breakdown by department of the entire problem of desertion and *insoumission* that dramatically demonstrated the contrasting reactions of different areas of the country. In some departments there was scarcely a problem at all: the Aisne, the Haute-Marne, and the Meurthe produced a rate of desertion of only 8 percent across these years, the Côte d'Or 6 percent, the Doubs 5 percent. Altogether, seven departments in metropolitan France produced desertion rates below 10 percent in this, the period of the greatest incidence of resistance to the new conscription law. In contrast, there were sixteen departments where the rate of resistance was in excess of 40 percent, and in four of these more than half the young men called to the colors either refused to respond or signed on only to desert once the conscription process was complete (157). The returns for the following years, from 1806 to 1811, point to a similar picture; although on this occasion Hargenvilliers did attempt to distinguish refractories from deserters, and although the overall numbers declared had decreased significantly, there was no common decrease or shared level of dissidence. Whereas in 1810 some departments were admitting to only a handful of deserters on their territory, others made returns that numbered their problem at 1,000 or more with the Aveyron topping the list at 2,530 (158). And in 1813, when both the Gironde and the Haute-Garonne accepted that they had more than 2,000 deserters and *insoumis,* there were twenty-three departments that claimed to have fewer than 100. In numerical terms desertion remained at the time of Leipzig what it had been back in 1793, a regional rather than a national phenomenon that can be understood only in terms of its local backdrop (159).

Ministerial correspondence throughout the period pointed to four areas of France where conscription problems were endemic, all areas where the nature of the terrain came to the assistance of men on the run. Jean Waquet, in one of a series of articles on popular responses to conscription, has aptly identified these as being the West of France, "depuis la Normandie et le Maine"; the Massif Central; the departments of the North close to the Belgian frontier; and the Southwest, particularly Aquitaine rather than Languedoc (160). These were the areas where the problem continued even after it had all but evaporated elsewhere. In stark contrast, the plains of the East and the Paris region were models of obedience and patriotic devotion. Reports from the various prefects in Year XII underline just how easy conscription had become in the eastern departments: in the Doubs "la désertion est rare"; in the Côte d'Or it was "presque nulle"; the Aube was declared to be "presqu'exempt du fléau de la désertion"; in the Ardennes desertion had never appeared "d'une manière allarmante"; in the Haute-Saône "la conscription s'exécute facilement" (161). In the Vosges the prefect could allow himself a certain degree of self-congratulation. In the Year VII the Vosges had acquitted itself well though perhaps not quite as well as the *commissaire* in Epinal liked to believe. He reported, rather rhetorically, that he had inspected the conscripts as they left and seen "la sérénité et la gaieté peintes sur tous les visages de la jeunesse des Vosges" (162). Throughout the Empire the department continued to record excellent conscription figures even in the most difficult years. And where there were defaulters, the prefect seemed to be informed of their every movement. In 1807 he could boast that of the *classe* of 1808, numbered at 549 men, only 5 had not left for their regiments. Of these, 1 was finishing his education in a *lycée* and a second training for the priesthood, 2 were already in the service of the army as carters, since they had been requisitioned at the end of Year XIII, and the fifth was temporarily absent from the department (only in this one case was there any reason to refer the question to the *conseil de recrutement*) (163). It was a record of achievement that would have been the envy of many of his colleagues in the Midi or, indeed, of Imperial administrators in the *départements réunis* where desertion rates remained stubbornly high throughout the Empire (164).

There is, of course, something very artificial about a map of desertion by department in this way. Departments were purely administrative divisions, determined for largely political reasons in 1790 by revolutionaries determined to break down the old provincial loyalties of the Ancien Regime. They did not represent any common tradition or political experience, nor did they necessarily present any geographical or economic coherence. The success of the recruitment process varied hugely not only between departments but also within departments, from mountain to plain, from village to village. In the Drôme the problem was heavily concentrated in the wooded, mountainous southern part of the department around Montélimar, Pierrelatte, and Saint-Paul-Trois-Châteaux; the more northerly reaches of the department and the valleys of the Rhône and Isère were relatively untroubled (165). In the Cantal, too, there were glaring contrasts between the recruitment records of different communes, to the extent that there were villages like Tournemire where desertion was an almost universal response in the 1790s (166). Some villages presented the authorities with few problems, whereas their neighbors developed an unenviable reputation as hotbeds of resistance. The very detailed returns made in Year VI in the Cantal illustrate this quite dramatically. In the canton of Chaudesaigues, for instance, some communes were fairly obedient, with one or two refractories apiece; yet Saint-Urcize had thirty-four refractories, and the tiny commune of Lieutadès had thirty-eight. The picture was very similar elsewhere, with marked pockets of resistance forming in remote rural communities. Boisset, in the canton of Maurs, had thirty-seven deserters and *insoumis,* a tally more than double that of the *chef-lieu de canton* itself. And in the particularly refractory canton of Montsalvy, which was continually to provide the authorities with conscription problems, resistance was again concentrated in a few small, tightly knit rural communities. Montsalvy itself had only eighteen refractory soldiers, an honorable record when compared with certain smaller communes under its administration like Junhac (with forty-six), Marcalès (forty-eight), Sénezergues (forty-nine), or Cassaniouze (sixty-six) (167). In their varying responses to military service localities could be very localized indeed.

These varying responses puzzled and irritated ministers throughout the period and were the subject of numerous reports and enquiries. Why should men from one part of France have served with the minimum of complaint, whereas those from another region responded with a continuous barrage of opposition and resistance? There was nothing markedly special about deserters. Like the *insoumis,* the average deserter represented faithfully the social structure of his local community (168). They were villagers like the others, and they often seemed to enjoy a degree of tacit support and approval from their fellows. The problem therefore came increasingly to be seen in terms of the responses of communities as much as those of individuals. Why did certain communities produce such a high proportion of deserters and refractories? Why were these communities so willing to provide them with shelter and protection? It was to such questions as these that ministers and prefects increasingly turned in an attempt to identify the character of the resistance that they faced and to diagnose its essential causes.

4

The Roots of Resistance

IF DIFFERENT AREAS of the country responded to the call to arms in such markedly different ways, how are these differences to be explained? Given the innate preference of the revolutionaries for narrowly political explanations, it is understandable that contemporary analysis placed heavy stress on the part played by counterrevolutionaries and royalist agents, who, it was widely believed, whipped up opposition among otherwise placid citizens to confound the Revolution and its works. In Year VII, for instance, the authorities in the Calvados convinced themselves that royalists were responsible for encouraging *insoumission* by infiltrating village conscription meetings, "leurs mains pleines de l'or de l'Angleterre" (1). In the Cher the story was similar. Not only were royalists spreading dangerous propaganda, but they were lying in wait for recruits as they made their way to their battalions, stationing themselves at key points along the highways "afin de les détourner de leurs devoirs par des promesses et même de l'argent" (2). The same obsessive fears led the authorities in the Lozère to claim that recruitment was being undermined, even in 1793, by royalist *embaucheurs* who sought to seduce the young men from their duty and persuade them to throw in their lot with the forces of counterrevolution. The damage that was inflicted on the Republic was magnified, it was alleged, by the unwelcome novelty of the whole recruitment process, since for many local families the royal army in the hills offered a valid alternative to the service of the Revolution (3). These reports and scores like them were based on more than casual gossip. There were royalist recruiters at work in many parts of the French countryside, and they had their successes; however, they do not provide a real explanation for the incidence of desertion. They merely point to royalism as a form of seduction, as yet another opportunity for the young to avoid a draft for which they had no stomach and as an offer of shelter that seemed less awesome than the long march to an unfamiliar lifestyle in an unknown country. In this sense the offers of royalist agents should be seen as just another of the temptations that beset conscripts on their first days on the road.

The fundamental reasons for a high rate of desertion or *insoumission* must be sought elsewhere, for royalism was no more than a catalyst stimulating a discontent that was already deeply embedded. Nor can desertion be satisfactorily explained in terms of the progress of French arms, the ups and downs that marked two decades of foreign war. In the short term, it is true, reports of victory could bring welcome relief from anxiety and act as a temporary fillip to flagging morale. They provided a valid excuse for celebration that allowed the authorities to divert attention from local miseries and political setbacks and to wallow in reflected glory. In the Vosges in Year VIII festivities were held to mark French successes in Switzerland, the Netherlands, and Egypt, festivities that involved the whole community in revelry and jollification. To the government *commissaire* in Epinal victory seemed the sweeter in that it dispelled so many of his problems. Public support for the war increased dramatically, complaints and petitions fell away, "chaque commune, chaque citoyen a pris part à la joie générale; on oublierait tous les maux passés" (4). Hard-pressed officials, like the prefect of the Lot in Year VIII, could use the welcome news to stimulate one last effort, one final sacrifice, calling on recruits to offer themselves willingly for what would be the last great push before the war was won: "Réquisitionnaires, jeunes conscrits de toutes les classes, l'heure des combats et de la gloire sonne pour la dernière fois . . ." (5). Public opinion was fickle, however, and the sense of jubilation soon passed. If victory could unleash immediate enthusiasms, so defeat could demoralize entire communities. In 1793 the approach of the Austrians was given as the principal reason for the reluctance of the young men of Cambrai to present themselves at the *tirage* (6). Defeats in Italy some years later had a similar effect causing, in the words of the prefect of the Hérault, both "découragement" and "répugnance" in the villages of his department (7). In frontier regions such discouragement could give way to outright panic, like that which ensued in 1793 when Spanish forces overran the French at Montalba, Fort Réal, and Corneillan and the remnants of the defeated French army spread fear and consternation in the villages of the Pyrénées-Orientales (8). Nothing undermined confidence as much as the tales brought back by soldiers of defeat and butchery on the battlefield. At Orchies in the Nord the local *commissaire* became highly agitated in Year V when he heard that five or six deserters from the cavalry were telling the local people exaggerated stories of the humiliations they had suffered. His fears were, quite naturally, for public order and for the future success of recruitment (9). That these fears were soundly based was demonstrated in 1814 amid the debris of the final collapse when panic spread uncontrollably from town to town and demoralization attacked even the *gendarmerie* (10). But again, such panics were short-term responses to bad news from the front. Across the twenty-year period of war the profound differences of response from one area to another cannot be explained by anything as ephemeral as the level of public confidence in the conduct of the war.

Many contemporaries concluded that the answer must run much deeper in the mentality of the people, in village tradition and popular psychology rather than in short-term bursts of optimisim or pessimism. Of course the introduction of revolutionary recruitment had amplified the fears of local people, but those fears were already there to be amplified (11). In rural Flanders Georges Lefebvre found that the old *milice* had been provided only as a result of extensive *remplacement,* and that opposition to the new demands of the Revolution reflected a repugnance at the idea of widespread personal service in the armies. The Revolution, in other words, was striking at the core of long-established village custom and "se heurtait tout simplement à des habitudes singulièrement fortifiées par le souci de la conservation personnelle" (12). Such traditions were closely tied to the ethnology of local communities. They were not limited to the question of military service, although the impact of the Loi Jourdan tended to place conscription in the very forefront of local grievances; often the attitude to military obligations was paralleled by that to taxation and to the extension of the role of the state in general. The theme of tradition is a recurring one in the reports that *commissaires* and prefects sent to Paris to explain the shortcomings of recruitment in their departments, one to which they returned when more immediate or tangible explanations failed them. In 1806 the prefect of the Lozère put tradition at the top of his list of explanations for a consistently high desertion rate, observing that the old Gévaudan had never supplied many troops for the royal armies of the eighteenth century and that those men whom it had furnished had generally been following local officers for reasons of tradition and family loyalty (13). His colleague at Privas, commenting on the recent arrest of twenty deserters for acts of banditry, went further, denouncing the "habitudes sauvages" of the country that he had been given to administer and lamenting that desertion was just one part of a long-established tradition of local anarchy based on family pride and vendetta. In the Ardèche, he said, Paris must not expect the rapid implantation of the rule of law "dans un pays où de tout temps chacun s'est fait justice à sa fantaisie et sans conséquences funestes." Change could only come slowly and result from an acceptance of new traditions, from "une longue habitude d'un gouvernement doux et ferme" (14).

In many regions of France tradition militated against the success of the recruitment effort. There were parts of the country, most notably in the Southwest, where not a single conscript was raised in Year VII in answer to the Loi Jourdan, and where apathy was so deeply engrained that even government officials became disheartened (15). In Corsica the new prefect of the Liamone admitted that unless he took exceptional and extreme measures the conscription exercise would have to be abandoned just as it had been abandoned by his predecessor. In view of the sullen resentment he encountered, he believed that he had no alternative but to use force, since he could not appeal to the sense of responsibility of the local community when every tradition in Corsican village life was against him (16). Tradition could cause far more than apathy or mild connivance at desertion. In the Midi especially local communities were repeatedly shown to view military service and its accompanying sacrifices with a mixture of disgust and incomprehension. In Year XI the prefect of the Bouches-du-Rhône reported gloomily that in some villages he had encountered a generalized revulsion at the very idea of serving in the army, a "dégoût bien caracterisé de la part des jeunes gens pour le service" that rendered recruitment virtually impossible (17). In many upland villages in the Var the response was equally uncompromising, and recruitment was reviled by local people as running counter to every instinct in their community, as constituting an intolerable *cor-*

vée de sang imposed by a distant government for a cause for which they understood little and cared less (18). Religion and village custom often strengthened the power of local intransigence. Bonds of family loyalty and an almost superstitious faith could prove more enduring than ties of citizenship and public duty. In some Breton villages the departure of conscripts was solemnly marked by a ceremony of an almost primeval symbolism as the anguished parents accompanied their son to the end of the village, where they would "ouvrir un cercueil et demander aux jeunes conscrits de se couper les cheveux pour les y jeter" (19). In others, as the prefect of the Finistère reported in 1807, the ritual was more specifically religious:

> La manière dont la plupart des bons habitants des campagnes du Finistère quittent leurs enfants appelés à la défense de la patrie est touchante et digne de remarque. Ils vont les conduire jusqu'à une certaine distance. Là ils les embrassent en leur disant un éternel adieu, puis, après les avoir quittés, ils retournent chez eux en récitant des prières, quelques-uns le *de Profundis*. Quoi de plus pénétrant que cette récitation religieuse . . . (20)

Such men might be driven to their regiments by a strong deployment of force, but they were unlikely to be converted into enthusiastic or committed soldiers.

The Cantal and the Drôme provide excellent illustrations of the kinds of problems that tradition could pose in matters of recruitment. In the Drôme resistance was largely localized in the mountains of the south and east, but in these regions tradition proved sufficiently tenacious to vitiate the army's most stringent efforts. The area around Die gave the authorities unending trouble, not because of any counterrevolutionary impulse or lack of loyalty to the administration, but because of an almost universal repugnance for soldiering, deeply engrained in the population and passed on undiluted from one generation to the next. The subprefect of Die commented that this repugnance had continued unabated during the thirty years in which he had been following local affairs, and noted that local people were still gripped by terror at the thought of serving in the armies even though conditions had so greatly improved and military victories had focused on the glory and success of the revolutionary cause. Attempting to explain this tradition, he emphasized the general economic condition of the population and the lack of real poverty that might encourage lads to seek a military career. He mentioned the anger felt at the payment of large sums by the rich to secure replacements and exemption from personal sacrifice; and he referred to the scandalous and depressing pictures of army life that were spread by deserters, whether real or fraudulent, who sought to "inspirer la compassion ou l'intérêt de tous les pères de famille dans les campagnes" (21). In short, the authorities were faced with a rooted popular conception of soldiering that no amount of logical argument could hope to dispel. In the Cantal as well there was a long-standing lack of respect for the military that undermined the efforts of a succession of prefects to meet their obligations. In part this was again a reflection of the *pays* and its economy: a country of mountain and upland grazing, of unyielding soil and sparse cereal cultivation, at least beyond the *planèze* of Saint-Flour and the hinterland of Aurillac. Life was hard and returns generally poor, and a large proportion of the able-bodied and the young had to emigrate each year if even the most basic subsistence were to be guaranteed. In many villages the only people remaining were the old, the sick, the women, and children too young to make the long and arduous journey (22). In such circumstances recruitment could never be easy, but in Cantal the harsh economic realities were compounded by the traditions that they had moulded in the people. Local administrators convinced themselves that the root of the problem lay in the mentality of villagers whose pastoral lifestyle, dispersed, remote from markets or modern communications for months on end, distanced them from both military considerations and civic responsibility. Their recalcitrance stemmed as much from psychological as from economic causes, with the result that the government could not rely on help from public opinion or village respectability. Moreover, the prefect was almost fatalistic in his dismal diagnoses of the problem, lamenting that it was his lot to be stationed in a region where he was struggling not only with the economy and the landscape, but with centuries of ill will and a country too poor to provide replacements. In the rolling plains of the north of France, he claimed, men were born soldiers and brought up with a conception of military honor, something that was beyond the comprehension of the people of the southern Massif. For him the North became almost an ideal, a world where the young marched cheerfully to war and where prefects could bask in their reflected glory. He dreamed of a posting there in

> une de ces heureuses contrées de la Picardie ou de la Lorraine, où toute la jeunesse est occupée à cultiver son propre païs, où le métier des armes est honoré, chéri, où le jeune homme qui n'a pas défendu sa patrie est souvent rebuté quand il cherche une épouse, où le fils de famille se présente gaîement au tirage, marche avec empressement ou trouve avec facilité un remplaçant . . . (23)

A spell in Arras or Douai would rapidly have disabused him of his more romantic views, but his point that the existence of some habit of soldiering was the most important single element in the success or failure of recruitment remains beyond dispute.

For there were parts of the country where tradition came to the aid of the recruiting-officer, where soldiering had long been regarded as an honorable profession, and where conscription posed no general problems of public order. In the Bas-Rhin, for example, the prefect observed in Year XIV that he had encountered little resistance among prospective conscripts. The only exceptions came from that small group of men who had been called up before their twentieth birthday, who were often absent from their homes and going about their everyday business in blissful ignorance of the recruiting procedures (24). So in the Vosges most of the problems encountered stemmed from the inadequacies of the bureaucratic machine rather than from the willfulness of the population (25). Again, areas regularly exposed to the passage of troops and accustomed to periodic billeting and requisition might take the fact of service very much for granted. Such was the case of the valley of the Rhône, constantly crisscrossed by battalions marching to and from active service with the Armée des Alpes (26).

The close proximity of an important military center or garrison town could do much to concentrate the minds of the local citizenry. Yet even in Versailles, perhaps the town in France with the longest tradition of regimental honor, conscription did not necessarily pass without incident. In fact, in Year VIII it was noted that the very strength of military tradition in the city and its environs was posing a special kind of problem. Such was the enthusiasm for army life among some of the young men of the area, and so deeply rooted were the traditions of individual regiments, that some who would otherwise have been available for conscription were being recruited directly by army officers into their own regiments, thus reducing drastically the size of the *dépôt*. Of the *classe* of Year VIII, more than 100 had enrolled as volunteers in prestige units, generally "dans des régimens de hussards ou de chasseurs", to avoid what they saw as the humiliating treatment that ordinary conscripts received (27).

Resistance to recruitment was generally characterized as a product of rural society rather than of urban centers, and it was in the countryside that the government's repressive efforts were concentrated. Revulsion was almost invariably described as a village response, the collective rejection of the army by rural rather than urban communities. In his report on conscription in Year VI the *commissaire* in the Pas-de-Calais made a brutal distinction between the enthusiasms of urban areas and the extreme reluctance shown by peasants when the recruiting season began. Rather than try to sum up the *esprit public* of the whole department, he wrote, he found it more realistic to divide it in two, sketching in "d'un côté l'esprit public des villes, de l'autre l'esprit public des campagnes" (28). The Vosges, too, illustrated this town–country dichotomy, for though it seldom presented real problems to the authorities, its obedience was subtly variegated. Even in 1792 when the department proudly sent its quota of volunteers to the front, it was the towns that rushed to conform and the villages and hamlets that had to rely on harassment, bullying and the ultimate resort to *tirage* (29). The implications of peasant resistance were not lost on urban opinion, and towns frequently protested that their sons were marching to the defense of the *patrie* while the peasantry continued to farm their lands undisturbed. Le Faouët in the Morbihan was one such town. In June 1793 it scornfully dismissed claims that the countryside was playing its part in the war effort and drew attention to the *malveillance* shown by farming communities when the recruitment decree was posted:

> Ils voulaient marcher tous, pour ne marcher aucun; quand nous avons vu les dispositions dictées par la malveillance, nous les avons engagés à rester dans leurs foyers, qu'ils n'avaient pas le moindre désir de quitter. (30)

Even the smallest urban centers, little more than local markets for the surrounding countryside, could point to a significantly better recruitment record than the villages and hamlets that they served. The commune of Laroquebrou, for instance, boasted that there had been no trouble from its own people when the *levée des 300,000* was raised; they had obediently turned up for the recruitment meeting, whereas the inhabitants of the outlying hamlets had responded by rioting (31). And although it is true that in this instance the rural population may have had good cause to riot, believing as they did that the whole operation was being callously rigged in favor of Laroquebrou, the same picture of urban docility and rural resistance was reported all over the country.

Yet it would be misleading to make too crisp a distinction between town and country or to imply that urban enthusiasm was universal. In the Nord, where the *commissaire's* report in Year VI had emphasized that recruitment presented no problems in towns, satisfaction proved to be short-lived. In *fructidor* of the same year he modified this opinion, cautiously remarking that even in the larger centers, like Dunkerque and Valenciennes, patriotism was less deeply rooted than might be wished, that it was a shallow facade, and that "on y lève le masque audacieusement depuis le départ des garnisons" (32). And if it was the rural backwaters that caused the most anxiety for government officials in the Cantal, they did not have a monopoly of intransigence. Even Arpajon, the town that had distinguished itself by its Jacobin loyalties, showed a conspicuous reluctance to provide soldiers for the revolutionary battalions (33). Towns offered refractory soldiers so much opportunity for escape and shelter. Their sheer anonymity offered valuable cover to young men on the run. This was especially true in the east of France and in regions near to military fronts where fugitives were frequently men from other parts of the country, strangers who would be easily spotted in country villages and who gratefully sought out the tightly packed rooming houses of the cities' poorer *quartiers.* Thus in the Ardennes it was the urban centers that were most suspect, towns like Rethel where deserters were known to be concentrated in considerable numbers, forming "conciliabules," seeking reassurance in one another's company, and causing outrage to the more patriotic elements in the local community (34). Strasbourg was another city where young men returning home without permission would seek shelter before setting out on their long and often hazardous overland trek. The authorities noted with some anger that policing in Strasbourg was dangerously lax, that few deserters were ever arrested in the town's inns or *chambrées,* and that fugitives flocked there because they knew that they could walk about in relative safety. Although few of the deserters at large in Strasbourg actually originated in the city, the municipal council was sufficiently alarmed by their reputation to appoint a *commissaire* to advise on policing measures (35). Other strategically placed towns and cities suffered in the same way. In Lille, for example, deserters from the Armée du Nord were reported to be living "fort tranquillement," mingling freely with the artisans and journeymen in the town's workshops (36). Paris through its sheer size and its richly diverse population proved an irresistible magnet for those fleeing the law. A list of those arrested in the capital in 1806 reveals that the deserters and *insoumis* among them came from a total of eighty-six departments of France and its appendages (37). Desertion in Paris was in no sense a Parisian affair.

It was generally the case that people deserted to cities rather than deserted in them. The high numbers of refractories and deserters in towns like Paris and Strasbourg do not imply a high level of disaffection in these cities and do nothing to dispel the image of desertion as a predominantly rural response. Only in the Southwest is that image forcibly questioned, where Bordeaux compounded its already unsavory reputation for royalism and a lack of patriotism by providing far fewer recruits for the armies than did most of the rural districts of its hinterland. The city's attitude was widely condemned throughout the rural Southwest, where it was suspected that the Bordeaux authorities were shirking their more unpleasant duties in the face of an ill-concealed popular hostility. The municipality did little to counter these charges, hiding behind a strictly literal interpretation of their powers and resorting to the argument that Bordeaux was already serving the Republic well through its prosperity and its overseas commerce. Prestige in trade could not substitute for service on the battlefield, however, and the city's casuistical arguments for special favors were greeted with scorn and anger in Paris (38). It is true that the regional economy offered encouragement to draft dodgers since the vineyards and the docks were havens of shelter and casual labor (39). The fact that the city was a great Atlantic seaport also magnified the problem by attracting runaways from all over the region. A typical case was that of a young man from Blaye, Sinsirgue *fils,* who fled to Bordeaux in Year III to lose himself in the *demi-monde* that frequented the lodging houses and *hôtels de passe* of the waterfront; it was in such a hotel that he was uncovered, living a calm and peaceable existence with the country girl who was his *petite amie* (40). He was only one of many lads from the smaller towns and villages of the Gironde who sought the anonymity of Bordeaux, the comforting security of a port town with a sizeable floating population, the safety net of a possible job on board ship if the police closed in too menacingly (41). Bordeaux, in short, both attracted outsiders and bred large numbers of refractories within its walls. It was the unchallenged capital of desertion in the Southwest of France. And yet, to the intense anger of its more obedient neighbors, policing was more active and repression more savage in the rural communities than in the city. The suspicion was darkly harbored that Bordeaux, not for the first time, was looking after its own interests at their expense (42).

Like all aspects of life in the countryside, rural desertion reflected very closely on local topography and the nature of the terrain. Mountains, dispersed habitation, upland pasture, rocks and caves, treacherous marshlands familiar only to the local population, smugglers' hill tracks that were part of a very private village *connaissance* all offered escape and evasion. *Commissaires* and prefects, reduced to near despair by the demands of Paris and by the inadequacy of their policing resources, placed the blame on all kinds of local circumstance, but again and again they turned to geography as the main impediment to their endeavors. Only the detail varied. In the Hautes-Pyrénées and the Puy-de-Dôme the *gendarmes* were thwarted by the high mountain ranges that dominated their departments, in the Mayenne by the natural protection that was offered by the *bocage,* in the Seine-et-Oise by the ease of access to Paris (43). The prefect in Mont-de-Marsan was appalled by the lack of modern communications across the wild wastes of the Landes, an untamed expanse of some 475 square miles that had been abandoned to nature, "sans chemins, sans routes frayées dans la plus grande partie de son étendue" (44). Deserters sheltering in the wooded and mountainous landscape of the southern Drôme found protection in caves and grottoes, and those threatened by starvation might be lured toward the main Lyon–Marseille road near Pierrelatte or in the Forêt des Blaches, where the regular passage of mail coaches seemed to offer rich pickings from the *deniers de la*

République (45). Farther north in the Nièvre they were concealed by the dense forests that covered one-third of the surface area of the department, "des forêts immenses, impénétrables aux recherches de la gendarmerie," or they could slip off undetected on one of the many timber trains that followed the rivers Yonne and Seine downstream to Paris (46). Throughout the South and Southwest vineyard country provided excellent and inviting cover from the searches of the police and army (47). In the Gironde conscripts could hide in the coastal marshes around Queyrac or benefit from the close secrecy and protective hospitality of the little fishing villages that lined the shores of the Bassin d'Arcachon (48). Every administrator seemed to suffer uniquely from the special properties and characteristics of his local area, its particular gift for furnishing succor and concealment.

Three areas illustrate as well as any the kinds of difficulty posed by geographic conditions for those in authority. The mountainous region around Saint-Girons in the Ariège gave Paris unremitting trouble throughout the war years, trouble that was largely attributed to its shear remoteness from the main axes of communication and from the principal theaters of war. The villages and hamlets around Saint-Girons had never developed any sense of involvement in France or French causes, and in consequence no sense of military urgency could be fostered (49). The wild, uncharted mountainsides covered in snow for months on end supplied natural protection for men whose "morosité" made them particularly prone to defy conscription. Indeed, as the subprefect tellingly remarked, the wonder was that any conscripts were ever induced to serve in a landscape so ideally suited to resistance, dominated by obscure hill tracks, by "les habitations disséminées, les granges escarpées qui servent d'asyle aux fuyards" (50). In parts of the Cantal the poverty of the soil and the difficulty of communications combined to create a generalized suspicion of the outside world that further impeded recruitment. Isolation restricted social intercourse and reduced any sense of national identity or civic responsibility. Conscription would always pose difficulties, said the prefect, in "un païs où la culture est peu de chose, où il n'y a pas une seule manufacture, et dont la plus grande partie, hérissée de montagnes et de rochers, est presque inaccessible pendant neuf mois de l'année" (51). In stark contrast to both the Pyrénées and the massif Central, the Nord was a region almost wholly bereft of mountain ranges; yet here too topography played into the hands of refractories and vitiated the efforts of the government. Here the fugitive conscripts sought the safety of the coast, where the *gendarmes* were frustrated by marshes and peat bogs, by "un terrain coupé de fossés" that became treacherous and impassable in the rainy season (52). Tracks between ditches, canals and abandoned mineworkings became obscured, the closed, self-sufficient nature of the people accentuated. One of the *commissaires* sent into the area in Year VII to revitalize the conscription effort reported that the local population was thinly dispersed across the landscape in isolated farms and cottages sprinkled across the fields, that fugitives were being assisted by local people wary of any interference from the state, and that there was little he could do to change their mentality. In several communes "les maisons sont tellement disséminées que les agents connaissent à peine leurs administrés" (53).

Yet again, topography could be directly linked to levels of desertion and *insoumission*.

If local geography made the task of enforcing the *levées* particularly difficult in certain parts of France, it was significantly aided by adverse weather conditions. Recruitment was consistently frustrated by snows and rains, frosts and mountain torrents, all of which could cut essential lines of communication and isolate villages for days or even weeks on end. In departments like the Ardèche snowfalls and drifting snow could interrupt normal communications at any time during the winter months, with the result that the *tirage* could not be held or decrees promulgated (54). In the Alps, the Pyrénées, and the massif Central, whole communities were abandoned every winter to their traditional autarchic ways. But it was not only in creating excuses and opportunities for resistance that climate adversely affected military recruitment. Unhealthy climatic conditions were a major source of illness and physical disability, contributing significantly to the large tallies of medical *réformes* in particular localities. Respiratory diseases and gastric complaints in low-lying parts of the Ain reached almost epidemic proportions, a product of local climatic patterns and especially of the fetid ponds that littered the landscape (55). Just as important was the effect that climate often linked to a mountainous terrain could have on the mentality of the local people, breeding an exaggerated sense of isolation and of alienation from the affairs of the nation. The Lozère was a case in point, where the snows and swollen rivers of the southern Massif could be expected to cut off hamlets and sweep away cottages during six months of the year. In the prefect's view these extreme conditions lay at the root of the refractory political behavior of the inhabitants, with the most outlandish regions producing the most backward attitudes. In contrast, he claimed, in the south of his department, where both the contours and the climate were gentler, the people were less sullen, more amenable to reason and to persuasion (56).

Frontier regions presented a rather special problem. For the deserter or refractory conscript there was the alluring prospect of safety and total anonymity, remote from the persecutions of the *gendarmerie* or the prying attentions of the village *notables*. For the young man on the run foreign soil assumed the charms of the Promised Land. Conscripts from the Haute-Garonne were sufficiently familiar with the Pyrenean topography and the tracks which crisscrossed the mountain passes to be able to take full advantage of their proximity to Spain, and in Year VII they were reportedly leaving "en foule" as soon as the outcome of the conscription was known (57). In those communes close to the Spanish frontier where there was a tradition of spending part of every year in Spain either to find laboring work or to pasture flocks, the exodus was even more pronounced, with the result that the district of Saint-Gaudens witnessed an "émigration en masse" every year of young men threatened with the draft (58). The level of policing in the more remote frontier areas was still very primitive. Although there were occasional dramatic and spectacular police operations along the tortuous Spanish border—like the massive ambush arranged in the Vallée d'Aran in Year VII in an attempt to surround whole units of French deserters returning from the front to bring in their harvest—these were few and far between and were often thwarted by lack of manpower (59). The *gendarmes* in a frontier region had so many different threats to counter, from spies and foreign deserters, refractory priests and *émigrés,* that blanket policing was impossible and the odds became heavily stacked in favor of the fugitive (60). In any case, France's land frontiers, to say nothing of her coastline, were too extensive to patrol thoroughly without deflecting men and materials from the war itself, and in many departments any systematic policing of the frontier would have meant the effective abandonment of inland districts to crime and banditry (61). Although the Pyrénées proved particularly popular with French conscripts, every frontier presented the authorities with intractable policing problems. From the east of France *insoumis* slipped across the border into Switzerland and the Valais (62). In the north conscripts were reported crossing into the Belgian departments and taking up permanent residence there to lose themselves from the civil records (63). Ironically, the same idea was popular with Belgian recruits, and men from the Lys often migrated in considerable numbers in the opposite direction (64). From the Italian front the prefect of Taro in Parma explained his high desertion rate by pointing to the ease with which conscripts could obtain river crossings into the Kingdom of Italy (65). All frontiers, it would seem, presented deserters with irresistible opportunities.

Desertion across national frontiers could often blend inconspicuously into long-established migration trends that traditionally uprooted thousands of young men each year. In some parts of the country migration had come to be regarded as a necessity if rural communities were to stave off famine and starvation. Only if the able-bodied members of the community left to find seasonal work elsewhere could the village survive throughout the agricultural year. Migration for several months of the year had become an essential part of what Olwen Hufton has termed the "economy of makeshifts" of the rural poor (66). As such it was welcomed as an escape route from misery, an acceptable alternative to the woefully inadequate charity available in the village; and it was recognized that its value lay not only in the earnings that were brought back at the end of the long months on the road, but also in the reduced requirements of the remaining villagers during the harsh winter. So few would condemn the habit of migration at the end of the eighteenth century, even in time of war, since few could envisage a rural economy that did not depend in part on income from elsewhere. When the prefect of the Cantal was asked to report on the value of migration to his department in 1812, he estimated that the annual income of migrant workers might be approximately 1,425,000 francs. Some of that money was brought back safely to the southern Auvergne where it helped to lubricate the local economy and provided employment and a modest prosperity for others (67). But the government was increasingly alarmed by other possible implications of large-scale migrations, of the regular crisscrossing of the French countryside by young men following their instinct and their elders along well-trodden paths to Paris and the Ile-de-France or from the mountains of the Centre and the Causses to the Mediterranean *littoral.* Much of the migration was southward, to the richer plains of the Midi or across the Pyrénées into Catalonia, to a farming economy where the harvests were more varied and the agricultural year more extended than on the bare uplands of the Massif Central; that was the essence of the appeal of the south, of the dream that Emmanuel Le Roy Ladurie has termed "le mirage du Midi" (68). By the height of the Napoleonic Wars, however, anxious prefects believed that the attraction was connected with the opportunities that it presented to reluctant conscripts. In an attempt to reduce these opportunities the government ordered a full-scale survey of the extent of seasonal migration in every department in France, the prefectoral *enquête* drawn up between 1807 and 1813 that has become the standard statistical tool for demographic historians of the subject (69).

If the quantitative value of the evidence provided by the *enquête* is strictly limited, the observations of local officials that it contains allow us to gain a very acute qualitative impression of overall trends and of regional contrasts (70). In all, there were perhaps 170,000 seasonal migrants each year setting out from their homes to find work as harvesters or in service, to pursue their craft skills or to sell their wares around the countryside (71). Most were peasants or *fils d'agriculteurs* seeking alternative sources of income when they were not engrossed with work on the farm, although the pattern varied with local craft traditions and the vagaries of the rural economy. Seasonal migration in the Pyrénées involved primarily agricultural workers and the poorer peasants, who traveled south to the Aude or crossed the frontier into Spain to sell their limited range of services to anyone who might buy, as laborers in the meadows, olive groves and vineyards of the Midi, or as *bûcherons* and *charbonniers* on the wooded slopes of the Pyrénées. Mostly their migration and self-imposed exile were timed for the late summer, once their own farmwork was complete for the season; but the Pyrenean frontier also produced a notable winter migration of *bergers,* shepherds who accompanied their flocks on their winter *transhumance* to the plains of the Roussillon (72). Frequently the journey across into Spain was so unremarkable that local peasants would not bother to obtain the legal passes they required; for some frontier families it was not even certain where the frontier lay, and neither the war nor the Revolution could dislodge age-old traditions. In the Ariège, for instance, emigration to Spain was highly concentrated in certain frontier cantons like Oust and Seix; the inhabitants of communes farther north such as Sainte-Croix and Saint-Lizier had no such tradition and, in the prefect's words, "n'émigrent pas" (73). Once war broke out on the Spanish frontier, the traditional migration became fraught with dangers of which many local people seemed quite oblivious. In Year II, for instance, three farmworkers from Seix who had crossed into Spain in the usual way found themselves prisoners in Spanish hands and obliged to join a Spanish army if they had any hope of survival. They joined the Spaniards in the hope of finding an opportunity to desert, and duly returned to the French frontier. But they were then tried for emigration and sentenced to death by a revolutionary court. This was a harsh sentence that was finally commuted by the deputy of mission in Toulouse, Paganel, who was moved by their appeal and by their ignorance because the three were all illiterate and had gone to Spain automatically in accordance with custom, quite unaware of the dangers that awaited them. They "n'ont eu d'autres vues que de gagner leur vie en fauchant des prés suivant leur usage ordinaire qui paraissent avoir été dans une ignorance absolue des loix sur les émigrés" (74). For Catalans and Basques especially the frontier presented no comprehensible cultural landmark, and it was almost impossible to persuade them to recognize its existence. Among the Basques of the Basses-Pyrénées it was established practice to cross into Spain during Lent to attend mass and confession celebrated by Spanish priests, a dictate stronger than any law from Paris (75).

The other area of France that regularly dispatched large contingents of migrant workers across the Spanish border was the southern Massif and especially the Cantal. Again, the tradition was long-established, especially in the mountain communes where upland pasture was the only source of income and where winters were long and unyielding. In the south of the department there was some variety, with chestnuts and fruit trees in the cantons of Maurs, Montsalvy, and Massiac, but even there poverty was endemic and the strong were encouraged to leave for a part of each year. Unlike the Ariège, the Cantal did not have such dominant emphasis on agricultural work. Its sons migrated for a variety of reasons, from sawing wood to selling cattle, from cutting hay to scouring the rural villages of surrounding departments as peddlars and tinkers (76). And unlike the seasonal harvesters, these peddlars—*chaudronniers, ferblantiers, colporteurs*—often stayed away for longer periods, for fifteen or eighteen months or even two years, until their supplies were exhausted or their rounds complete. Others were apprenticed to a trade and were away from the department on their traditional *tour de France,* their whereabouts uncertain and the date of their return unknown (77). Within the Cantal traditions were highly regionalized, the young men setting out on long, reassuringly familiar journeys in the footsteps of their fathers and fellow villagers. The commune of Lugarde near Condat was one of several where almost all the young men were *colporteurs* (78). Chaudesaigues, in contrast, cherished its long tradition of producing skilled and powerful sawyers (79). Pleaux produced a steady stream of young men attracted by the town's reputation for *chaudronniers,* who set out willingly to mend the pots and pans of the nation. In 1806 *chaudronniers* from Pleaux were to be found in departments from the Somme to the Lot-et-Garonne, with particular concentrations in the Charentes, in the East (especially the Ardennes and the Moselle), and in the Ile-de-France; they had also made their way to foreign destinations like Holland and especially Spain (80). They were carrying on a village tradition every bit as strong as if they had been farming the ancestral land in their native hamlet. But for the recruitment-officer their migration was a source of extreme difficulty because it was natural for the young, the most robust to be away from home during the winter months returning only in the late spring. There were communes in the Cantal where every single man included in the year's conscription was away from home on business. Overall, in the rural areas of that predominantly rural department approximately one conscript in three was absent, a legitimate migrant in search of work elsewhere (81). The prefect, anxious to exonerate himself from the charge of conspiracy at *insoumission,* could point out that in any year the Cantal sent some 40,000 workers to jobs in other parts of France and some 3,000 or 4,000 across the Pyrénées into Spain (82). Fully aware of the difficulties in attempting to persuade these migrants to return for the *tirage,* he even suggested using Auvergnat merchants and commercial agents in Spain as supplementary organizers of his departmental levies (83).

Although the pattern of migration was heavily regionalized, most areas of France exported or imported some labor for seasonal tasks, and only ten departments claimed that they had no movements of population in the course of an average year (84). Even the Cantal was an importer of labor on a modest scale, since the mass emigrations southward left the countryside denuded of hands at harvest time and placed the crops at risk. The prefect reported with obvious distaste that while his *administrés* were leaving home to sell their wares elsewhere living lives of *ivrognerie* and *libertinage*, local farmers were dependent on seasonal harvesters from the surrounding departments—the Lot, the Corrèze, and the Haute-Loire—at considerable cost to the local economy (85). In consequence those wishing to avoid military service were frequently exposed to the temptation of joining an established exodus across a national frontier or departmental border to the security of exile. Migration provided what seemed a marvelous opportunity to escape from a local officialdom that already knew too much about one's whereabouts and civic obligations. The habit of migration in a community provided even more: a sense of self-preservation on long route marches, an empathy with the terrain and understanding of the lie of the land that could assist escape, above all a collective mentality among migrant workers and travelers that created a mutual bond among them, particularly in the face of local hostility. No amount of political education or patriotic propaganda could undermine this protective instinct. If the *procureur* in Aurillac was blaming emigration for his poor recruitment figures in 1792, the prefect in 1820 was still telling much the same story: that emigration took its annual toll among young men aged fourteen years and older, that for some it was an annual expedition that they would undertake for the rest of their lives, and that the habit of migration was largely responsible for the widespread antimilitarism that characterized his department (86). Many, of course, returned from Spain or the Mediterranean at the customary time and found themselves conscripted into their local battalion. But many more took advantage of the migration experience to evade service altogether, using forged papers and assumed names in a bid to sublimate their identity in the anonymity of their itinerant lifestyle. Denis Verrier from Marcenat was unlucky enough to get caught while moving around the villages of the Nièvre peddling his paltry wares, and the authorities duly returned him to his native village (87). Others, especially those who had crossed national frontiers, might enjoy better fortune and escape the recruiting-officer by simple attrition. Where emigration had previously been seasonal following a strictly observed timetable, it was prone to become more open ended, even semipermanent, as young men stayed on in their adoptive surroundings until all danger of being conscripted had passed. It was, in the opinion of the prefect of the Haute-Vienne, an abuse of confidence and tradition that enjoyed the conspiracy of the community at large (88).

More generally, the absence of large numbers of young workers during the recruitment season combined with poor communications to sow confusion and acrimony in the communities they left behind. Could a village include in its quota men who might be hundreds of miles away and not immediately available for service? Were host communities entitled to include seasonal workers in their own *listes de tirage*? How could contact be established with wandering *colpor-*

teurs who were probably illiterate and whose lifestyle was little different from that of rootless vagabonds? The ambiguities were most troublesome during the revolutionary levies, before the Loi Jourdan clarified and bureaucratized the individual's obligations to the army. In 1793 the communes of rural Cantal were particularly exercised by the problem of absentee workers, pleading to be allowed to include them in their quotas, and protesting that if they were given exemption the villages would be quite unable to meet their obligations. Injustice there was, injustice to those unfortunate enough to be at home during the recruiting season. But how could injustice be avoided? If absentees were included in the communal quota of their village, they could hardly be guaranteed fair treatment, especially where selection was by means of *scrutin* (89). Yet any alternative system was even more open to abuse since the suspicion remained strong that migrant workers were always likely to be poached by the districts through which they had to pass for inclusion in their quotas. Seasonal laborers, indeed, were often forced to submit to the ballot twice, in two separate villages, an outrage against the whole spirit of revolutionary law. Protests flowed in, like that of the Prunet brothers, cowherds at Thiézac in Cantal, who survived the *tirage* in their own commune only to find themselves designated for service at Saint-Cirgues in the Lot (90). Migrant communes ever vigilant in such matters added their voices to the protest. Saint-Bonnet in the district of Murat expressed the outrage of its peers when it learned that three men from the village, although supplied with certificates allowing them to pursue their trade as *marchands forains* in the Champagne, had nonetheless been arrested at Clermont and compelled to submit to the *scrutin*. It came as no surprise when they were selected to serve because Clermont had a reputation in the Auvergne for recruiting those passing through to form part of its contingent (91). Communes in the Aveyron were equally suspect, for it was widely believed that they specialized in the incorporation in their quotas of unsuspecting Cantaliens on their annual journey back home (92). While conscripts could be monopolized by towns through which they passed in the course of their migrations, bitter disputes of this kind were impossible to avoid and feuds between rival communities were kindled anew. Yet to incorporate them into the units from their own villages could be administratively cumbersome, with the onus of making contact with their sons often left to harassed parents uncertain of their exact whereabouts (93). One father from Mirepoix in the Ariège had to trace his son's movements in Year X to save him from an unjust condemnation as a deserter. The son was an apprentice locksmith away from home on his *tour de France* when he was called up for a supplementary levy, and his father's enquiries followed his progress through lodgings and love affairs from Pont Saint-Esprit, through Avignon and Montélimar, until he had found work in Lyon. It was a laborious piece of detective work (94). When conscripts were traced, moreover, their return could be equally laborious, a forced march of several weeks across half of France, so that in extreme cases men might submit to their medical examination on the spot rather than trudge back from their migration. Jean Comte, a conscript from the Charente, was such a man. He was working in Rambervillers in the Vosges when he learned of his luck at the ballot of 1806 and petitioned the authorities to examine him locally in Epinal (95). Even those migrants who were in no way recalcitrant could cause the army great expense and confusion.

Migration, in short, affected recruitment in several distinct ways: in creating administrative complexity, in providing opportunity and cover of a type so natural as to be almost instinctive, and in shaping the outlook and mentality of whole communities. In the process it could add to the sharp contrasts of tradition that already existed between neighboring villages and create additional bones of contention between them. Where such rivalries and animosities were deep-seated they could only thwart the conscription process, as communes jealously guarded their own youngsters at home and tried to shift the brunt of the sacrifice on to their age-old rivals. Revolutionary recruitment did not create such rivalries, which owed more to popular tradition and religious atavisms, to memories of slights and wrongs perpetuated in a thousand *veillées*. The division of France into communes and cantons had, however, the effect of resurrecting half-forgotten causes and giving localism a new lease on life. Typical of its effects were the events that rent the canton of Montbrun in the Drôme during the *levée des 300,000*, when each commune attempted to manipulate the *scrutin* to the disadvantage of its traditional enemies. Men who should have been serving the national cause came close to blows in the poisoned atmosphere that prevailed; in the words of the *commissaire* despatched somewhat anxiously from Nyons, "les plaintes se multipliaient, les troubles se propageaient, les esprits de part et d'autre étaient fort agités, les habitants enfin de ce canton étaient à la veille d'en venir aux prises" (96). In this respect recruitment was no more than a further catalyst to a well-established tradition of intervillage feuding, an integral part of the popular culture of rural adolescents who picked quarrels with the youth of neighboring communities with all the excitement and clan loyalty of present day football supporters. On one level it was simple fun, but it was fun that could rapidly turn sour. The fair at Foix in Year XI was the scene of a particularly bloody encounter between the young men of two rival communes, Serres and Brassac, in which their traditional antagonism about grazing rights was quickly revived by quarrels over recruitment quotas (97). Such encounters were always variations on the same theme, that the other party was escaping too lightly, that the burden of one's own village was palpably unfair, that the others were deliberately cheating in order to send them away to be killed. Flimsy rumors soon assumed the authority of proven fact as families eagerly clutched at them to justify their wishes and their apprehensions. In the recrimination that followed the national interest suffered.

Rivalries of this sort were generally between rural communes, and migration was overwhelmingly of the rural poor, seeking an extension to their traditional economy. In these as in other respects resistance to the draft was seen to be an archetypically rural response. More precisely, it was a response by agricultural and pastoral communities that could claim that the loss of vigorous young workers inflicted grievous damage on the economic base of their traditional way of life. Cultural remoteness may have contributed to this attitude, but so does the simple fact that farming in the eighteenth century was highly labor-intensive, especially in the *pays de petite culture,* and that the effect of recruitment was to deprive the countryside of the labor it needed to remain viable. An artisan could, in principle, return from the war and resume his old place at the lathe or in the printshop; the peasant feared that his land would be lost to cultivation forever. And there is no doubt that in many parts of France the farming economy was put at risk. In the Ain the success of the grain harvest was jeopardized by the combined effects of recruitment and requisition, the loss of labor being compounded by the seizure of horses for military duty (98). Near Narbonne the shortage of harvesters had risen wages to such a point that peasants could no longer afford to employ them and the crops were being left to rot in the fields (99). In the Ariège lands were being left fallow for want of the labor needed to maintain them in cultivation (100). Not surprisingly such disasters had their effect on the enthusiasm of local men for military campaigning, and desertion frequently assumed a distinctly seasonal profile. In the Basses-Pyrénées the desertion rate increased violently when it became clear that the harvest was threatened (101). In the Nord recruits were reported to be abandoning their units in droves to return home to help sow the new season's crop (102). Even amid the relative calm of the Vosges it was observed that both conscription offenses and instances of petty theft increased in July and August, the months when the countryside hummed with activity and when labor was at a premium. Begging and vagabondage were widespread in the same months, which also saw a predictable increase in the number of reported fights and barroom brawls (103). Desertion and *insoumission* were merely one aspect of a pattern of economic activity and rural sociability.

It was in agricultural and pastoral regions that the personal motivation to desert was most pronounced, the personal loss that service involved most exaggerated. In mountain communes in the Pyrénées the shepherd or rural artisan could find his business destroyed or his flocks dispersed by the loss of a son to guarantee a continuity of labor (104). Especially in the South, with its smallholdings and tradition of *métayage,* the fear was prevalent among peasant boys that if they remained absent from their village for more than a very limited period, it was their future, their security and ability to build up a small family farm that would be placed at risk. The sacrifice they were being asked to make seemed so open-ended; there was no firm time limit placed on service, and once a young soldier had reached his battalion, it seemed that the generals had a vested interest to keep him there. When the lists were drawn up in 1814 of those soldiers who abandoned their corps in the chaos of the final rout, the extent of their sacrifice often became clear. Among the men listed for the district of Rambouillet in the Seine-et-Oise, for example, were conscripts of every *classe* since Year VII, as well as a few unfortunate individuals from the *levées* of 1793, who had accepted the inevitability of a lifetime in uniform before finally deserting in the confused final days of the Empire (105). Countrymen who might have been prepared to serve for a summer campaign and then return home for the harvest were repelled by the thought of signing away their lives in the service of France. They knew only too well the lot that befell soldiers once they became too old to fight. Every village had its veterans, old soldiers without farm or family, thrown back on charity, public sympathy, or the local poorhouse. Peasants understood with unerring clarity that for them security meant the investment of years of back-breaking labor, first in working as a farmservant for someone else while savings were painstakingly accumulated, then in laboring for themselves in building up their own sparse *métairie*. Denied the best years of their lives through military service, they feared for their independence, their capacity to find a wife and start a family, especially for their old age. A young man needed credit if he were to succeed in farming or any other kind of business venture, he needed to establish himself in the community, and again military service could put all his hopes and ambitions at risk. Jean Péchaud from Chavagnac in the Cantal expressed the feelings of many when he protested at his selection to serve in his absence in 1792. He was, he submitted, "jeune encore, il est peu fortuné, il a par conséquent besoin de maintenir sa réputation et son crédit, ces deux choses influenceraient trop sur le reste de sa vie pour qu'il en fît le sacrifice" (106). Military service could condemn a young peasant to a lifetime of labor for the account of someone else, and with it to a position of marginality in the village community. The degree of the sacrifice involved explains the extent of *insoumission* and desertion in many of the poorer areas of the country, where infertile soil and fragmented holdings conspired to make families even more loath to see their sons depart.

In many small farming communities opposition to conscription and the determined defense of local youngsters threatened by the recruiting-officer seemed almost to become second nature by the early years of the Empire, a central element in the collective psychology of village society. What is more difficult to explain is the change, sometimes quite drastic, that appeared in these attitudes over time, to the extent that villages that had openly defied the government's commands in 1793 or Year VII were by 1810 and 1811 filling their military quotas with only the minimum of protest. Why? In part government persistence had been rewarded and the habit of soldiering had penetrated into the most defiant rural communities; obedience had been shaped by two decades of continual friction. In large measure, too, the new found cooperation reflected the more determined and professional approach of the state to policing the problem, a subject to which we shall return in some detail (107). Conscripts, in other words, came forward not out of any love of France or respect for the Emperor, but one of simple fear. That is a significant part of any explanation, though the demoralization of the final conscriptions of 1813 and 1814 and the increased incidence of refusal that demoralization entailed might seem to give the lie to any notion that France had been successfully educated or subjugated into obedience. If Years VII and VIII stand out as particularly critical years in the recruitment process, perhaps 1810 and 1811 should be regarded as exceptionally and untypically good years for the government rather than as the natural outcome of years of patient politicization. They were also the years of the worst economic crisis of the Napoleonic era, when harvests failed on an unparalleled scale and misery became a tragic reality for thousands of peasant families.

There is little doubt that the state of the economy and the propensity to desert or to avoid the draft were closely linked, although the nature of the connection is not a straightforward linear one. It is certainly not the case that in normal years the poorer members of society were eager to serve as conscript soldiers, even if they might be attracted to serve for profit so as to rescue their families from distress. In Year II, for instance, it was noted that a very large part of the troops provided by the district of Hennebont in the Morbihan "sont des mercénaires et chargés de famille, qui n'ont d'autres subsistances que le fruit de leurs travaux et de leurs peines" (108). The willingness of men to offer themselves as *remplaçants* reflects the same economic motive, a preparedness to fight and if necessary die, but for money, as mercenaries, in the time-honored fashion of the poor. Conscription was a very different matter, especially for the peasantry, who without substantial hope of financial gain had every reason to stay on their farms. Poverty was in no sense a catalyst to obedience, at least for as long as poverty did not become out-and-out starvation and the hope of security did not fade utterly. In an ironic way, the poorer peasant might be the least likely to feel threatened by the Imperial police, since the principal sanction that could be used against him, the imposition of a heavy fine on his family, was so obviously beyond his means as to be uncollectable. Officials found themselves thwarted by their inability to take any effective reprisals against deserters from poor families, and the offender might hope to escape scot-free while his more affluent counterpart would be deterred from desertion by the certain knowledge that his property would be sequestrated (109). The subprefect of Béthune even suggested, quite plausibly, that the reason for his lack of success in bringing conscripts to book was the social chance that "le sort est tombé sur une foule de malheureux" (110). In his frustration he equated poverty with resistance, and in normal years during the Consulate and Empire he was probably right. Napoleon did, after all, ensure that the peasantry generally enjoyed a much more secure return than that to which they and their forebears had been accustomed. But if that relative prosperity meant that even poor peasants could hope to establish some sort of *patrimoine* and thus accentuated the reluctance of rural communities to serve in the armies, the crisis years after 1810 came as a cruel and unexpected shock. Grinding misery and the inability to find food for their families effectively reduced many poorer peasants to seek the traditional outlets that had been their lot for so much of the eighteenth century. For many this meant the end of any dream of independence and swiftly undermined the collective instincts that had sustained peasant villages. Real hardship drove men to find what sources of sustenance they could and, just as they had always done, the poor were forced to consider soldiering as a simple means of staying alive. The army, after all, reduced the number of mouths to be fed in the starving village community, provided food, shelter, and a modicum of pay. Even children of fourteen years of age were begging to be admitted to a military career as an alternative to a life without hope, as the prefect of the Nord rather harrowingly reported in October of 1811:

Il se présente journellement à la Préfecture, à la mairie de Lille et des autres villes, des enfants de 14 à 16 ans qui demandent à servir dans la marine ou dans le régiment des pupilles de la garde. Ces enfants, sans travail par suite de la suspension de plusieurs ateliers, appartenant à des familles pauvres, fatiguent autant la surveillance de la police que les administrations de secours. Il est à craindre que pendant la saison de l'hiver le besoin ne les porte à commettre des désordres. (111)

In the years after 1810 the downturn in the economy combined with sustained police activity to persuade the mass of the population to accept their military obligations and submit to the law.

If the economic climate played a significant part in forming the attitudes of the civilian population, those who deserted from their regiments were often swayed by their firsthand experience of what soldiering really meant. For as much as the government of the period might strive to make the welfare and supply of the army their very highest priority (112), there were persistent complaints from the ranks that the reality of army life was itself a major factor in swelling the numbers of those opting for the insecurity and ignominy of desertion. Their misery began in many cases during the long and lonely march to join their battalions, a march that they were frequently forced to make without company and in the greatest discomfort, like those men from the Morbihan who were reported by an outraged district council at La Roche-Sauveur to be walking "isolément" and "nu-pieds" in *messidor* Year III (113). In later years such solitary marches were increasingly replaced by a more regimented approach, with groups of raw recruits escorted to their destinations by *gendarmes* or military *conducteurs,* whose task it was to ensure that they did not slip away during the journey. Yet in many cases these drivers contributed to the high rate of desertion, for they rapidly acquired a rather unsavory reputation for deceit, cupidity, and physical brutality. In the Southeast many recruits complained that they were systematically starved during their journey so that the *conducteur* could pocket their rations (114). In Brittany drivers seldom had any knowledge of the Breton language or of Breton customs, with the result that they mocked their young charges mercilessly for their dress, their manners, even their style of eating (115). It was scarcely a propitious initiation into the strange and rather terrifying rites of military life. Nor did the frequent allegations that these drivers were brutal men, given to bouts of heavy drinking and a rather macho bravado, do much to allay the fears of the fainthearted. Those employed were often former soldiers or too old to serve, men with a grudge to bear and an unreassuring tendency to physical violence. Cases abound of reported beatings and outbursts of violent anger. Neither man nor beast was safe at their hands. In the Ariège in Year IV it was alleged that many of the drivers were not of the quality that the job required, and that their lack of compassion and understanding of others was a major cause of the mass desertions that the area had witnessed. Even the official in charge of the *dépôt des chevaux* was roused to protest at the treatment his horses received at their hands:

> Ce n'a pas été sans indignation que nous avons vu maltraiter de gaieté de coeur des chevaux attachés au pied d'un arbre, et les frapper jusqu'à leur faire mordre la poussière. Il n'est pas surprenant s'ils dépérissent tous les jours, car bien loin de les soigner suivant que leur état l'exige, on ne cherche que leur perte en les assommant de coups. (116)

Too often, it seems, their treatment of their fellow human beings followed the same pattern, and denunciations of *conducteurs* seen abusing young conscripts make unpleasant reading. One such, in Year VIII, got as far as the Minister of

War, who was moved to take the allegation seriously. The revolutionary rhetoric only serves to deepen the impression that the incident must have made on the young minds of those involved:

> Hier une quarantaine de recrues destinées pour la marine marchaient dans la rue du Faubourg Antoine, la plupart pieds-nus; il tombait une averse, et ces enfants de la patrie avançaient gaîement sous des flots de pluie, en chantant des hymnes Républicaines. Deux ou trois d'entr'eux s'écartent un peu des rangs; aussitôt leur conducteur tombe dessus à grands coups de sabre et les repousse ainsi dans les rangs. Sont-ce des Russes ou des Français qui traitent de cette affreuse manière les jeunes Républicains qu'ils sont chargés de conduire? La justice et la politique exigent également que cette coupable brutalité ne reste pas impunie. (117)

For many conscripts the first weeks in their regiments only compounded the feelings of resentment and misery that had beset them ever since the day of the ballot. Of course any army, and especially a conscript army, will produce its list of complaints and grievances, but as the years passed and the scale of French war aims widened, it became more and more obvious that finance and administration were frequently inadequate to the armies' needs and that the men in the regiments were suffering very real privations. Even for volunteers who had joined up with a real and passionate enthusiasm the disappointment could be sobering; for the average, rather reluctant conscript the conditions he encountered could easily be transformed into thoughts of desertion. Food was often in short supply and of very poor quality; the gangrenous bread supplied to troops at Ax in *thermidor* III aroused fears of contagious and debilitating illness (118) and the rotting meat distributed to soldiers at Epinal four years later sparked off a minor insurrection among normally passive conscripts (119). For many the lack of fresh clothing was a more serious deprivation than the inadequacy of rations. Long months of marching through mud or bivouacking in the mountains of Piedmont could only be borne if warm and dependable uniforms were supplied and in many cases they were not. Letters home told doleful tales of months spent in the same spot waiting for the enemy, running a serious risk of fever through having to wear the same damp clothes (120). Soldiers from the Nord serving in the Armée de la Moselle in 1792 were forced to march through frost and snow for two weeks without even the elementary protection of a tent, such was the failure of military supply (121). And the level of deprivation suffered by the men of the Drôme, again on the Moselle, is eloquently described by one of their number in *frimaire* II. He notes that his battalion "se trouve dans le plus grand dénuement possible, enfin de vray sans-culottes, puisque nous sommes du premier au dernier sans souliers, rongé de la galle, et mangé par la vermine" (122). Physical hardship on this scale was not easy to bear with equanimity and contributed significantly to the general sapping of morale that encouraged desertion.

There seems, indeed, to have been general agreement among all the parties involved, civilian as well as military, that conditions in the French army were actively contributing to the problem of desertion. The army may have been reformed and spared the abuses of the Ancien Regime, but shortages and temptations remained that were beyond the powers of the legislator, and at times even the generals accepted that their troops were suffering misery and degradation on an intolerable scale. Money for the soldiers' pay failed to come through from the treasury, and starvation threatened. Soldiers in the Marseille battalions were reduced in 1793 to eating roots if they were not to die of hunger (123); and in the Var in Year VIII the men of the local regiments had to beg for alms to feed themselves (124). Low pay, postal costs if they were to communicate with their families, the lack of proper weapons for soldiers in fighting regiments were cited as contributory causes of anger and demoralization. So in turn were boredom, the dreadful, wasting boredom of soldiers who had no war to fight and were kept in readiness for months on end, and physical exhaustion, generally exacerbated by the cramped and disease-ridden conditions into which the conscripts were herded in barracks and camps. So bad were these conditions in one *dépôt* at Digne in the Basses-Alpes that the local departmental administrators wrote to Paris in protest, insisting that "des esclaves trouveroient moins de rigueur chez un peuple barbare qu'on en faisait éprouver à nos conscrits." How could their troops display their patriotic fervor," they demanded, when "outre les menaces, les paroles outrageantes qu'on leur prodiguait, ils étaient consignés dans les lieux les plus malsains, couchés sur le fumier, manquant de tout" (125)? What made such conditions even less bearable for many soldiers was the news that their dependents at home were also being neglected despite the promises and the undoubted good intentions of the revolutionary governments. Soldiers serving in the Vendée in the Year II, for instance, were appalled to learn that pension payments to their wives had been arbitrarily suspended in the interest of economy (126); and an angry infantryman in Year IV was driven to protest that while part of the population was making fortunes out of *biens nationaux,* the dependents of soldiers were reduced to such misery by an ungrateful government that they had to beg for food and officers' wives were compelled to sleep with Jews to keep themselves and their children alive (127).

Behind many of these complaints lay an implicit sense of betrayal. Men who had been recruited to protect *la patrie en danger,* who had been lulled into a sense of security by the brave words of the Revolution's reforms, discovered by bitter experience that the realities of soldiering were still brutal and demeaning, and they blamed the government for abandoning them and failing to honor its promises. Often the fault did lie with the government, with its administrative failings and its financial collapse, but on other occasions the best-laid plans of generals and ministers foundered on personal greed and deceit on the part of officials and middlemen. It was frequently alleged that those in charge of supply were corrupt and were deliberately holding back essential foodstuffs for their own profit (128). Elsewhere it was bedding that was fraudulently sold off while the soldiers suffered from lice and vermin. At Fruges in the Nord, for example, profiteering by military suppliers resulted in a total lack of straw for the troops, which meant that the same filthy straw had to be used for four successive detachments of men (129). Cynicism came quite easily to soldiers suffering from such dilapidations, who saw their comrades dying of fever in fetid hospital beds while speculators appeared to escape unpunished, or who found themselves encouraged by their officers to indulge in pillage to avert starvation in the regiment. And that cynicism, as the officer who reported the incident at Fruges readily acknowledged, was a major factor in loosening the bonds that tied an individual to the army, in spreading disillusionment, and in explaining the disturbingly high desertion rate prevalent among his troops.

Any discussion of the problem by contemporaries soon returned, however, to the question of nostalgia, of the *mal du pays* that the eighteenth-century armies feared so deeply (130). Nostalgia was more than severe homesickness, a longing to see fields and animals, family and friends. It was, as Marcel Reinhard showed in his classic piece on the subject, a genuine illness, though it was never quite clear what proportion of that illness was physical and what proportion psychological (131). What is evident from military reports throughout the Revolutionary and Napoleonic period is that armies continued to be destroyed by *melancholie* and by the debilitating fevers that accompanied it. It was recognized by leading medical specialists of the day that even if *nostalgie* was difficult to diagnose in terms of physical symptoms, it gravely weakened the patient's level of resistance to other illnesses and could often make relatively minor ailments serious or even mortal. On several occasions its incidence reached almost epidemic levels. Reinhard cites the Armée de la Moselle in Year II, the Egyptian campaign of Year VII, the Armée des Alpes in Year VIII, and the various armies at Mainz in 1813 and 1814 as particularly deadly instances of widespread melancholia (132). It was also accepted by doctors at the time that the conscription laws and the farflung reaches of French military ambition in these years did much to worsen the problem, sending young men hundreds of miles from their homes for very long periods and condemning them to the boredom of interminable inaction, long waits for new orders, and endless uncertainty about where they would be sent next. Those lacking willpower and determination, those unable to read or write, country boys who did not really know how to entertain themselves during the long months in army encampments, these were the groups most at risk and most likely to decline into lassitude and poor health or most likely to desert. The armies tried all kinds of remedies, from purgings and bleedings by regimental doctors to the prescription of games and amusements, even of drink and female company, to overcome these symptoms. It was the high incidence of melancholy that led to the abandonment of the universalist ideals of the revolutionary *amalgame* and to the institution of units recruited regionally, so that boys from the same villages could defuse severe attacks of homesickness in one another's presence. And when, in 1793, Jourdeuil ended all *permissions de convalescence* in the Armée du Nord in an attempt to stamp out desertion, it is significant that he made one important exception: those suffering from *nostalgie* were still to be allowed to return to their *pays,* since there was no other known cure for their medical condition (133).

The individual circumstances that drove men to desert varied widely as with any army. Among French deserters were men repelled by the conditions of regimental life, blinded by feelings of guilt and responsibility, and saddled with debts in their units which they could never hope to discharge (134). There were those among them who deserted every year for the harvest or once the campaigning season was over who could never be persuaded that soldiering was now a full-time occupation. Some continued to plead in mitigation that they had never had the regulations explained to them and that they assumed it was their right to slip off home when the work of the year was over (135). A few even tried to turn this to their profit, leaving their units not to return home but to sign on with another regiment and pick up a second bounty, a refinement on the custom of *billardage* that had been so common in the Ancien Regime (136). Others abandoned everything for a love affair left unfinished in their *pays,* like Guérin, from Soullans in the Vendée, who was persuaded to desert by his mistress with whom he withdrew into the treacherous marshes that surrounded her village "d'où il continua ses assiduités auprès d'elle" (137). Others again were little different from criminals, men suspected of theft or murder in the armies whose desertions were a means of escaping the consequences of their actions. For four young conscripts from Romans desertion seemed the only means of escape in Year III when they were discovered selling off army stores to a local innkeeper (138). In the Morbihan, Jean Valois and François Soval stole some liquor from a bar and got involved in drunken horseplay; for them, too, desertion presented itself as a logical alternative to a spell in prison (139). But if the decision to desert might be a highly personal one influenced by circumstances that had little to do with the conduct of the wars, the overall phenomenon of desertion and *insoumission,* affecting, as we have seen, hundreds of thousands of soldiers cannot be dismissed simply as the aggregate of these individual crises. In large measure those electing to desert or to avoid service did so in a climate that favored their actions, where they could be assured of a degree of support or at least of understanding from their own communities. If the government was ever to break local strongholds of resistance to recruitment, it was not just individual conscripts that it would have to convert to the cause of the *patrie,* but whole families, entire communities. Until that happened the option of life on the run outside the law would always seem worthwhile to a wide spectrum of reluctant soldiers.

5

The Deserter and Civilian Society

WHEN THE unwilling soldier knew that he would receive a warm welcome from his family and friends, desertion and *insoumission* could appear to provide easy options. But did they? Was the decision to desert one that a conscript could ever make with any degree of assurance or equanimity? The powerful image left to us last century by Emile Erckmann and Louis Chatrian of Joseph Bertha, a young conscript from Dagsbourg in Alsace, learning that every hoped-for exemption had been refused and that he must leave for the front, but unwilling to leave his village and his fiancée, being pulled this way and that by the conflicting advice of relatives and friends, is a difficult one to erase (1). In this fictitious scene, duty conflicts with sentiment, nation with family; his aunt in particular is open in her advocacy of flight as the only sensible course to follow, promising that his family will offer him every support and even join him in hiding or exile should circumstances make it necessary. In her mind there is nothing shameful about refusing to serve. Many of the other lads of the village were doing the same with apparent impunity. "You shall not go," she tells him. "You shall go and hide in the forest with Jean Kraft, Louis Berne, and all the bravest lads in the place. You shall cross the hills and go to Switzerland, and Catherine and I will come and join you there, and wait until this work of extermination is finished" (2). It is all made to sound beguilingly easy, a natural path to follow in such unhappy circumstances. Only Joseph's employer, the watchmaker Melchior Goulden, counsels against this view, pointing to the disadvantages that might pursue him in later life. Speaking as an ex-soldier of the Republic, Goulden urges young Joseph to think carefully before placing himself outside the law because in Alsace there would be a social cost to pay:

> Joseph would then be a deserter, and after playing such a trick no man would be respected anywhere. He could no longer have father, mother, church, or country, having shown himself unable to fulfil the first of all duties—that of defending his own country, even if that country be in the wrong. (3)

In Erckmann and Chatrian's account, Joseph does indeed allow himself to be persuaded by these patriotic arguments and he duly leaves for Germany. But hundreds of thousands of young men faced with a similar choice elected to break the law and risk the consequences. They did so in the full knowledge that a deserter's lot could be lonely and brutalizing and that everyday life on the run could not hope to be easy. They understood the risks and the deprivations that lay ahead; but they considered them well worth facing in order to escape from the military and the miseries that service implied.

The risks were clearly greater for the army deserter than for the refractory, if only because he faced greater isolation and unfamiliar environment. The refractory would generally be able to live in or near his native village and mix with his family and friends during those hours when police activity was slight, but the deserter might have to cover hundreds of miles before he reached his *pays* and to cope with strange dialects, unknown terrain, and an uncertain welcome in villages and hamlets where he had no contacts and where his very presence might seem to pose something of a threat. Especially after the introduction of annual conscription, he would seem dreadfully visible and vulnerable in the communities through which he passed—a young man, obviously of the age for military service, with the accent and manners of another part of the country, uncertain of his way, and without any means of support and sustenance. It is hardly surprising that the *gendarmerie* were always more confident about arresting conscripts outside their native villages than on home soil (4). If stopped on the highway, he would have no papers, no passport, no plausible reason for making his journey. In other words he would be a prime candidate for arrest and further investigation (5). Since such investigation would almost certainly reveal inconsistencies in the young man's story or bring to light such incriminating evidence as forged passports or hospital permissions, few deserters arrested far from their native province could expect to prove their innocence or to be acquitted by the courts.

Many of those arrested were indeed discovered far from home, crisscrossing France along the same trajectories as were used by new recruits in the opposite direction, or by vagrants and migrant workers in whose company they might seek anonymity. This was especially true in eastern departments and those close to war fronts where the deserters reflected less the pattern of local conscription than that of army movements, with the composition of the waves of *fuyards* subtly changing from one year to another as different regiments took up duty in the Alps or in Germany. In contrast, departments of the interior and those that were protected from the passage of regular battalions on their way to and from the front showed a more markedly regional character. The Lot-et-Garonne is a case in point: in Year XI, before the flurry of excitement in the Peninsula brought thousands of men through the Southwest, those arrested in the department were for the most part lads from the immediate region or migrant workers from the Auvergne; besides those from the Lot-et-Garonne itself, who were in a large majority, the largest contingents came from the Pyrenean departments: the Lot, the Gers, and the Haute-Garonne (6). Similarly in the Midi, there was relatively little through traffic, and this is faithfully reflected in the arrest figures. In the Hérault, for instance, more than 700 local men were arrested for desertion between Year XIII and 1814; the next largest figures related to other southern departments, both neighbors like the Gard (which supplied 45 names) and the departments of the *causses* and southern Massif: the Aveyron (62), the Tarn (26), and the Lozère (21). Those deserting from foreign armies were more numerous than those from the northern half of metropolitan France (7). Departments in the North and East presented a very different picture. In the Doubs, a very typical eastern department, men arrested as deserters came from the widest possible geographical catchment. Besides local boys, they included conscripts from seventy of the eight-five departments of the *hexagone* and from seventeen of those annexed by Napoleon; and their number was swollen (and the *gendarmes'* task complicated) by considerable numbers of foreign soldiers: Spaniards and Italians, Russians and Austrians, Hungarians and Poles as well as Swiss from across the border (8).

The Vosges, too, had a pattern of arrests that reflected its status as an eastern department. The captives came from fifty-five of France's metropolitan departments and from nineteen of the *départements réunis*. In a few cases they were stopped by the *gendarmes* when they were discovered wandering in the woods on their own, their willpower broken and with terrible tales of misfortune to relate. The only deserter from the Calvados to figure on these arrest sheets had stayed with his regiment until he had to seek medical care for his swollen feet at Neufchâteau. Once he recovered he gave up the attempt to rejoin his fellows and set out for home. Another from even further afield (as a native of Perpignan he could hardly have chosen a less convenient spot to fall ill) deserted after hospital treatment for fever, and was found alone on the highway. But it was exceptional for deserters to tackle such long journeys without some companionship, and usually the decision to desert was taken collectively by a group of friends from the same unit. Not infrequently their quest for freedom was to end collectively too. In April 1806 thirteen soldiers from the Basses-Pyrénées, all from the same regiment, were arrested in the same bar at Dogneville; in the same month ten conscripts from the Haute-Garonne were caught as they hid from the *gendarmes* in two groups near Chatel-sur-Moselle and Mirecourt. Similarly, in 1811 a frightened group of nine young deserters from the Ariège was disturbed in the village of Relanges. With their Mediterranean appearance and their heavy southern accents they stood little chance of escaping the attention of the *gendarmerie,* and their rather unrealistic dream of traveling together back to their villages along the Pyrenean frontier came to a predictably premature end (9).

Those deserters who remained at liberty were condemned to lives of fear and deprivation for months or even years on end. They were outlaws who could not have recourse to the authorities when they suffered attack or theft at the hands of others; they had no civil status, hence no civil rights at law. For other desperate travelers on the highways of rural France deserters could therefore seem an easy prey, and there were cases where they became the victims of men more ruthless or more cynical than themselves. They were often forced back on their own society and formed themselves into bands, groups of hungry and frightened men roaming the hills in search of food and shelter. They might be tempted to turn to crime to keep themselves alive, and some *bandes* did acquire an unsavory reputation for terrorizing lonely farmsteads. But the fact that others were threatening the local population only made the task of the bona fide deserter, the simple peasant whose criminal imagination stretched no further than the avoidance of the *gendarmes* and a safe passage to his native village, more difficult. Most of these deserter bands posed little threat to society, living peaceably in the woods or passing through rural villages without doing harm to anyone. Their aims in banding together were more social than criminal, a quest for mutual support and companionship in their long and arduous travels (10). Like the *maquisards* of the Resistance, army deserters were marginalized by their very desertion. They could not risk being seen walking openly along country roads in daylight hours, and with few exceptions they traveled by night, taking advantage of the hours of darkness to pass through villages and hamlets while spending the daytime hiding in foresters' huts or shepherds' mountain retreats or more commonly in thickets and ditches or caves on remote hillsides (11). They were often intensely hungry, except where friendly local people could be persuaded to come to their aid, and like all vagrants and *marginaux* they thieved and begged to survive. In winter the intense cold of the upland regions of France presented them with yet another danger, especially since it was the hills and mountains that provided the best cover and were particularly favored by men on the run. The snows could be long and unyielding, blocking roads and tracks for five or six months of every year in parts of the Pyrénées and the massif Central. In one sense, as the prefect of the Puy-de-Dôme recognized in 1808, these conditions favored the deserter because police patrols had to be called off and the intense misery that the cold created could evoke the sympathy of local people; however, such conditions—"la grande quantité de neiges et l'âpreté du froid, surtout pendant la nuit" (12)—could also kill.

The combination of undernourishment and cold could be as lethal for conscripts on the run as it was for those of their colleagues who were still in uniform. Like them, they had to forego most of the restorative benefits of dry beds and fresh linen, hot meals and human understanding. One young man, Jean Marmiès from Montignac in the Lot-et-Garonne, got no further than the Drôme on his abortive journey home from the army. He died in a local peasant's kitchen the victim of simple weariness and neglect. He told the mayor, who came to interrogate him the evening before he died, that he had been starving and that for the previous three days he had been desperately begging from farm to farm in a bid to stay alive (13). Another, Pierre-Joseph Copin, died in a wood not far from his home at Saint-Amand in the Nord. He was being sought by the *gendarmerie* for a murder committed in the vicinity, and he had been in hiding for some days, unable to show himself in public for fear of arrest. His father, a smallholder in the village, was asked to identify the body which had been discovered a few days earlier "sur le chemin de la Croisette à la taille des anchois" where he had died from weakness and exhaustion (14). They were not alone; exposure, fever and hunger took a heavy toll. So did physical violence, which of necessity dogged the lifestyle of the deserter. The people among whom they lived and with whom they sought shelter in woodland huts and on mountain sheepruns were often prone to violence, and young deserters naturally figured among their victims. The case of François Renaud, whose body was found in a ditch near Saint-Ciers-de-la-Lande in the Gironde, demonstrates in a grimly bloodthirsty way the risks run by many young men forced to experience the marginal society of woodcutters and charcoalburners:

> Il était étendu sur le ventre, la tête dans l'eau, les pieds sur les bords du fossé. Il était dépouillé de tous ses habits qui étaient étendus sur lui. Plusieurs empreintes de pieds d'hommes qui se remarquaient autour de lui ont fait présumer qu'il avait été retenu de force dans cette position, jusqu'à ce qu'il fut étouffé. (15)

Whether from cold or hunger, the cupidity of local criminals or the ever-increasing vigilance of the *gendarmes, la vie en marge* could be a dangerous and highly uncomfortable existence. It is hardly surprising that considerable numbers of deserters changed their minds and voluntarily turned themselves over to the police. Deserters, like soldiers, frequently had second thoughts when they came face to face with the implications of their action. In 1806, for instance, the Minister was able to report to Napoleon that of sixty-four deserters that year in the Morbihan, thirty-nine had surrendered voluntarily to the authorities (16).

Others deserted persistently throughout the war years undeterred by the risks and deprivations implicit in their chosen lifestyle. Louis Isnard from Mérindol in the Drôme was one such man. When he was taken prisoner in Year II, it was suggested by the military authorities that because this was his third arrest for desertion, a punitive example might be made of him so as to discourage others of like mind. He had already enjoyed a *permission* because of poor health, and on his return to his regiment had stayed for only 2 days before heading for the hills. With visible irritation, his commanding officer listed his previous offenses: "Il était l'année dernière grenadier dans le bataillon qui était en garnison à Romans, il en déserta. Avant cette époque il était engagé dans le régiment ci-devant Boulonnais, il en déserta aussi, et il est d'autant plus coupable d'avoir quitté sa compagnie qu'il y était en remplacement après avoir touché une forte somme" (17). Recidivism of this kind could easily become habit-forming. In the Nord it was noted that year after year the same names appeared on the lists of deserters, men who continued to slip off home to see their parents or to tend the harvest and who would not be deterred by the threat of severe punishments like a spell in a *dépôt colonial* (18). Sometimes the habit was so implanted that the conscript's time with his regiment never exceeded a few days, each period of incorporation punctuated by spells of freedom in his home village and by terms of imprisonment for past crimes. The recurrent pattern of freedom, capture, and sentence was accepted, like the rigors of the escape itself, as the price that had to be paid for the normality of civilian existence (19). To the army persistent deserters of this kind were more than simply a source of passing irritation. Their very presence in the battalions could serve as an example to others and, though increasingly as the wars continued the first priority was to get deserters back in uniform, seasoned officers knew that they were not solving the fundamental problem. The district of Montélimar put this very succinctly when discussing the course of action they should take with unreformed recidivists. "Vous sentez, citoyen," they wrote to the Minister of War, "le danger qu'il y a que ces hommes en soient arrêtés et ramenés de suite à leur corps dans un instant surtout où l'on lève de nouveaux corps pour se porter en masse contre les ennemis coalisés de la République" (20).

It was the army's goal to isolate the deserter from the rest of French society, to make his lifestyle intolerable and his arrest and punishment more certain. To this end a wave of laws and decrees was introduced throughout the war years, prescribing punishments not only for deserters themselves but for those who offered them any form of help or protection (21). Draft dodgers, too, were more systematically tracked down. The *gendarmes* and columns of regular troops sent into rural villages had instructions to root out all those found of military age, whether they had ever been incorporated or not. Repression became more effective and as a consequence the refractory's lifestyle became significantly less secure. Whereas in the 1790s he could have hoped to spend most of his time at home or with relatives living a life indistinguishable from that of his friends and contemporaries in the village, he was increasingly forced into the surrounding countryside, searching out caves and hiding-places that would offer protection until the forces of law and order had passed through. Increasingly he, too, was being forced into clandestinity, spending months on end in the mountains, living rough in a manner already familiar to the deserter, coming down into the village for food or to perform some casual laboring, maintaining his links with his community, but condemned to increasingly long periods of isolation and hunger *en marge* of ordinary society. It is true that unlike the deserter the *insoumis* might hope to benefit from the concern and friendship of his fellow villagers, a level of support and sympathy that ensured that he was unlikely to be betrayed and that information about troop movements would be passed on to him (22). Increasingly he might have to share much of the physical deprivation of the deserter, to seek the anonymity of remote countryside, even to form bands for mutual self-defense.

Throughout the war years bands of deserters and refractories became commonplace in many areas of the country, especially in the vicinity of national frontiers or in border regions between departments where policing was less coordinated and where the young fugitive recognized that he had a better chance of survival. The crossing of a departmental boundary came almost to acquire a symbolic significance for many conscripts, a conscious act of breaking out from familiar ties and obligations. Often it had provided the occasion for the original desertion, for many young soldiers innocently believed that they stood a much better chance of escaping detection if they stayed away from the territory of their own *département*. Hence we find that conscripts from the Ariège frequently deserted the moment they crossed into the Aude (23); those from the Cantal when they encountered the welcoming terrain of the Aveyron (24); or men from the Nord when they crossed into Belgium or on to the plains of the Somme (25). The same logic led bands of deserters and *insoumis* to position themselves in areas from which a quick escape across an administrative boundary was available because they knew that the *gendarmerie* had a very limited geographical brief and that a change of department would bring a temporary respite from pursuit. Prefects noted wearily that such tactics made the task of policing much more difficult, especially where the deserters had an intimate *connaissance* of the locality and knew every stream and sheeptrack for miles around. Deserters in the Lozère could pillage government funds and steal firearms with impunity in the knowledge that they could then slip swiftly through the mountains into the Ardèche or the Haute-Loire (26). Troubles in the frontier regions of the Southwest led to active consultation among the prefects of the Landes, the Gers, the Gironde, and the Basses- and Hautes-Pyrénées, where it was accepted that the authorities were powerless to combat highly mobile bands of armed men (27). And many departments, like the Rhône, were given to blaming the extent of freedom enjoyed by deserters in their areas on the proximity of other departments to which they could readily abscond after committing some outrage or act of bravado (28). For the same reason certain communes, handily placed near frontiers, became favored spots for deserters to congregate. Saint-Urcize in the Cantal was one such town, situated on the very extremity of the department and adjacent to both the Lozère and the Aveyron; it was ideal for deserters' purposes, being, in the words of the prefect, "une commune ... dont la population, qui s'élève à environ 1700 habitants, est disséminée sur une vaste étendue et cultive un sol montagneux et très infertile" (29). Similar benefits existed on the boundaries of almost every rural department, and help to explain the continued presence of deserter bands in selected towns and villages like Saint-Girons in the Ariège or La Charité in the Nièvre (30).

If refractories were less likely to form permanent bands in this way, they too developed the collective psychology of the fugitive during the years of their ordeal, avoiding habitations by day, setting lookouts to warn them of the approach of the *gendarmes,* eking out a precarious living as best they could. For many experience of life as an outlaw would be protracted, since the period of service for men in the battalions was not fixed and only amnesty was likely to allow the fugitive to breathe freely again. The arrest reports tell a poignant tale of men captured after long years of fear and running. Louis Bergès, from his experience of the problem in the Southwest, cites some random instances: Jean Austrandié from Agen, a conscript of Year VIII, finally caught at Marmande in January 1808; Joseph Colonges from Auch, who deserted shortly after his incorporation in Year XI and stayed at large for twelve years; or Pierre Bayssac, another young Agenais, who remained on the run from his desertion in Italy in Year VII until his arrest in April 1812 (31). Many long-term deserters had, of course, returned to their home villages long before their arrest where they lived lives that were in no sense different from those of their fellows who had never consented to be conscripted in the first place. At one level village society regarded deserters and *insoumis* through very different eyes. The refractory was their own son or nephew or farmservant, someone who had a right to be in the village and on whose behalf risks had to be taken, whereas the deserter might be a stranger to whom they had no responsibilities and about whom they knew nothing. At another level, however, their lot and circumstances were very similar. Both were poor generally to the point of beggary and near starvation; both were actively pursued by the authorities, especially under the Empire; and both were in various ways highly dependent on local people for their safety and their basic everyday needs.

Poverty and destitution were almost universal. In the case of deserters, their circumstances often explained the degree of their deprivation, a lifestyle necessarily based on temporary expedients and palliatives. They would be very unlikely to bring any reserves with them because the armies were poorly paid, often months in arrears, and men serving in the French battalions were generally dependent on pillage and on the generosity of their families if they were to avoid severe hardship (32). The *réfractaire,* however, would be very little better off despite the contacts he could hope to maintain with his fellow villagers. As we have seen, the belief prevailed in many country districts that it was the poor who were being asked to make all the sacrifices through military service, and the resentments that this caused among the poorer sections of the community were often translated into sullen defiance and *insoumission.* Once the government tried to prevent draft dodging by seizing the land and property of the parents, an approach much favored during the Empire, officials frequently reported that it was those without property and with nothing to sequestrate who were taking to the mountains and defying the law. The position in the Cantal was typical in this respect. The lists of fines drawn up by the *bureau* in Aurillac in Year XII recorded, time after time, that the family of refractory conscripts could not be prosecuted because they lived in total penury and had already been granted a *certificat d'indigence* (33). At Le Cateau in the Nord officials were similarly forced to accept defeat when of the first sixty-four individuals they managed to identify, fifty-four came from families that were patently unable to pay anything, and the fines had simply to be written off (34). Prefects referred to the same theme in their reports to the Minister of the Interior. It was the poorer sections of the community that were defying the law and not only the conscripts themselves but their entire families united in an act of family solidarity. In the Pyrénées ariégeoises, "les pères et les mères des insoumis ont encore plus mauvaise volonté que les enfants, la plupart sans propriété ou n'ont qu'un champ, un pré, une grange, une chaumière sans meubles, quelquefois un peu de bétail qu'ils tiennent cachés ou qu'ils laissent errer sur des pâturages communs" (35). In such cases their marginality in the community could reinforce their determination to resist. Groups like the *bordiers* in the Pyrénées who did casual labor on other people's farms, proved particularly recalcitrant:

> Les mutations presque annuelles qui ont lieu parmi les bordiers de ce pays, gens sans propriétés et ne tenant à rien, sont la cause la plus ordinaire de l'insoumission, et il est très difficile de les atteindre parce que, habitant toujours des campagnes isolées, ils y sont souvent ignorés et ont beaucoup plus de moyens que les autres de rendre inutiles les perquisitions. (36).

As early as Year II it was noted that in the Morbihan it was those families who had no fixed abode that were most actively encouraging their sons to avoid the draft on the grounds that because they had no stake in the community they therefore owed that community no sacrifice (37).

Impoverished, probably hungry and cold, tracked like wild animals by the *gendarmerie,* and forced into a mutual dependence is the picture of everyday life, both for the deserter and, for long periods, for the refractory, which is ineluctably emerging. But it is a picture that implies also a considerable measure of collusion from the local community. It is unrealistic to think of these men, young, vigorous, sexually active, gregarious, living out the years of their youth in total isolation. They needed contact with others, whether to help them on their journey or to relieve the grinding boredom of their enforced lifestyle. Many deserters were grateful to shepherds and cowherds for advice on the most discreet route across the mountains, avoiding major settlements. Shepherds in the Pyrénées, taking their flocks on the annual *transhumance* into Catalonia, were especially appreciated as guides and companions for young men seeking to elude the *gendarmes* and the border guards. Along coastlines and where major rivers cut their proposed route, it was to boatmen and ferrymen that deserters were forced to turn. Boatmen on the Rhône were particularly open to temptation, given the large numbers of men eager to return to their homes from the armies in the East and in northern Italy. One *battelier* who was caught had charged two deserters six francs for the short journey from La-Roche-de-Glun across to the other bank (38); and the government *commissaire* at Loriol was sufficiently alarmed at the extent of this traffic that he urged in Year VI the institution of systematic identity checks for all those crossing the river by *bacs* (39). Along the Channel coast fishingboats played a similar role for men escaping from Belgium and the armies in the North. At Dunkerque, local fishermen and ferrymen plied the town's canal system inside the military fortifications, seeking out deserters from the garrison and ferrying them to freedom (40).

Even once they had returned to their *pays,* refractories and deserters yearned for the everyday sociability that was denied them while they were in hiding. They longed for simple fun, the atmosphere of a bar or cabaret, music and dancing, and the company of friends and relatives. Those living close to their own farm or village would emerge from hiding whenever they thought the coast was clear to return home, and it was rare for parents to turn them away. Many, indeed, continued to live at home more or less openly, depending on village gossip and warnings from neighbors and well-wishers for the intelligence they required about the approach of the *gendarmes.* The information collected by the *gendarmerie* about the whereabouts of deserters and the evidence turned up during police raids both confirmed an evident truth: that very large numbers of conscripts were in fact being harbored by their own families for considerable periods of their supposed disappearance (41). When questioned, of course, the parents would plead their innocence or their helplessness. Joseph Pothevin from Saint-Ybars, whose son was known to be roaming the district with conspicuous ease, protested that he had done everything possible to persuade him to serve, even taking him to the prefecture in Foix and pressing his *feuille de route* into his hand; it was not his fault if his son had subsequently changed his mind (42). But was it? Conscripts knew very well that they would be welcome around the family hearth, given a hot meal and a change of clothing, and might even be expected to do some work on the farm before they returned to hiding. They knew, too, that at certain times, notably after nightfall and on Sundays (43), it was relatively safe to emerge from hiding. The *gendarmerie* were continually frustrated in their work by the open connivance of most parents in the *insoumission* of their sons, and could only take action when a conscript was surprised at home *en flagrant délit* or when, to the intense embarrassment of the parents, a refractory soldier died at home while staying there without permission. When

Pierre Carrette died of fever at his father's home in Tourcoing in 1811, for example, his name was taken off the list of local refractories, but his death in turn exposed his father to legal action (44).

The young conscript also longed for the company of his friends and contemporaries, the peer group within the village that formed the basis of adolescent sociability. In the regiments he deeply missed his friends, the young males of the community who formed his natural social milieu. In letters home he was forever asking after them, their exploits, the jobs they had obtained, their fortune in the *tirage* (45). During his lonely night marches and days in hiding, the joys of youthful laughter and drink and merriment seemed all the more pressing and, like any young man from a remote settlement or any stranger passing through a village, he was drawn to the atmosphere and instant affability of the *auberge* or *estaminet*. The *gendarmes,* too, understood the value of bars as social centers for the lonely, resorts of criminals, and centers of antirecruitment propaganda where the refractory would be guaranteed a warm reception (46). They knew that many *aubergistes,* responsive to local opinion on the matter, favored the cause of young deserters and offered them whatever protection they could. They therefore took a particular interest in wayside bars, the natural focal points for the surrounding countryside, places where fugitives could meet by arrangement before returning to another week of discomfort and hunger. At one such establishment, Craywick in the Nord, the brigadier noted on entry that a hush fell over the room and that "il y avait de l'embarras dans les manières d'agir du cabaretier et de la cabaretière"; he ordered the search of the premises and three young men of the previous *levée* were discovered hiding in an attic (47). They were unlucky. In many parts of the country bars came to be regarded by refractories as safe houses where they could enjoy a drink with their friends free from disturbance. In strongly refractory areas like the Ariège, it was in fact the *gendarmes* who might have difficulty being served. Police enquiries in 1809 established that at Couflens, a hamlet in the borderlands around Seix, the landlord and his son-in-law "non contents de refuser le logement à un militaire sur un billet du maire, se sont permis les injures les plus grossières contre l'autorité locale." At Mérigon François Bergé received in his bar "à toute heure de la nuit des jeunes gens de famille" and especially refractory conscripts. At Ercé, another *cabaretier,* Paul Merniguet, "donne à boire, à manger et à jouer à toute heure de la nuit et reçoit dans son cabaret les conscrits réfractaires qui s'y réunissent pour commettre ensuite des désordres et même des délits dans la commune" (48). Elsewhere *aubergistes* allowed their premises to be used by those who sought to sell *remplaçants* to young conscripts or by fraudulent means to impede the workings of the conscription law (49).

It was but a short step from visiting the local cabaret to attending one of the highpoints of country sociability, the village fair or *bal champêtre.* For the young of the village these *foires* were the principal occasions when they could let off steam, get drunk, participate in wild ritualistic dancing, and, most importantly, make conquests among the village girls. They were occasions when the *jeunes gens* established their own values and challenged outsiders. At *foires* long-standing jealousies and intervillage rivalries often became inflamed into pitched battles between the young men of neighboring communes. For all these reasons they were occasions that the young country lad did not want to miss, and deserters and refractories often took a calculated risk in attending a village dance or local fair, mixing with the dense crowds of revelers in the hope that the sheer numbers present would mask them with a certain anonymity. At Le Roussay in the Seine-et-Oise a refractory was spotted enjoying some wine with his friends in the wine-tent seemingly unconcerned by the presence of the local *gendarmerie* (50). At another local *foire* at Chalabre near Limoux the police tried to intervene when they identified a number of deserters and *insoumis* mingling with the crowd, but were insulted and ill-treated by other revelers much to the indignation of the Minister of the Interior, who was sensitive to the impact on public opinion of an incident where his men had been humiliated in so public a place (51). Deserters would come a long way to enjoy a village dance in relative security, to meet their friends and plot future coups. A *bal champêtre* in the next department could seem even more attractive to men on the run and anxious to avoid their local mayor or local *gendarme*. At Sainte-Colombe in the Lot-et-Garonne, for instance, a local dance in 1811 attracted an enthusiastic crowd, among them "des réfractaires des communes voisines, presque toutes étrangères au Département" (52). Not all, of course, came for innocent enjoyment. For some, as in so many aspects of youth culture, the main attraction lay in the possibilities for fighting and disruption. Take the case of Pierre Carnelle, nicknamed "Langeac" after his native village in the Haute-Loire, who toured the village *fêtes* for miles around looking for trouble. He was a seasoned deserter who had already been condemned to death for the murder of a shepherd, and he was eventually killed in a shoot-out with the *gendarmerie* in a bar near Saint-Flour. As the *sous-préfet* reported with obvious relief, "son caractère pétulant et emporté était connu tellement que dans toutes les fêtes de ces environs, où il y avait des querelles et émeutes de la jeunesse, il en était toujours l'auteur" (53). For others the major reason for attending a village fair lay in the pickings it might offer. Jean Lavigne, another deserter, attended the fair at Calvinet in the Cantal so that he could rob one of the *colporteurs* with a stall there and thus obtain money for food (54). Whatever the individual motivation, the presence of refractories at *foires* and country *bals* in significant numbers helped to reduce their sense of isolation and to provide some contact with the rest of rural society.

That sense of isolation could, of course, be dramatically reduced if the deserter were lucky enough to find some amenable female company. One of the principal attractions of returning to his village was, quite naturally, that of meeting once again his former fiancée or girlfriend, abandoned when he had been forced to leave for his regiment or for the protection of the hills. But for most *fuyards,* that was an Elysian solution, consigned firmly to the realm of dreams and fantasies. In more practical terms, any woman would do, and the risks accepted in attending *foires* and village dances reflected not only a craving for sociability and drunken revelry, but also a strong desire for female conversation and sexual relationships. In the more established *bandes* of deserters, just as in their criminal counterparts like the Bande d'Orgères, the womenfolk were an integral part of the community (55). They were the exceptions, however, and for most the company of women had to be a casual affair. Like any group of men deprived for weeks on end of the pleasures of civilization, deserters would turn eagerly to prostitutes whenever they had money to spare, or more generally to those village women who were prepared to sleep around fairly indiscriminately and who were attracted by the element of daring, and the slightly exotic appeal of a young fugitive who would slip away in the morning for the safety of the wilds. There was a sense, indeed, in which the prostitute offered an element of security to the deserter on the run. He would have a roof over his head, secure until dawn from the attentions of the *gendarmerie,* without any of the police surveillance and registration that a night in a hotel or lodging house necessarily entailed. The prostitute, quite apart from any sexual charms, offered the relief of anonymity akin to the turkish bath in the cities, and deserters, criminals and others *en marge de la société* were glad to profit from it. Often, of course, such activities attracted the prying interest of neighbors, and the anonymity was breached. Women of uncertain morality were kept under police surveillance and subjected to police threats precisely because of the men with whom they associated; women like Jeanne Manset, a widow from a small village in the Lot-et-Garonne, who "menne une conduite immorale" (in itself not a primary matter of concern to the authorities), "sa maison étant le refuge nocturne des gens sans aveu et des conscrits réfractaires" (56). A happier solution for the deserter was to establish a more lasting relationship with some local woman in the *pays* who would offer him protection and a permanent home, would arouse none of the suspicions and animosities that rained down on the prostitute, yet would satisfy his frustrated sexuality and bring to an end, at least temporarily, his endless travels. François Eynard, a young deserter from Tournon in the Ardèche, found just such a companion in Erôme (Drôme), a widow who took a fancy to him, "qui le recelait et avec laquelle il vivait." Yet even his illicit idyll was short-lived, ending in arrest in the summer of 1809 (57).

The most immediate need of the thousands of young men on the run was much more basic than companionship or entertainment, however. Their first thought was of how to stay alive, how to find the food they needed to maintain themselves for another day. If they were to attain that goal legally without antagonizing the local community through theft and deceit, this implied that they would have to earn money by taking some sort of employment to finance their flight. For refractories hiding in the immediate environs of their village, this posed relatively few problems since they could generally be assured some casual or seasonal work on their parents' holding or on lands farmed by one of the village *notables.* They benefited from the protection of the extended family, and the fact that village culture was close-knit and defensive and could be generally relied on to defend "les nôtres" against the incursions of the outside world. In the area around Bazas in the Gironde, police enquiries found that the majority of their draft dodgers were living quite openly in the community, either doing farmwork for their own fathers or being hired by others as *métayers, journaliers, cultivateurs* (58). Parents accepted the risks involved in sheltering outlaws readily enough. Neighbors and friends gave their own reasons when they were interrogated, but they are reasons that underline the cohesiveness of village society: "C'est parce qu'il était voisin de ce conscrit et un des principaux habitants de la commune"; "c'est un oncle de ce conscrit, et de plus un des principaux habitants." These reasons were quite sufficient in a Pyrenean community where there was no stigma attached to desertion, where the majority of the young men were hiding out in *cabanes* on the mountain slopes, and where it was accepted that brothers and sisters brought them food at times when they were unable to come down into the village to work (59). Assistance was not limited to lads with established connections in the village, however. Deserters passing through could also hope to gain temporary employment, especially in agricultural areas drained of manpower by the continual *levées* for the armies. Deserters might be regarded with a certain suspicion, as would all young men unknown to local people, who might steal or attack them and who in many instances would be armed; but they had the virtue of being physically robust, and their desperate circumstances and lack of civil status meant that they provided a welcome source of cheap labor at times when it was in high demand. However much they might cloak their actions in the language of charity, the farmers and artisans who offered employment to deserters and refractory conscripts did so with an acute sense of their own self-interest.

Much of the temporary work available in rural France was of necessity agricultural, helping out on the farm in labor-intensive seasonal tasks like sowing or harvesting. In one sense it was work that was particularly well-suited to the needs of the conscript because it did not require any special skills and was geared to the basic *connaissance* of any country lad. He would welcome work by the week or even by the day since he would be under pressure to move on to maintain his anonymity. It was in his own interests to change commune and employer at fairly regular intervals to avoid detection. Furthermore, agriculture was an occupation of an essentially seasonal nature in which everyone was in the habit of employing day-laborers or taking men on for the duration of the harvest. Since many such laborers were migrant workers or itinerant beggars even in normal times, it was a milieu into which the deserter could merge without attracting too much attention or scrutiny. And since the law insisted that proof be provided that an employee was hired on a permanent basis (a *serviteur à gages* properly contracted) before he became his employer's responsibility, relatively few prosecutions were brought for the hire of deserters on farms, and the agricultural community continued to make use of whatever labor was available without making too detailed enquiries about its exact provenance. Yves Calvèz, a smallholder from Kergos in the Morbihan, was one of the few farmers to be convicted for employing a deserter in this way, but he was unwise enough to admit that the man had been employed "pour la récolte" for a period of four or five weeks, and the court decided that that constituted a contract of employment (60). In contrast, Pierre Nuc, who farmed a smallholding at Le Bosquet near Marcolès (Cantal), succeeded in persuading the local tribunal that he was innocent of any crime when he hired a deserter as a casual laborer despite the fact that the *gendarmes* had unearthed the young man's army rifle and had discovered his bedding in a barn on Nuc's land. The case might seem to have been cut and dried, but witnesses were produced to say that the harvester was well-known and trusted in the area, that no one realized that he was a deserter, that he offered his services freely to anyone who had need of them on a daily basis, and that he walked about the village quite openly, going to mass on Sundays and frequenting the local bars and inns (61). He was, in short, sufficiently well-integrated into village life that Nuc was justified in hiring him without making any special investigations about his past, and the fact that he was employed by the day absolved the farmer of any moral or legal responsibility. Courts were notably reluctant to convict in such cases, which in turn meant that farmwork continued to provide a rich seam of employment for conscripts on the run.

On farms and in the countryside casual labor might be very casual indeed, payment in kind of food and shelter for small tasks or services rendered. *Bergers* might take on a conscript to help them look after their animals during the *transhumance* or peasants make use of the cheap labor that deserters provided to carry out odd jobs of construction or maintenance around the farmyard. Pierre Lamblin, a *journalier* from Marchiennes in the Nord, employed a deserter to help him with building work on his house, but again the court acquitted him on the grounds that the man had been paid by the day and that the work involved was rather trifling: "il s'agissait de la réparation d'un mur, conséquemment d'un travail momentané et de circonstances" (62). Neighbors and farmworkers were forever performing little services for one another and helping with jobs on other people's farms to the extent that in rural society the definition of employment could become rather blurred. In the Southwest the *vendanges* provided excellent opportunity for temporary labor in an activity that had always been highly dependent on migrant workers from the surrounding departments. Therefore the same migration patterns that provided young men with a means of easy passage from their own villages also supplied them with employment once they arrived at their destination (63). Similarly in sheepraising country, there was work to be found in cleaning and combing the wool or in helping with sheep-shearing. In the Drôme, for instance, deserters were employed both to tend the flocks on the mountainside—an occupation that allowed them to earn a little money without renouncing their hiding-places or their clandestine lifestyle—and to card the wool after it had been cut. The small scale of the rural woollen industry again worked to the deserter's advantage. When Jean-Pierre Champon was eventually challenged in 1808, it emerged that he had been living quite openly in the village of Allex because "il est cardeur de laine et paraît s'être soustrait jusqu'à présent aux recherches de la force armée en travaillant de son métier chez divers particuliers" (64).

Local industries were also well-placed to benefit from the traditional skills that many of the deserters practiced and from the windfall of cheap labor that they constituted. In the Saône-et-Loire some fifty refractories and deserters had formed themselves into a band of woodcutters, and the local economy had become dependent on their labor, with the result that both the *entrepreneurs* and the *acheteurs de la coupe* had become their protectors (65). Stonecutting was another trade in which masters frequently found themselves tempted to employ conscript labor. At Coulours in the Yonne considerable numbers found jobs in the small masons' yards that proliferated in the woods around the commune (66). In the Seine-et-Oise refractories were welcomed by quarrymasters desperate for able-bodied masons and quarrymen, mostly in centers like Châtillon that served the lucrative Paris building trades (67). Iron-foundries, too, were often glad to use conscript workers, especially because so many country boys had some primitive knowledge of the trade, and the fact that many forges were small, rural enterprises hidden in the forests made regular patroling by the *gendarmerie* improbable. Deserters were regularly employed in the small forges of the Ariège and the Vosges (68), and even in major enterprises like Le Creusot where, in the words of the departmental administration, "une multitude d'individus sans passeports, de réquisitionnaires, de conscrits trouvent asile" (69). Any rural area with difficult terrain and a wealth of small industrial enterprises was ideally suited to the young man on the run from the armies, since it could provide him not only with a means of concealment but with the regular source of income that deserters generally lacked. The Nièvre, well-endowed with rural industry and blessed with a river network that allowed wood to be floated directly to the Seine and Paris, emerged as a deserter's paradise:

> Ceux des jeunes gens qui cultivent les terres trouvent dans les vastes forêts qui les avoisinent des asiles impénétrables aux gendarmes qui ont ordre de les chercher: ceux qui font flotter le bois exploité se réfugient, à la faveur des trains, dans les villes situées sur tout le cours de la rivière d'Yonne; et ceux qui travaillent aux forges et fourneaux sont les soutiens de familles ordinairement indigentes, et que la crainte de les abandonner à la misère porte à se cacher où ils peuvent lorsqu'il est question d'une levée ou qu'ils sentent l'approche de la gendarmerie qui, d'ailleurs, n'y va peut-être pas avec trop d'assurance. (70)

In these circumstances it is hardly surprising that men of conscriptable age often sought to acquire the necessary skills for jobs in trades like metalworking, and obtained certificates from their mayors to vouch for the level of their attainment. Work in a quarry or a forge became suddenly prized, and ideas of social promotion were rapidly transformed. In the Nord, among other regions of France, "on a vu tout à coup le fils de cultivateur, le commis, le marchand, le rentier devenir forgerons" (71). Given the country's appetite for weapons in the war years, it was a trade in which opportunity seemed limitless.

Larger firms could be just as tempted as small ones to capitalize on cheap available labor, and coalmines were among the industrial enterprises where deserters found refuge in considerable numbers. At Aniche in the Nord, one of several mines to be raided by the *gendarmerie,* the owners angrily denied all knowledge of their workforce and insisted that no law could prevent them from taking on labor wherever it could be found. If there were conscripts working underground, they implied, the responsibility lay with the *chef d'atelier* in whom was vested the power to hire and fire. In any event, after careful study of military files, the *gendarmes* made seven arrests, but it was clear to them that the employment of strong, powerful miners would continue regardless of their origin, protected by the industrial muscle of the mining companies (72). The government could never escape the fact that at a time of acute labor shortage refractory conscripts provided an unparalleled black market in diverse skills. By the age of twenty or twenty-one years many of these young men had completed their *tour de France* and were fully fledged craftsmen eager for the opportunity to exercise their trade. Some were even away from home on their *tour* at the moment of their conscription, and returned to find that their names had already been included in the lists of refractories. Such was the case of young Alibert, a locksmith from Mirepoix, who had carefully waited until after the *levée* in *messidor* X before setting out to Pont Saint-Esprit to begin his apprenticeship. Then the government announced a *levée supplémentaire,* and Alibert was shocked to find himself sentenced to five years' imprisonment in his absence (73). He was forced, like many others, into hiding armed with his trade and a saleable commodity to any employer. In towns, especially, there was a lively demand for skilled craftsmen, from tailors to bakers, metalworkers to carpenters, and they soon found work if they looked for it. In Bordeaux deserters and refractories were to be found in shipbuilding and in all the river trades (74). In Caen it was noted that while the unskilled drifted toward farmwork, those with skills were earning their living "chez des fabricants ou des maîtres ouvriers" (75). Blessed with literacy, a deserter could hope to find a clerical job in a country starved of clerks and administrators, sometimes even in the public service. Henry Reynier was a Swiss who had deserted from the army in Piedmont; yet by Year IV he was firmly ensconced working for a local *notaire* at Aouste in the Drôme valley, a pillar of local society lodging in the same house as the curé (76).

Reynier lived in a comfort and a degree of security that were in no way typical. His circumstances would make very bad caselaw; however, he is a salutary reminder that for many hard-working and otherwise law-abiding citizens, refractories and deserters were real people with whom they came into contact on a fairly regular basis and whom they did not think of denouncing to the authorities. Conscripts lucky enough to find jobs would generally work openly in the fields or in the *atelier* in front of neighbors and fellow villagers, and there is little evidence that they felt in danger or that the rest of the village regarded their presence as in any sense criminal. Everyone knew that their neighbor had a son in the mountains, that he came to see them under cover of darkness, that food was being left for him in a shepherd's hut or in a ditch by the roadside. Refractory conscripts were not pariahs. If they evoked any emotion it was likely to be one of sympathy and fellowship. This does not mean, of course, that long months spent hiding in the caves of the Drôme or in the snowy wastes of the Massif Central were any less miserable or the Piedmontese wolves any less ferocious for the young man on the run. But it did mean that if he was utterly starving or overcome by fever, he would be more likely to throw himself on the mercy of local people with some measure of hope that he would not be turned over to the *gendarmes.* A tale of misfortune might, with a bit of luck, elicit assistance. When a deserter turned up on his doorstep at Aulnay in the Seine-et-Oise, Etienne Robillaird, the village miller, listened patiently to his story, invited him in, and was finally persuaded to cut his chains. His motive, it seems, was pure compassion:

Un homme inconnu s'est présenté vers les huit heures du soir à la porte de son moulin demandant le chemin de Roissy. Luy ayant ouvert sa porte pour lui indiquer ledit chemin, il s'est introduit chez lui. S'étant aperçu qu'il était enchaîné, il l'a invité de se retirer; mais après ses instances réitérées, s'étant dit déserteur et déclarant n'avoir quitté son corps qui était en marche que pour aller voir sa femme et ses enfants, qui étaient audit Roissy, et se proposant (suivant son dire) de rejoindre ensuite son dit corps qui devait passer sous huitaine à Meaux . . . (77)

Like beggars and others who had to throw themselves on the mercy of their fellow men, deserters no doubt learned to polish up their tales of misfortune. But in every village there were men and women who would shelter them or offer assistance despite the penalties prescribed by the law. Nor was the answer to be found in increasing these penalties or securing exemplary convictions since, in the words of the *commissaire du Directoire* in Epinal in Year V, "les loix pénales trop rudes sont toujours éludées" and juries would simply refuse to convict (78).

In extreme cases where refractories enjoyed the sympathy and confidence of the entire community, they could conduct themselves in public virtually as they chose, secure in the knowledge that they were among friends. In Pamiers in Year III deserters were reported to be disporting themselves freely in the city streets, chatting peaceably with their friends, and even meeting for a friendly drink with those of their companions who were in uniform (79). There would seem, indeed, to have been surprisingly little friction between those who had been compelled to serve and those remaining in their homes. In one incident in the Drôme in 1792, connivance went so far that a troop of local soldiers participated in a prison break by four men incarcerated at Crest for desertion (80). Even later in the Revolution when attitudes had hardened considerably, incidents were reported that revealed the relative ease of movement enjoyed by those on the run from the law. Cases of open fraternization between deserters and *gendarmes* were not unknown, and they were not always the prelude to an attempted arrest. The *agent municipal* in Foix complained in Year IV that "si la gendarmerie a l'air de poursuivre vivement ces déserteurs, elle n'a réellement que l'air, et il paraît certain que plusieurs fois depuis leur arrivée plusieurs d'entr'eux ont bu et mangé avec ces individus." There was no real attempt to arrest them, or even to restrict their liberty: "Tous ces déserteurs étaient à la dernière foire de Tarascon, et c'était de notoriété publique. Quelqu'un d'entr'eux jouait du violon dans un bal de sociètè. Quelles démarches a fait la gendarmerie ce jour-la?" (81). It was a reasonable question, one asked again by the Minister of Police in 1813 when he taxed the *gendarmerie* in the Seine-et-Oise with willful inaction over deserters who were known to be working in the quarries at Châtillon. Significantly, he suggested that the only solution would be to bring in *gendarmes* from elsewhere to arrest one known deserter, Edme Colas, who was working at the quarry and living in the inn run by Courtaz at La Croix d'Arcueil. His reason was his lack of confidence in the local men "qui sont journellement avec ledit Colas et qui lui dépensent son argent avec promesse de ne pas l'arrêter et de lui donner avis des ordres qu'ils pourraient recevoir à son égard" (82). Such cases of open collusion were rare perhaps, but they undermined effective policing, caused the authorities grave embarrassment, and demonstrated for all to see that refractories and deserters could socialize freely without fear of arrest or denunciation.

It is interesting that when deserters *were* denounced to the authorities, an element of personal grievance often lay behind the denunciation. The government could usually count on village squabbles to produce a rash of denunciations and counterdenunciations. At Génat in the Ariège the *garde-forestier* was sufficiently jealous of the mayor, Vincent Viguerie, that he built up a systematic dossier against him revealing that a conscript who had never left for the armies was not only known to the mayor but had visited him, eaten at his table, and worked on his property (83). At Lesparre in the Gironde the Imperial *procureur* himself was denounced for not sufficiently prosecuting deserters but again the act of denunciation was shown to be malicious, the work of an *instituteur* in the town embittered by an imagined slight and looking for advancement in the community (84). Another case in the Meurthe in which a village mayor was accused of harboring deserters had its roots in an act of private vengeance. The *dénonciateur* had previously been convicted of the self-same offense, and was rather crudely trying to take revenge on the mayor (85). Sometimes denunciation was spurred on by intercommunal jealousies, like that which divided Aurillac and Saint-Flour (86). More commonly the origin of the grievance was to be found in personal circumstance, in a sense of outrage that others were avoiding service while one's own family was paying an unreasonable price. In Year V, indeed, *pères de famille* were explicitly invited by the government's *commissaire* in Colmar to denounce deserters, suggesting that their desertion was directly responsible for their own sons' presence in the armies (87). Serving soldiers sometimes shared the resentment felt by their parents when they heard that their fellows were living peaceably at home while they suffered the torments of life on the Italian or Spanish front. A number of conscripts from the Vosges were sufficiently angered by the fact that their friends were still working happily on the farm and that "ils ont toujours été tranquil" that they petitioned the commissaire in Epinal to do something about it. They described what they themselves had felt when they had had to return to their units after a *congé,* and bitterly resented those of their peers who had failed to do so (88). There were individual cases too where men who tried to avoid service by procuring medical certificates that were obviously false found themselves denounced by fellow villagers, especially by those whose sons and nephews had been forced to leave in their stead. The unfortunate Antoine Lambaut, who got himself exempted by the *conseil de révision* at Pauillac, was the victim of just such a denunciation, in his case by the other conscripts from Lesparre who had found no loophole and resented his fraud. Perhaps his leg was too badly injured to allow him to march, they said, but it had always been strong enough when it came to dancing, as the whole of Lesparre was well aware:

> Non seulement nous, mais tous les habitants de Lesparre pourraient vous le prouver, il a dansé avec nous presque tout le carnaval, il était membre d'une société que nous avions formé pour danser, il s'est absenté au moment qu'il a su qu'il fallait tirer au sort pour mieux jouer son rolle. (89)

Lambaut made the mistake of openly reveling in the deception he had perpetrated, which contributed to the resentment that the others felt.

Despite the government's obvious interest in encouraging denunciation of this kind, it enjoyed only a very limited success, usually in cases of extreme unhappiness or exaggerated resentment. A father, distracted by the life of "agiotage" and "libertinage" that his deserter son was leading in the fleshpots of Paris, requested that the authorities save the family a great deal of anguish by arresting the young man and compelling him to serve (90). A widow, embittered by her experience a decade earlier, when a deserter to whom she had offered protection had repaid her by seducing her daughter, went to considerable lengths to get her revenge. She not only indicated to the *gendarmerie* the whereabouts of every deserter currently hiding in the village where she lived, Saint-Quintin in the Ariège, but submitted a very specific dossier accusing those who were sheltering them, and especially the mayor against whom she harbored a particularly corrosive grudge (91). On occasion social envy might play its part, and the authorities from time to time received allegations, generally unsigned, that rich and privileged members of the community were being shown undue partiality or protection (92). The *gendarmerie,* of course, did what it could to foster such malcontents, especially where they showed signs of crusading zeal. There would always be some individuals—a fact of which we were reminded all too dramatically by the *collaborateurs* and *collaboratrices* of the Vichy period—who took a certain perverted delight in making trouble for others. At Hesdin in the Pas-de-Calais, for example, one young man who had neatly avoided service by a timely marriage, a "réquisitionnaire marié avant le premier germinal" as he described himself in his letter, discussed the problem of *insoumission* in his locality with all the gleeful enthusiasm of a seasoned police spy, claiming that local lads were "déterminés à ne point partir," that they "ont acheté de la poudre, des balles, et qu'ils sont pourvus de munitions," and that "c'est dans les cabarets, les jours de dimanche, que les réquisitionnaires et les conscrits se rassemblent et forment leurs complots." For good measure he promised to find out more and to pass on any new information that he uncovered (93). But it is worth stressing that such instances are very few, even in the period of greatest revolutionary fervor. Moral outrage and wounded patriotism played little part in the denunciation of deserters and refractories.

Except in relatively rare circumstances, the young man on the run could depend on village solidarity and on the uncertain rapport of many villages with the *gendarmerie* to offer him a degree of protection. Local people had no reason to denounce him unless their own domestic interests were affected deleteriously by the deserter's presence in their midst. They had no desire to bring the *gendarmes* into the village, to involve them in private village matters that they were accustomed to settling without outside interference. Besides, the intrusion of the police into their private world could prove dreadfully embarrassing for everyone, unearthing the many irregularities and petty offenses which were an unquestioned part of their daily routine and which made significant contributions to the economy of the community. It was the mission of the *gendarmerie,* as we shall see in a later chapter, to interrupt this cozy self-sufficiency and to prove to country people that consorting with outlaws was not compatible with their own self-interest (94). In the case of refractories, generally their own flesh and blood, men who had an acknowledged role to play in the life of the community, that mission would never be easy to accomplish. With deserters, men from outside their community to whom the villagers felt less of a bond and no direct obligation, collective opinion was less firmly united. Deserters were tolerated, given work, and provided with food and straw for bedding partly through sympathy on the part of people who were in many cases themselves the parents of *réquisitionnaires,* and partly through blatant self-interest. That tolerance was always brittle and might snap in those cases where the deserter failed to fit in with the established ways of the local community, or where his presence came to be seen as a threat to their property or their personal security. A deserter who had no job, did not work, or was not useful to local people, above all one who affronted their established morality or put their family life at risk, might find himself rebuffed by the community or even denounced to the authorities. Guy Fleuriot, a *réquisitionnaire* hiding in one Norman village in Year VII, placed rather too much strain on the tolerance and generosity of his involuntary hosts with the result that he was virtually handed over to the local *gendarmes:*

> Fleuriot n'a jamais joint son bataillon, il a toujours éludé la loi. Il est sans profession. Il n'occupe aucune place. Il n'a pas craint de porter le trouble et la désolation dans un ménage, en déterminant une jeune femme qui a deux enfants en bas âge à provoquer un divorce dans l'espoir de l'éspouser. Ces faits sont constants. En conséquence nous avons lieu d'espérer que vous ferez usage des moyens qui sont en votre pouvoir pour faire joindre à ce jeune homme les drapeaux de la République dont jusqu'à ce jour il s'est aussi lâchement éloigné: en satisfaisant à la loi vous rétablirez en même temps l'union dans une famille divisée. (95)

Patriotism did not enter into this denunciation. The author was the girl's uncle, anxious to protect his family's honor, not the state's. But there can be little doubt that he spoke not just for himself but for the general consensus of opinion in the village.

6

Desertion and Criminality

ONE ASPECT of the deserter's lifestyle that could materially affect the attitude of local people toward him was the extent of his participation in criminal activity, especially where his crimes caused actual harm to the local community (1). It was only to be expected that young men on the run, often miles from home and desperately hungry, would from time to time resort to crime to satisfy their most pressing needs, not out of any desire to hurt other people but from a simple primeval urge to keep themselves alive. Their lifestyle in so many ways resembled that of the *errants* and vagabonds who infested the roads and villages of eighteenth-century France, and who had come to be regarded with less and less charity as the century progressed. Even the courts did not always find it possible to distinguish clearly between them. The *tribunal correctionnel* at Valence, for example, found itself faced with the case of a vagabond called Brochier in Year V. The tribunal knew that he came from Granne in the district of Die, and his offense was that of simple vagabondage, but there was no means of telling whether his lifestyle concealed the more serious crime of desertion. After substantial enquiries, they were left with little hard evidence. His municipality duly provided the information that "ce particulier est en effet originaire de Granne, qu'il n'y a point d'immeubles, qu'il y a plus de vingt ans qu'il n'y réside plus, qu'on ignore où il demeure habituellement, qu'on on a dit qu'il a déserté de plusieurs régiments, que c'est peut-être la raison pour laquelle il n'a pas de passeport" (2). Like many deserters and others deprived of a regular means of earning their livelihood, Brochier had been marginalized and compelled to adopt a way of life that depended on the fruits of petty crime.

The authorities were in no doubt that crime and desertion were inextricably linked, that where a region suffered a perceptible increase in its crime rate, young men, footloose and without responsibilities to local people, were almost certainly to blame. In Year VII the government's *commissaire* in the Lot-et-Garonne specifically linked desertion to the spate of crimes against property and the person that he had encountered in the department. Forty deserters had taken over a country inn and were creating havoc on neighboring farms. Elsewhere they were responsible for antigovernment slogans. In a cluster of villages around Monclar they had wreaked a dreadful vengeance on the local community, "ils ont pillé trois maisons, incendié une grange, assassiné un citoyen, violé une jeune fille" (3). Similarly in the Sarthe, both civilian and military authorities recognized that deserters were increasing the levels of lawlessness in rural areas where *brigandages* were becoming ever more frequent and where "il n'est que trop reconnu que les bandes vagabondes et nocturnes qui se portent à ces excès sont en partie composées de déserteurs" (4). Petty crime, thefts from barns and isolated farmhouses, in some instances of corn still growing in the fields, constituted the major part of this increase, and the assumption that men on the run were responsible was one that not only officialdom, but whole rural communities, readily drew (5). The government did not view these developments with equanimity. In 1813 a report from the Minister of Police pinpointed the increase in the crime rate over the previous few months, and was in no doubt about the underlying cause. For in that period, "le nombre de déserteurs et de réfractaires s'est accru avec une rapidité et dans une proportion inconnue jusqu'à ce jour." Surveying the crime figures for 1810 when there had been, officially at least, 164,770 *déserteurs* and *refractaires* at large on the territory of France, the report stressed that each and every one of them was liable to resort to crime. For 164,770 deserters meant that

> 164,770 individus obligés de se cacher, de se soustraire aux regards de l'administration, ne pouvant se livrer avec sécurité à aucune industrie, a aucun projet d'établissement, obligés d'errer sans asyle et sans état, conduits par le besoin à tous les crimes et livrés par l'habitude du mal à la mercie du premier factieux qui pouvait les réunir sous les étendards du brigandage armé. (6)

As we have seen, this analysis is facile in the extreme, a propagandist picture of the deserter and refractory as an enemy of the people, painted in all the strident and unsubtle colors of an *image d'Epinal*. Yet there was clearly a considerable correlation between the presence of *fuyards* in an area and the increase in that area's crime rate. How valid is the image of the deserter and refractory as a cynical criminal? What crimes did they commit? And in what measure did these crimes impinge on the everyday lives of those in whose midst they lived?

Again, it is perhaps timely to draw a clear distinction between the crimes committed by deserters and those that were the work of village boys hiding in the surrounding woods and thickets. Inevitably, local communities were liable to view the offenders differently, and to show far more indulgence toward their own sons; but the distinction is not entirely one of favoritism. The *insoumis* were seldom as desperate or abandoned as the deserters, they knew which farms they could approach for food or shelter, and they had no reason to rob or plunder to stay alive. Indeed, they would be very unwise to do so since their continued liberty depended on their ability to work with the peasant community of the area in their shared opposition to the state and its officials. The deserter, on the other hand, might be left with no choice but to risk antagonizing the villagers if he were not to die of cold or malnutrition. Therefore, while crimes of violence stemming from youthful revelry were common to both deserters and refractories, robberies, housebreaking, and arson—actions that threatened local people and undermined their meager welfare—were far more likely to be the preserve of deserters from elsewhere, passing through the community, without roots or *connaissances,* and without the work from which the refractory could hope to extract a small but invaluable income. Of course, *insoumis* got involved in fights, in barroom brawls and drunken assaults on third parties, in intervillage *rixes* at fairs and markets. But these were incidents that caused the village little trouble. These draft dodgers were in no way a class apart, but were behaving like all young villagers of their age, unmarried males without family responsibilities who had always caused affrays at *bals champêtres* and expended their youthful energy in colorful *charivaris.* Village society was well accustomed to such excesses.

Similarly, conscripts might become involved in the ordinary criminal activities of the village without arousing any anger on the part of the local population. This is especially true in the case of poaching, of the *délits forestiers* that were commonplace in every rural community, even the most law-abiding (7). That deserters sleeping out of doors on cold nights should steal firewood from local forests seemed quite natural to villagers who not infrequently made nocturnal visits to the communal woods with an identical purpose (8). The forest laws were in any case very difficult to enforce. Relatively few villagers were ever brought to justice, and those who were could hope to escape with the very lightest sentence, especially if the case were heard before the local *juge de paix.* In the Seine-et-Oise the Minister noted angrily that one *juge* had treated the offense so lightly that he was insulting the *gardes-forestiers* and making their task quite impossible. Men found carrying away faggots of wood from the *forêt nationale* at Saint-Germain had been allowed to leave the court freely after paying a paltry fine, "une somme modique, dont ils sont remboursés, et au-delà, par la vente d'un seul fagot" (9). *Insoumis* were particularly prone to involvement in *délits forestiers* because they knew instinctively where to go and had an invaluable local knowledge of trout streams and rabbit runs; as local lads they were doing neither more nor less than they might have been expected to do had there been no question of military service. On occasion their offenses were committed jointly with civilian friends from the village itself, a final proof, if any is needed, that poaching was seen as an acceptable economic and social activity in which any villager might become involved. In one instance, in the Ariège, conscription offenses were neatly linked to breaches of the forest laws. A father and his two sons, both *conscrits réfractaires,* were arrested in 1808 after *gendarmes* had stumbled on their illegal enterprise close to the Spanish frontier. The father was accused of protecting his sons and of flouting the law on communal woodland since "il les entretenait sur la frontière d'Espagne chez un maréchal ferrant, ces jeunes gens venaient parfois couper du bois sur les montagnes, le père le vendait ensuite, soit à Seix, soit ailleurs" (10).

Smuggling was also a form of criminal enterprise that came easily to countrymen, especially those near national frontiers or the old boundaries between *pays d'état* and *pays d'élection.* The population in these regions was generally well-schooled in the art of contraband. There was no stigma attached to the crime, nor any antipathy toward those involved; hence it was a lucrative pursuit in which a young fugitive could involve himself without risking the ire of local people. Even when the smuggling involved the passing of goods from France to a country with which France was at war, the villagers seemed to view smuggling bands with a nagging respect, in part, of course, because they themselves often benefited from the trade and shared directly or indirectly in the prosperity that the smugglers created. In *brumaire* Year III, for instance, the Haute-Garonne reported that villagers from the frontier commune of Aspet near Saint-Gaudens were passing mules across the Pyrénées into Spain under cover of darkness— "qu'il existait des hommes assez ennemis de leur patrie pour faire passer des mules et des mulets au tiran de Castille," in the official language of the time— but the department's sense of outrage was not shared in the settlements in the mountains (11). Where customsmen did try to intervene and make arrests, there was every likelihood that the local population would riot or impede them, as happened in the villages of Suc and Lavelanet in the Ariège in 1810, where the *douaniers* were sufficiently foolhardy that they tried to intercept bands of smugglers more than one hundred strong (12). What Paris never adequately appreciated was that in many of these frontier communities smuggling was a fundamental part of local culture involving the domestic economy of every family. Whole villages took part, from the most humble to the wealthiest farmers, the *notables* of local society (13). Often these richer farmers were the natural leaders of the smuggling rings in the same way that they were the natural leaders of the community, and there are instances where officials themselves were involved and where locally recruited regiments reverted to their traditional nocturnal pursuits (14). Contraband was symptomatic of a more general lawlessness and contempt for officialdom that was common in remote mountain areas where the writ of central government did not run. In the more inaccessible villages of the department of Taro in northern Italy, smuggling, highway robbery, and desertion were natural bedfellows, reflections of the extreme misery and deprivation of the inhabitants. At Monchio "une misérable cabane, quelques chèvres, et quelques chataîgniers—voilà toute leur fortune: aux approches de l'hiver ils se rendent en Toscane et campent dans les campagnes." At Morfasso crime and smuggling were even more endemic, with the inhabitants branded as "contrebandiers avant que ce pays fût passé sous le régime français, et voleurs de grand chemin depuis." In Carpaneto smuggling was the mainstay of the village economy in a region where the peole were "presque tous des muletiers: ils se rendent souvent dans la Ligurie, et sur le territoire de Bobbio; c'est là que se réfugient nos conscrits" (15). In the Pyrénées conditions were very little different, and again the economy of whole districts was dependent on contraband. Smuggling in the Andorra valley was believed to involve eighty or more men on a regular basis, exporting French grain and importing coffee and colonial produce. It was a lucrative trade centered on most of the major mountain settlements along the frontier such as L'Hospitalet, Siguer, Auzat, Conflans, Aulos, Ustou, Sentein, and Bonac, a map that corresponds quite tantalizingly with that of *insoumission* in the region. The customsmen did not know the terrain sufficiently to identify the passing places in the mountains where trading was done, and a veil of secrecy was successfully maintained over the identity of those involved. What was known with some certainty, however, was that smugglers consorted with deserters and refractories in their mountain fastnesses, used their services during their journey, and devoted part of the profits of the trade to providing them with food and clothing (16).

Poaching, stealing firewood, smuggling grain through mountain passes did not constitute crimes in the eyes of local communities where everyone, even the most law-abiding, might do the same from time to time. A refractory conscript who tried to keep himself alive by such means would merely underline the fact that he was well-integrated into the mores of the village or hamlet where he was hiding. He might be seen as an unwelcome competitor by the local *braconniers,* but in no sense could he be construed as threatening the welfare of local people. Because of his misery and desperation, the deserter was far more likely than the refractory to indulge in criminal activity that harmed the interests of villagers and thus overstepped the bounds of local tolerance. The majority of these crimes were crimes against property, thefts involving an element of violence or destruction, *vols avec effraction.* Throughout the period of the wars, indeed, there were regular complaints from all corners of France that the number of thefts and burglaries was increasing alarmingly, largely because of the social disruption caused by war, with thousands of people on the move or in hiding from the authorities, removed from the calming influence of their families and communities and hence more likely to flout social convention (17). Often the offenses seem trifling enough, acts of petty pilfering to keep body and soul together. At Dunkerque it was noted that thefts of food were particularly numerous, committed generally on impulse by men who had no idea where the next meal was coming from, "le tout pour parvenir à se dérober aux poursuites qu'on faisait après eux" (18). Sometimes they would steal small objects and items of clothing from stallholders or from houses in the villages they passed through in the hope of selling them again at the first opportunity. Often their victims were poor and vulnerable. When two naval deserters were arrested at La Brède in the Gironde, "on les a trouvés nantis d'effets volés, notamment de treize mouchoirs enlevés à une pauvre famille de Cadaujac," a rash theft that persuaded local mayors to look out for the two fugitives (19). Deserters could, of course, set their sights on more ambitious targets, like those in the commune of Arsac who burgled homes, waylaid one of the richest farmers in the district, and drove away two flocks of sheep in one brief orgy of criminal activity (20). Those eager to make a quick getaway might attempt to steal horses from stables or from fields, a crime that caused fury in the farming community. Yet to country boys the theft of livestock could seem a very obvious way of making the money needed to stay alive because horses not only guaranteed instant mobility but were always saleable commodities at the many horsefairs and markets held in nearby towns (21). Lonely farmhouses and isolated cottages were favored targets for thieves, although in parts of the Nord they turned their attentions to parish churches generally left unlocked and unguarded even after nightfall. Again they seemed to provide easy and guaranteed pickings. At Oost-Capel near Dunkerque, three men were reported as having broken into the church and stolen "deux calices et un ciboire," one of the chalices being pure silver (22). Yet because of the nature of the crime, it was twenty-four hours before the *gendarmerie* were alerted, and the thieves were safely out of the vicinity. Of the three men, one was a deserter, another an *échappé aux galères,* an interesting alliance between the fugitive and the hardened criminal. Their thieving was in no way casual pilfering, but highly organized crime involving churches in a score of villages and small towns. They had all the attributes of a professional gang who, in the words of the magistrates in Dunkerque, "à l'aide d'une patente de marchand, rodent de commune en commune et ont des relations avec des juifs qui achètent tout" (23).

If individual thefts could be tolerated, acts of collective banditry were perceived as posing a much more serious threat to rural communities. Although the deserters often grouped together for their own protection, they could seem very menacing to local people, and their criminal activity risked spreading panic from farm to farm, rather as had happened during the *Grande Peur* of 1789. In the years of general lawlessness that followed the dismantling of revolutionary government, such crimes became commonplace in many parts of the country, sparking off a rash of alarmist accounts and denunciations. Even when the thefts were restricted to the basic necessities that the men required for their survival, like those committed by a band of six to eight deserters in the mountains around Châtillon, alarm spread rapidly at the very thought of bandits, "armés jusqu'aux dents," and the *sous-préfet* at Die admitted that with such offenses "la peur peut être pour quelque chose" (24). Fear was essential to the successful operation of such bands; without it they would have been reduced to impotence. Near Bourganeuf in the Creuse groups of between fifteen and twenty stalwart conscripts, "des plus beaux hommes," were sighted roaming the countryside, begging for food at remote farms with abundant use of threats and menaces (25). They would hide in the woods during the day and emerge only at night, secure in the knowledge that the whole community lived in fear of their ravages. In many cases they did receive a degree of protection or at least of mute tolerance from the local community, which made them very difficult to hunt down. Around Sainte-Foy in the Gironde, for instance, bands of deserters were reported to be playing on the emotions of local farmers, using the requisition laws as a lever to excite the anger of young *cultivateurs* and to build up a spirit of opposition (26). Generally, however, they relied on simple terror. After one attack near Castelmoron, the authorities noted that breaking down the wall of silence in the local community was the greatest single obstacle they encountered in pursuing the band responsible. Rougier, the *adjoint du maire* in the village of Rimons, had been the victim of this crime, and the whole community shared his terror:

> La plupart de ces brigands se tinrent postés en dehors du logis. Ceux qui y entrèrent avaient le visage barbouillé de rouge, et aucun ne fut connu. Ils se firent indiquer par le citoyen Rougier le lieu où était son argent. Ils visitèrent ses meubles et ne prirent que le numéraire qui s'y trouva. Leur proie fut de 450 francs, avec une certaine quantité de pain et d'autres comestibles dont ils dirent avoir besoin pour *bouffer.* Ils affectèrent, en se retirant, de mener le citoyen Rougier au milieu d'eux pour lui faire remarquer en quel nombre il était et le menacer de venir le tuer s'il osait parler de leur visite. (27)

Since the villagers believed that the band contained between forty and forty-five *brigands,* these were threats that they took very seriously indeed.

Bands of deserters were frequently indistinguishable from the ordinary brigand bands that caused so much havoc in the French provinces during the Thermidorian and Directorial years. In several notable instances deserters merged with civilians in such formidable groupings as the "bande de Salembier," which ravaged the Nord, the Pas-de-Calais, and wide tracts of the *départements réunis* in Year IV and Year V, using the frontier as a welcome means of escape when they felt themselves threatened (28). Salembier's enterprise was on a considerable scale with approximately sixty brigands, men and women, at his beck and call. The charges against them related to twenty-six different crimes, from ordinary thefts to "vols avec des circonstances atroces," from attacks on passers-by to "assassinats horribles"; targets included farms, mills, lock-keepers' houses by the canals, and churches in lonely villages. The band roamed the northern plains, striking generally by night in groups of ten, twelve, or fifteen, heavily disguised to avoid detection (29). Salembier was not alone in realizing that deserters were by sheer force of circumstance ideal fodder for inclusion in brigand bands. In the Sarthe eyewitnesses spoke of up to forty deserters organized in large *rassemblements,* spreading terror in the countryside, where they "se font livrer des armes, des subsistances, et même de l'argent" (30). Along the northern frontier "brigands travestis et armés" who tied up the inhabitants of a lonely cottage and ransacked the house in search of money "pourraient bien être des conscrits et réquisitionnaires réfugiés dans les bois" (31). The same kind of identification between deserters and brigands was made by officials across the whole of France. In the Ardèche in Year VIII the *commissaire* reported glumly that "les bandes de brigands qui nous désolent" consisted primarily of "conscrits et réquisitionnaires" who ought to be incorporated in the armies as a measure of public safety (32). In the Drôme in 1809 the authorities convinced themselves that the very considerable problem of lawlessness in the department could be effectively stamped out if desertion were eliminated, and the dossiers of captured brigands would seem to bear out their judgment. They referred repeatedly to their military service and to the circumstances in which they left the army as being at the root of their drift into crime: "Répond qu'il a servi pendant six ans dans la 100e demi-brigade; il s'est retiré avec son congé"; "répond qu'il n'a servi que quatre mois il y a sept ou huit mois, dans un bataillon auxiliaire qui fut ensuite licencié"; "répond qu'il a servi neuf mois dans le 11e Bataillon de la Drôme, qu'il vint à son pays en convalescence, et qu'il s'est marié depuis" (33). In the same year the prefect of the Mayenne offered his rather perceptive explanation as to why refractories and deserters should be so prone to serious crimes of *brigandage*. In hiding, he suggested, many of them became tired and bored, unable to work or to socialize because of the activity of the local *gendarmerie*. They came together into bands for company. The first thefts were timid, almost desultory affairs, but their success led to further and more ambitious plans.

> Quelques-uns d'entr'eux se réunirent en petites troupes, armés d'abord de bâtons et de menaces, ils s'introduisirent dans les maisons isolées, se firent donner des subsistances; bientôt ils enlevèrent les fusils; leur audace s'accroissant insensiblement, ils formèrent de plus grands rassemblements, imprimèrent la terreur dans les campagnes, et finirent par attaquer la gendarmerie et

par lui enlever leurs camarades qui avaient pu être arrêtés. Enfin ouvertement rebelles aux lois, il prétendaient forcer les jeunes gens, disposés à s'y soumettre, à partager leur rébellion. (34)

So tight was the link between brigands and deserters that in the countryside around Nyons thieves and highway robbers sought anonymity by passing themselves off as deserters. The *sous-préfet* observed in *frimaire* X that by means of this disguise "les brigands ont trouvé un abri dans les montagnes de cet arrondissement, sans faire naître la méfiance ou le soupçon" (35).

Brigandage is a somewhat indiscriminate term used by the authorities to cover a confused multiplicity of crimes ranging from political murders of republican officials to the most banal kind of highway robbery with no motive beyond that of enriching the perpetrators. In the South and the West particularly, armed attacks in the period after *thermidor* often did conceal political or counterrevolutionary aims, and deserters from the Republic's armies were quite prominently involved (36). In the West they frequently wore the uniform of the Republic when engaged in their murderous attacks (37). And though in that area the uniform may have had political connotations, elsewhere brigands might mount their night raids in military uniform out of a kind of bravado, surrounding themselves with an element of military pomp. In the Drôme, for example, the prefect reported in Year XIII that after some years of calm the problem of *brigandage* had resurfaced in the mountainous terrain between Die and Montélimar where "des vols de mulets, des vols de divers effets dans des maisons écartées" had once again become widespread. There was no question of these being political attacks since the aim was clearly gain rather than reprisals and the objects chosen had no political or symbolic significance. A police spy had provided helpful details of their lifestyle and their current activities. There were in all some fifteen members of the *bande* although only four had as yet taken part in raids. Of these four, three were army deserters and they wore uniforms for their exploits, a *carmagnole* and a *pantalon de velours*. According to the spy, they were armed with "une carbine, deux pistolets, et un poignard"; they had several known hiding places, generally in uninhabited barns and they posted a lookout to warn them of the approach of the *gendarmerie* (38). Even in their new and rather hazardous experience of civilian life, they preferred to retain certain elements of their old military organization and swagger. Stripped of its political significance, it was a powerful way of impressing and overawing the local population.

The extent to which local people were cowed by such bands reflected the extent to which they felt threatened. Where brigands restricted themselves to fairly precise political targets, like republican mail coaches or treasury deliveries, the local peasants were relatively unperturbed and might continue offering them their protection. Similarly, large sections of the population would experience little fear where brigands were wreaking retribution on former Jacobin officials, or on those villagers who had rushed to buy *biens nationaux* back in the Year II. In fact, when they attacked a symbol of authority that was the object of widespread popular loathing—like the *octroi* posts at Bourg-lès-Valence in 1808, which were smashed up by a gang of men armed with sticks, pikes and pitchforks—local citizens even joined in (39). Attacks on arms stores or powder magazines did little to upset the mass of local people (40). Even when bands indulged in robbery, they might choose their victims with care so as not to antagonize the country communities on which they depended for shelter. Attacks on strangers, complete outsiders passing through the area, were viewed differently from those that placed local lives in jeopardy. Hence merchants might appear to present ideal targets for brigands. They were outsiders from a different social milieu and they could generally be depended on to carry worthwhile sums of money on their person. In Year IX a band of brigands attacked a Swiss merchant on the road from Cambrai to Bapaume, seizing his horse, his wallet, and his moneybelt, and leaving him by the roadside with "les mains liées, les yeux bandés, laissé par terre avec un bâillon dans la bouche." It was without question a cruel attack on a foreign businessman, but one that had no very dire consequences for the local community, who might even hope to share in part of the spoils (41). It was very different when the livelihood of local people was put at risk. Deserters in the Aisne ravaged grain supplies in Year III, particularly in the area around Chauny. They inspired fear among local farmers, giving themselves chilling *noms de guerre* drawn from the annals of war and banditry (Dumouriez, Cartouche, Lafayette, Mandrin) and warning the peasantry that they would not require any hired labor for the harvest since they would find their crops harvested for them (42). Then the *gendarmes did* get a degree of cooperation from the farmers, anxious to avoid a year of enforced dearth. There were, it is true, larger-than-life figures among bandit leaders who so terrified local populations that they commanded respect despite the damage they caused. Jean-Pierre Bouisson, known in the southern Cantal as the "voleur d'Alpuech", could depend on the warmest reception and the best food and drink whenever he came visiting. He, however, enjoyed the reputation of being a local Mandrin, carrying several pistols on his belt wherever he went, and telling of his adventures to anyone who would listen, including the time when he had got the length of the scaffold in Orléans but had leapt into the crowd and escaped (43). He did have as his audience a relatively gullible mountain people who were ready to transform him into a folkhero. More commonly the attitudes of local people to brigand bands were intensely pragmatic, and were well-summed up by the prefect of the Lot-et-Garonne in Year VIII:

> Quand les brigands n'attaquaient que les diligences . . . les citoyens mettaient moins d'ensemble et d'activité dans leur surveillance et leurs perquisitions; depuis que les propriétés particulières ont été menacées, leur zèle pour écarter et détruire le brigandage est plus général et plus efficace: la crainte de provoquer la vengeance des malfaiteurs les retenait, la nécessité de se mettre à l'abri de leurs entreprises les excite. (44)

If deserters were particularly prone to commit crimes against property to stave off hunger, their loneliness and deprivation could drive them to other excesses that did more to antagonize the local population. Men on the run, far from their own village and thus cloaked in a certain anonymity and without the company of a wife or *copine* were perhaps more liable than others to resort to rape or harassment in a bid to satisfy their sexual desires. Certainly village opinion tended to place the blame for unexplained attacks on those without social obligations, driven to desperation by long months in hiding, and village opinion could be unforgiving on this matter. When the daughter of an innkeeper, Cathérine Claudel from the commune of Ainvelle in the Vosges, was found raped and murdered in a wood in 1810, the local community was quite naturally outraged. She had been savagely attacked with blows to her stomach before being strangled with "une ficelle" with such violence that the *gendarmes* were at first inclined to believe that more than one man had been responsible. They revised their opinion only after the arrest six weeks later of a deserter from La Folie in the Haute-Loire "refusé dans les auberges et arrêté sur la route par des charretiers à cause de son travestissement en fille ... Les habits qui formaient son déguisement ont été reconnus être ceux de ladite Claudel" (45). Of course, soldiers did not have to have deserted to commit rape, and popular distrust extended to garrisons and passing regiments as well as to those on the run. In the same department, for example, a twelve-year-old girl from Nomexy was the victim of an assault by the fencingmaster from the local regiment (46). As with any crime, the fact that the assailant did not belong and came from outside the commune helped to seal the impression of a community that had been violated, and feelings ran very high. As Jean-Pierre Gutton has shown, girls were still regarded as being in some sense the property of the village, of the "groupe de la jeunesse," a traditional concept that was reaffirmed at every *bal champêtre* and symbolized in the "multiples rites de mariage" (47). The rape of any village girl by a man from elsewhere was therefore doubly offensive to village mores and gave rise to a widespread desire for retribution and vengeance.

   The psychological pressures that turned men to rape could also lead to more generalized violence, and the presence in a commune of deserters or refractories was always liable to result in an increase in the number of assaults and killings committed on its territory. Therefore when murders were reported in small towns or villages, or when bodies were discovered in ditches by lonely roadsides, the *gendarmerie* and the villagers were united in believing that conscripts were probably to blame. When an obscure individual was murdered on a lonely road near the departmental boundary between the Cantal and the Puy-de-Dôme in Year XI, *le bruit public* was quite adamant that deserters were responsible, and such exaggerated rumors were circulating that "on ne voyageait plus dans cette contrée qu'en caravane." The *sous-préfet* at Murat was sufficiently alarmed to order an immediate search of the woods, mountains, and *burons* (the huts occupied by shepherds on the higher slopes) to assuage local fears, but with no success (48). In that case it was the sheer randomness of the killing that most alarmed the local population, the fact that any traveler was placed at risk. In other instances the victim had been chosen with care and the murder executed with clinical calculation. When a *garde-champêtre* was found dead in a wood at Haumont in the Nord, there were few doubts in anyone's mind that the murder was the work of deserters because the *garde* had a reputation for severity and punctiliousness and had been responsible for the arrest of numerous *conscrits réfractaires*. What shocked public sensibilities was less the fact of his killing than the manner of it. "Sa tête était fracassée, ses yeux crevés, et son corps était transpercé à l'endroit du nombril par un bâton de noisetier" (49). Particularly vicious attacks could only have the effect of exacerbating ill-feeling towards deserters. At Galgon near Libourne an old lady living alone was bludgeoned to death by her *domestique,* a deserter from a neighboring village whom she had taken in and protected. The motive was presumably gain and there was evidence of premeditation, but it was the excessive violence of the attack that horrified opinion: "On lui avait fracassé le crâne à coups de massue, et sa poitrine était frappée de plusieurs coups de couteau" (50). News of such crimes only increased the sense of insecurity that was already rife in many areas of the French countryside. Faced with the miseries and tribulations of months and sometimes years on the run, conscripts might, it seemed, be driven to almost any outrage. No one in remote areas of the country could consider themselves truly safe. One young deserter living in the woods near his home village in the Cantal uttered wild threats against his father and his stepmother whom he accused of harboring prejudice against him and making his life intolerable. On 26 July 1809 he could take no more. He entered the family house and "a frappé sa belle-mère de cinq coups de couteau, dont quatre ont porté sur la tête et un sur le bras gauche; on craint beaucoup pour les jours de cette femme qui était enceinte" (51). Of course this attack was the kind that followed many a family quarrel in rural France, often about inheritance and the division of land; it did not necessarily follow from the fact of desertion. Nevertheless the strains placed on frightened, often rather immature young men by their life in clandestinity accentuated existing family tensions, and public opinion was not slow to connect such attacks with the rough and violent lifestyle of their fugitive existence.

As with any *fait divers,* public outrage could generally be measured by the brutality and callousness of the crime. When two women and a baby were found battered to death in an isolated farmhouse at Sainte-Croix near Die in Year XI, the thirst for vengeance was understandable. The killers were both deserters, *cultivateurs* from Die, who had called at the farm claiming that they were looking for two *remplaçants* to whom they had paid considerable sums the previous Sunday and who, they had good reason to believe, had since gone into hiding. This was, however, no more than a pretext to gain admission to the house. On asking whether there were no young men around the farm buildings, they were told that the women were alone, the husband and uncle being away at the fair in Saillans and the brother-in-law out in the woods collecting firewood. Reassured, the two murderers set about their gory task, clubbing the occupants with their freshly hewn *bâtons* and leaving them for dead before setting fire to the farm to destroy any evidence of their crime. The story sent a *frisson* of horror through the locality, and large crowds turned out to watch the execution of the two killers on the main square of Valence (52). Deserters already condemned in their absence faced severe military penalties if they were recaptured, and some of them responded as men with nothing to lose, killing and robbing with carefree abandon. But few can have been as indiscriminate as Pierre-François Fautrel, who had deserted from several regiments in and around Lille, and who on the eve of his execution for murder confessed to a whole series of killings over the previous few years. A Norwegian soldier, an Italian whom he had met on the road, the mayor of a Belgian town through which he had passed and a woman in whose company he had staged one of his escapes all figured on his list of victims, usually for purposes of theft. There was something chilling about Fautrel's casual approach to the deaths of others. The woman, for instance, who had helped him to desert, simply outlived her usefulness, whereupon he pushed her into the Rhine near Nijmegen on the grounds that she had become a burden to him, "dont il ne savit plus que faire." Even more horrifying, if his rather cavalier deathbed confession is to be believed, was his admission that for two of his crimes others had been convicted and executed. While serving in the Twenty-fifth Light Infantry he had killed a fellow soldier "à coups de bâton et à coups de sabre" in the citadel at Verdun. He was, he said, charged with the crime along with a *tambour* in the same regiment, but whereas he had been acquitted by the *conseil de guerre,* Thomassin, his alleged accomplice, "qui n'avait nullement participé à son crime, fut fusillé." Again, he alleged that he alone had been responsible for the murder of the mayor, near Berg-op-Zoom, having held him up on a lonely road to steal his money. He had deserted his regiment along with another soldier, and he had since heard that this man "le nommé Jouvinot de Lille, qui était déserté avec lui mais qui l'avait quitté quelque temps avant cet assassinat, fut arrêté et condamné ainsi que lui Fautrel à la peine de mort par un conseil de guerre, qu'il sait que ledit Jouvinot, quoique innocent, fut exécuté et que lui il avait le bonheur de se sauver entre Berg-op-Zoom et Breda" (53).

Many of the killings ascribed to deserters were not of local people, however, but were rather incestuous affairs within the twilight world of the fugitives themselves. Conscripts leaving home to make the long and often hazardous journey to join their regiments could generally be counted on to have a certain amount of money on their person, usually in the form of the *prime* they had received from the recruiting-officer, supplemented by gifts from parents and relatives on the eve of their departure. They therefore made obvious targets for theft, especially by those who knew the timetable and habits of new recruits, and the periodic discovery of their bodies on public highways caused considerable anger among government officials (54). Young conscripts could be terribly naive and trusting, lured into a false sense of security by their uniform and by the comradeship of the journey. At Asnières-sur-Oise (Seine-et-Oise) in 1806 the body of a conscript was found, hurriedly concealed in a communal wood. On investigation it was revealed that he had been persuaded by another recruit to take a shortcut away from the main road shortly before his disappearance, that the two men had been discussing money in a bar before the murder, and that the victim had revealed to his companion that his father had given him several gold coins before he set out on his long tramp from Mende to join his battalion at Boulogne. His loose, excited conversation and open, trusting nature were sufficient to ensure that he would never again see the wilds of his native Gévaudan (55). In the Midi there was sometimes reason to believe that soldiers killed by gangs of deserters were political victims of White Terror rather than the targets for simple theft, since young conscripts were frequently expected to make long and solitary journeys in the uniform of the Republic across countryside where Royalist brigands roamed unchecked (56). Usually, however, there was a sad, mundane predictability about such killings. At Autreville in the Vosges, passers-by found a young soldier dying in a derelict *baraque* by the roadside. Again, he had been robbed of all his cash by his two *compagnons de route* to whom he had vouchsafed the information that he had received 300 francs from his father, a huge sum in the eyes of the majority of twenty year olds, to help him on his long journey to the front. Almost clinically they had steered him toward the shed and "à portée d'un coup de fusil et à coups de sabre le laissèrent pour mort, le déshabillèrent et répandirent ses habits pour ôter la trace qu'il fut un militaire" (57). In this case the *gendarmes* seem to have known exactly what to do because they ordered the search of all local bars and the dilapidated and disreputable inns that were known to shelter criminals, where they quickly arrested one of the murderers. Once again, it soon became evident that this was a murder among soldiers because all three had come from hospital in Nancy and were on their way to rejoin their unit. The killers even knew their victim. They set up the robbery in a quiet spot, did their utmost to remove any signs of his identity, and took to the woods leaving behind any thoughts of rejoining their regiment. It was the second killing of its type on the same lonely stretch of road within six months; on the previous occasion a *militaire réformé* had attacked another young recruit in almost identical circumstances.

Much of the crime for which deserters and refractories were responsible was crude and ill-considered, the quickest means to the very simple end of laying their hands on a little money to ease the hardship of their lot. The victims were often chance acquaintances, those whom they encountered on the road, in a bar, or whom village gossip suggested were rich. But it would be a mistake to dismiss all the criminal activity of these men as falling into such predictable categories, or to imply that they were incapable of planning and premeditation. Frequently attacks were made less from a quest for gain than from a burning desire for revenge on those who were held responsible for reducing them to the straits in which they found themselves. This was especially true where large bands of fugitives lived in close proximity to their own village, most probably *insoumis* who maintained contact with the other villagers and who knew which of the local people were cooperating with the authorities. Public officeholders were especially at risk from attacks of this kind, men whose position in local society seemed to justify the belief that they were traitors to their own people, *mouchards, collabos* whose attempts at ingratiating themselves with the prefect or the *gendarmerie* had condemned the young men of the area to their current very marginal existence. Village mayors, compelled by law to organize the *tirage* and supervise the recruitment process, could find that their land or their livestock had been the target of a night attack. Being country boys themselves, the majority of deserters knew only too well how to wreak the maximal amount of damage. At Poujols in the Hérault, for instance, the vineyards of the *agent municipal* were seriously damaged in just such a surreptitious night raid. All the buds were chopped off his vines over an area of three *ares,* and young plants on another part of the farm were systematically uprooted (58). The rich vines of the Gironde would appear to have been especially at risk, and mayors throughout the Bordelais were made to pay for their zeal in denouncing offenders to the prefect. After one particularly severe attack at Mouliets in 1811, the *procureur-général* in Bordeaux explained that the department had been subjected to such outrages for years and that the devastation was the work of "des individus qu'on crôit être des conscrits réfractaires ou insoumis. Il paraît que ceux-ci ont voulu se venger du maire qui a donné des renseignements à la colonne mobile sur le lieu de leur retraite" (59).

Millers, too, might find their *moulins* destroyed by arsonists as acts of revenge or warning to the rest of the community. There was no question that such fires were accidental, and blame for them was generally placed on the shoulders of the young, of "conscrits fuyards qui s'y livrent au brigandage," as in the case of one fire at Sainte-Croix-du-Mont, near Cadillac:

> Le bois, la charpente, le bled, tout a été la proie des flammes, à l'exception des meules qui se sont brisées dans leur chute. Les débris n'ont pu engloutir un rase de terre dans lequel on a trouvé du soufre en fleur et des javelles sèches que l'incendiaire avait apportés, sachant bien que personne ne couchait dans le moulin. (60)

In many communities mills were numbered among the most profitable of local enterprises, and the miller would be a leading figure in village society—rich, linked by ties of family with the other village *notables,* a possible aspirant for mayoral office in his own right. Just as significant in the eyes of refractories was the fact that he was often a highly unpopular figure with local people, suspected of accumulating his wealth by cheating and by every form of perfidy, holding back flour and siphoning off grain, and overcharging and abusing his monopoly position at the expense of the poor and needy. As Steven Kaplan has demonstrated in his study of the granary areas supplying Paris in the eighteenth century, the very word "miller" developed shameful connotations in the popular mind, and millers suffered a bad reputation that came with their job, which they did not in any sense have to earn (61). By attacking mills and their owners, therefore, the *insoumis* knew that they risked little obloquy in the community, and they could strike a warning note to others who might be tempted to betray them. As with the vines, they knew the best moments for mounting their attacks. In the Nord in Year XIII, for instance, they struck with great precision so as to make the most indelible impression. It had been a good year, grain supplies were plentiful, and "l'incendie d'une meule est un objet important. Voilà plusieurs incendies de ces meules depuis peu de temps" (62). The local notables were being made to suffer as an example to others.

Acts of revenge of this kind ranged widely across the whole gamut of rural life. Deserters caught committing offenses against the forest laws turned against *gendarmes* and *gardes-champêtres.* At Haverskerque in the Nord a *garde-forestier* who had brought charges against conscripts found on his return from Lille that his home and his various outbuildings had been razed to the ground. The house had been built of *paillotin,* of straw and mud, and the roof had been thatched, with the result that it burned like a torch (63). *Juges de paix* rash enough to press charges were also liable to attack, and in one incident at Landrecies, a horse belonging to the local justice of the peace was killed by deserters as it was grazing in a field, a symbolically powerful reminder to a rural community that could never quite make the necessary distinction between law enforcement and personal interest that it was deserter bands that effectively held sway across large tracts of peasant France (64). In the Nord, indeed, terrorization of this sort was especially widespread, with deserters adapting to their own requirements the terror tactics already used by local bandits, the device of the *sommation minatoire.* The *sommeurs* would leave a chilling note with their chosen victim, generally a farmer in the heart of rural Picardy, instructing him to place a designated sum of money at a selected spot "sous différentes menaces et particulièrement sous celle d'incendie"; those refusing to answer this summons would find their barns, outhouses, and hayricks destroyed in an unexplained blaze. The crime in this form was almost unknown outside the North where governments had been grappling with it throughout the eighteenth century. In 1722 the Parlement of Douai had attempted to force farmers to declare any *billets* they received from *sommeurs*. In 1763 it had been noted that the crime was reaching epidemic proportions despite the most severe punishments (*sommation* had been regularly punished by breaking on the wheel). In 1812, in response to public anxiety at the frequency of attacks, mostly by deserter bands in the Nord and the Pas-de-Calais, a *Cour Spéciale Extraordinaire* was established at Douai with exceptional powers (65). In its new form *sommation* was particularly used as a device to deter overzealous public officials, a means of personal intimidation rather than of revenue-raising (66). Its full potential is illustrated by the multiple attacks and threats made on the *commissaire du Directoire* in the canton of Berlaimont, an official known for his outspoken comments on the execution of the conscription laws. The *commissaire* was given to understand in a very forthright manner the likely consequences of further action on his part:

Le 17 vendémiaire dernier il revenait de la commune de Locquignol, où il était allé faire la lecture d'une circulaire concernant le départ des jeunes gens de la première réquisition; en passant dans la forêt de Mormal, il fut arrêté par deux de ces jeunes gens qui lui déchirèrent ses habits et qui se disposaient a l'assommer, s'il n'avait fait une résistance vigoureuse et s'il ne fut parvenu à s'échapper de leurs mains.

Le quatre de ce mois on ravagea ses propriétés, on bêcha son champ avesti de bled, et on fit au milieu une fosse de la longueur, de la profondeur ordinaire des fosses sépulcrales, comme pour le prévenir que l'on venait de creuser son tombeau. (67)

The Minister of the Interior suspected that his *commissaire* had indeed been effectively silenced, since the campaign against draft dodging in Berlaimont came to a suspiciously sudden end.

Berlaimont was not the only rural commune where the government's recruitment efforts were effectively undermined by the criminal activities of deserters and refractories. Mayors were frequently dissuaded from carrying out their duties too punctiliously by a timely reminder of the power still exercised by those of their citizens living in clandestinity. In the Ariège attention is frequently drawn to their lack of cooperation with the government in conscription matters; in the Cantal, to their unhelpful attitude and "esprit municipal"; in the Dordogne to the sheer apathy that they displayed (68). Almost everywhere mayors showed increased reluctance to enforce the law or to interpret their duties legalistically, since to have done so would have resulted in their increasing alienation from important sections of village society. *Insoumis* were, through their presence in the community, forming themselves into a considerable pressure group over local opinion. Similarly, the *gendarmes* could not ignore the threat that deserters and refractories posed. They also became discouraged by their isolation from the community, and by the fact that when they *did* succeed in capturing a deserter in the woods or in a mountain cave, they often found themselves ambushed by other deserters as they attempted to steer their prey down a lonely hillside. Often they were compelled to release their captive, and their standing in the community suffered accordingly. There were many cases of this. In the Deux-Sèvres two *gendarmes* were killed when a band of deserters discharged forty or fifty shots at them in the course of freeing two of their comrades (69). Near Saint-Rémy in the Cantal the *gendarmes* escorting Jacques Chaussau to prison were forced to turn him loose by the appearance on the mountainside of a menacing band of his friends, "dix-neuf hommes masqués et armés de fusils à deux coups" (70). Near the commune of Blessy in the Pas-de-Calais, deserters again freed one of their number from police custody as the *gendarmes* were picking their way along a path, hidden from the village by high hedgerows. Again, fifteen or twenty men were supposedly involved in the attack "armés de fusils, fourches et autres instruments aratoires" (71). On occasion, the ultimate humiliation for those escorting them, deserters captured and bound by *gendarmes* succeeded in making their own escape. Near Cannes, for instance, seven prisoners, among them deserters under arrest, turned on their escorts in a lonely gorge, breaking their chains and hurling themselves on the astonished gendarmes. "Ils se jettent sur leurs conducteurs, mettent le gendarme Barbe hors de combat par trois coups de stilet, et aprés une demie-heure de lutte arrachent leurs armes qu'ils cassent sur des pierres, brisent les fers de leurs camarades, et se sauvent tous dans une forêt voisine" (72). Police reports of such incidents always tend to exaggerate the danger, the ferocity of the conscripts, the numbers in a gang, and the odds against which the *gendarmes* were struggling. The fact remains, however, that there were scores of incidents like these, and that local people did nothing to assist the officers who found themselves under attack. For the *gendarmerie* the arrest and escort of conscripts was not only a dangerous and unpopular assignment, it was an activity that lost them much of the local good will on which even the most basic policing was dependent.

The reluctance of mayors to report the presence of deserters in their communes, combined with the ineffectiveness of the local *gendarmes* in the face of organized resistance from conscripts at large in their areas, had the effect of throwing open the countryside to terrorization by the deserters themselves. Village *notables* might bear the brunt of vengeance killings and attacks on crops, but few isolated farmsteads could consider themselves truly safe. The sheer violence of such attacks and the gratuitous destruction that accompanied them helped generate panic in the community. In the Lozère in Year VI, for instance, fear spread from hamlet to hamlet as rumors of the approach of brigand bands reached a petrified local population (73). When the conscripts struck the effect on a peacful household could be quite shattering. At one farmhouse near Remiremont in the Vosges, the full fury of a band of some fifteen deserters hit the building, and the effect was like that of a minor hurricane. The men smashed down the front door and indulged in an orgy of destruction in the kitchen, before settling down to enjoy the fruits of their victory. They "y ont brisé toute la vaisselle de terre et de faïence, les verres et les bouteilles; y ont fait cuire un fromage, avec trois douzaines d'oeufs qu'ils ont pris, avec deux à trois livres de boeure *(sic)* frais et recuit, s'en sont regalé, en se rendant maîtres de la maison; ensuite ont fracassé toutes les vitres" (74). Yet, at five o'clock in the afternoon, there was no resistance; no one moved against them. Nor did the community rush to react, since attacks of this kind did recur from time to time, and the population was hushed into silence by the fear that united them all. The farmer and his family did not dare to denounce the assailants, their neighbors would take no part in the affair through fear of reprisals, and even the public officials whose job it was to keep the peace showed little inclination to press charges. The *juge de paix* was apparently unperturbed by the incident, preferring to take no action "dans la crainte encore d'encourir la haine des malveillants." Fear, in short, had taken over the whole community, and the forces of order were unable to combat it. In such circumstances it was even doubted whether the arrest of any individual deserter or band of deserters could have any impact on the sagging morale of local people (75).

Of course the main purpose of all the criminal activity of both deserters and refractories was to remain at large and to avoid the threat of military service; other aims were no more than ancillary. Therefore it is only logical that some of the most spectacular crimes of these years were those perpetrated to destroy the evidence on which recruitment was based, the dossiers of the *état civil* that designated the dates of birth and marriage and that, after the introduction of conscription in Year VI, were the principal documents used to condemn twenty year olds to army life. Criminal damage to these documents was common in rural areas, often with the abetment of mayors and municipal officials, but the most organized attacks were those mounted against the duplicate copies that were held in the districts and departments. At Murat in Cantal, for example, only the alertness of a twelve-year-old boy playing near the stables of the *sous-préfecture* averted a serious disaster. He stumbled on a lighted wick placed near some piles of straw and fodder and raised the alarm. The subprefect was in no doubt that deserters had lit it and that the conscription records were their target (76). In one department, the Ariège, a series of fires effectively rendered conscription impossible to administer. In Year VII conscripts were assumed to be responsible for a blaze that swept through the *maison commune* in Saint-Girons, destroying not only the *état civil* for the entire district, but also the local prison, making it impossible for the *gendarmerie* to take effective action against such deserters that they surprised in the surrounding hills (77). The destruction of the records was enthusiastically greeted by the lads of the local villages, and their joy was only increased in Year XII when another suspicious fire destroyed the duplicate records held at Foix, burning down the entire *préfecture* at the same time. All the administrative dossiers were consumed in the blaze, which had been started by setting light to a pile of firewood directly below the library. Witnesses reported smelling traces of sulphur in the debris, and the delighted reactions of local people left the authorities in little doubt that the fire was an act of deliberate *malveillance*. One witness recorded that

> au moment où les flammes se manifestèrent, il entendit plusieurs personnes parler, sur la place publique, et dire *voilà le joly feu*. Un autre avoir aussy entendu dire, *ca va et ca ira*. Un troisième avoir ouy dire à un individu inconnu, rencontré sur le chemin de Foix à Pamiers le matin de l'incendie, que la Préfecture de Foix avait été incendiée et que malheureusement on n'avait pu y bruler les oizeaux. (78)

The consequences, especially in the rural areas of the district of Saint-Girons, were extremely grave because the only records still extant were those held by individual mayors and were often kept in chaotic disorder and constantly open to fraud and forgery. Although the law was explicit that items of the *état civil* destroyed or lost during the Revolution must be made good, in practice very little was done because there was very little that the authorities could do (79). Rumors spread unchecked, given that any hint of relief from conscription was avidly welcomed by local people. When a lawyer in Quérigut spread the rumor that to be eligible for an exemption a young man did not have to be married at all, merely to have lived with his wife before the date of the conscription law, a whole generation of country boys breathed a sigh of relief and refused to turn up for the *tirage* (80). After Year XII, for all practical purposes, the government was no longer able to maintain even a pretense of orderly recruitment in the villages along the Spanish border (81).

In their bid to remain at liberty, by their actions and by their very presence in a community, deserters and *insoumis* increasingly involved third parties in their crimes and unleashed a whole gamut of secondary criminality. Parents, friends, mayors, and public officials, all those who offered them help or who condoned their activities, became increasingly enmeshed in the web of complicity to which desertion gave rise. We have already seen the extent to which life in hiding depended on the good will of local people, and frequently on their open assistance: the provision of food, the passing on of warnings about police movements, the hiring of labor. All these activities were illegal, and those caught offering such assistance were liable to severe sanctions from the courts. To constitute a criminal offense, harboring a conscript had to be entered into consciously, "sciemment" in the words of the decree, which did have the effect of providing numerous loopholes and which gave juries opportunities for considering acquittal. Rural juries in particular were often ready to listen to the most implausible excuses as suspects denied that they had consciously taken part in any act of concealment. A farmer in the Gironde, faced with the indisputable fact of a deserter's presence on his land, tried to argue that his crime was inadvertent, that his children had offered the man protection while he was out harvesting. The tribunal gave him a hearing but in that case it did not believe him (82). More fortunate was a farmer from Charmes in the Vosges accused of hiding two *réquisitionnaires* on his farm and tried by the *tribunal correctionnel* in Mirecourt in Year VII. When the *gendarmes* had raided the farm at daybreak, they had overheard the farmer banging on his windowpane and shouting a warning that they took to be a prearranged signal because almost immediately two young men had raced naked out of a neighboring barn, pulling on their trousers as they ran. Yet the court refused to believe that the conscripts were employed on the farm, or that the farmer knew of their presence there, and he was acquitted (83). All kinds of personal and sentimental attachments could lead individuals to take the risk of offering protection to a deserter or *insoumis,* quite apart from the possible economic interest of having an able-bodied young man on the premises. But again, public sympathy was easily aroused, especially when the *gendarmerie* tried to prosecute mothers for harboring their own sons or wives for harboring their husbands (84). The government persisted in the belief that exemplary punishment of *receleurs* would solve the problem, and even the periodic amnesties offered to conscripts were never extended to include those aiding and abetting their crimes (85). Yet in so many cases judges and juries were able to find mitigating circumstances. A widow who sheltered a refractory was deemed to be frail and therefore worthy of a degree of leniency when she appeared before the tribunal in Vannes: "si l'amende a été réduite au minimum, c'est que cette veuve, fermière d'une assez forte métairie, a sept enfants, une mère octogenaire, et deux frères fous, tout cela chez elle et à sa charge" (86). When a peasant from Haspres (Nord) was caught harboring his two sons and one of their friends "cachés dans un souterrain dont l'entrée était masquée par des fourneaux," the fact that he was moved to break the law by strong family loyalties helped keep his sentence to a minimum (87). Similarly with the mayor of the village of Anor (again in the Nord) who could show that the deserter whom he had been sheltering had been living with his daughter and had got her pregnant, this too moved the tribunal to leniency (88). Local people, in other words, were well aware of the pressures that were brought to bear on parents and neighbors, and were reluctant to antagonize important sections of the population. These penalties could not be effectively enforced because, in the words of the government *commissaire* in Epinal in Year V, "les loix pénales trop rudes sont toujours éludées," and juries would simply refuse to convict when they thought the penalty out of all proportion to the offense (89). The sheltering of refractory conscripts was one area where the threshold of tolerance was clearly very wide indeed.

It was never really regarded by public opinion as a criminal activity; the same can be said for the employment of refractories and deserters, which, as we have seen, was so vital to their everyday existence (90). A more positive act of collusion, and one which more clearly crossed the thinly drawn line between lawful and unlawful pursuits, was the conspiracy that often accompanied the frauds and deceits employed by conscripts to avoid service. Even though many of these frauds were purely individual acts by the young men themselves, everyone in the village knew what had happened and the vast majority offered their mute approval. Self-mutilation is a case in point. Because the conscription law insisted that those liable to serve should be strong and healthy, and because it was common knowledge among village boys that no one could be considered for the army who lacked either the trigger finger of his right hand or the front teeth required to reload a musket, one possible if a very painful road to salvation was known to all, and from all over France came the same familiar reports of drastic acts of homespun surgery. A report by the Minister of War in Year VII lamented the alarming increase in such incidents, regretting that "des pusillanimes incapables de vouloir contribuer au succès de nos armées ont néanmoins le lâche courage de s'abattre un pouce ou un doigt de la main droite pour se soustraire au service militaire" (91). The two young men of the *classe* of 1810 against whom the *conseil de recrutement* of the Dordogne initiated proceedings for this kind of fraud were textbook stereotypes of the art: "l'un s'était coupé ou fait couper la première phalange de l'index de la main droite, et l'autre s'était fait arracher les dents incisives de la mâchoire supérieure" (92). To make doubly sure of his *réforme* a conscript from the Saône-et-Loire, uncertain perhaps which finger would obtain his release, unflinchingly severed three (93). In one village in the Gers, four young men turned up on the same day to present their bleeding stumps to the recruitment-officer (94). The anger of government officials is easy to understand, and there were various attempts to establish *enquêtes* to assign responsibility for such injuries. But the stubbornness and recalcitrance of villagers made such a task nearly impossible. Every incident had its accomplices, its willing or unwilling aides: the parents who helped nurse their son back to health, the *chirurgien* who might advise on the best method to adopt, the *aubergiste* who kept watch for the *gendarmes,* the brother or family friend who administered the blow or helped to anaesthetize the victim before the blow was struck. Even when there were no witnesses, no active participants in the incident, villagers would suppress embarrassing rumors or they would repeat the same unlikely tale in answer to the *gendarmes'* questions. When Baptiste Sauzeil cut off his index finger in 1807, he was working alone in the communal wood at Vicdessos (Ariège) and claimed that because of rheumatic pains he had been obliged on that day to saw left-handed. It was an implausible story but no one could be found to deny it, and various villagers agreed that they had indeed observed him using his left hand or noted that they had heard that he was suffering from rheumatism (95). In their lack of cooperation with the *gendarmes* they too were being drawn into the web of complicity.

For those who lacked the courage or who were endowed with too much imagination to think of chopping off their fingers, other routes to a medical *réforme* could seem less agonizing. It was altogether easier, for instance, to pretend to be epileptic because no verifiable signs of the disease were demanded. What the conscript had to provide was sworn testimony by ten fellow villagers that he was subject to occasional epileptic fits. And the "evidence" of sympathetic friends and neighbors was not very difficult to collect, particularly since there was no way of making the witnesses answerable by law for the truth of their testimony (96). Deafness was also impossible to verify with any accuracy during the army medical, with the result that once again the authorities depended on sworn testimony. But so unsatisfactory was this procedure that the Imperial administration intervened to make the mayor personally responsible, forcing him to provide testimony that he knew that one conscript had been deaf since birth, or that another was given to seizures or fits (97). Drugs, caustic substances, ointments and lotions were all tried, either swallowed or rubbed into wounds, in an attempt to appear ill or maimed. In the Creuse in Year IV, for example, there were complaints that conscripts were swallowing harmful concoctions that affected their pulse (98). The prefect of the Seine-Inférieure described in graphic detail the range of "maladies simulées" feigned by conscripts in his department during the war years.

> Ils s'étaient fait arracher toutes les dents pour ne point servir, d'autres étaient parvenus à les carier presque toutes en employant des acides ou en mâchant de l'encens, quelques-uns s'étaient fait des plaies aux bras ou aux jambes par l'application de vésicatoires, et pour rendre ces plaies pour ainsi dire incurables, ils les ont pansées avec de l'eau impregnée d'arsenic. Beaucoup se sont fait donner des hernies soufflées, quelques-uns appliquèrent sur les parties de la génération des caustiques tellement violents que les médecins doutent qu'ils puissent échapper à la mort. (99)

Not all these ruses, of course, deceived the authorities; nor did all the young men who placed their hopes in such remedies survive their self-induced illnesses. An inquest on one young conscript, Jean Gizolme from Laveissenet (Cantal), showed the tragic results of his ill-advised medication. He had died painfully and unnecessarily, "à la suite d'une plaie faite à la partie interne de la jambe droite avec du poison corrosif, qui après avoir corrodé cette partie s'est insinué dans la masse du sang et a occasionné la mort de l'individu" (100).

Those who sought fraudulent medical treatment of this kind usually involved others in their frauds. Families and friends shared in the secrets of those lucky enough to succeed in their deception, and faked injuries were imitated long afterwards by others hopeful of gaining a *réforme*. Jacques Biralleau, a strong, healthy lad from Saint-André-de-Cubzac, managed to convince the *capitaine de recrutement* that the ugly swellings on his right leg made him unfit for service. When his younger brother duly attained the age of eighteen years, he merely passed on the necessary advice. In consequence, the recruiting-officers found themselves faced with the second member of the same family to sport identical injuries, since the young man "s'est fait venir du mal, comme son frère, à la jambe droite, de manière qu'il se trouve être à l'hôpital de Bordeaux, en croyant de se sortir comme son frère a fait" (101). Or again, the fact of having been injured in a genuine accident, like Pierre Rolland from Clavières (Cantal) whose foot was gored by an ox, could be turned to the young man's advantage, if necessary with the aid of a fraudulent substitution (102). Doctors and medical orderlies were notoriously easy to bribe or convince into complaisance, and minor ailments would frequently be sufficient to justify a *réforme*. Individual hospitals developed a local reputation as places where exemptions were easily obtained, in the Somme, for example, the *hôpital militaire* in Amiens was much favored by the young (103). Even the doctors employed to examine conscripts at the *conseil de révision* came under suspicion. In 1806 the prefect of the Vienne drew attention to the "friponneries" committed by the medical staff on whom the army relied. "Je les change à chaque conseil," he explained in some anguish; "Je les prends dans toute l'étendue de mon département, je ne préviens de mon choix que la veille, et j'ai toujours lieu de craindre qu'ils ne se laissent gagner" (104). In the Gironde in the same year the measures taken were even more exacting, the prefect explaining that the name of the *chirurgien* was announced only fifteen minutes before the hearing, and that the doctors were always changed daily since "celui de la veille est immédiatement accablé de visites et de lettres" (105). Some doctors were themselves becoming alarmed by their new found reputation for fraud and deceit, and they accepted that the ease with which conscripts could arm themselves with *congés* was a reflection on the lack of scruples being shown by their colleagues (106). There *were* those among them who would agree to produce fraudulent medical certificates in return for cash payments (107), who would distribute drugs and *caustiques* that could be used for enflaming open wounds (108), or whose services were so warmly appreciated by the conscripts they examined that they could build up a wide clientele and still charge six francs for every visit (109). Whether out of sympathy or cupidity, doctors could always be found to conspire in frauds or help create the symptoms of serious illnesses, and those desperate for a *réforme* or a *congé* knew that they could enlist their aid as willing accomplices. Some conscripts even had the effrontery to wander from *médecin* to *médecin,* systematically seeking out the one expert opinion that would allow him to remain in the safety of his village (110).

It was not only doctors and medical orderlies who were open to corruption. The presence of deserters or refractories in a commune placed at risk any person who was in an official position or who enjoyed some level of jurisdiction in matters of conscription. Money did not always change hands, although favors generally did, sometimes in kind. A *huissier* in Bordeaux was rash enough to accept a case of wine in part payment for his assistance, though he later discovered that he could not deliver his part of the deal and was driven to suicide by the shame of threatened exposure (111). Rank favoritism could also arouse suspicions of fraud, as when two mayors' sons in the Loire-Inférieure were both given exemptions by the *conseil de révision.* In such cases had not local deals been unofficially struck among the notables (112)? Generally, however, exemptions were being bought in the same way as medical certificates, with corruption spreading like a cancer through some parts of the administration. No one was above suspicion, and the courts in these years heard cases involving the bribery of army officials, recruiting-officers, and jurymen and members of the *conseil de révision* (113). In the Morbihan the *syndic des marins* at Locmariaquer was condemned for taking money from the families of conscripts, "soit pour les dispenser du service, soit pour faire cesser les poursuites contre des déserteurs" (114). The *gendarmerie* were also under constant surveillance by a government that feared, often rightly, that they were not above taking bribes in conscription cases. In Year XIII, for instance, two conscripts who had been taken prisoner by the *gendarmes* in the village of La Bastide-de-Bouzignac (Ariége) were subsequently released in return for payment; in the men's defense it was pointed out that it was "la semaine du carnaval" and that the cash involved was only drinking money (115). Similarly when a *gendarme* from Laroquebrou (Cantal) allowed the two prisoners whom he had under escort to break free, a jury had little hesitation in deciding that he had taken a bribe. The conscripts had been bound and handcuffed at the time when they escaped, and the *gendarme's* account of events was less than convincing. "Je crois que c'est avec les dents qu'ils ont brisé la corde qui était attachée aux menottes; et la corde ainsi brisée, ils ont pris la fuite à toutes jambes . . ." (116). What is interesting in such cases is the underlying assumption that conscripts were different from other criminals, that they were fellow human beings with whom officials might strike a deal or from whom *gendarmes* might think of accepting money. In some instances the corruption spread right into the ranks of the prefectoral staff itself. In the so-called "affaire du Cantal" a plot was uncovered involving the corruption of 104 different people, all engaged in the process of selling exemptions and false papers (117). And in 1812 the prefect of the Rhône, in commenting with favor on the sentences recently passed on three *gendarmes* convicted of conscription offenses, added that examples were sorely needed since in the Rhône "la plus grande partie des gendarmes s'immisçaient indûment dans les affaires de la conscription" (118).

More than any other single group, village mayors and their *adjoints* were open to temptation and influence in matters of conscription. It was mayors, after all, to whom the recruitment procedure was entrusted at communal level, and it was on them that pressure from the local community bore most heavily. As has already been shown, mayors were often suspected of partiality during the *levées,* of favoritism toward their friends and relatives; and as early as 1792 there were isolated instances of village mayors being accused of fraud or concealment, either to avoid serving themselves or to offer protection to their sons (119). The *état civil* remained throughout the period the key to any young man's salvation, and the fact that the mayor kept and referred to it on behalf of the community opened the door to frauds and forgeries. The dates of births and marriages could be deliberately falsified; the papers of younger brothers might be mistaken for those of the designated conscript so that he could be excused on grounds of height; and dead relatives might be exhumed from their administrative graves to help provide *réformes* for the living (120). Pages were removed from the communal records without anyone apparently knowing when it had happened or who had been responsible; collusion in cases of this kind was very hard to break (121). There were communes where by some freak of nature only girls were being born so that, twenty years afterwards, no one from the village would find himself faced with the need to serve (122). Sometimes mayors became known as specialists in arranging marriages for those in pressing need of a wife. At Bréaugis in the Nord, a commune which, according to Expilly, contained no more than ten *feux* in the eighteenth century, the mayor masterminded a marriage industry during the Napoleonic Wars, spreading his favors far beyond the commune itself and implicating in all some forty-eight different people (123). Colombier-le-Vieux in Ardèche was another village where the authorities felt bound to intervene when they received complaints that the mayor had made "un trafic honteux de son ministère" during the period from Year III to Year VI and that he had even consented to the marriage of a conscript to a woman who had been dead for twenty years; however, the enquiry was inconclusive because of the chaotic state of the records and the refusal of local people to offer the slightest assistance with the investigation:

Cette longue série de mariages, leur rapprochement et l'état des jeunes gens qui les ont contractés en font soupçonner fortement la légitimité et donnent à penser qu'ils ont été intercallés longtemps après dans les registres par l'of-

ficier public dans les vues de dispenser les jeunes gens de la conscription ou
de la réquisition; mais comment en prouver la simulation, ni qu'ils ont été
antidatés, si ceux qui y ont figuré comme parties contractantes ainsi que les
témoins en soutiennent la sincérité? (124)

Therein was the primary problem in investigating allegations of fraud by mayors
and their associates. Many villages saw nothing harmful or criminal in such
manipulation and had no interest in bringing it to an end.

Whereas some of these frauds were isolated personal favors to friends or
omissions made for the minimum of personal gain—one mayor in the Cantal
forged papers out of straightforward friendship, lubricated by a few bottles of
wine (125)—forgery could also be big business, with the mayors working as part
of a larger syndicate. Sizable sums of money changed hands, and the degree of
damage inflicted on local administration was often considerable. In one commune in the Ariège the former mayor and his *adjoint* had secretly set fire to the
état civil for a forty-year period from 1751 to 1790, thus erasing any evidence of
a young man's date of birth and making the conscription laws unenforceable
(126). Particularly damaging to the government's credibility were those cases of
fraud where members of the prefect's staff were involved in orchestrating activities, where a dozen or a score of mayors were falsifying their village records with
the full connivance of the prefect or subprefect. At Bazas, for instance, substantial payments in cash to the *sous-préfet* or his secretary were sufficient to ensure
that one's name would be removed from the list of those condemned to serve.
The ring, orchestrated by the *sous-préfet,* involved two of his employees, a *commissaire du gouvernement,* a local clergyman, and a handful of mayors (127).
Similarly at Cambrai in the Nord the *sous-préfet* was found guilty in 1812 of
frauds involving the mayors and *adjoints* of various towns and villages in his
area, encouraging them to seek out trade from the families of conscripts, and
issuing *réformes* in exchange for money. The *sous-préfecture* was the center of a
complex plot and the *sous-préfet's* own involvement was assumed to be considerable; however, the man convicted of organizing the crime syndicate was his
former personal secretary who had corrupted local mayors and brought the
administration into contempt, and for this he was sentenced to eight years'
imprisonment and to being branded as a *faussaire* (128). Not surprisingly, it was
in the Pyrénées, always one of the least patriotic areas of France and one where
the conscription laws were treated with scant respect, that some of the most
wide-ranging forgery rings were operating. In the Ariège the problem was
endemic. The *sous-préfet* at Saint-Girons was himself implicated in the crimes,
and mayors and their *adjoints* were involved in the majority of communes
within his jurisdiction. In all, reports sent to the Minister of the Interior listed
fifty-one communes where crimes of *faux, recel,* or *escroquerie* involved public
officials, and sixteen where armed attacks had been mounted on the *gendarmerie*
in denfese of deserters or refractories (129). Between Year XI and 1806 the prosecutor in Saint-Girons produced evidence of 379 forgeries, which involved the
complicity of at least 160 people. The social damage that had been done in the
area was, he said, incalculable. One of the mayors most deeply implicated, Bor-
ret from the village of Lacave, not only forged documents and sold them for a

standard fee (between twelve and twenty-four francs for a marriage act and between thirty and sixty francs for a passport), but even hawked them around local fairs and markets in search of custom. Throughout the mountain villages, mayors and their accomplices were committing every known form of forgery. Darmaing, the fanatical judge on the *Cour de Justice Criminelle Spéciale* established at Foix to examine these allegations, found that "les faux consistent en une foule d'altérations commises sur les actes, ils présentent des noms dénaturés, des prénoms substitués aux véritables, des garçons désignés comme filles, des décès supposés, de faux actes, de fausses dates, des actes rédigés en doubles, ou portés après coup sur des feuilles déjà batonnées comme nulle" (130). Darmaing and the government were right to be concerned because in places like Saint-Girons it was the governance of the area that was at stake.

The majority of these frauds resulted from willing collusion between conscripts desperate for a device that would let them escape the army and officials who, through sympathy or greed or both, found themselves in a position to dispense an administrative favor. They went largely unchecked for lengthy periods because no one within the local community was directly harmed or prejudiced, even if the families of the men nominated to replace those reprieved might subsequently see things rather differently. Neither party to the fraud could feel aggrieved. The only overt loser from the deal was the rather opaque, impersonal interest of the state. Not everyone, however, was so scrupulous, and the desperation of those conscripted was an element that could be played on and abused. After all, to many gullible families overcome with grief by the news that their son was included in the next *levée*, the only important goal was to get hold of a piece of paper that would liberate them from their misery. In such circumstances *any* piece of paper with a semi-official appearance would seem convincing, and there were those who were all too eager to capitalize on their innocence. It was a terrain tailor-made for tricksters and conmen. Many of the passports produced by deserters were no more professional than that clutched by Louis Bourguignon, who had deserted from the 56e Régiment de Ligne in 1808 and who had bought a crudely amateurish document from another young man he encountered on the road. The *gendarmerie* were not deceived:

> On le trouva porteur d'un papier imprimé à l'usage de passeport et qui sans doute avait été enlevé à quelque municipalité: on l'avait garni de manière à ce qu'il ne pouvait servir à celui qui en était porteur, puisque le nom de la commune de Crépol d'où il semblait qu'on aurait voulu le délivrer n'était écrit qu'à moitié: qu'il ne s'y trouvait aucun nom de porteur, que le nom du maire de la commune avait été remplacé par un nom supposé, enfin que toute sa contexture le rendait évidemment inutile à quiconque eut voulu s'en servir, puisqu'il ne se ressemblait à un passeport que par la qualité du papier qu'on avait employé. (131)

Elsewhere the market for false papers was so buoyant that their forgery grew into a lucrative enterprise, with papers copied, signatures forged, even seals appended in an attempt to deceive the authorities. One firm in Bordeaux had established a commercial business in such forgeries before their printshop was discovered. What surprised the prefect was their concern for detail, the professionalism of their approach, especially in copying the subprefect's seal, which indicated that the forgery was the work of an artist (132). Another forger, who had already escaped from prison after a previous conviction, was surprised in his workshop in 1808 surrounded by the specialist tools of his highly profitable trade. He obtained blank passport paper by forging the signatures of various mayors from around his department, the Nord. At the time of his arrest he was equipped with "quatre sceaux à l'aigle impériale ayant la légende, l'un de la commune, le second de la sous-préfecture d'Hazebrouck, le troisième de la préfecture du Nord; l'espace de la légende du quatrième était en blanc" (133).

Many of the frauds committed by those claiming to befriend the conscripts and their families were cruel and costly confidence tricks. One gang in the Vosges peddled false papers as a lucrative sideline to their principal activities of theft and highway robberies. For them the traffic in *faux* was simply another opportunity for gain thrown up by the years of annual conscriptions (134). In the Nord gang members scoured the countryside looking for young men of the age and build to provide *remplacements,* and an almost professional trade in *remplaçants* was rapidly organized (135). In Aurillac swindlers were touting for business among the country lads who had just arrived to present themselves for their medical (136), and in Bordeaux they were waiting like vultures on the quayside for young recruits to disembark (137). At conscription time the roads of France were crawling with innocent and frightened young men often away from home for the first time in their lives, fearful of the fate that lay in store for them, and easy game for the *fraudeur.* In many cases the replacements they offered failed to meet the army's specifications, or slipped away leaving the conscript to serve in person; but by then the *escrocs* had also disappeared, having duped the despairing *cultivateur* out of his savings or his son out of his signing-on bounty (138). Bars were their favorite haunts and innkeepers their frequent accomplices. They would note the arrival of new customers, gauge the nervous looks and youthful depression of each in turn, and allow their premises to be used by the gangs, whose profits they would generally share in recompense. No fraud was too unscrupulous, no victim too vulnerable. Antoine Caillet, though physically disabled and mentally retarded, was anxious that he would be forced to serve, and was defrauded of 1,500 *livres* in Valence in 1807 as the price of a *congé* to which he was already entitled (139). The fact that Caillet was known to be simple-minded merely made him a more attractive victim for deception.

If frauds of this kind were concentrated in country areas, it is because of the desperation of peasant families to extract their sons from the draft, but also because of the gullibility and superstition that still characterized much of eighteenth-century rural society. The *fraudeur* knew very well that he could play on that gullible nature, that the innocence of country people in the affairs of the wider world would help him trick and cheat them as he saw fit. Jean Lavigne was one *fraudeur* who exploited rural credulity to the full. Armed with a forged certificate, he toured the more remote villages and hamlets of the Aude and the Haute-Garonne raising money for the ransom of French soldiers who were, he revealed, being held and tortured by Algerian captors. He described their imaginary calvary in the most moving terms, appealing to "les âmes sensibles" to come to his, and their, assistance (140). His plea did not go unheeded. Similarly, money might be sought in return for a magic intervention to prevent a son or husband from drawing a low number in the *tirage,* for sorcery and black magic were still a potent force in the lives of many peasant families and conscription offered an excellent opportunity to exploit their simplicity. Nicolas Lecomte, described as a "charpentier et marchand de vin" at Asnières-sur-Oise, was one trickster condemned for sorcery of this kind. A mother from the rural area behind Asnières complained to the authorities that she had given Lecomte 100 francs "à titre de magie pour lui faire tirer un bon numéro." Unfortunately the young conscript had drawn twenty-six and found himself in uniform, and the embittered mother denounced the supposed *sorcier* for fraud despite the fact that he had shamefacedly returned her money, and, most interestingly, despite the violent opposition of other members of her family to any such denunciation (141). In rural areas where tales of ghosts and devils still enjoyed wide credence, *escroquerie* of this kind was legion. If the victim so desperately wanted to believe in the cure, any story might seem persuasive. Yves Vauban, an artisan from Saint-Amand in the Nord, swindled peasant families of some 5,000 francs over a period of years by building up false hopes, "à l'aide de l'espérance chimérique qu'il leur donnait de les exempter de la conscription, leur persuadant de porter pour cet effet une bouteille pleine d'eau et de suif et leur en faisant boire" (142). The case of three *sorciers* operating in the rural Gironde illustrates the full extent of peasant gullibility. They played mercilessly on local superstition and turned it systematically to their profit. Two of them were former priests, itself an undoubted advantage when they claimed magical powers of healing since the faithful needed no further conviction. The remoter parts of the department, noted the prefect, were full of such men, "médecins empiriques," known for their powers to cure sterility between man and wife, or revered because they cured "hommes et bêtes avec des prières et des signes de croix." Palais, the principal accused in this case, was arrested after offering to provide conscripts with the false symptoms of a disease that he would subsequently return to cure. His reputation in the countryside, however, was already solidly established because he was known as a *devin* with magical powers: "Pour se mettre en réputation, il fit enlever sa femme par le diable. Elle criait de toute sa force que le diable l'enlevait: tout le quartier accourut" (143). Village culture and popular superstition were powerful allies for *fraudeurs* preying on the fears and anxieties of peasant families.

Crimes of violence committed by deserters on the run; crimes against property by men starving and desperate; crimes of collusion perpetrated by local people who, for whatever motive, came to their aid; crimes committed at the conscripts' expense by those to whom the opportunity for personal gain seemed too attractive to resist were all contrasting ways in which the crime rate increased as a consequence of desertion and *insoumission,* especially in the countryside. There is little doubt that thousands of crimes, mostly of a petty kind, were committed that never came to the attention of the *gendarmerie.* Of those that did, many were never solved or did not lead to conviction, in large measure because throughout the revolutionary and Napoleonic period popular sympathies remained ambivalent, with many Frenchmen blaming the army and the politicians rather than the unfortunate young men who were enmeshed by the recruitment laws. The bulk of these crimes were, in any case, minor matters like poaching and petty pilfering which could easily be contained by the village community itself. For the most part, therefore, the increase in criminality did little to estrange deserters (and even less *insoumis*) from rural society and little to promote the cause of the army in villages lacking any *esprit militaire*. There were crimes, of course, that did frighten and anger local people—rape, brutal assault, murder or banditry that spread fear through their communities—but these were relatively infrequent and were not the sole reserve of deserters from the armies. The most menacing of these crimes, that of *brigandage,* of armed and ruthless gangs thieving and maurauding across wide tracts of countryside, was not immediately associated in the public mind with desertion or *insoumission,* even though deserters and refractories were frequently involved. In many instances, indeed, its motive could be political as much as criminal, especially during the White Terror that ravaged much of the Midi after *thermidor* and in the counterrevolutionary areas of Brittany and the West. There, religion, antirepublican fanaticism, or simple vengeance were the most common motives for robbery and murder. Any link with desertion might seem to be almost incidental. But was it? It is an appropriate point to turn from the role of deserters in ordinary criminality and to examine the part they played in the kindred activities of *chouannerie* and counterrevolution.

7

Desertion and Counterrevolution

THROUGHOUT the revolutionary period republican politicians continued to regard desertion and counterrevolution as twin manifestations of a common mentality. Although their suspicions were absurdly exaggerated—the majority of deserters and refractories quite manifestly had no political axe to grind—they cannot be dismissed out of hand as nothing more than opportunist propaganda. For the language of royalism was too often used in these years, and the white flag of the Bourbons too persistently raised, for charges of political counterrevolution to be ignored or minimized. Besides, recent experience served as a powerful reminder of the damage that royalist loyalties could inflict on the revolutionary armies. If the line army inherited from the Ancien Regime had become seriously depleted and demoralized by 1791, the reason was primarily political. In the highly charged atmosphere of these early years desertions were frequently motivated by political idealism and by attitudes to the new political order. Among ordinary soldiers, it is true, desertion had generally reflected a reluctance to serve under noble or counterrevolutionary officers, and the rash of mutinies and desertions in 1789 and 1790 had more to do with patriotic or republican loyalties than with counterrevolution. Frequently the former soldiers of the line deserted to re-engage in the more politically committed units of the National Guard (1). But among the officer class desertion could often be ascribed to political conservatism and to the rejection of the constitutional regime that they were now called on to serve. Both the timing and the circumstances of their departure imply a highly political motivation. The majority of the officers who left their posts or who resigned their commissions did so in the months after the King's flight to Varennes, when they were forced to take a new oath of loyalty to the nation which made no mention of the person of the monarch. Moreover, the King had already given them an example, and it was a route that thousands of officers would follow in the ensuing months. Sam Scott has calculated that by the end of 1791 some 6,000 officers had emigrated from France, often without any formal resignation, in some instances leaving entire units without any com-

146

mand structure (2). Their dereliction of duty caused distrust and mutiny among the ranks of the armies they had led, expedited a fundamental reform of the military, and left an indelible suspicion in the minds of the political leadership. *Causes célèbres* like the Dumouriez affair served only to convince Republicans that their instincts in this regard were soundly based. When counterrevolutionary movements erupted in Brittany and the West, or after *thermidor* in large tracts of the Southeast and Southwest, it was only natural that they would see in refractories and army deserters a rich vein of potential support for the insurgent cause.

The intelligence that they collected helped substantiate their suspicions and focus their attention on the political dangers inherent in desertion and in draft dodging. For much of the disorder and *brigandage* in country areas, especially in the years that followed the dismantling of the Terror, did seem to be integrally linked to counterrevolution and to the politics of vengeance. Armed gangs roamed the villages and hamlets of the South of France searching out political victims, terrifying, maiming and murdering those who had rashly agreed to serve on the local revolutionary tribunals or committees, join battalions of the *armée révolutionnaire,* or make a name for themselves as advocates of Terror at their club or popular section during 1793 and the Year II. Those suspected of aiding and abetting the terrorist authorities or those especially who were known to have informed on their fellow citizens became prime targets for retribution once Robespierre had been overthrown and the principles he represented had been denounced and vilified. Networks of counterterror were established across the countryside where the Paris government seemed no longer to retain any degree of police control; and courts proved quite unable to enforce the law in face of a public opinion that united against the *hommes de sang* of the previous regime. In many parts of the Southeast and the Rhône valley justice became the preserve of armed gangs of royalist youths, and it was administered by callous, self-righteous killers who identified their chosen target, often over the counter of the local *cabaret,* before setting off into the Provencal night to despatch him with a clinically aimed bullet on the threshhold of his cottage or farmstead (3). In the South, as in Paris, such political violence was the privileged sphere of the *jeunesse dorée,* the gangs of young thugs masquerading under such fanciful titles as *compagnies de jésus* or *compagnies du soleil,* who spread hatred and sedition from village to village and who rushed to answer Fréron's call that they should mobilize to root out every last vestige of Jacobinism and "exterminer les égorgeurs" (4). In Paris the assault on former republican officials was paralleled by the more blatantly social attack on those members of the *classes populaires* who could reasonably be identified with the now scorned *sans-culottisme* of the early part of the decade, and those who blamed the Jacobins for the drabness of their lives and the loss of their youth hurled themselves mercilessly into the boisterous pleasures of the "guerre des théâtres" (5). Even more serious for the government was the renewal of *chouan* activity in the West and the outbreak of royalist insurrections in the Southeast and Southwest of the country, insurrections that enjoyed a large measure of support from the peasantry of their respective areas and that threatened France with another taste of civil war and the self-destruction of a second Vendée (6). By Year VII lawlessness was endemic in many of the more peripheral regions of the country, and this lawlessness seemed increasingly to be legitimized by its association with the banners of Christ and King.

But how political was such lawlessness, how clearly distinguishable from the banal, generalized violence and criminality with which it so often merged? There was little doubt about the political pedigree of the leaders of such revolts, who included counterrevolutionary nobles and returned *émigrés* committed to avenge the wrongs and indignities that their families had suffered during their enforced absence from France. In the case of the insurrection in Languedoc in the last years of the decade, for instance, a movement that was largely concentrated in the two departments of the Haute-Garonne and the Gers, the leaders were committed royalists, and the successes and failures of the insurgents were followed with the greatest interest by royalists in Bordeaux, the Landes, and throughout the Southwest. Associated with its organization was the royalist *Institut Philanthropique,* and among those who threw in their lot with the rebels were committed royalists like Mailhos and Dupont-Constant, leaders of the *Institut* in their respective departments of the Gers and the Gironde (7). But if the leaders were committed to the restoration of the monarchy and the overthrow of much that had been instituted since 1789, the same cannot be said with any confidence about the thousands of villagers who were persuaded to join in their revolt. Nor can it be assumed in these highly political times that everyone using the language of politics was necessarily dedicated to a political cause. The language of counterrevolution might easily be used to give a degree of respectability to simple self-aggrandizement. Those thieving and murdering in the name of the King were not always clearly distinguishable from common bandits. The atmosphere of fear and suspicion that reigned in many parts of the Southeast and Southwest after *thermidor* gave encouragement to the greedy and the self-seeking as well as to those who harbored political principles or ambitions for vengeance. This was especially true in the Midi, that territory defined by Colin Lucas as stretching from the Bas-Languedoc eastward to Provence, including the Comtat and the Vivarais, and stretching northward into the Velay and the Gévaudan and up the Rhône valley as far as the perpetually turbulent city of Lyon. This was in the eyes of many contemporaries the natural home of a politics of violence, where the Revolution stirred up hatreds and a thirst for revenge, and where political killing was always ambivalent, part of a muddled tradition of counterrevolution, personal vendetta, criminality, and communal violence. The Midi, says Lucas, had a distinct character during the revolutionary years. It was "the unquiet land of the Revolution, where parish-pump politics merged into national issues, activating beneath a revolutionary language longstanding personal issues, communal and confessional animosities into a polarisation towards extremes, distinctive patterns of collective action and the frequent rejection of national norms" (8). In such parts the national discourse of Revolution made relatively little impact on people's minds or their behavior. What was frequently resented was not so much the specific policies of the Jacobins as the fact that they presumed to intrude into the private realm of communal affairs. Tim Le Goff, discussing the attitudes of local people in the Vannetais, emphasizes the importance of such resentments, the collective opposition of whole communities to the "offence to local lifestyle" that revolutionary decrees increasingly represented (9). Peter Jones, studying the response of rural communities in the southern massif Central, relates the extent of politicization to landscape and habitat, suggesting most convincingly that the impact of the revolutionaries became increasingly irrelevant in the *pays de petite culture* of the Causses (10). Precise explanations for this sense of alienation differ from area to area. In the West, for example, Paul Bois and Charles Tilly have both suggested in their differing models of peasant counterrevolution that town–country divisions lie at the heart of the problem, with rural communities resisting the encroachment of urbanization and a market economy (11). Elsewhere, scholars have warned against any simple monocausal explanation, preferring to point to the opposition aroused by any form of intrusion by the state into communal affairs (12). It is the sheer extent of the rejection of such intrusion, and with it of the Republic itself, that leaves its mark on the historian of rural violence. As Le Goff and Sutherland remark with reference to counterrevolution in Brittany:

> By 1795–96 a majority of French citizens were probably in some sort of revolt against the Republic, a regime founded, ironically, on the basis of popular sovereignty. Draft-dodging, vendettas, stagecoach robberies, tax evasion and religious recusancy became the customary manifestations of this resentment almost everywhere. (13)

Suspicion of outsiders, the taxes and impositions of the state, and the laws and justice of the Revolution had the effect of encouraging widespread support for those who openly held the outside world in contempt. In this regard it made little difference whether the aim of local brigands was the overthrow of the Republic or the lining of their own pockets. Provided that they did not turn their threats and their violence against the villagers themselves, brigands were likely to maintain a strong bond of local support in their home communities. A campaign that was perceived by local people as a crusade directed against the taxman, the urban merchant, the usurer, or the landlord, did not lose any of its charm whether or not it was being conducted in the name of the King or of the Catholic church. Since in the Revolutionary period it was primarily the state that was attempting to extend its control over the countryside, to bring even the remotest of communities within the rule of law, it was only logical that the state and its agents should appear as prime targets for community anger. Therefore there was nothing very harmful or damaging about armed attacks launched by bands of local men against stagecoaches carrying the state's mails or the government's tax revenue, two of the principal forms of *brigandage* engaged in by those who claimed to be fighting against the French Republic. Counterrevolutionaries needed the product of such raids to buy arms and to finance their political campaigns; common criminals were equally relieved to land on such an attractive haul, especially in times of grinding hardship such as the Year IV or Year V. In the Bordelais in this period the bands of supposed royalists who infested the main roads around Bordeaux and Libourne were indistinguishable from bandits, tying up their victims and resorting to torture in the traditional manner of the *chauffeur* (14). In the Gard, one of the southern departments where royalist bands wreaked havoc at the expense of republican officials and the republican mails, political terrorization was by 1800 giving way to open criminality. Even when the bands holding up government stagecoaches went through the motions of shouting royalist greetings to identify themselves to their victims, they had in reality crossed the line from political activity to simple banditry, robbing to stay alive and pursuing a lifestyle that was little different from that of vagrant beggars (15). Yet this change in role made little difference as far as the local community was concerned, and villagers continued to offer them shelter and protection just as they had done at the height of the royalist revolt in the region.

Nor is there any reason to believe that deserters or *insoumis,* driven by fear into hiding and dependent on the local community for food and protection, would necessarily be deterred from joining a brigand gang simply because it affected royalist sympathies or attacked republican targets. Refractories generally shared the sympathies and outlook of the community at large, and in areas of the country where republican propaganda had made little impact the young men of the villages would have little reason to oppose the counterrevolutionaries on ideological grounds. As for deserters, they had quite deliberately abandoned the armies of the Republic, for which they had little affection. For many the difference between the service of the Republic and the service of the King amounted to the simple contrast between serving the nation and serving their local community, and the local community understandably won. There is, of course, a certain irony in a situation in which men who had taken great risks and faced enormous deprivations to avoid service in one army promptly allowed themselves to be incorporated in another, even in some cases wearing the distinctive uniform of the *muscadins* and accepting a rival military discipline. In the South, the royalist *bandes* generally fitted out their men in the bright, ostentatious colors of military units, referring to themselves as *chasseurs* or *hussards* and exploiting the reflected glamour of their uniforms to impress and sometimes intimidate the local peasantry. This was far more than youthful bravado. The *muscadins* were faithfully re-enacting the customary ritual of a southern youth movement and, given the local character of their cause and the fact that they saw themselves as the defenders of their traditional community against outside aggression, what could be more natural than for the young men of the area, strong and proud of their physical prowess, to rush to its defense (16)? Seen in this light, the organization of local terrorist bands falls squarely into the tradition of communal rivalries and of the squabbles, fights and vendettas that had from time immemorial marked the encounters of the young at fairs, carnivals, and village dances.

Joining a royalist *bande* or lending support to local *chouans* might, in other words, have little to do with political conviction. The deserter in particular was already condemned to a marginal existence during the months or even years that he spent returning to his native region, and banditry could seem attractive when the alternative was the constant threat of starvation. Counterrevolutionary bands offered much the same comfort and assurance as ordinary criminal gangs: food, clothing, a share in the spoils, and an end to the desperate loneliness that was the deserter's lot. They drank and laughed and swore and damned the consequences, reveling in their shared conquests and enjoying a sense of compan-

ionship that contrasted with the solitude of life in hiding or the dreary predictability of another night's trudge once darkness had fallen. Evading the
gendarmerie might be hazardous, but holding up republican mails added a certain zest to their existence, and celebrating their triumphs, often publicly and
with carefree generosity, could provide an unaccustomed injection of fun. Royalist leaders like Saint-Christol or Froment or Dominique Allier assumed all the
stature of the great bandit chieftains of the past, and were worshipped by their
followers with the same fervor. In some cases, in fact, their leadership was essential to the band's continued existence, as is witnessed by the collapse of several
royalist units once their *chefs* had finally been captured and executed (17).
Involvement with such *bandes* allowed a young man to regain a certain self-
respect, at least in the eyes of his peers and frequently in the community at large.
He was, after all, at the stage in his life when fighting and military swagger would
come naturally to him, however reluctant he might have been to accept conscription into a formal national army. Most important of all, the royalist presence provided him with an opportunity to use his youthful strength in the furtherance of interests that he could identify as his own. He was a soldier, trained
in the use of weapons; in all likelihood, he still had his army rifle along with the
rest of his kit. It was a temptation that many were unable to resist. Joining a
band of royalist *brigands* might provide the only tangible means of escape from
hunger and economic distress. In the Drôme in Years VII, VIII, and IX, the
incidence of brigand attacks increased significantly during the winter months
when more young men were tempted to throw in their lot with the local outlaws
in their quest for survival (18). Royalists also suffered from desertion, and when
spring came some members of these bands were slipping away to continue their
journey home.

But equally, there were good reasons why in areas where royalism already
enjoyed a measure of popular support, deserters and *insoumis* should have been
drawn into alliance with them. For if popular opposition to the state had its
origins in the perceived intrusion of the outside world into essentially local matters, there was no field of activity where that intrusion was more brutal or more
stark than that of military recruitment. The deserter who had been forced to
leave his village and the refractory whose lifestyle had been disrupted by the
state's demands were, more than any other members of village society, the victims of that intrusion. In many instances their political consciousness was awak-
ened by the fact of having to pass before the *conseil de recrutement* and to accept
the reality of military service. From the time of the first *tirages* there was always
a pool of dissident youth in hiding or protected by the local population, a society
en marge that demonstrated that there was an alternative to obedience and
whose existence encouraged a spirit of rebellion in others. Moreover, from 1793
any attempt to round up these refractories or to repress their insubordination
was bound to attract sympathy from their fathers and mothers, brothers and
friends, with the result that punitive action by the government could easily play
into the hands of their opponents. Royalists, in particular, were ready to profit
from any rash move by the gendarmerie or the republican armies in areas like
the West and the Southeast. They could with considerable ease assume the man-
tle of localism, winning sympathy from the ranks of the young and from those

who felt themselves unjustly prejudiced by the new recruitment laws (19). It was a battle for men's minds that the state found very difficult to win since by definition it was the state, in the guise of the communes and districts, that had responsibility for the recruitment procedures, and the state, through the army and the *gendarmerie,* that attempted to enforce them (20). In the eyes of rural communities, military service was, *par excellence,* the preserve of the state and its agents. The *bandes,* consisting overwhelmingly of men from the immediate neighborhood, were thus able to score important propaganda points in the psychological war between the local population and the Revolution's new secular officials (21).

In this campaign royalism might be almost incidental. The enemy was what mattered, and the enemy was clear to all—the Republic and its officials, with their insistence on over-government and their imposition, often in the most crass and unsympathetic way, of urban values and urban administration on the French countryside. The formation of semipermanent *bandes* in revolt against the state began in 1793, when recruitment first alienated a sizable segment of the community from the government in Paris. But these *bandes* soon became involved in a struggle with much wider implications, in the defense of traditional values against the representatives of the new authority. In March 1793 peasant bands attacked the towns in Brittany that symbolized their new oppression, occupying La Roche-Bernard and Rochefort and attempting to lay siege to Auray, Pontivy, Redon, Fougères, Vannes, and Vitré. This was done in the context of anticonscription riots, and it was certainly the promulgation of the new recruitment law that sparked off the violence. But, as Donald Sutherland explains, the implications of this anti-urban attack was far wider, bringing into question the republican administration itself:

> The attack on the towns in March 1793 took place within this context of changed governmental relations between town and country. The peasants were conscious that they were attacking not the towns *per se* or even a particular social class which inhabited them, but centres of republicanism. That is, the particular enemies were the Districts and their administrators. (22)

It was a context that the royalists and their supporters were uniquely placed to exploit.

Royalists might also hope to win converts in areas where the peasant dislike of revolutionary government was reinforced by a strong and resilient religious faith. Of course, the revolutionaries were always quick to seek out religious interference and to blame any form of dissent on the pernicious influence of refractory priests, but in the process of recruiting royalist *bandes* that influence cannot be wholly disregarded. Refractory priests who enjoyed the trust and confidence of local people could play their part in obstructing the recruitment effort and in turning the young conscripts to other causes. *Fanatisme,* stated the *commissaire* at Villefranche-sur-Saône in Year III with typical dogmatism, was at the root of the disobedience that he was encountering in the more mountainous parts of his district, engendering in the inhabitants a spirit of resistance that discouraged service, spread lawlessness and political dissent, and brought the *assignat* into disrepute (23). His colleague in Vannes in Year V was more specific in his allegations. Attempts to round up deserters and refractories in the western departments, he warned the minister, risked causing rioting and a renewal of civil war in the region. And refractory priests were waiting for just such an opportunity to stir up sedition among the rural population:

> Les prêtres réfractaires qui rentrent en foule alimentent dans les chambres, les granges, là où ils célèbrent leurs cultes, l'esprit de sédition et de révolte contre le gouvernement républicain. Vous sentez que les prédictions sanguinaires sont encore plus chaudes dans les confessionaux. Ces incendiaires sont parfaitement secondés par les anciens chefs de chouans, leur bien digne milice. Je sais qu'ils parcourent en armes les cantons, s'y rassemblent, y tiennent des conférences, et ressèment l'alarme dans les campagnes. (24)

Abolishing refractory influence in the countryside was a formidable task because the returned priests could generally depend on a certain lingering good will in their former parishes, while the sheer harshness of the law made the uncommitted disinclined to turn them over to the authorities. They were frequently offered protection from their friends and families. Sometimes mayors and public officials were themselves discovered harboring or encouraging them in their anti-republican activity. The mayor of Pénestin in the Morbihan was suspended in Year X when it was revealed that he had been paying a salary to a nonjuror out of communal funds (25). At Narnhac (Cantal) it was the *adjoint* who found himself dismissed in Year VI for offering hospitality to men hostile to the Republic, "pour avoir fait célébrer la messe chez lui par des prêtres réfractaires, leur avoir donné asile, entendu leur messe dans tous les lieux où elle se dit, et les avoir invités à manger" (26). These were far from being isolated instances, and in the counterrevolutionary heartlands of the Midi the influence of refractory clergy was rightly feared by local and national officials alike. By the mid-1790s they were slipping back into France with the express aim of stirring up strife, and some of those who had previously sworn their loyalty to the government and accepted the Civil Constitution were withdrawing their commitment and urging the peasants to rebel. At Lavelanet in the Ariège these were deemed to be the most dangerous of all, "ceux qui, ayant prêté le serment, l'ont retracté devant un délégué du pape, ont annoncé à leurs fidèles brebis que tout ce qu'ils avaient fait auparavant était nul, qu'il leur fallait deux mois de pénitence au bout desquels ils pourraient seulement reprendre leurs fonctions" (27). Throughout large tracts of Catholic countryside the spiritual prompting of these nonjurors posed a constant threat to the Republic, especially in areas of open counterrevolution where they could profitably throw in their lot with the *chouans* or *émigré* nobles. The respect which their office commanded in Catholic villages ensured their safety and guaranteed that their views would get a fair hearing. In the Drôme, it was reported, they counted *insoumis* and deserters among their congregations (28). In the Cantal, the arrest of a nonjuring priest caused an immediate riot at Chaudesaigues, a community that the government *commissaire* described as "et fanatisé et chouanné" (29). As in other parts of the French provinces, these were characteristics that went hand in hand.

The connections between the refractory clergy and rural counterrevolution do not need to be repeated here. They are already well known and discussed by every historian of *chouannerie,* of the Vendean revolt, or of southern royalism. Religion, like conscription, constituted an area of activity where the involvement of the state was resented and frequently rejected; worship and religious observance were private matters for the village communities themselves (30). The constitutional priest who was imposed on unwilling villagers was often treated as an *intrus,* a man whose interests and outlook were those of another culture, that of the Jacobin clubs and of the towns. It is therefore no accident that those communities that defended their identity against one form of intrusion should have resisted just as strongly other forms of imposition, no accident that areas with problems of *insoumission* frequently coincided with those where the government encountered religious dissent. When they demanded the return of their parish priests, Breton peasants were indirectly "asking for the return of an institution which affirmed their consciousness of themselves as men and as a community" (31). Moreover, the defense of the *curé,* like the defense of the village economy or of the village honor against the imposition of change from outside, would naturally fall on the young, those same young men who on a personal level so bitterly resented the imposition of conscription (32). In communities that remained loyal to the Catholic church, the bond of mutual reliance established between the priest and his young parishioners could become one of the mainstays of communal politics, and the *curé* might be drawn into offering them his protection in return. This he could do through all sorts of small but significant gestures: by providing casual work for *insoumis* who had stayed behind in the village, by forging certificates or falsifying registers, and by agreeing to marry conscripts religiously without first checking that they were eligible for marriage in the eyes of the civil authority (33). The priest, in short, might assume the role of their ally against the Republic and its laws, and his approval might extend to more open acts of defiance and rebellion. So extensive was the problem that in Year XIV the Archbishop of Toulouse was forced to take action against those of his priests who were caught protecting draft dodgers (34). In the Ariège the assistance of the clergy could take an openly political character. In one case in Year VIII the *curé* of Aulus was denounced for whipping up anger and resentment against the state, urging on the young men of his parish when they armed themselves with rifles and attacked the property of a prominent local Republican, Jean-Pierre Souquet. Souquet suffered considerably when they pillaged his sawmill, removed the millstones from his flourmill, and finally returned to burn the flourmill to the ground. All this occurred immediately after they had attended the *curé*'s somewhat inflammatory version of mass, and because the properties in question were all national lands acquired at the expense of local *émigrés,* it was reasonable to assume that the attack had been politically inspired and that the priest's role had been openly provocative (35).

Some priests took their antirepublican principles to even greater lengths, schooling the young men of their parish in royalism and encouraging them to commit acts of *brigandage* against the agents of the state. In one parish near Lille the *curé* led regular counterrevolutionary choir practices with the sixteen to twenty year olds of the locality, joining in lusty renderings of the "Réveil du peuple" and spreading scurrilous rumors about conditions in the republican battalions (36). And there is ample evidence from other areas that some at least among the clergy took an active part in their own underground war against the French Revolution, pitting what they believed to be God's law against the law of the country. In Year VI, for instance, priests and local draft dodgers were held jointly responsible for a series of thefts and murders along the road from Hesdin to Arras that had all the hallmarks of those brigand attacks which were more common in the Midi. Their victims included a *brigadier de gendarmerie nationale* intercepted as he was conducting captured deserters to prison in Arras, a merchant who had the misfortune to be mistaken for a man from Saint-Pol traveling to the *chef-lieu* on government business, and a constitutional priest who was savagely attacked by *réquisitionnaires* on the same stretch of road between Saint-Pol and Arras (37). If such cases are to be found in the relative security of the Pas-de-Calais, how much more did disillusioned clergy become involved in royalist bands in the counterrevolutionary heartlands of the West, the Midi, and Languedoc. In the Ariège, at the height of the insurrection of Year VII, local authorities complied with clerical demands and trees of liberty were rapidly replaced by *croix de mission,* while one of the first initiatives taken by the royalists at Mirepoix was to recall the orders of penitents (38). In Brittany priests not only acted as correspondents for Puisaye's royalist network, some even spied for the royalist cause, recruited its soldiers, took charge of arms dumps, and served as chaplains when the *chouans* mounted an attack (39). Catholic royalism in the Gard, where revolutionary politics could not escape the influence of the long-standing religious tension between Catholics and Protestants, gave the clergy an even more prominent role. Many of the brigand leaders had long anti-state pedigrees, having served their counterrevolutionary apprenticeship in the royalist *camps de Jalès* between 1790 and 1792. The bonds between the Church and the *égorgeurs* were strong and enduring, and to many there seemed surprisingly little contradiction in exchanging the cure of souls for the leadership of a terrorist band, avenging the sufferings of their church through acts of savage butchery and political murder. François Froment, for example, belonged to a devout family from Nîmes, supposedly of noble stock, and was sufficiently favored by the bishop to have been granted the post of receiver of the revenues of the cathedral chapter. He and his family were even given rooms in the episcopal palace, a rare and much cherished honor. Several of the other gang leaders who devastated the countryside around Nîmes were also the products of seminaries and holy orders. Among them were such prominent *égorgeurs* as the abbé Solier, who was guillotined at Le Vigan in 1801 for his career in terrorism and revenge killing, and Claude Allier, the brother of Dominique, who was executed in 1793 for his part in the federalist revolt in Lyon (40).

For many in the southern half of the country the intrusion of the state in matters of military recruitment and religious belief only paralleled another form of intrusion—the Revolution's concern for individual property rights and apparent contempt for custom and communal land. To smallholders in the *pays de petite culture* the whole question of *partage* seemed both irrelevant and potentially damaging because in areas of poor soil or upland pasture the division and allocation of the commons was never an economically realistic option. It is true that under the Jacobin Republic there was no legal obligation to disperse the commons in this way, as the law on *partage* remained a piece of permissive legislation, to be enforced only if one-third of the male inhabitants of the commune voted in favor of the change. But the debate on *partage* was often divisive and acrimonious, pitting the interests of the richer farmers and landowners against those of the poor and landless. Communes frequently intervened to prevent division of their lands, and those owning property threw themselves into a bitter struggle to prevent the kind of egalitarian division that the law prescribed. At Salers the *société populaire* protested in *germinal* II that "L'égoisme et la cupidité portent (les riches) à chasser de leurs maisons les locataires, croyant par là les priver de leur droit dans le partage des communaux" (41). In fact, throughout the South, there is little evidence that the law achieved widespread enactment, and the customary practice of the area, which alone provided the basis for the long-established emphasis on *vaine pâture* and *droit de parcours,* emerged largely unscathed. Custom yet again proved more powerful than statute (42). Yet, however muted the impact of legislation in this domain, and however limited the practical advance of agrarian individualism, this law and those that succeeded it after *thermidor* were widely perceived in the southern and more mountainous regions of the country as another instance of government interference in the most intimate affairs of the rural community. In departments like the Drôme, the Gard or the Ariège, the new communes rallied in defense of their traditional rights and defended them as essential contributors to their economic welfare. In the granary belt of the North, *partage* may have made economic sense—Florence Gauthier talks of it as offering "le début d'une solution radicale . . . de la crise agraire" (43)—but it could have no such application to southern *métayers.* For them individualism was an irrelevancy, and a most damaging irrelevancy, which demonstrated once again the distance that separated them from the Parisian legislators. The decree of 25 *thermidor* III served only to accentuate this feeling of alienation because it stressed once again the rights of the proprietor over the entire produce of his harvest by excluding villagers from their traditional gleaning rights after the first reaping of the crop (44). Faced with this legislation and with the stricter application of the *code forestier,* the southern villager was driven into more and more frequent clashes with the law, and these experiences could only serve to alienate him further from the Republic. In Gwynne Lewis's opinion, there is little doubt that the success of Catholic royalist brigandage in parts of the Southeast "was linked to the offensive launched by the *journalier* with his *lopin de terre,* the *cultivateur* with his small herd of sheep or goats, the small *vigneron,* the *bûcheron* and the *charbonnier,* indeed, by all those who depended on the rights of access to the forests and the fields" (45).

Opposition to republican officials and suspicion of republican laws could, in other words, drive whole communities into a rejection of the Republic itself. In such communities royalism often provided a logical alternative, especially to those who dreamed nostalgically of a world in which they had been left alone, undisturbed by Paris and its interminable legislation. Whole communities might be won over to the cause of the King, not through any deep-seated belief in the institution of monarchy but because of an ineradicable attachment to old ways and traditional freedoms. In such communities, often remote villages in the *pays de petite culture* where tradition was loath to die, nonjuring priests found shelter, republican festivals remained uncelebrated, and mayors committed frauds in favor of refractory conscripts secure in the knowledge that they enjoyed a wide measure of local support. Saint-Paul-Trois-Châteaux in the Drôme was a typical instance of a southern community where conscription was always difficult and where the state was never able to supplant the dictates of local tradition. Saint-Paul lacked any instinct for the Revolution or the Republic; it provided ideal cover for deserters, brigands, and royalist *chefs* alike. On the state of public opinion in the commune, General Merck could only report in Year VI that no progress whatever had been made, to the point where the local council was not even capable of mounting a simple republican festival:

Dans la commune de Saint-Paul aucunes fêtes républicaines ne sont célé-brées, on ne veut point les reconnaître. On n'a point fait la fête de la reconnaissance et des victoires le 10 prairial, il n'en a pas même été question; le commissaire du directoire n'ose pas publier l'arrêté qui prescrit l'usage du calendrier républicain, l'agent de la commune et le président de l'administration sont d'une criminelle insouciance, et depuis l'établissement du chef-lieu du canton à Saint-Paul, l'administration ne marche plus. (46)

In such circumstances opposition and non-cooperation were at every level of society, and it was deemed dangerous to think of raising an armed force from the local community to tackle the problem of *brigandage.* Administrators did not have trust in their own officials, and even local notables seemed suspect; furthermore, arms were so widely available in the badlands of the southern Drôme that almost any initiative was fraught with possible danger. The *sous-préfet* of Montélimar was sufficiently anxious to advise against the formation of *colonnes mobiles* to police royalists in Year VIII since they would almost certainly be infiltrated by the *bandes* themselves. Saint-Paul was not a place where such authority should be given to local people, for the *brigands* enjoyed support "dans toutes les classes des citoyens. Ils en ont partout: ils en auront dans les colonnes mobiles; et je suis très embarrassé par la crainte de donner une portion d'autorité militaire à des hommes qui peuvent en abuser" (47).

Where the political loyalty of the village at large was so feeble, it is hardly surprising that enthusiasm among the young for military service was rarely to be found. Villages opposed to the Republic produced very few conscripts, and *insoumission,* with the full approval of parents and local *notables,* was generalized. It is therefore quite natural that those who turned instead to fight for the *égorgeurs* in the Southeast or for the *chouans* in the West should have been *réfractaires* more than deserters. In such villages so few youngsters were incorporated in battalions that the rate of actual desertion could be very low. In Brittany, for instance, military deserters, as opposed to draft dodgers, played only a marginal role in *chouannerie:* of 81 men who surrendered at Dol in 1796, only 5 were deserters; of 602 in the Morbihan, only 9; and of the thousands of royalists captured at Quiberon Bay in 1795, only 12 were designated as deserters from the republican armies. In contrast, because they were young and vigorous, a very high proportion of them had been subject to conscription, and the fact of being a draft dodger and hiding from the authorities provided the opportunity and a certain impetus to take part in a more positive form of resistance (48). In the bands of the Southeast and Southwest, deserters played a more prominent part than in the Vendée and Brittany, though again it is *insoumission* that holds the key to the size and ready availability of the royalist units. The deserter, once back in his native village, would blend spontaneously into the brigand bands that controlled the local countryside, rejoining in their ranks those of his friends who had resisted the blandishments of the recruiting-sergeant. He had not abandoned his regiment out of any deeply held royalist faith or opposition to republicanism as a political ideal; such principles lay well outside the collective consciousness of peasant communities. Rather he had deserted for the usual, mundane reasons that drove hundreds of thousands to desert across the length and breadth of Europe: because he was cold and miserable, or hungry, or simply bored; because he felt abused by the military or had a grudge against his officers; above all because he listened to the familiar sound of his local *patois* and felt smitten by homesickness and simply left. But once he was back in his village, he would naturally resume the role that was expected of the young, that of defending, and if necessary fighting for, the freedoms and traditions of the community.

Royalism as a question of faith was very rare among the deserters and *insoumis* who took up arms in its name. Yet royalist shouts and songs, used as rallying cries or as symbols of collective defiance, were widespread and gave the Republican authorities some reason for panic and pessimism. In Year VIII, for instance, when conscripts from the village of Ouaine in the Yonne arrived at Auxerre to be prepared for departure to join their battalion, it was noted with alarm that they uttered cries of "Vive le Roi!" in the city streets. The incident went no further, and there is no evidence that the cries constituted a threat to the Republic, although the department almost as a matter of course expressed its feelings of outrage and asked that exemplary punishment be meted out to those identified and convicted (49). More threatening to authority were outbursts of royalist singing and chanting in towns and *bourgs* where antirepublican sympathies were known to be strong. Royalist chants could so easily be transformed into expressions of generalized opposition to everything that the government was trying to achieve, and there were occasions where mayors and town councilors demonstrated their solidarity with the young conscripts by joining in their defiance or by refusing to take any action against them. At Donzère in the southern Drôme, for example, the *jeunes gens* had little to fear from a complaisant local authority, and they took advantage by persecuting the local *gendarme* for whom they showed the most ostentatious contempt. The unfortunate officer, isolated by public opinion, could only report to his superiors of the humiliation he had suffered, when, on the night of 3 *vendémiaire* VI,

> il vit, sur les neuf heures du soir, une trouppe de jeunes gens rassemblés avec des bâtons, qui chantèrent pendant la nuit, dans presque toutes les rues de Donzère, le *Réveil du peuple;* qu'à environ minuit, ils se rendirent à la maison ou il était couché dans son lit, qu'ils le forcèrent à boire, quoique son hôtesse

ne voulut pas leur donner du vin à une telle heure; qu'il a bu avec eux contre la force n'y ayant point de résistance. (50)

At Mauriac in the Cantal, the identification of some of the town council with refractory conscripts (they appeared in public in a *rassemblement* in the center of the town, joining in their rendition of the *Réveil du peuple*) assumed an even more destabilizing aspect, since the same councilors had been agitating against the *acquéreurs de biens nationaux* in the area and had remained unmoved when sacred objects were stolen from the constitutional church for the use of nonjurors (51). In such cases the singing of royalist songs had been transformed into a deliberate device to undermine legal authority. When the commander of a detachment of soldiers sent to Pierrelatte in Drôme to arrest deserters heard some of them singing the royalist anthem, he ordered their immediate arrest; but to no avail since "le citoyen Théoule, adjoint municipal, arrive et de son autorité il les fit mettre en liberté" (52). Where a dissident community rallied round its conscripts, as in Pierrelatte, there was little that the military or police officials could do. The *Réveil du peuple* had been used to taunt them, to poke fun at their impotence, and to underline the solidarity of local people in their opposition to state intrusion.

If Paris consistently exaggerated the part played by royalism in stimulating desertion, it was justified in fearing the effects of desertion and *insoumission* in regions where royalists already had a hold on public opinion. There is little doubt that the simple fact that a man had refused to serve the Republic or had, after experience of the armies, elected to desert aroused the interest of the *chouan* and royalist leaders. A deserter or an *insoumis* could not turn to the legal authorities for help, and this in itself made him somewhat vulnerable to such pressures as might be brought to bear on him. Moreover, his rejection of the Republic served to win faith among the community of outlaws and bandits that encompassed rural royalism. The deserter especially enjoyed a certain prestige in their eyes as a man who had undergone a kind of *rite de passage* and who had not been found wanting. His military experience limited as it was could appear invaluable to the rebels because he would know how to use a rifle, would probably bring with him his arms and ammunition, and would retain some residue of his former military discipline. It is therefore in no way surprising that royalist recruiters worked relentlessly to win over refractories and deserters to their cause. Besides all other considerations, the fact that they were young and living in local villages made them the natural recruitment fodder, arguably the *only* recruitment fodder, for the forces of Catholic royalism in the South and for the *chouan* bands of the West.

Royalist *embaucheurs* were generally local men who understood very well the temperament of the villagers, their fears and their traditional loyalties, and they often showed great skill and patience in wooing them to the counterrevolutionary cause. At first their actions might consist of nothing more than spreading "mauvaises insinuations" to the young men affected by the requisition that they could with total impunity stay in their village rather than leave for the front (53), or they might ring the church bells in a succession of villages at the moment chosen for the selection of conscripts, a device that conspired to spread panic and rumors that the countryside was overrun by troops (54). In the cities royalists distributed pamphlets stirring up hatred of the government; in the countryside word of mouth was far more effective. In Bordeaux in Year VI two men, a medical student and a printer, both of known royalist sympathies, were arrested for writing and selling a tract entitled *Aux Jeunes Gens,* which specifically urged them to resist conscription and which tried to whip up their animosity toward the *colonne mobile* whose job it was to police conscription in the city. Those who joined the *colonne,* readers were informed, were recruited from the dregs of Bordeaux society, from among "tout ce qu'il y avait de plus vil et de plus abject" in the city (55). More commonly, the *embaucheur,* like the foreign agent, worked surreptitiously, talking to men looking dejected after the *conseil de révision* and hanging around local bars on the day of the *tirage.* His part was little more than a whispered conversation, which made it difficult to secure convictions, but those engaging soldiers in friendly chat in the *auberges* and cabarets of garrison towns, or accosting them during their march to join their regiments, were particularly suspect. Julien Quentin was probably a typical *embaucheur,* a traveling salesman who bought and sold livestock, who frequented the bars around fairs and markets, and who was denounced at Saint-Cloud in Year IV by three soldiers whom he had sought out and to whom he had offered a drink (56). At times the scale of the subversion was rather more spectacular, and the charges more serious. In Year VII at Lille two men were arrested and charged with trying to instigate rebellion among the conscripts from the Cher and Loir-et-Cher who were making their way to their regiment. According to the troops, who on this occasion remained loyal, these two men, well-dressed, claiming to come from Paris and Lyon, had approached them between Gien and Nogent while their company was resting,

"parcourant les différents groupes des conscrits, leur conseillant d'abandonner la cause de la liberté, de déserter même en masse, en se défaisant de leurs chefs, leur promettant le secours des honnêtes gens, leur disant (grossière absurdité) qu'ils ne peuvent se rendre à Lille où est l'ennemi, ainsi qu'à Lyon, à Grenoble, que la République est perdue et que les défenseurs seront perdus . . ." (57). The military authorities took the allegation very seriously, and the two strangers were handed over to the *juge de paix.*

In refractory villages recruitment for the royalist cause was often crowned with success and posed a major threat to the government. The royalists held trump cards that were denied to the Republic, openly playing on the fears and resentments of local people against the imposition of bureaucracy. While the Republic might offer signing-on bounties to stimulate recruitment, it was obliged to pay such bounties in *assignats,* even though the paper notes were dismissed as worthless by the peasantry. Royalist *embaucheurs* suffered from no such constraints. At Valence, for example, they recruited fifteen young men in Year IV by the promise of payment in coin, while "à Donzère, Montélimar, Pierrelatte et Voulte l'on engage secrètement pour une armée qui se forme dans l'Ardèche, frontière de la Lozère, l'on prétend qu'il y a déjà un fort noyau de formé, qu'une caisse considérable est déjà établie, que tous les frais se payent espèces son-nantes, que là le soldat est autant payé en numéraire que la république paye en assignats, ce qui fait beaucoup de prosélytes" (58). The success of such tactics was all the more resounding in that men serving in the Republic's armies were often paid months late in devalued *assignats* or found increasingly that they received no payment at all. Royalists might also put their local knowledge and familiarity with local custom to good use, turning up at *fêtes* and *bals publics* and converting them into demonstrations of political strength. At Puymirol in Lot-et-Garonne they showed their anger at the inclusion of republican propaganda in the village carnival by taking it over and using it as their own private stage. Suddenly, in the midst of the gaiety and dancing, "on voit les cadenettes et costumes ridicules se multiplier, puis deux masques de ce même parti travestis en roi et en reine, précédés de deux postillons qui faisaient claquer le fouet, paroissent tout à coup sur la place publique" (59). It was not simply a daring jest that was certain to grab the attention of all present; it was a powerful reminder that even at a carnival, the central social point of the municipal calendar, the new authorities lacked the muscle needed to keep them away. The timing, the sense of occasion, the style and swagger of the demonstrators were guaranteed to capture the maximal attention and to convert a popular social gathering into a moment of political triumph. Bribes and inducements were vital to the success of royalist agents, but their impact was increased by skillful public relations and a talent for impressing simple folk in ways to which they could relate. When for example two *embaucheurs* entered a bar in Rambouillet to try to subvert soldiers garrisoned in the town and win them over to the Vendean cause, they did not content themselves with offers of cash. Rather they sought to leave an indelible impression on the minds of their audience. While one of them created a distraction in another corner of the bar, his accomplice dropped hints about the huge sums he had to distribute in bounties and tried to dazzle the prospective recruit with his credentials. He was subsequently accused "d'avoir offert 6000 livres d'engagements à ce citoyen, de lui avoir montré différents papiers qu'il lui a dit être des lettres du comte d'Artois et de Charette, et qu'il déserterait sous deux jours" (60). The fact that they frequently used deserters and refractories as recruiting agents only emphasized their identity of interest with the young men they were seeking to win over; again, a clever ploy that helped to convince peasant boys who were confused and flattered by such attention (61).

In such instances the act of recruitment was planned and deliberate, an integral part of the royalist war effort in areas where loyalties were uncertain. Around frontiers and near seacoasts such campaigns were traditional, and they were only accelerated by the political nature of the revolutionary wars and by the scope they presented for ideological subversion. Foreign armies also benefited from campaigns conducted in border regions, offering bounties far beyond the dreams of French conscripts and bribing individual recruits into service as mercenaries. Rumor spread rapidly about the activities of English, Austrian, and Prussian *embaucheurs* in towns and villages along France's frontiers. Refractories were the usual target for such agents, and their presence was noted with consternation in virtually all the outlying areas of the *hexagone:* in the streets of Foix, along the Swiss border, among troops in the Doubs, and in the farms and hamlets of the Breton countryside (62). Many of these recruiters were involved in what was really a form of criminal conspiracy, making substantial sums of money for themselves by passing young men to their foreign paymasters and involving entire rings of conspirators in the cause of subversion. Félix Lamy was one such *embaucheur,* working out of the bar he owned in Dunkerque and devoting himself to the corruption of sailors from the Nord and surrounding departments. When he was arrested, police found thirteen different passports on his premises which, he claimed, had been supplied to him by the "commissaire des relations commerciales du royaume de Hollande à Dunkerque," a rather shadowy individual who was eventually tracked down and questioned. What emerged was a mesh of intrigue and corruption. Lamy bribed the young seamen to abandon the republican navy and serve instead on corsairs, in private employment. The so-called *commissaire,* Casteleyer, directed them to Dutch ships and seacaptains which another conspirator, Sophie Labbé, was paid to provide the seamen with accommodation undeclared to the authorities at her Dunkerque lodging house (63). Lamy and his accomplices worked for foreign interests, and their main concern was gain through commerce in human beings. More dangerous to the French government was the organized trade in men for the Austrian army or the *chouan* forces in the West. The department of the Morbihan, for instance, proved a happy hunting ground for rebel armies in their quest for recruits, since large areas of the department were beyond the means of the *gendarmerie* to police. The government's *commissaire* in Hennebont was convinced by Year V that many communities had in practice been abandoned by the Republic to the attentions of the *chouans,* whose leaders were only too ready to take full advantage of this surprise windfall. Reports from all over the region repeated the same allegation, that the rebels had a recruiting agency in Hennebont whose sole aim was to subvert republican troops by the offer of bribes, often of English money. As they passed from mouth to mouth, the rumors gained shape and substance. "C'est, dit-on, un négociant de Lorient qui fournit les fonds pour le recrutement des déserteurs, les déserteurs s'aperçoivent dans les campagnes par bandes nombreuses, le bagne de Brest, mal gardé suivant les apparences, fournit grand nombre de ces scélérats . . ." (64). The republicans would build these individual rumors into a conspiracy of colossal proportions organized around a highly efficient and well-financed counterrevolutionary administration. Yet everything that we know about the counterrevolution, especially in regard to *chouannerie,* suggests that such powers of organization were far beyond the capabilities of what was a very fractured movement, often living precariously from hand to mouth (65).

Chance and muddle were just as likely to have been responsible for the recruitment of a republican soldier, especially where counterrevolutionary forces held the upper hand and could bully or coerce the local population. Joining the *chouans,* for instance, might be less the result of a deliberate act of persuasion than the consequence of a lack of policing or of a temporary loss of control by the Republic. The members of a passing royalist contingent could so easily exert a direct pressure on their peers, especially on those *réquisitionnaires* who lived in fear of capture or who had already been condemned *par contumace* for their act of rebellion. In addition, by taking a young man prisoner, they could effectively transform him into a *chouan* rebel. Whether he fought actively against the Republic or not, he was likely to be denounced and condemned for his association with the enemy (66). Among those tried for royalism in the Southwest in Years VII and VIII were many whose counterrevolutionary careers had begun when their village was invaded by the royalist armies and when the peace of their everyday lives was rudely shattered. They were seldom committed antirepublicans, but local boys whose youth and physique made them useful soldiers and attracted the interest of the rebel battalions. Again and again we are told that their involvement with the rebellion had been a chance affair, the result of an unfortunate encounter with royalist soldiers. Until then they had shown no taste for any form of political action beyond that of refusing to be drafted, "s'étant assez bien conduit jusques à l'époque du passage de l'armée royale," or "ayant été fait prisonnier par les royaux à l'affaire de Carbonne et entraîné par eux jusques à Saint-Gaudens" (67). Although it was obviously in their interest to minimize their commitment to the enemy, the evidence of many of these so-called rebel soldiers appeared to ring true, and in some instances even the republican tribunals before which they appeared accepted that their brief flirtation with royalism was not of their own volition. At Blagnac in the Haute-Garonne the royalists sent in more seasoned troops, themselves *réfractaires* from the republican armies, to spread panic among the villagers and to seize all the young men of military age. Their captures were the result of simple terrorization: "ils arrêtèrent des patriotes, devastèrent la commune, et brûlèrent les papiers publics" (68). They disarmed the local farmers and threatened death to those who refused to follow them in their crusade against the Republic, just as all over the Southwest threats and menaces were part of the standard armoury of royalist *embaucheurs* sent into the local community (69). In the face of brutality and strong-arm tactics of this sort, resistance could appear somewhat futile, with the result that in many villages all the strong and healthy males were systematically rounded up in dawn raids and incorporated in the rebel armies. For some, of course, service in the royalist cause had few charms, and those incorporated by force often tended to desert as soon as an opportunity presented itself. There were royalist "soldiers" who stayed with their new units for no more than a few days or hours. There were others who, with greater calculation, made use of the royalists to escape from republican custody but gave little in return. One young man from Aurignac (Haute-Garonne) found the arrival of the *brigands* happily fortuitous but who was in no sense himself a royalist: "lorsque l'armée des brigands y entra," reported the government *commissaire*, "il fut délivré et retourna dans ses foyers, d'où il n'a pas bougé depuis" (70). In countryside in the grip of civil war where counterrevolutionary forces were in charge, joining them, however briefly, could be the only means of escape, the only way of staying at liberty or of continuing one's journey uninterrupted. Simple expediency might dictate that it was the only feasible path to follow, the latest of that long series of expedients to which the deserter or refractory was condemned by the exigencies of his life outside the law of the Republic.

Nowhere was this more true than in the West, where *chouan* bands and Vendean armies controlled large areas of the countryside for lengthy periods, and where the border between republican and rebel-held territory shifted remorselessly back and forth. For young refractory conscripts this presented an endless series of risks, but it also furnished opportunities for escape as they learned to play off the competing aims of both sides to retain their precious liberty. *Chouan*-controlled communes had the huge advantage for those seeking to escape conscription that the Republic's officials were powerless to execute the government's decrees, and it was reported throughout the West that young men of the *première réquisition,* instead of joining their designated units, were making long overland journeys to find shelter in the deepest recesses of rebel Brittany. In the Calvados, it was even suggested that the fathers and mothers of these youngsters were encouraging them to do so since, in the words of the *commissaire* in Caen, "l'esprit de contre-révolution leur fait préférer pour leurs enfants le service des brigands à celui de la République" (71). Such claims aroused feelings of panic among local republicans, who often believed that the problem of *chouannerie* was simply a dangerous politicization of the problem of *insoumission*. Between 1793 and the Year III when *chouannerie* was posing a major threat in large areas of the West, all those arrested for desertion or for draft dodging were automatically assumed to be in collusion with the *chouans,* to be their spies or agents, or to have vital information about their organization (72). This belief was often proved to contain some substance, since the interrogation of men suspected of being *insoumis* provided the authorities with a wealth of valuable information about *chouan* activities, stock piles of weapons, the movement of units, and the hiding-places used by their soldiers (73). In fact, the two categories, *insoumis* and *brigands,* proved impossible to distinguish with any precision. When the *chouans* entered a village, their first action was generally to order all the young men to march behind their banners. At Le Faouët in Year VIII, for example, "les jeunes gens ont reçu de la part des chefs des rebelles l'ordre formel de se tenir prêts à marcher sous peu de jours" (74). Equally, when the authorities attempted to round up local *chouans* by means of a military operation, a *battue générale* of the outlying hamlets and all the known hiding-places on the surrounding *bocage,* they were likely, as occurred around Josselin in Year II, to find only a substantial haul of refractory conscripts (75). So close was the identification of *insoumis* and rebels in the minds of the departmental officials that every draft dodger became automatically a potential counterrevolutionary and every recalcitrant republican soldier an assumed royalist recruit. And the real, often unspoken fear of the authorities was that throughout the West the old *chefs de chouans* would seek to restore their power and influence by calling on every deserter and refractory to mobilize behind the cause. The very thought of this eventuality drove otherwise moderate men to consider the most extreme solutions, even the total evacuation of villages where royalist sympathies were known to be strong. How else, asked the *commissaire* in Le Mans rhetorically, could the *chouans* be deprived of a regular source of manpower in their war of attrition against the Republic? He proposed, somewhat desperately, the deployment of the army against recalcitrant villages since "il faudrait enlever tous ceux qui habitent les communes connues par leur complicité avec les Brigands royaux ... pour les embarquer et les transplanter dans les armées employées hors du territoire de la République" (76).

The evidence provided by trial records and by individual interrogations amply confirms this impression that it was random circumstance that generally transformed a refractory conscript into a *chouan* or royalist, seldom a hardened political conviction. Under the right leadership acts of simple pillage and banditry in response to need and hunger could easily drift into counterrevolution (77). Or the ringing of church bells could spread panic among the village population and send the young men scuttling off in defense of their community against an imagined enemy. At Belz in the district of Auray, for instance, it was the tocsin, the traditional ringing of the bells to signify an emergency, that called the villagers to arms and launched them on an attack against the republican soldiers. Suspects were questioned about the meaning of the tocsin, about the interpretation placed on it by local peasants as they tilled their fields, and about the identity of the men who had given the order that the bells be rung. But such questioning achieved very little. Like René Maho, a twenty-four-year-old *laboureur* suspected of taking part in the rising, those questioned denied all knowledge of the perpetrators, saying simply that "à son retour on lui dit que c'étaient des enfants de dix, douze et treize ans environ" who were responsible (78). In country areas where *fanatisme* provided a support for tradition and superstition, the ringing of the church bells had always been a signal for alarm, for the approach of a storm, or for the urgent convocation of a village meeting. During the periods of active conscription, it could easily be turned into a warning signal to all the young men of serviceable age that troops or *gendarmes* were approaching, and many village mayors and councils were dismissed by the Minister after breaches of this kind (79). But the meaning could not always be clearly defined. At Moulis in the Ariège, for example, the bells started ringing in Year VII at the very moment when the recruitment was getting under way; but it was admitted that *mauvaise volonté* was very difficult to prove, that "le son des cloches à l'approche des troupes de la commune coïncidait avec le vieux préjugé du fanatisme de sonner les cloches pour dissiper l'orage, qui à la vérité grondait sur leur tête avec impétuosité" (80). The recruiting officers were left with little more than their suspicions that the church and the commune were seeking to raise the standard of revolt in Moulis.

Throughout the West suspects consistently denied that they joined the *chouan* revolt out of well-defined political conviction, placing the responsibility on an impulse of the moment, misunderstanding, or rumor. When the *jeunes gens de la réquisition* marched on Vannes from rural communities in the Morbihan in Year II, they did so for religious rather than political motives, responding to an appeal to "tous les fidèles catholiques" of the *pays* to march to save their faith and make way for the return of their "bons prêtres" (81). If this is to be taken at face value, and there is little reason to believe that the courts were more generous in their treatment of *fanatiques* than of royalists, it would imply once again that the young were acting as representatives of their communities, angered by urban intrusion into their religious lives and matters of traditional conscience. Others insisted that their commitment to the royalist armies had been brief and forced, originating not in counterrevolutionary ideas but in simple compulsion. This was a more natural form of defense, a desperate attempt to slough off any element of personal responsibility and to place the blame on the faceless, unnamed fanatics who served in the royalist recruiting units. In turn they stressed that they were wholly apolitical, just ordinary villagers caught up in events that were beyond their comprehension and outside their control. And they called other villagers as witnesses to the fact that their service with the enemies of the Republic had been the result of constraint. Joseph Daigny was caught as he slipped home from the royalist army after its defeat at Montréjeau. Captured red-handed, he could not deny his service in the King's cause, but played down his importance, insisting that

> il n'a été que simple fusilier, que lors de l'organisation qui se fit à Saint-Gaudens il refusa le grade de capitaine qu'on lui offroit. Ajoutant que machinalement il portoit son fusil, et qu'il ne brulla point une amorce et qu'il ne s'est jamais mêlé de rien organiser, ny de donner aucuns ordres. (82)

Jean Raimond, a thirty-four-year-old *tisserand* from Miramont, agreed that he had been forced to join the rebels when they invaded the town, but claimed that he had stayed with them for no more than one week, the period when they were in Miramont, finding the first possible occasion to desert. Interrogated about his role during that week, he accepted that he had been opportunistic and had played along with the group that was in control at the time; as a consequence he was rebuked by the court and given the lightest of prison sentences. Raimond scarcely appeared a convincing man of principle, in anyone's cause:

> Interrogé s'il n'a crié Vive le Roy, prêté et exigé le serment de fidélité pour luy et pour la religion.
> Répond ne l'avoir fait prêter à personne, mais qu'il l'a prêté avec la troupe parce qu'il fut forcé.
> Interrogé si depuis longtemps il n'engageait les gens de sa connaissance à entrer dans son parti en leur faisant entendre que c'était pour soutenir la religion et pour avoir un Roi. Répond et nie, ajoutant que quand on le lui a proposé, il a répondu qu'il voulait rester du côté du parti le plus fort. (83)

One after another of those accused of taking part in the revolt of Year VII in the Haute-Garonne and the Ariège repeated the same story, insisting that they had been forced to march, to swear an oath of loyalty to the King in front of the assembled royalist forces, even to wear the enemy's white *cocarde*. Like Arnaud Latour from Miramont, they persisted in their claim that theirs had been no more than an auxiliary role, that of mounting guard at night or of preparing meals for the rebels. In no circumstances would they admit to the more serious charge of taking up arms against the Republic (84).

The testimony of royalist commanders and brigand leaders who were brought to trial lent support to these claims. Louis Maury, the "fameux chef de bande" from Pamiers who was tried and executed in Year VI for *brigandage* and murder, made it clear in a deathbed confession that the royalist units under his command were composed of just such footloose young conscripts, generally alienated from the Republic by the simple fact that they had been conscripted.

In the Ariège, he claimed, he could command a rebel army of 1,500 *jeunes gens,* almost all army deserters and *insoumis,* but he added that they were not generally men marked by any form of political ideology. The vast majority of them were royalists of circumstance, young men who had been temporarily misled and who could easily be won back to republicanism. He had forced them to swear an oath to the King to fashion them into an effective fighting unit, the "serment des chouans" of his own Breton youth which "se prêtait la main sur l'Évangile placé sous les poignards" (85). Even if his statement supplied the authorities with no new information there is no reason to call into question this part of Maury's testimony since none of his friends or accomplices was directly implicated. Furthermore, his claim was endorsed by two other bandits who were due to be guillotined with him on the main square of Foix. There is evidence that *brigands* not only relied on deserters and refractories for manpower in their bands, but had frequently themselves served in the republican armies in their youth. This was true, for instance, of many of the most prominent brigands who roamed the sparsely policed border area between the Drôme and the Vaucluse during the 1790s. Among them were men like Dumaine, *dit* Montauban, one of Saint-Christol's chief lieutenants and a much-feared *égorgeur* in his own right. His previous career makes interesting reading. In *brumaire* Year VI, shortly after his death in a shoot-out with the local *gendarmes,* his father tried to explain his son's involvement in political terrorism by recalling details of his childhood and adolescence:

> que jusqu'à l'age de 16 ans il a fait tout son possible pour corriger les fautes de son fils, qu'il n'a pas pu malheureusement en venir à bout, qu'ensuite il s'engagea dans le régiment de Chartres . . . qu'à la formation des bataillons de volontaires il se mit dans un bataillon de Vaucluse . . . qu'il y a environ deux ans il revint dans sa maison, que deux ou trois mois après il fut arrêté comme déserteur . . . qu'il désertait de Milan deux ou trois mois après et revint chez lui où il ne voulait pas le souffrir . . . et qu'il y a environ deux mois il ne faisait que courir d'un endroit à un autre, que depuis l'attroupement de Saint-Christol il n'a paru que deux ou trois fois chez lui, et que toutes les fois qu'il le voyait il le réprimandait . . . et s'il est mort il ne regrette pas. (86)

Yet another military career had ended in desertion, and that act of desertion had facilitated Dumaine's relentless drift into a life of crime and antirepublican banditry.

During the years when royalism flourished in the wilder parts of the West and South of the country, there were few who doubted that refractories and returned deserters played a major role in the rebel bands. In the Lozère deserters were flocking to join bands led by royalists already under sentence of death (87); in the Haute-Loire it was feared that as many as 1,500 *jeunes gens* were involved, wandering the mountains around Monistrol "comme des chouans." In the view of Bonnet, on mission to the area, they presented an equal threat, given that "ils insultent et désarment les républicains; ils crient vivent les royalistes; ils maltraitent les prêtres assermentés; ils ont abattu les arbres de la liberté dans Montfaucon; dans cette dernière ville un prêtre a eu une oreille coupée" (88). There were some communes where all the men listed as being suspected of royalism were, without exception, on the run from the republican armies. Such was the case in the village of Brax in the Haute-Garonne, where all nine known *insurgés* were either *réquisitionnaires* or refractory conscripts, including some who had held office as *officiers municipaux,* quite illegally, since the time when they had avoided the draft (89). In the canton of Léguevin, whose territory included Brax, many of those implicated in the royalist cause had previously been conscripted. Some, indeed, appeared to have divided their time between the service of the Republic and that of the rebels, a conflict of roles that caused them and their community little unease. The two leaders of the rebellion were both nobles who gathered around them the refractory and malcontent youth of the surrounding district; one was noted as "ayant gardé chez lui pendant plusieurs mois des réquisitionnaires et des conscrits," the other as "vivant dans le ci-devant château avec ses camarades conscrits ou réquisitionnaires." Their closest helpers had had similarly checkered careers, one having held the rank of captain in the national guard, while another had played a devious double game while still nominally in the service of the Republic. His loyalties were already doubtful, and "étant sentinelle à un poste avancé il reconnut les royalistes et sans mot dire il les conduisit au corps de garde, qu'il n'avertit pas: ainsi il fit prendre les patriotes et leurs armes" (90). To villagers the contradiction implicit in such careers would have seemed unremarkable, and few would have passed moralistic judgments on their relatives and close friends. After all, desertion and *insoumission* were themselves widely tolerated without reproach and were recognized as part of the same tangled web of resistance to the government as were royalism and *brigandage* and the assertion of communal traditions. Concepts of national identity and treason were still only dimly understood. Throughout the Revolution and for much of the Napoleonic period this was to remain a simple fact of life in many parts of rural France that governments in Paris seemed singularly reluctant to accept.

8

Desertion and the French Armies

THE EFFECTS of desertion and *insoumission* were felt most keenly by the armies themselves. Generals and military *commissaires* were unanimous in their assessment of the damage inflicted on French fighting strength by what they termed the scourge or "fléau" of desertion. For although individual acts of disobedience might seem unspectacular, their total effect was to impose a constant and enervating drain on military resources and to place at risk the success of French military ambitions. By the later years of the Revolution, when desertions were particularly endemic, the armies were both embarrassed and depleted. It was this, not any commitment to the principle of conscription, that led to the acceptance of the loi Jourdan in Year VI and the abandonment of any pretence that France had a national force based on voluntary recruitment (1). Military tactics were seriously undermined by the loss of manpower. The revolutionary *demi-brigades* were supposed to be flexible and highly maneuverable forces that could hurl themselves at the enemy and take full advantage of surprise and speed. Yet desertions were running at such a level that, even at the height of the Jacobin Revolution, some commanders had to admit that they had not the resources that the tactic demanded (2). By the beginning of the Consulate the problem had become so serious that it was costing the military, by their own admission, some 200,000 men, many of whom were technically inscribed in their units even though they had never left their villages. Desertion on this scale could scarcely be tolerated year after year, conscription after conscription; it posed a massive threat to Napoleon's soaring military ambitions. There was in any case an increasingly serious shortage of young men, both for the armies and for agriculture. By 1812 nearly 80 percent of young Frenchmen of conscription age were being trawled into the military, and the total losses in dead and wounded had reached nearly one million (3). In such circumstances desertion and resistance became luxuries that the armies could no longer afford.

The effect on the military varied from regiment to regiment and from one army to another. It was particularly severe in the infantry and in certain artillery units, but relatively mild in the elite cavalry regiments (4). But in those sectors where the habit of desertion became widely practiced, the damage done to both military capacity and morale was acute. It was no longer a case of occasional individual decisions to desert, but rather of collective refusals, of units that threatened to melt away without ever firing a shot in battle. The trickle had quickly turned into a major flow, affecting not just the soldiers themselves but many of those engaged in ancillary services. André Réal, on mission to the Armée des Alpes in Year III and Year IV, reported bleakly that in some units the majority of the men had already disappeared; desertion, he added, "a fait des ravages effrayants dans l'armée des Alpes, soit parmi les volontaires, soit parmi les conducteurs et charretiers des transports militaires" (5). Similarly in the navy those workers who were drafted to serve as ropemakers and ships' carpenters joined the sailors in mass desertion, generally taking advantage of those propitious moments when their ships had docked in other ports to make their escape (6). Among men in the infantry regiments desertion often spread quite uncontrollably. Of seventy-one soldiers from Aurillac despatched to Saint-Flour in the spring of 1793, only nineteen were still at their posts by mid-August (7). In Year II thirty-one men of the Compagnie Borel from Crest in the Drôme took a collective decision to escape and mutinied to gain their freedom. Their officers found them in a determined mood, prepared for their long journey home with their packs and weapons on their backs, uttering defiant threats and bloodcurdling menaces, their leaders "ayant le sabre nu à la main" (8). From the South and Southwest in particular the stories reaching Paris were alarming and dreadfully repetitious. By the end of the decade whole armies were disappearing and supplementary levies were made necessary because of the erosion caused by desertion. Of the 1,300 men conscripted in the Creuse in Year VIII, for example, only 300 found their way to their regiments (9). In the Haute-Loire nearly 1,100 members of the first auxiliary battalion deserted out of a total strength of 1,400 (10). In the Landes in Year VII, of 1,200 men who left for their units, only 60 were still in uniform after a single day on the road (11). In the following year 333 left their native Ardèche to join their assigned regiment at Dijon, but a meager 6 managed to complete the journey (12). Desertion, in other words, was no longer the response of a small minority but was decimating the forces at the generals' disposal. For unhappy or unwilling soldiers it had come to seem one of the most natural courses to follow, at least for as long as the government took no effective action to stop it. Ministers like Petiet and Schérer saw one of their principal tasks to be the provision of palliatives, of measures that would help the army retain its *effectifs* in time of war and reduce the damaging incidence of desertion (13).

Not all desertion was as spectacular and not all was premeditated or pre-planned. Men might return to their homes to say goodbye to their families or collect personal possessions for the journey and be distracted from their duty by the "perfides conseils" of relatives and friends (14). Or they might learn of others who had deserted with impunity and be tempted to follow in their footsteps; but everywhere desertion was highly infectious, spreading by the power of example. In the words of the prefect of the Seine-et-Oise, "il ne faut que la vue d'un militaire rentré impunément dans ses foyers, sans permission, pour que tous les autres se croyent autorisés à en faire autant" (15). As early as 1793 some recruits in the Drôme were refusing to leave or were deserting after only a few days' service on the somewhat spurious grounds that others had deserted before them and that it would be an outrage to equality if they were forced to serve (16). The military were particularly sensitive to the danger posed by the existence of so many deserters on French territory because their mere presence helped to give resistance an air of security and even respectability. Those already at liberty encouraged others by their example. Frequently lads from the same village deserted on the first or second night of the march, and once it became standard practice to send boys from the same towns to the same units, the army was appalled by the large-scale mass desertions that ensued. As a policy it was better geared to curing *nostalgie* than to preventing desertion (17). Just as village solidarity had helped ensure that the young men left their *pays* in cheerful spirits, so it allowed unhappy conscripts a degree of companionship and shared experience in their long days and nights of clandestinity. The presence of others created hope among their peers just as the departure of friends created despondency in the regiments they left behind. In the Meuse lads from the neighboring frontier departments were wandering from village to village disguised as *colporteurs,* offering the young men of the country areas a job and a guaranteed wage if they would join them (18). At Douai deserters were blamed when an anticonscription pamphlet was posted in the town outside the inn on the very day of the *tirage* in 1807, warning the local population that "on fait la guerre aux pères de famille, on mène nos enfants à la boucherie" (19). The armies were aware that desertion had to be curbed if an example was not to be given to the next generation; in the context of rural France especially, desertion could so easily foster more desertion.

The loss to the military was not confined to the loss of manpower, serious though that was. Other men could, after all, be conjured up through the unpopular device of supplementary levies, or by forcing communes to provide replacements. Under Napoleon such measures were resorted to year after year, but at a very considerable price to local communities, to farming, and to the economy. If the men replaced were deserters hiding in the hills or *insoumis* living precariously on the edge of their communities, the economic contribution that they could make in no way compensated for the loss that the removal of others in their place—in almost every case young, capable *pères de famille* who had benefited from exemption or had been placed in the reserve—necessarily implied. There was an economic cost to be paid, and it was the local civilian population, not the army, that had to pay it. That is not to say, of course, that the army did not in turn suffer from this policy. As farming areas never tired of reminding the government, it was they who produced the foodstuffs that the military relied on, at least during their periods on French soil. Poor harvests and high prices had the most deleterious effect on the value of the French battalions as fighting units (20). And the replacement of the deserter with a man of similar age and physical strength, if we assume that the law was carried out to the letter, did not compensate for the months or even years of training that had been lavished on him. Especially as the armies became more professional and relied less on the massed attacks of the Revolutionary years, training and tactical instruction were important to their efficacy as fighting units. A man with some years' experience was more useful to his commanders, more prepared for the ardors of warfare, and less fearful and panic-stricken in battle than the raw recruit being blooded in his first campaign. It was for this reason that generals were so loath to release seasoned veterans after years of service, and that the military sacrifice demanded of young soldiers so often appeared despairingly open-ended. For this reason, too, they continued to see the desertion of trained infantrymen as a crippling blow to their fighting strength.

Desertion affected not only the strength and experience of an army as a fighting unit, but also the key support services that were necessary to success in the field. If the army relied on its active combatants, it also required regular and guaranteed supplies of food and clothing, arms and munitions. The provisioning of a military effort on the scale of the Revolutionary and Napoleonic Wars demanded a level of mobilization in the community as a whole that was without precedent. It demanded the requisitioning of carts and barges, the call-up of carters and boatmen to steer and drive them. It required horses both for fighting and for transport duties. It demanded the mobilization of gunsmiths and millers, seamstresses and hatters; they, too, were an essential part of the militarization of France. When farmers refused to turn over their horses to the army, when carters squabbled about payment and sulked in their villages, when administrative bungling or public bankruptcy prevented uniforms from being ordered or delivered, it was the troops and their welfare that inevitably suffered. In Year II each of France's armies was desperately short of guns and ammunition, to the extent that one man in ten was issued with a firearm that would not fire, and generals were even thinking of equipping some units with pikes to face the enemy (21). The quest for powder for those guns that were in working order meant counting on the patriotism and civic responsibility of all Frenchmen, and especially of the *sans-culottes*. They were to clean out their barns and cellars collecting saltpetre for the war effort and taking it to their sectional workshops to be processed (22). The extent to which these support services were stretched both by the scale of the war and by the lack of an efficient army administration in the 1790s can scarcely be overstated. Their contribution was vital if whole regiments were not to starve or be reduced to despondency and impotence. Again and again deprivation is cited as the principal cause of desertion by soldiers whose tolerance had finally snapped. Supply remained tenuous throughout most of the war and on the majority of military fronts, and the loss of wagonloads of corn or of consignments of jackets or shoes could be as serious as the loss of the soldiers themselves.

The desertion of men in these support services, or their refusal to continue to work for the armies without being paid—a very real problem in a period when those on the government payroll were being made to wait weeks and even months before receiving any remuneration, and when that remuneration finally trickled through in the form of devalued and near-worthless *assignats*—remained persistent thorns in the side of the military. So did the fraudulent disposal of army property and the pillaging of rations and supplies, both by the soldiers themselves and by their civilian suppliers. It was this constant drain on foodstuffs and weaponry that led many deputies on mission in Year II to turn the full weight of their authority against *fraudeurs* and that encouraged Saint-Just in the Nord to adopt as his emblem the punitive slogan, "Subsistances militaires, guerre aux fripons," accompanied by the unambiguous device of the guillotine (23). For the military authorities, the cost of desertion involved not only the loss of trained and seasoned soldiers, but also the theft of whatever equipment they happened to be carrying at the time of their departure. Reporting from the Armée des Pyrénées-Orientales in Year II, Soubrany and Milhaud emphasized the importance of such losses of equipment, especially of bayonets, and reminded the French public that persistent thefts of arms and clothing could have an effect on the military strength of the country every bit as serious as the loss of the recruits themselves (24). Their fears were echoed throughout the war years, with ministers issuing appeals to areas of the country where losses were deemed to have reached intolerable proportions (25). The law came to make distinctions between acts of desertion, judging their gravity by various criteria, including the question of arms and equipment. Had a man deserted his post "avec" or "sans bagages?" By Year XII the answer to this question could make a fundamental difference to the fate that awaited the deserter. The death sentence was prescribed for any deserter who "aura emporté ses armes ou celles de ses camarades"; hard labor ("le boulet") for the man who "aura emporté des vêtements ou des effets appartenant à ses camarades," the same penalty as was reserved for those who deserted on foreign soil (26). The way in which the law was framed was an accurate guide to the level of public alarm about losses of army tunics and military hardware. By 1808 the sale of even part of one's uniform after deserting from the armies led automatically to an appearance before a *conseil de guerre* (27).

Yet the disappearance of large quantities of army equipment was not stamped out by such Draconian legislation; it continued to anger officers and civilian administrators throughout the Empire. This can be explained in part by the fact that men deserted on the spur of the moment, or when a favorable opportunity presented itself, and it was more than likely that they would be in uniform at the time. Short of stripping naked, most soldiers had little alternative but to take their army-issue clothing with them when they left. It could single them out in a crowd as likely deserters and betray them to the villagers on whose charity they were so dependent; but until they had the opportunity to sell it or to exchange it for less distinctive raiment, they were effectively obliged to remain in uniform. In any case, clothing was expensive, and French peasant boys were well aware of the value of the cloth on their backs. Whatever the danger, it would not come easily to them to throw away good material that could keep them or others in their family warm on winter nights. One temptation, therefore, was to disguise the uniform with ribbons or patching, or to tear off telltale indications of its military origin. Pierre Sers and the departmental administration in the Gironde showed a keen understanding of the care and frugality of the average peasant when they suggested that uniforms were more frequently "dénaturés" than destroyed, which should have made the policing of desertion somewhat easier at least in rural areas (28). It was not just chance or circumstance, however, that dictated that men deserted with their equipment wherever possible. The long weeks or months on the run would have to be financed, and their uniforms were their most immediate form of currency. Traveling merchants, second-hand dealers, *forains,* in fact anyone out to make a quick profit might be expected to offer money or civilian clothing in return for a uniform in a decent state of repair. At Languedic in the Morbihan two men were arrested in 1806 for exchanging their own rather ragged clothes for the uniforms of returning soldiers (29). At Versailles, more ominously, Pierre Lamy was charged with receiving stolen uniforms as part of a commercial racket. It was noted that he specialized in the purchase of army jackets and trousers and that his premises were stacked with stolen military property. He was well-known to deserters in the neighborhood as an unscrupulous dealer to whom they might hope to unload the goods they had taken at the time of their desertion or had carried home on their backs after making their escape (30). For the man who signed on without any real intention of soldiering, who took his bounty and looked for his first chance to escape, the equipment that he was issued could help supplement his financial gain. The case of one recruit from the *levée des 300,000* in 1793 is perhaps instructive. A laborer from the village of Spycker in the Nord, he got as far as Douai before deciding that army life was much too hard and miserable, having spent most of his signing-on bounty of 250 *livres* by the time of his desertion. Asked if he still had his arms and uniform, he gave an illuminating account of the ready market for military property in the area. He told his interrogators

qu'il a vendu son habit d'uniforme au cabaret de Saint-Roch à ce qu'il croit un des fripiers de Douay, à un homme de la maison, moyennant trente livres, et qu'il en avait déjà acheté une autre couleur marron à un dragon, qu'il a vendu son avresac sur la place dans une cave, moyennant cinq livres, à un étranger, qu'il a laissé son fusil dans sa chambre, et n'a vendu ses effets qu'à l'instigation de deux dragons qui l'avaient engagé . . . (31)

The rest of his clothing, his trousers, two shirts, and two pairs of shoes, he had sold to a friend who could make use of them, and he admitted that he had parceled them up and sent them off on the mailcoach to his friend's home in Wormhout. Finding a market for good clothing never presented a problem.

The traffic in army surplus was not restricted to boots and tunics, and some deserters opened themselves to the charge that their appropriation of state property amounted almost to wholesale looting. Horses, always marketable in country areas, were particularly favored by those fleeing from their regiments because they both helped the initial escape and raised revenue once a safe distance had been reached. In peasant France there were few who could not be tempted by the opportunity for a bargain where livestock was concerned, and horse fairs were notoriously corrupt, the natural habitat of thieves and swindlers. The large numbers of horses maintained by any regiment during this period created an obvious focus for temptation, especially in those moments when discipline became lax in the French ranks. In 1793, for instance, dragoons from the Third Regiment of the Nord were known to be circulating among the fairs and markets of the country around Avesnes offering army horses for sale, using deceit and cunning to persuade potential purchasers of their integrity. In the words of the departmental authorities, angered by the suggestion that their fraud was being in any sense condoned by officialdom, they "ont la bassesse de vendre leurs chevaux et leurs équipages, sous le prétexte qu'ils sont désertés de l'ennemi où la lâche trahison de Dumouriez les avait conduits" (32). Some deserters, more brazen than others, set themselves up in trade on the basis of their thefts, apparently using the camouflage that this gave them to avoid suspicion and possible arrest. One man who worked in the army stables had taken full advantage of his position of trust. When he was arrested, again near Avesnes in Year II, he had three army horses in tow and three foals that he had been in the process of training. In addition, he had the bridles and harnesses for the animals, also a very valuable commodity, and a wide range of assorted booty plundered from military stores:

> Sur deux desquels chevaux étaient deux grands sacs, dont un contient du houblon et l'autre des linges, habillements de femme et d'enfant et deux tentes que nous ignorons si elles servaient à l'usage des Républicains français ou des Autrichiens. (33)

He looked, in other words, less like a deserter from the Armée du Nord than a bona fide merchant, making his rounds of the local markets and livestock fairs.

The losses that most alarmed the military were those of firearms and ammunition, which remained in short supply throughout the greater part of the war and which at times undermined the effectiveness of individual units and threatened the security of particular fronts. For the man on the run from authority, the advantage that a rifle or shotgun gave him was not in doubt. He had an immediate means of self-defense, it deterred the officious bystander who might have been tempted to curry favor by turning him over to the *gendarmes,* and, like other pieces of equipment, it had an instant market value when the need for food or money became too great to bear. The army conscript, unless he deserted in the first hours of his service, would have benefited from some basic training in its use. The possession of a gun not only frightened others, it boosted his morale and gave him a degree of status in the rather macho world of peasant France. The law on the possession of firearms was precisely framed to limit the potential damage to public order. In the Dordogne in Year XII, for example, ordinary citizens could not freely carry guns and rifles around the countryside on the pretext that they needed them for hunting; only *gardes-champêtres* and national guardsmen enjoyed that privilege. For others the privilege was conditional on obtaining a certificate from the local mayor, who was in turn restricted in his largesse. He was allowed to give permits only to landowners and other citizens who had fixed residence in his commune and were "d'une solvabilité notoire," and before being valid these permits had to be countersigned by the chief of the local *gendarmerie* (34). The authorities were well aware of the threat to security posed by the large number of armed soldiers who had taken refuge in the countryside, of men sufficiently desperate to use their weapons if they were cornered or threatened with exposure. They also recognized that hunting parties were often little more than a cover for other crimes, that "le délit de la chasse n'est souvent que le prétexte et l'occasion de crimes" (35); however, in practice little was done to restrict the established freedom of the countryman to carry a shotgun and defend his property. Large-scale desertion in an area simply increased the already sizable number of firearms in circulation and opened the countryside to greater violence and lawlessness. In parts of France close to military fronts vast arsenals of weapons were soon circulating from hand to hand, sold by fleeing conscripts to local villagers "qui les ont metamorphosées en armes de chasse," with an immediate effect on the level of poaching in the vicinity (36). Demand seldom slackened. As soldiers passed through villages and hamlets they were frequently importuned by local people seeking to buy guns and cartridges for purposes that almost certainly were not permitted by law. In the West, indeed, it was suspected that purchases from impoverished deserters were going straight into the armories of *chouans* and royalists, even if the actual purchaser might seem innocent of any political involvement (37). Unscrupulous merchants quickly realized that this was a market they could turn to their advantage. When a gunsmith's shop at Nivelles in the Nord was raided by police in 1814, it was discovered to contain an Aladdin's cave of military equipment, bought cheaply from deserters and offered for sale to the village community. Among these trophies were an unworn gray military greatcoat and a pair of white army trousers. The arsenal of stolen weapons included rifles of both French and foreign manufacture, pistols and shotguns, a total of 216 firearms in working order and suitable for the defense of France (38). Human greed ensured that there would always be gunsmiths ready to exploit the insatiable appetite of rural society for shotguns and other weapons. And deserters would always be tempted to risk the higher penalty that desertion with their rifles generally incurred.

If the general staff was concerned by the cumulative effect of all these losses on the capacity of the army, it was equally alarmed by the implications of large-scale desertion for those soldiers who were left behind. For the serious immediate effect of losing comrades through desertion was not to strengthen the determination of those still in the ranks, as army propaganda liked to pretend, but rather to corrode what morale existed among the soldiery. The fact that others were leaving seemingly freely for home only served to remind the men who stayed behind that they were also homesick and wanted to see their families. They too longed for the open road, for the smell of cut hay on their farm and the open skies of their *pays*. To many young conscripts service was bearable only because it was a shared experience first and foremost with others from the same villages and same valleys. Companionship was the more vital in that so many of the normal creature-comforts were denied them. In their letters home from the front, it is striking how often it was the other lads of the village about whom they craved news and gossip—seldom the girls (39). The army as a social unit depended so utterly on adolescent male sociability, and when they were deprived of their friends, either through maneuvers or death or desertion, the crippling effect on their morale was felt. Lads from the Drôme condemned to the hostile landscape of Savoy in 1813 made their dependence on one another very clear in their hastily written notes to their parents. Jean Chuilon made no pretense that the soldier's life had any appeal for him. In "ce maudit pays de la Savoie" he had been exposed with the others to an endless series of deprivations and degradations. "Nous y avons été logés comme des pauvres malheureux," he wrote, "dans les écuries avec les animaux, sans draps ni couvertures, en un mot dans toutes sortes de saloperie." But he found solace in the company of others from his *pays,* including twenty-two from his own rural canton, a fact that gave him strength in even the most taxing conditions (40). Equally, it was when this source of reassurance was removed that the soldier became most inconsolable, most destructively *grognard.* When Louis Berton from near Crest found himself separated from his friends from home, he was miserable and dejected. It was then, for the first time, that he began to curse his luck in being incorporated, to admit to his parents and anyone else who would listen that "si j'avais sçu comme il se passe dans l'état militaire, jamais je n'auray parti" (41). The desertion of a soldier's friends made him want to desert and certainly made him unwilling to play the part of a dutiful and cooperative soldier. It evoked wails of distress and self-pity from men who saw no future for themselves but drudgery, discipline, disease, and probable death far from their farms and families. Soldiering, wrote François Crosnier in 1811 to his parents back in the Oise, was "le plus triste sort que l'on puis avoir dans le monde. Car je donnerais bien la moitié de ma vie pour en être sorti . . ." (42). Of course those with a grudge against the Revolution could make mischief with such sentiments and could stir up a sense of revolt; but the demoralization often ran deeper. As Claude Petitfrère has rightly noted in the context of Toulouse in 1793, "ces abandons ne manquent pas d'avoir une conséquence déplorable sur le moral des soldats restés fidèles" (43).

This in turn made it difficult for the French armies to deal effectively with the problem of desertion in their own ranks. How severely could they afford to repress cases of *désertion à l'intérieur,* where the security of the troops was not directly affected and where no charge of treason could be brought? If they repressed too enthusiastically, there is little doubt that they would have lost the sympathy of the majority of the men who were, even in normal circumstances, dangerously reluctant to condemn those of their number who abandoned their posts. It was a source of intense embarrassment to officers who had to walk a very thin line between imposing strict discipline and antagonizing the opinion on which they remained dependent for their success. Though attitudes became visibly fiercer as the war continued, there was an understandable reluctance to impose the sort of harsh sentences that would recall the *hussards* of the Ancien Regime (44). In any case, it was not always easy to get such a rigid and penal approach implemented, as the troops responsible for arresting fugitives and bringing them to justice were themselves less than enthusiastic about the role they were expected to play (45). Increasingly, as is well documented, deputies on mission and *conseils de guerre* did attempt to deter others by meting out exemplary justice, by ordering individual deserters to be shot in front of their comrades as a means of encouraging the patriotism of those who remained. Terror of this kind, however, could be terribly counterproductive in a force in which commitment and morale were so very vital to performance and self-sacrifice. The troops lined up to witness the execution of one of their number for abandoning his unit did not necessarily cheer the firing squad or rally to a rousing chorus of a patriotic anthem. In the eyes of many of these youngsters the penalty exacted was out of all proportion to the crime, and while the sight of an execution might indeed deter others as the generals intended, their acceptance was often placid, fatalistic and bitter. Desertion to many soldiers had the character of an everyday incident, not a criminal act implying wickedness or the desire to inflict harm. One young conscript, writing home from Italy in 1813, described the shooting of one of his friends for desertion in tones of pity:

> Nous avons fusillé un de nos camarades et cela m'a fait beaucoup de peine, parce qu'il n'avait pas fait du mal, il n'avait que déserté. (46)

In those few plaintive words he gave vent to the feelings of many of the men who served the Emperor in Italy and Spain—an understanding of the plight of deserters and of the strains that had led them to desert, a complete lack of censure or anger that they had abandoned their colors and their comrades, and a hint of realization that the man on the *peloton d'exécution* could so easily have been themselves.

Desertion put military discipline at risk as well as the morale of the troops. The cohesiveness of the units was undermined as was the authority of the officers. But, more seriously in the revolutionary period, any breach of military discipline could easily be translated into a slight or a deliberate insult directed at the Revolution itself. The war had become by the Year II a political war, a propaganda war as well as a purely military engagement, and the political education of the troops was one of its fundamental aspects. Addresses from the ministries in Paris, patriotic bulletins and newspapers directed specifically at the soldiers, and visitations from deputies on mission whose rhetoric was always political before it was military were all reminders of the educational role that recruitment was seen to be performing (47). Indiscipline and insubordination therefore had implications that extended far beyond those in an ordinary army. The soldier, after all, had rights as well as obligations; to defy military authority was a more comprehensive act, a more deliberate political statement, when his political liberties were guaranteed by law. Saint-Just was merciless in his treatment of those who defiled their status as soldiers of the Republic. For him the strength of the French armies lay precisely in their political character, in "une loyauté envers la nation . . . alliée au métier de soldat de carrière" (48). He saw desertion as the refusal, the betrayal of that loyalty to the nation, to the Republic, and to France itself. For Robespierre the soldier's obligations were those defined by military law. He had no right to question or to overturn military regulations or to disobey the orders of his superior officers unless these officers strayed from the purely military arena and tried to deprive him of his basic political rights, the rights that were bestowed on him by his French citizenship:

> Le soldat a le droit de faire tout ce que la loi militaire ne défend pas. Ainsi qu'un soldat manque à l'appel, à la revue, à quelque exercice, qu'il déserte un poste ou refuse d'obéir aux ordres que ses chefs lui donnent dans l'ordre du service militaire, il viole la discipline, il doit être puni selon les lois. Mais si ces mêmes chefs étendent plus loin leur empire, veulent lui interdire l'exercice des droits qui appartiennent à tout citoyen, si un officier par exemple s'avise de vouloir lui défendre de visiter ses amis, de fréquenter des sociétés autori-

sées par la loi, s'il voulait se mêler de ses lectures, de sa correspondance, pour-rait-il invoquer la discipline et exiger l'obéissance? (49)

In military matters Robespierre, like any other political leader, could only lend support to the authority of his generals and insist on the maintenance of discipline within the armies. In his own words discipline was "l'âme des armées" without which they would be reduced to utter impotence. The denial of discipline, the encouragement of individual decision making among the soldiery or the condoning of desertion could lead only to anarchy, mutiny or to the sorts of problems that the Revolution had suffered at Nancy in the early days of 1790.

Desertion was perceived as a many-headed monster, attacking the armies in various ways: depriving them of manpower, deplenishing their already over-stretched stocks of arms and equipment, threatening military discipline, and placing a strain on the continued loyalty of their troops. Just as importantly, desertion and *insoumission* on the massive scale of these years put at risk the sympathy of the civilian population for the new military institutions of the Revolution and Empire. And if the volunteer and conscript armies were dependent on a certain goodwill from the adolescents who became their fighting strength, so they relied on a measure of empathy from the population at large. The *nation en armes* lost much of its moral authority if it was fighting against the instincts and loyalties of its own population. Yet in many parts of the country the military had indeed forfeited public support by the end of the 1790s, not only through the deep-seated horror of recruitment that colored attitudes in much of the countryside, but also in response to their experience of the armies in their own communities. After ten years of war civilians knew so much more about the armies, or at least had mental images of army life created by their own experiences or by those of sons and brothers at the front. Men returned to their villages on sick leave, or returned wounded and maimed as a result of military action. Others sent searing descriptions of army life in long and self-pitying letters to parents whom they never expected to see again. But for many Frenchmen their mental picture of the army was that provided by the young men they met in the village or on the farm on a daily basis, the *insoumis* and army deserters who had every reason to spread tales of woe and rumors of cruelty and deprivation. The presence of hundreds of thousands of these youngsters, each with an axe to grind against the military, was a powerful agent of antimilitary propaganda throughout the years of conscription and war.

Carefully planted rumors helped to foment these impressions, of course, and the enemies of the government were well aware of the strength of antimilitarism as a stick with which to beat the authorities. In the Drôme in Year VII, for instance, it was noted that "les bruits exagérés" were being avidly listened to in the villages and hamlets, especially in the *pré-Alpes*. These rumors centered on the fate and poor condition of the armies, "sur le dénuement absolu de nos armées, sur l'impunité des dilapidateurs, sur les succès de nos ennemis, sur la pénurie des bras et du numéraire" (50). Public opinion was particularly susceptible to rumors of this kind, and it was ready to believe that recruits were starved and ill-treated by their officers, because deserters in their own communities had done ample groundwork in preparing them for such revelations. The mayor of

Saint-Girons reported in July 1793 that recruitment had become impossible in his commune after rumors had spread like wildfire about the miserable conditions of men fighting on the Spanish front (51). The local people, here as elsewhere, sympathized with the plight of their own brothers and sons and were prepared to believe the worst of army regimentation and army discipline. Moreover, some instances of cruelty and brutality were damningly public, leaving a damaging scar on civilian attitudes to the military. At Langon in 1808 an officer ordered that corporal punishment be meted out to a soldier of the reserve in the course of the periodic review of the troops, an occasion that was watched by hundreds of local people. When they saw the unfortunate victim being beaten with the flat edge of a sword, they reacted angrily, adjudging the treatment "avilissant" and degrading. Violence broke out between the troops and the villagers, with blows exchanged and stones thrown (52). Similarly in 1813 a display of brutality by officers of the Fifty-fifth Regiment in Dunkerque aroused the local population to fury. In this instance firm discipline would seem to have merged into ill-treatment and torture. On a public square in the town, reported the *procureur,* near the theater,

> des officiers du 55e Régiment se sont permis pendant l'exercice de leur troupe d'y attacher à un arbre deux conscrits et de torturer l'un d'eux sur le prétexte de lui redresser la jambe gauche. Ce révoltant spectacle fixa l'attention des passants et attroupa les habitants du quartier et les femmes du voisinage. On s'indigna de ces mauvais traitements, les femmes mères de famille se demandaient si leurs enfants au service de l'état étaient traités de la même manière. Plusieurs officiers se respectaient assez peu pour répondre à ces propos par de grossières injures, une femme fut frappée et une autre arbitrairement arrêtée. Il n'en fallait pas davantage pour exciter beaucoup de tumulte dans un rassemblement aussi nombreux. (53)

Officers in the new mass army could not disregard popular unease with the same equanimity as their predecessors in the Ancien Regime had done, for public opinion now affected the army, and incidents of this kind only served to strengthen the bonds that shielded deserters from arrest and denunciation. Too often isolated cases of abuse or tales of cruelty took their toll on public sympathy and undid much of the effect of revolutionary and Napoleonic propaganda about the national interest and military heroism. When the body of a young soldier was found hanging from a tree near Bordeaux in 1811, his fellow villagers shared in his despair and immediately assumed that he had been repelled by army life and driven by the army to seek escape in suicide (54). They did not stop to question this assumption. To them it was glaringly obvious that the degradation of life in the camps and the savage discipline of the officers bore total responsibility for his untimely death.

Deserters did not single-handedly create a crisis for the armies or turn domestic opinion against the military. Rather they were one ingredient in a complex potpourri of attitudes and experiences. Relations between the army and the civilian population of France were always fluid and uncertain. Like all armies, the men in the colors of the Revolution and the Empire could both stimulate pride and patriotic enthusiasm and cause untold misery and grief among those they met. They were young, buoyant, and often belligerent; they became drunk and violent; they left trails of human devastation in the form of broken hearts and unwanted infants. The relationship between the military and the towns in which soldiers are billeted is never an easy one, and the points of maximal tension were usually to be found in garrison towns along the frontier and in the various *villes étape* that they used along their route. Local people were quick to complain when they felt that their interests were being affected adversely. At Montélimar it was noted rather sourly that the regular passage of men on their way to the Armée d'Italie put intolerable pressure on meat supplies and forced local people to go hungry (55). In rural parts of the Drôme soldiers were held responsible for an alleged deterioration in moral standards. After two decades of exposure to troop movements, the women of the area were turning to prostitution in alarming numbers, assured of a welcome supplement to their meager income whenever a new regiment was passing. There was, it seemed, little that could be done to check the spread of this trade, for the "filles et femmes de mauvaise vie" had become by 1811 "comme des insectes que la saison enfante par milliers"; even the local *curés* had declared themselves unable to suggest a solution (56). It is true that the army could be terribly insensitive in its relations with the civilian population, sheltering behind the belief that in wartime everything must reasonably be subsumed to the cause of victory. Thus feeding the troops must take precedence over the creature-comforts of civilians; and the diseased peasant women of the Drôme had to be sacrificed to the demands of rest and recreation. But was there any excuse for the sort of crass insensitivity shown by the military authorities in the Nord when they simply dumped the effects of the dead in bundles on the village greens for their families to collect without first issuing prior warning or even informing them of their loss (57)? Or for the decision to exhume and re-bury a Protestant soldier who had died in hospital, on the grounds that his Protestant burial amounted to intolerable *fanatisme* (58)? Antics of that kind did little besides inflaming the religious passions of country communities and turning their anger against both the army and the men who served it.

As the scale of the war escalated and more and more troops were deployed, the instances of conflict with the communities through which they passed became more numerous. Soldiers gained a reputation for violence and brawling that may have been exaggerated, which certainly was not unique to the armies of this period, but which nonetheless did much to sour local opinion. In garrison towns in particular everyone seemed to have their story of gross misbehavior by the soldiery, whether at their own expense or that of other townsmen (59). Punches and sabre cuts were doled out fairly indiscriminately. There were serious incidents between soldiers and local conscripts (60), between soldiers and *gardes-forestiers* after disputes about game and hunting rights (61), and even between soldiers and local *agents de police* who had a different view of what the law stipulated (62). When a *gendarme* tried to break up a fight at a *bal public* in Versailles frequented by *vélites* from the garrison, he was insulted and wounded with several sabre thrusts to the head; his colleague saved himself from injury only by sheltering beneath a bar stool (63). Most of the violence, however, stemmed from disputes and drunken arguments between soldiers and the youth of the local community, their peer group in a sense, but with different accents, different clan loyalties, and a resentment of the arrogance often displayed by the military. Disputes over drink could spark off violent *bagarres* involving dozens of people, and inns could be turned into battlefields by the refusal of the barman to serve unwanted guests (64). A silly incident, like a local boy urinating too close to a military post, could rapidly be transformed into an antimilitary riot (65). Cultural differences and language difficulties only served to fuel the flames. In Montélimar, where there had been a long history of bad blood between the men of the garrison and the townspeople, a major confrontation developed in 1806 between the Ligurian troops who were at that moment on garrison duty and the young of the city. It began innocently enough, when one group of local lads passed comment on the harsh treatment that a soldier was meting out to a prisoner in his charge. Tempers became frayed, the soldiers rallied around their comrade and became abusive, and it all ended with the Ligurians, bayonets drawn, advancing menacingly on the local population as they streamed out of church (66). Rowdy high spirits could so easily turn into ugly incidents. At Saint-Cloud in Year VI troops newly returned from the Vendée went on a drinking spree in the town's bars. All might have passed quietly had they not stumbled on a wedding party, whereupon fighting broke out and the wedding celebrations rapidly assumed the guise of a gangland vendetta (67). Tension was rarely absent in the relations between communities and the military personnel imposed on them. Their violence was resented all the more strongly because they were outsiders, people for whom the commune felt, despite the government's efforts, little responsibility or fellow-feeling. There were occasions, indeed, when the traditional battles between journeymen's confraternities, so much a part of the eighteenth-century urban landscape, were transferred to contests between local artisans and soldiers from elsewhere, identified as a collective interest just like the traditional groups of *gavots* and *dévoirants*. Police reports refer to battles between soldiers and several journeymen from the same trade, pitched battles that suggest a certain formality, certain familiar ground rules. At Chaudesaigues in 1807 one such battle between *cordonniers* and soldiers ended tragically, with one of the shoemakers left dying by the roadside (68). The locals often felt that the authorities, whether the *gendarmes* or the courts, looked on soldiers with unwonted charity after such incidents, and there were demands that military killers should be treated like any others. Again the general feeling was that the state tended to protect its own, and that the violent excesses of the troops were too easily condoned. When, for instance, a dragoon killed a local coachman in a brawl at Versailles in 1809, it was pointed out in his defense that he was one of the finest soldiers in his regiment and that "sa rixe nocturne avec un cocher yvre n'a été qu'un malheur causé par les ténèbres." He got off very lightly with a year's jail sentence, and local people were entitled to ask whether the law provided them with any protection against a murderous soldiery (69).

Bullying and the use of violence were not the only habits that soldiers picked up while serving abroad and inflicted on their countrymen once they returned to French soil. In Germany and Italy rape was widely tolerated, and it was even expected that local girls would provide sexual pleasure for French troops. But back in France there was understandable outcry when soldiers on garrison duty expected the same services from the local population. In Nantes in Year IV there was an angry howl of protest against the licentious behavior of men from the Eighth Battalion of the Seine-Inférieure, who attacked two local women, one of them barely sixteen years old, in a night of drunken orgy. One was dragged behind the Faubourg Saint-Clément and beaten with nettles; the other was the victim of a gang rape and seriously hurt. "Elle éprouve," in the words of the medical report, "dans les organes de la génération des douleurs avec chaleur et engorgement produites par la répétition d'actes effrénées qu'ont exercés sur cette citoyenne, avec violence, plusieurs militaires" (70). Public opinion was not easily assuaged. When a seventeen-year-old girl was attacked and repeatedly raped in the Forêt de Rambouillet in 1813 by a number of lads from the Ecole Militaire at La Flèche, local people came to her defense and injuries were inflicted in the fighting that ensued. But again it was alleged that the army too easily covered its tracks and prevented the guilty parties from being brought to justice. In this case the young men concerned were subject to military discipline only, and the light sentences imposed—the two ringleaders were charged, and one of them was given a month in prison—did nothing to restore confidence among local people (71). Women, it was widely felt, were not safe in military towns; nor, only too frequently, was property. When garrisons were short of supplies, the temptation to steal and pillage proved hard to resist, especially for those who had just returned from campaigns across the Rhine. On foreign territory the French armies, like all other forces at the time, had few qualms about feeding itself by wholesale pillage, and booty was one of the principal goals of the serving soldier and one of the few ways in which he might hope to turn the war to his personal advantage (72). In his memoirs Philippe-René Girault expresses his reservations about the morality of the policy, but most went about the job of looting with unbounded glee. In Girault's words, looting parties were military "expeditions" like any other, planned and organized:

> Nous partions de notre camp la nuit, ayant à notre suite une cinquantaine de voitures, nous tombions à l'improviste sur un village qui était livré à la dévastation. On chargeait les voitures de tout ce qu'on pouvait ramasser, de tout ce qui pouvait être emporté. Les paysans étaient maltraités, tués quelquefois, les femmes violées, tout était permis. (73)

Such habits died hard. Inns were smashed up by men desperate for drink (74); pigs, sheep, and horses were all stolen by soldiers who were little different from livestock rustlers (75). When a battalion of volunteers from Nyons feared that bread rations were about to run out, their response was both violent and panic-stricken. They attacked and looted local bakers' shops, stealing bread with the same impunity they would have enjoyed in a Dutch or German town. Their justification for looting was very simple, a justification that had long and insidious ancestry in the annals of the military, "qu'on voulait les faire mourir de faim, que cette seule crainte les avait fait agir contre celui que leur ôtoit leurs vivres" (76). Soldiers did not find it hard to convince themselves that local civilians were making fewer sacrifices than they were themselves, and that the civilian population therefore owed them a decent standard of living. But to civilians such acts of theft and banditry were a source of fear of abuse and violence at the hands of the very men who were supposed to be there to protect them. It was indefensible, as the department of the Seine-et-Oise clearly recognized following a spate of thefts around Rueil, when "des hommes . . . armés et salariés pour la défense commune ne seraient que de vils brigands et d'infâmes assassins" (77).

When soldiers on active service came into close contact with civilians, incidents of this kind were difficult to avoid. Although conscripts came from the same sorts of background as the people they antagonized, army life, with its artificial restrictions on movement and its rather forced masculine sociability, reduced their tolerance of others and sharpened their native aggression. Soldiers too often showed their contempt for *pequins* and translated their contempt into brusque words and rough treatment. At Macon men of the sixty-ninth *demibrigade* amused themselves during the burial service of the bishop in Year XI by tying one of the mourning bands around a dog's tail and listening to its yelps. This caused them great hilarity, but it deeply shocked devout Catholic opinion in the town (78). Gratuitous physical violence was equally unwelcome. Near Ercé in the Ariège a number of soldiers were given the task of intercepting a shepherd who was believed to have stolen a flock of sheep from someone else's barn. Local people approved, until the men used such force on their unfortunate victim that he died of his injuries (79). Authority and vandalism were never far apart in garrison towns, and soldiers were prone to make themselves unwelcome guests. The town council of Pierrelatte made it clear just why having troops billeted in a community was seen as something of a burden. The dossier of misconduct and wanton destruction was overpowering. One unit had been responsible for theft and vandalism on an epic scale, with cases of wine stolen, bills left unpaid, houses wrecked, and the *billets de logement* torn up by men intent on finding themselves more lavish accommodation. The town survived the visit, but felt as though a plague of locusts had descended on it (80). It was where the troops felt that they had a grudge to settle or that they were morally justified in wreaking revenge that the worst excesses were committed. In the Vosges, for example, the countryside around Rambervillers was laid waste by troops who claimed that they were rooting out brigandage and punishing the families who sheltered the perpetrators (81). And in the Vendée the self-righteous assumption that all *Vendéens* had lent their support to counterrevolution meant that army units felt at liberty to pillage and loot as they would in enemy territory. The soldiers believed that they had every right to punish people whose sympathies they condemned, and they cited the authority of the Committee of Public Safety in their defense. The result was almost total destruction in selected areas, like Cholet. Animals were seized, fodder looted, buildings set alight. "Le domicile du patriote," complained the municipal council of Challans, "est pillé, incendié, comme le repaire des brigands . . . rien n'a été épargné par les militaires qui étaient envoyés pour protéger les propriétés des bons républicains" (82).

As the war continued it is not difficult to appreciate why relations between soldiers and civilians could become somewhat fragile, or why towns that had not been officially designated to receive troops objected loudly when soldiers were allocated to them (83). In this climate of distrust and suspicion that had been created, deserters could rely on added sympathy, refractories shelter more securely in the bosom of their community; and they did not hesitate to take advantage of this new found confidence to stir up further animosity toward the military. As for the army itself, it was well aware of the dangers that such complicity posed both for its reputation and for future recruitment. It tended to shelter behind the myth that the youth of France was naturally brave and patriotic, and that the antimilitarism that had grown up in much of the country was the work of *malveillants*. There were, in the view of one divisional commander, no limits to the intrigues and seductions to which local communities were a prey. False rumors were being spread to cool the ardor of the young, scare stories about the reality of life in the regiments, lies about the imminence of peace and the disbandment of the armies. Pity and humanity might lie at the heart of such stories, but they did incalculable damage: "Dans quelque communes on s'apitoye sur leur sort, et pour les dégoûter du métier des armes on leur assure qu'arrivés aux dépôts généraux ils seront enchâinés" (84). Sometimes the damage was more subtle and more deliberate. Villages in the Finistère where conscripts were billeted on their way to join their units were accused of abusing their trust by attempting to spread revulsion among their young guests. Far from honoring them as the nation's heroes, they were putting temptations in their path, "on les isole dans des fermes où sont apostés des embaucheurs et autres gens contre-révolutionnaires, et on les met à contribution pour leur procurer un gîte que la loi leur accorde sans rétribution" (85).

The military saw it as their duty to protect young conscripts as far as was possible from the contaminating influences of civilian society, and stressed to the troops the perils that could result from too ready fraternization with the local communities through which they passed. Regulations were deliberately devised to prevent men on garrison duty from mixing too freely with the day-to-day life of the inhabitants. Civilians found hanging around army barracks were assumed to be up to no good. Women offering to sleep with conscripts in the towns and villages that lay in their path were suspected of seducing them away from their duty (86). Letters from the outside world were likewise regarded as a possible source of contamination. The Minister of War was alarmed in Year XII to find that men who had returned from army service to enjoy a peaceful, undisturbed existence with their families, including many who had deserted, were corresponding with their friends in their old regiments, urging that they too should desert, and assuring them that they had nothing to fear once they were back in their *pays* (87). Letters from parents to their sons in the armies were sometimes intercepted when it was suspected that they could be inciting disobedience, letters like those written to two young men stationed with their infantry regiment at Blaye in the Gironde in 1814, which specifically pleaded with them to desert and come home to help on the farm (88). The implication was quite clear that army discipline was carefully constructed around the myth that desertion was rare and would be severely punished, and that the puncturing of this myth, from whatever source, would undermine morale and the strength of the armies. The logic of this was that men should be kept as far from the contaminating effects of civilian society as was reasonably possible so as to keep the myth intact and to maintain tight control over information and propaganda. The danger of *mal du pays* meant that the military tried to keep men from the same area together in the same unit; but they were equally keen to avoid letting units remain too close to their native village lest the temptation to desert prove overwhelming. In Year III General Perrin expressed regret that a battalion from the Drôme would have to spend a substantial period of time on garrison duty in Avignon, since the proximity of their homes "les engage peut-être à s'y rendre sans s'inquiéter des règles de la subordination" (89). Those local administrations on whom responsibility fell for ensuring that their units did not desert were equally uneasy when they were posted too close to home. Pamiers, for instance, wrote to the military authorities in Year III to complain that volunteers from the Ariège were being incorporated in the Armée des Pyrénées-Orientales at Perpignan instead of being sent farther afield. "La proximité de leurs foyers," they wrote, "est la principale cause de leur désertion. Il serait très à propos de les faire passer dans des armées plus éloignées de leurs familles" (90). There seemed to be a rare shaft of unanimity in this regard. Everyone agreed that if desertion were not to continue to ravage the armies of the Republic and Empire, civilian and military society must be kept rigorously separate.

As long as desertion did maintain its ravages, as long as the state failed to convince civilian society of its military duties, the French armies necessarily remained weakened, both numerically and morally. The lack of harmony between civilian and military administrations was a persistent cancer in revolutionary France and one that lasted well into the Empire. And the army's image remained to that degree tarnished in the eyes of the population at large. This in turn had serious implications for successive levies and conscriptions and was clearly a matter of concern to central government. It was impossible to divorce the army from its image. Soldiering was about *élan* and style, a certain swagger and bravado, and a successful army was made by more than laws and decrees. The first volunteers back in 1791 realized this only too well. As the men of the First Battalion of the Cantal reminded their political masters, it would take more than the promulgation of a recruitment law to excite patriotic sentiment in the young men of the southern Auvergne. In their words, it took *fêtes* and *farandoles* and a certain gaiety of spirit: "Quelques volontaires, avec un tambour, des cocardes tricolores, et la bouteille à la main, feraient plus de prosélytes pour défendre la patrie que tous les discours et lectures possibles" (91). It was a message that Paris was forced to take to heart. The image of the military had somehow to be improved, and the damage inflicted by deserters on that image to be undone. The threat to the success of the armies was too grave and too immediate to be borne with equanimity.

9

The Build-up of State Repression

FOR THE STATE, desertion and *insoumission* posed a double threat: to civil order that emanated from the widespread defiance of the recruitment laws and the subsequent increase in crime and counterrevolutionary activity, and to military order that resulted from the refusal of large numbers of soldiers to serve in their designated units. Given the scope of governmental ambitions, these were threats that had to be taken seriously, and tolerance for deserters or respect for their freedom of conscience were never marked characteristics of the period. The concern for the individual rights of the soldier that were so loudly vaunted in the early months of the Revolution soon gave way to an insistence on more traditional virtues, like obedience and military discipline. In Year II Baudot might proclaim that it was Jacobin philosophy that officers should henceforth be held responsible for errors, not ordinary soldiers: "La démocratie," he insisted, "commande l'humanité pour le soldat et réserve la terreur pour les généraux" (1). But if there was ever much humanity shown toward the soldier, it was short-lived. Such was governmental alarm at the rate of defiance in the ranks of the army that the crushing of desertion and *insoumission* were soon counted among the very highest objectives of the state. By Year III the "discipline consentie" of the Jacobin years had already given way to what Albert Meynier has termed a "discipline imposée" (2). A new disciplinary code introduced harsher penalties, including the death sentence for a whole cluster of military offenses, such as desertion to the enemy, *abandon de poste,* or the surrender of a garrison position before it had been militarily breached (3). Desertion within the frontiers of France generally earned five years in the hulks; desertion abroad, especially in those cases where soldiers allowed themselves to be seduced by foreign *embaucheurs,* could mean a sentence of death. In Year VI alone there were 349 such executions, with the condemned man publicly humiliated before the massed ranks of his comrades before being handed over to the firing squad (4). Ministers were unanimous in seeking a penalty that would deter others, so as to keep the maximum number of soldiers at their post.

187

Under Napoleon penalties were stepped up further and military law was firmly imposed, but always with that same aim of deterring waverers and supplying the generals with the largest number of active troops. Napoleon's military code was severe, but it was not intended to repel French opinion and remained far removed from the barbarism of the Ancien Regime. The framework of Napoleonic repression was established by the decree of 19 *vendémiaire* XII, which set up eleven *dépôts militaires* for those convicted of *insoumission* and which established mandatory fixed penalties for both refractories and army deserters. Refractories were given a fixed sentence of five years in one of the *dépôts,* along with a fine of 1,500 francs; for deserters the fine was double that figure, and the prison sentence varied according to the circumstances of the individual offense. Recidivists, those deserting with their equipment, and those deserting on foreign soil were condemned to ten years' *boulet* in the hulks, while the offense of simple desertion incurred a two-year detention with hard labor on a public works scheme. The death sentence was prescribed for the most serious categories of desertion only: desertion to the enemy, desertion abroad with subsequent incorporation in an enemy unit, the leadership of a band of deserters where it could be demonstrated that the leader induced the others to revolt, and acts of violent insurrection by those already sentenced to the *boulet* against their guards or overseers. Whereas refractories were judged by ordinary courts, special *conseils de guerre* passed sentence on those charged with desertion. The distinction between the two categories, the one defined as civilian offenders, the other as in breach of military law, was now quite clearly drawn. The refractories had a rigorous regime in the *dépôts,* being organized in military companies and receiving the same bread supply and the same pay as ordinary soldiers, but deprived of pocket money, billeted in a barracks apart from the rest of the army, denied the right to leave their barracks except by special permission and in the company of a *sous-officier,* and condemned to live on half-rations. They wore a special uniform and wore their hair especially short, performed the normal fatigues and exercises required of other soldiers, but were required to exercise with rifles without bayonettes for reasons of security. The convicted deserters, in contrast, were expected to perform their military exercise and their labor without pay; they were no longer considered to be active soldiers during the period of their sentence (5). These penalties remained in force until 1808, when they were increased once more, especially for the considerable number of deserters convicted for the second or third time. And in 1811 the death penalty was further extended to cover those men who benefited from an amnesty for their crimes of *insoumission* or desertion, and who subsequently deserted a second time (6). As the armies became more and more embroiled in Russia and in the Peninsula, Napoleon became increasingly impatient with those who left their units or who persistently refused to perform their military service.

How effective was this legislation in persuading the public of the seriousness of the state's resolve? Much depended, of course, on the willingness of the courts to convict and to impose sentences that many in the local community regarded as too severe. Since refractories were tried throughout this period before ordinary district tribunals, it was generally against them and those who had offered them assistance that the government found it most difficult to secure convictions. In many parts of France courts seemed less than enthusiastic in their approach to such cases, and even when the charge involved acts of violence and armed rebellion, local tribunals were apt to regard the outcome with supreme indifference (7). In the Gironde there was complaints that those accused were being acquitted because of "la funeste indulgence du jury" (8). More serious for the government was the overall lack of cooperation in *chouan* country, where it was sometimes impossible to assemble a jury of any kind, given the fear that the journey to attend the court inspired in most potential jurors (9). Cases of *insoumission,* even when aggravated by brigandage, were foundering in the Drôme because once again courts were refusing to support the government's cause. In Year V the *commissaire* of the Directory in Pierrelatte, one of the most lawless areas of the Southeast, protested angrily that his job had become impossible because of the protection offered by the district tribunal to those criminals who enjoyed a measure of local sympathy. The courts, he suggested, "autorisent les citoyens dans le refus qu'ils font de payer les impôts ou d'obéir aux réquisitions" (10). The irritation of officials thwarted in their attempts to secure propaganda triumphs was often evident as they lashed out angrily at the laxity with which justice was administered. In the Pyrénées it was noted that a successful prosecution in recruitment cases often depended on the social standing of the family of the accused, and that in some instances the local *procureur* was making minimal efforts to bring cases to court (11). Even where the evidence against a refractory or deserter seemed quite overwhelming, it did not necessarily follow that he was prosecuted. Take, for instance, the case of Thélot, a *réquisitionnaire déserteur* arrested in the Eure in Year VIII on what looked like substantial grounds for suspicion. For Thélot "a été trouvé saisi de trois pistolets en bon état et d'un poignard. Il avait cinquante cartouches de calibre et une assez forte provision de poudre. Il a déclaré hautement qu'il était royaliste, de la compagnie de Huigaud et Frotté, dont il espérait de prompts secours. Il a menacé les citoyens qui l'ont arrêté de les assassiner s'il recouvrait sa liberté . . ." (12). Yet there seemed a real danger that he would never be put on trial, given the strength of local sympathy and the significant fact that the director of the jury chanced to be his father. It is little wonder that some prefects felt that their efforts were blocked by the influence of the families of the accused, or that, in the words of the prefect of the Cantal, "l'action des tribunaux" often risked being "neutralisée" (13).

The general unpopularity of conscription ensured that local opinion could seldom be relied on to add weight to the government's cause. Often the pressures on local tribunals blatantly favored the accused, and there are numerous cases in which administrators could only stand by while the spirit of the law was flouted. Humanitarian reasons could so often be found to justify a reduced penalty or to provide grounds for acquittal, with the result, for example, that mayors who had shown indulgence to refractories were being acquitted to the Drôme on the somewhat spurious grounds that they had done so out of pity for the accused and not for personal gain (14). To the prosecutor such decisions constituted a travesty of justice, with local officials and judges destroying months of careful preparation and police work. At Douai, for instance, the civilian court had refused to impose the death sentence that a *conseil de guerre* had passed five years previously on a deserter who had been arrested for his part in a "rassemblement séditieux et armé" near Arras. The judges argued that that sentence had been passed *en contumace,* before the accused had been captured, and that the judgment had been given under a law that had since been repealed. But to the military authorities it seemed like just another instance of the weakness and indecisiveness of criminal justice where desertion was concerned (15). Such accusations were especially prevalent in the West, where courts were reluctant to arouse the locals by imposing harsh sentences on men who enjoyed a wide measure of popular support. Even the prefect in Vannes was willing to reduce the fine levied by the court on men who had deserted on their way to join their units, "attendu que tous sont enfants de cultivateurs, fermiers, artisans, ou manoeuvres" (16). Yet by this time the courts were supposed to be imposing fixed penalties, with crushing fines of 1,500 francs on all parents of *réfractaires,* regardless of their personal circumstances. In practice in the Morbihan, and perhaps elsewhere, courts were choosing to ignore that law and were allowing themselves the luxury of discriminatory sentencing. In January of 1806 no consistent policy was being pursued by the four district tribunals in the department, for if three of them, at Vannes, Lorient, and Napoléonville, were applying the full fine to all those they convicted, the fourth, at Ploërmel, was systematically showing greater sympathy to its conscripts by cutting their fines to 500 francs (17).

The suspicions and anger of officialdom alighted especially on the most local of all jurisdictions, that of the *juge de paix.* For he was invariably a local man, elected by the people of his canton, and answerable to them in the exercise of his functions. If civil courts in the districts were suspected of laxity, how much more vulnerable to pressure and influence was the *juge de paix,* often isolated among his rural community and cut off from the influence of the prefect and the departmental administration. In some areas their elections were subject to fraud and manipulation, and at Saint-Lizier (Ariège) it was remarked that even deserters on the run in the surrounding mountains somehow managed to cast their votes (18). Ignorance of the law and cowardice in the face of local opinion were the two charges most commonly leveled against the justices. In the West, where that local opinion was frequently counterrevolutionary, this could mean that the application of the law was being left to enemies of the revolutionary cause. The result was highly prejudicial to the implementation of law and order, as the prosecutor at the Tribunal Criminel in Vannes explained in uncompromising terms:

Dans les campagnes la majeure partie des juges de paix est composée de laboureurs qui en général ont été choisis par le crédit des ennemis de la Révolution. Ces juges de paix sont sans connaissance: quelques-uns savent à peine lire et écrire; ils ne sont pas en état de se diriger par eux-mêmes. La plupart ont été élevés par des prêtres qui ont refusé de se soumettre; ils en ont contracté les préjugés, ils se laissent diriger par l'influence de leurs premiers instructeurs, ils ne répondent point à ce que la loi exige d'eux. (19)

Individual cases illustrate graphically the dangers of leaving the policing of desertion in the hands of men whose first loyalty was to their peers and to their own community. What hope had the state of imposing fines on the parents of deserters when the *juge de paix* himself had a son who had deserted, as occurred at Mèze in the Hérault in Year IV (20)? What chance had the army of winning public support for military justice when a *juge de paix* felt free to appeal against its rigors, attempting to overthrow a ten-year sentence on a local deserter on the somewhat spurious grounds that he was already an experienced horseman: "Il est naturel à un excellent homme de cheval de ne pouvoir s'accoutumer aux apprentissages durs et pénibles de l'artillerie" (21)? In the Vosges one rural *juge de paix* was denounced for refusing to take action against local deserters when it was revealed that several of his close relatives were members of a deserter band that was terrorizing the surrounding countryside (22). Another, at Marly in the Seine-et-Oise, not only refused to charge a young man arrested in his canton without a passport, claiming to come from the *dépôt* at Courbevoie, and bearing a certificate from a Paris hospital in the name of another conscript (all reasons for suspicion of desertion), but went so far as to raise a collection from local people to help him on his way (23). Ignorance, corruption, fear, and sympathy were all faults imputed by government administrators to the humble justices of the peace, all reasons why they had little confidence in their abilities and regarded them as the weak link in the chain of judicial authority.

Suspicion of influence by the community on local justices, combined with an increasing distrust of juries in trials involving recruitment offenses, led the governments of the Revolution and Empire to demand greater use of military courts and special tribunals to try major cases without recourse to a jury. The use of the *conseil de guerre* to judge army deserters and those whose crimes were committed while they were technically serving soldiers was intended to guarantee a severe and consistent sentencing policy and to avoid the intercession of public opinion. And where conscription frauds reached epidemic proportions or where rioting in support of deserters posed a major threat to public order—as occurred in the Ariège in 1806 and the Nord in 1813—exceptional measures might be taken to remove jurisdiction from ordinary criminal courts and to establish special courts entrusted with the single goal of rooting out the cause of disobedience (24). Punishments were intended to be severe, as a deterrent to those in the community who were tempted to desert or to offer assistance to men on the run. For those forging documents to deceive the authorities or offering physical resistance to the *gendarmerie,* sentences of ten or even sixteen years of hard labor were common in 1806 and 1807, as the prefect instructed the judges in Foix to purge the department of conscription conspiracies (25). *Conseils de guerre* were also well-known for their lack of sympathy with those who deserted from the armies, and the government could generally rely on the seasoned military men who handed out justice to view the crime with a clear perspective. Military judges suffered none of the conflict of loyalties that marked their counterparts in civil courts, and the sentences passed reflected this single-minded concern for the welfare of the armies and dedication to the interests of the state. Their jurisdiction was a wide-ranging one, involving crimes of any kind committed by serving soldiers or those who worked for the armies and therefore came under military discipline. As early as Year III the law established their competence, so that "tout délit commis par un militaire, ou par tout autre individu attaché aux armées ou employé à leur suite, sera jugé à l'avenir par un conseil militaire." Accordingly, as the Minister of Justice explained, "quelque soit la nature de délit, quelque soit le lieu ou il est commis . . . il est jugé par un conseil militaire; il suffit que ce soit un militaire pour que la poursuite du délit soit faite devant un conseil militaire, car l'article est sans exception" (26). As a result, where members of the same *bande* included both deserters and civilians, the same crime could be pursued before very different courts, and the sentences imposed varied considerably. Those who were judged by a *conseil de guerre* were frequently given savage sentences of hard labor or even death, whereas their fellow-accused were being lightly treated at the hands of civilian courts. Ironically, this often proved even more of an embarrassment to the army than the leniency of local judges, since those receiving severe punishments were liable to appeal and have their sentences quashed on the basis of parity and the dictates of natural justice (27). In general, however, the government was well content with the performance of the *conseils,* which could be depended on to carry out national policy and apply the standard recommended penalities (28). In the eyes of the public at large, however, they acquired a reputation for harshness and arbitrariness, to the extent that even the threat of the *conseil* was sufficient to persuade deserters to return to their units (29). Even government officials occasionally hesitated before referring cases to military justice. At Bazas in Year IV the *commissaire du Directoire exécutif,* considering a case in which two local lads had fired on the *gendarmes* to try to free a friend arrested for desertion, conceded that the offense merited military judgment but held back from signing the necessary order. For even he had no desire to see them shot:

> Les faire juger militairement, cependant, ils ont de grands risques à courir, et la peine de mort est là. Tout bien considéré, j'aimerais mieux en faire des soldats vifs que des soldats morts. (30)

In a letter to the department of the Gironde some weeks later he was to emphasize the same point, that on no account should soldiers be lost to the Republic through the over-zealous demands of military law (31).

If tribunals were used by the government to punish deserters and to deter their comrades-in-arms, they were effective only in cases where the offender had already been arrested and could be brought to trial. Therein lay the government's biggest single problem, as is witnessed by the high percentage of judgments handed down *par contumace* in the absence of the accused, who must be presumed still to have been at liberty in his village or in some mountain retreat. The most effective method of dissuasion for the thousands of young deserters and *insoumis* who risked retribution from the courts was less the example of a few severe sentences than the near certainty that their offense would not go unpunished. It is no accident, therefore, that the bulk of government activity over recruitment was directed at the policing of the levies, ensuring that the young men of each *classe* were informed of their duty, that they turned up for medical inspection and for the *tirage,* left their village on the designated day, and duly completed the journey prescribed in their *feuille de route* to reach their regiment. This was a task that demanded keen vigilance and close policing of the community and that could not be properly executed without a well-defined administrative structure.

The recruitment procedures, as we have seen, became increasingly centralized as time passed, with authority being transferred from the individual mayor—on whom the onus of preparing the first revolutionary levies had rested—to the *sous-préfet* and the *conseil du recrutement* (32). Of course, there was never any possibility of excluding the village mayor from the recruitment process, if only because he alone could provide invaluable information about the personal lives and circumstances of those called, and he alone kept the rolls of the *état civil* in the local community. But his part in the procedures of conscription was systematically cut back, with authority passed first to the canton, then to the *arrondissement,* where the young man's fate was decided by the *conseil* presided over by the subprefect himself (33). In Napoleon's eyes this was a way of eliminating the local variables that had so bedeviled the first conscriptions—the favoritism shown to certain individuals, the lack of understanding of the height and health regulations, the refusal of individual mayors to cooperate in the recruitment operation. In this way, too, it was believed that the multiple opportunities for fraud that had led to so many mayors being put on trial in some parts of the country would be ended. It is true that a few *sous-préfets* were to be implicated in fraud and a number of prefects dismissed for the failure to fill quotas (34); but the chain of administrative command was clearer, the loyalties of the officials undivided, the air of bureaucratic efficiency, and above all of simple normality, finally achieved. If it did not end conscription problems, the administrative centralization of the Empire certainly played a major part in accustoming a reluctant and sometimes rather bemused population to the cold facts of their civic obligation. It is a case where administrative reform must itself be seen as a part of the policing process. So, indeed, must certain of the policy decisions taken with regard to the operation of conscription. The decision, for instance, to levy the Vendée and the rebel areas of the West at a lower rate than the rest of France was, as Jean Tulard recognizes, in essence a simple policing measure: "pour désarmer l'opposition, Napoléon épargne la Vendée: le poids de la conscription y est moins lourd que dans le reste de l'Empire; pour la surveiller, il décide la fondation d'une ville au coeur même de la Vendée et choisit en 1804 le site de La Roche-sur-Yon à la limite du bocage" (35). It was, in other words, less a question of principle or of equity than a policing device, a contribution to the program of pacification in the West. In the same way, the decision to reintroduce *remplacement* in the months following the Loi Jourdan, and subsequently to extend the scope of the law on replacements and substitutes, must be seen as a means of appeasing the wealthier sections of the community, again, as a device to help in the policing of recruitment (36).

Effective policing of this kind was doomed to failure unless the departmental administrations received a flow of information about the whereabouts of refractories and the people who were offering them protection. The capture of deserters was largely dependent on such help, and if *insoumission* were ever to be broken, the authorities knew that they had to establish good relations with at least sections of the local community. In part the information they required could be obtained by bureaucratic means, forcing everyone to register at the *mairie* and to carry official identification whenever they were away from their village. The law of 10 *vendémiaire* IV laid down the terms on which strict surveillance of individuals' movements could be maintained. It stated explicitly that "nul individu ne pourra quitter le territoire de son canton sans être muni et porteur d'un passeport, signé par les officiers municipaux de la commune ou de l'administration municipale du canton" (37). In this way the mayor and local council were obliged to cooperate in providing the infrastructure of police activity, or opened themselves to prosecution for failing in their duties or committing acts of forgery. Once the principle of annual conscription had been accepted, the policing of the young became much easier, as anyone who looked as though he might be of conscription age was liable to be stopped and interrogated as a possible suspect. Harvesters and casual workers who could not easily get their credentials checked by members of the local community were particularly prone to arrest, though anyone who was young and male was vulnerable to police interest, especially at those moments when Napoleon was calling up the reservists of the previous years. Often the interest was aroused by the conscript himself and by his behavior when the troops or *gendarmes* approached the village. Such was the case of Pierre Teychenné, a deserter from the *dépôt* at Perpignan, who ran away when he saw the *gendarmes* on the road from Rimont to Serres in 1808 (38). Others arrested, however, were innocent farmworkers who just happened to be young. At Sartrouville in the Seine-et-Oise in Year VII where, in the words of the *juge de paix,*

> Deux jeunes gens revenant de la moisson, l'un se disant être Etienne Sers, âgé de vingt-quatre ans, et l'autre Maximilien Serre, âgé d'environ vingt ans, one été arrêtés ce matin par la garde nationale et conduits à la maison communale où ils resteront jusqu'à ce que vous ayez certifié que ni l'un ni l'autre n'appartiennent à un corps militaire ou ne sont pas désignés par les lois pour en faire partie. (39)

The insistence that ordinary citizens carry papers and produce them on demand effectively placed the onus of proof on the individual and provided the authorities with a powerful channel of information about the age, commune of residence, and military record of the young.

Information could also be gleaned from people over whom the administration had some control, whose cooperation they were able to obtain by a mixture of threats and inducements. Such people included prostitutes, always operating outside the law and dependent on police tolerance if they were not to spend long months in the *dépôt de mendicité* or local *hôpital*. The police knew very well that prostitutes flourished in periods of war, taking full advantage of the passage of troops through previously peaceful communities and providing deserters with both sexual favors and a safe dwelling-place for the night. Down the Rhône valley it was noted that by 1811 "les poisons de la prostitution ont gagné les campagnes . . . le mal est devenu si grand que la cure en est regardée, pour ainsi dire, comme impossible " (40). Yet what for the health of the community might seem to pose a considerable threat provided the local police with valuable contacts in their campaign against desertion and *brigandage*. Similarly, the authorities could bring direct pressure to bear on innkeepers and lodging house owners through their control of the *patente* that allowed them to remain in business and to sell food and drink (41). In their quest for deserters, just as in the policing of other marginal and itinerant groups, the police turned instinctively toward the local *auberge* as the likely haunt of brigands, criminals, and men on the run from the law. They recognized only too clearly that deserters remained at large because of the complicity of innkeepers who failed to carry out the precise and detailed prescriptions of the police regulations: to enter in an official register "les noms, prénoms, qualités, domicile habituel, dates d'entrée et de sortie de tous ceux qui coucheront chez eux, même une seule nuit." And, noted the prefect of the Cantal rather savagely in 1808, that regulation did not apply only to inn-keepers, but to anyone who offered a room to a stranger or passer-by, to those landowners, peasants, artisans, merchants and *métayers* who hired labor and who received into their own homes "comme commis, employés, ouvriers, ou domestiques, des individus qui n'y ont pas leur domicile habituel" (42). One result of such regulation was to give innkeepers and *logeurs* a responsibility that was beyond their means to honor, since they could not always be in the bar watching customers come and go, and had no means of checking the identity of every stranger who entered their premises. Jean Laroussinie, an *aubergiste* at Arpajon near Aurillac, was charged with *recel* when a deserter was found in his bar; however, he successfully defended himself by pointing out that when the man had arrived, only his *servante* was present and his wife had been away vis-iting a sick relative, while he himself was in another room negotiating with a local farmer about the purchase of some corn (43). Equally, strict police sur-veillance of bars and inns had another effect. For *aubergistes,* often in breach of the law in some other regard, could be pressured by the *gendarmes* into provid-ing the information they required until they became, for all practical purposes, police spies or informants. In frontier areas like the Nord they were a particu-larly valuable contact for the policing of *émigrés* as well as army deserters, and the local administrators deliberately put pressure on them to cooperate (44). In this respect they were only building on well-established patterns of behavior. In Richard Cobb's telling phrase, "the police had what no historian can acquire unless he is working on a near-contemporary movement: experience" (45).

The systematic use of civilian informants such as *logeurs* and *aubergistes* was one aspect of a wider approach to the policing of desertion. For throughout the Revolutionary and Imperial period local administrators and *lieutenants de gen-darmerie* turned increasingly to spies and agents in the local population to iden-tify draft dodgers and those offering them protection. Their employment was essential, it was argued, if deserters and refractories were ever to be brought to justice, otherwise they would have every opportunity to slip off into the dense undergrowth undetected or to seek shelter in one of the many safe houses that existed outside the law. The prefect of the Nord put the case for espionage very bluntly in *fructidor* XIII, after finding his conventional methods of policing frus-trated at every turn. Policing would never produce results, he said "à moins qu'elle ne fût puissamment secondée par des personnes apostées pour leur indi-quer les traces, l'asile des délinquants, et le moment de les arrêter." That in turn implied the existence of a secret fund to offer payment to those who proved helpful because assistance would not be forthcoming otherwise. The spies were helping the government at considerable risk to themselves only in return for cash bribes, and there was no point in pretending that the government could appeal to their patriotic sentiment. In the prefect's words,

> J'observais que l'emploi de ces personnes exigeait que des fonds fussent alloués pour les païer, attendu qu'elles ne passeraient pas leur temps à épier les démarches des conscrits sans l'expectative d'une indemnité. (46)

There was little self-deception on the part of the authorities. They realized that they were appealing to the basest of motives, and the Minister was rightly cautious lest the use of espionage had the effect of turning communities against themselves and encouraging acts of vengeance (47). For what the government was asking was that villagers betray one another and hand over members of their own communities to the forces of order. The failure of conventional police methods to break the solidarity of rural society meant that deceit and treachery were needed if recruitment policy was to have any chance of success. As the prefect of the Mayenne admitted, it was the only means at his disposal if the law were to be other than a complete travesty:

> Ce n'est que par des intelligences secrètes que je suis parvenu à mettre les plus criminels sous la main de la justice. Ils n'ont été arrêtés que parce qu'ils m'ont été en quelque sorte livrés par des habitants animés de l'amour de la chose publique ou excités par des récompenses. (48)

The fact that the conscripts' families were frequently at the center of the conspiracy to protect them against the law made the use of informers seem all the more indispensable (49).

Once the principle was accepted, the reliance on spies became increasingly extensive, and considerable sums were earmarked for undercover work of this kind. By 1814 in the Nord it had become standard practice to allocate moneys for secret policing in all villages where there had been evidence of sedition or instances of rioting against the enforcement of conscription, "pour dissiper les mouvemens séditieux" by the quickest possible means (50). Money was paid to villagers in the Seine-et-Oise in return for what was little more than suggestive gossip about the whereabouts of men suspected of *insoumission* (51). In the Ariège, local people from the valley of Andorra were being recruited to cross into Spain and report back to the authorities on the activities of their fellow Frenchmen, particularly those who were rumored to be sheltering on the other side of the frontier to avoid the army (52). Where the opportunity presented itself, deserters themselves could be most effective agents to report on other fugitives. A *battue générale* in and around the commune of La Plume (Lot-et-Garonne) in 1806 achieved only a moderate degree of success, with a few arrests recorded in an area infamous for concealing refractories. Rather than admit to failure, the authorities changed their tactics and granted immunity to two of the young men they had captured in return for information about the movements of their friends (53). In another case the fact that a deserter chose to give himself up voluntarily was seized on by the prefecture as evidence of his willingness to cooperate. Philippe Duhem from Sédequin fully expected that he would be put in prison or sent back to his regiment. He was only too eager to accept the offer made to him, and agreed that "s'il pouvait obtenir d'être renvoyé dans ses foyers avec un congé, il ferait arrêter des conscrits réfractaires" (54). It was an important breakthrough for the harassed officials, even if it also constituted a serious breach of established police practice. In extreme circumstances military agents were sent into the community with the express intention of winning the confidence of local people and obtaining information about the activities of army deserters. This was most prevalent in areas of brigandage and counterrevolution where the villagers might be too frightened to entrust their safety to *gendarmes* or government officials. But the activities of men like Gély, a rather shadowy figure used by the army in Year IV to extract news of deserters and refractories hiding in the badlands of the Drôme and the Ardèche, show the extent to which the authorities were prepared to go to infiltrate the local community. Gély was busily employed passing back to his military masters snippets of information about the spots where deserters were likely to be hiding so that the divisional commander in the Drôme could take the appropriate action against them (55).

After the Concordat of 1801 ended the open rift between Church and State that had deprived the governments of the Revolution of any assistance from the pulpit, the Catholic church was once again available to government as a channel of influence and information. And there is ample evidence that it was a channel that was extensively used in the cause of bringing *insoumission,* in particular, under control. This was a two-way process, with the Church once again providing spiritual guidance to the faithful on what were essentially political matters, while certain clerics went so far as to cooperate with the authorities by furnishing valuable information about their parishioners and their response to the law. A compliant Church could be useful to the civil administration in so many ways, especially where the refractory conscripts came from devout Catholic homes and where the sensibilities of parents could be cynically played on. The clergy, moreover, were a privileged group under the Empire. Not only could the government expect a degree of gratitude from men whose right to preach and to minister to their congregations derived from a political decision by Napoleon, but they were themselves exempt from military service by an Imperial decree of 1806 (56). Portalis, as Minister for Religious Affairs *(Ministre des Cultes)* had no qualms about profiting from the moral capital that this gave the state, issuing circular letters to his bishops to remind them of their civic responsibilities. The bishops frequently complied, using, or arguably abusing, their episcopal authority in the interests of the Empire.

Examples abound of episcopal letters from politically committed bishops that went far beyond their religious sphere. Writing to the *curés* of his diocese in 1803, the bishop of Saint-Flour stressed that military service was a civic obligation that they should encourage families to accept if family life itself was not to suffer. He called on the priests to make use of the special influence that they alone could exert:

C'est à vous, que la confiance appelle si souvent dans les conseils de famille, à faire entendre le langage de la raison et de la religion. C'est à vous à épargner aux paisibles habitants des campagnes les maux incalculables qui peuvent résulter du refus que font plusieurs jeunes gens d'obéir à la loi qui les appelle à la défense de la patrie.

And he added, as if to seal the bond of obligation between Church and State, the following little homily:

Et en effet nous nous devons à la patrie, c'est une vérité que la raison a reconnue et que la religion consacre: nous ne saurions trop l'inculquer aux fidèles. Cette patrie a le droit d'appeler ceux que leur âge, leur santé et leurs forces rendent propres à la défendre; et il est d'une stricte et rigoureuse obligation pour tous de se rendre à cet appel. (57)

This was the kind of active cooperation that the Minister had in mind, although sometimes the political involvement of bishops could verge on the slavish and become almost embarrassing. The bishop of Vannes had so drilled his clergy in communicating the policies of the government that, in the Minister's words, "jamais je n'avais vu un concert plus unanime entre tous les ecclésiastiques" (58). The bishop of Besançon's pastoral letters could become indistinguishable from eulogies of the Emperor, effusive to the point of idolatry:

Il en est de notre Empereur comme du soleil. Sa présence échauffe, anime tout dans son Empire. Son éloignement y est suivi d'un certain rafroidissement. C'est l'hyver de certains coeurs. (59)

Individual bishops, bullied and persuaded by overanxious prefects, could exceed their powers by threatening those members of the Church who failed to obey the law on recruitment with spiritual as well as temporal retribution. The bishop of Mende, for example, at the bidding of the prefect, urged his clergy to refuse the sacraments to any family that contained refractory conscripts and that failed to hand them over to the civil authority. In 1813 the prefect reported to the Minister of the Interior that the bishop was wholly devoted to the government's cause, that: "J'ai trouvé dans Monseigneur l'Evêque et son clergé le véritable esprit que la Religion commande, l'amour du Souverain et le désir que les loix soient exécutées" (60). Fortunately, perhaps, Paris did not share his enthusiasm and ordered him to restrict himself to measures sanctioned by the law. To withhold holy communion might only serve to stir up hatred of the regime, and if the bishop's instruction were followed to the letter, it would undermine the purpose and authority of the priesthood (61).

The government sought to take advantage of the trust in which the *curé* was generally held, at least in strongly Catholic communities, to harness public support for the recruitment effort and to root out families who were supporting refractories. *Curés* could and did help in a number of different ways. In country areas their literacy and level of education commanded a degree of respect which in turn gave their words an added element of leverage (62). Their prestige stemmed also from the almost superstitious acceptance by many peasants that the priest and he alone held the key to their salvation; it was not for them, therefore, to challenge his wisdom or judgment. Consequently the involvement of the *curé* with every stage of the recruitment process, from the initial conscription meeting to the police activity against the recalcitrant, gave a moral authority to the interest of the state. In the diocese of Vannes the priest had, at the bishop's prompting, assumed the symbolic role of officiating at the *tirage* and accompanying each of his parishioners to the cantonal meeting that would determine his fate (63). The clerical presence was equally strong in other parts of Brittany, notably in the villages around Rennes, where the priests would again identify with the conscripts and their families by saying mass early in the morning of the recruitment meeting, "une messe de très grand matin qu'ils ont appelée la messe de la réunion" (64). In this way the whole process of conscription was sealed within the Christian symbolism and familiar ritual of Breton village life. Pastoral visits were organized in such a way as to alert the clergy to the ways in which they could give active assistance to recruitment. The efforts of the archbishop of Bordeaux in the rural areas of the Southwest, for instance, were deemed to have "bien disposé les esprits" in villages whose sympathies had previously seemed to veer in the support of refractories (65). Increasingly, indeed, priests were urged to involve themselves and their clerical office in what amounted to acts of policing. One *curé* in the Aveyron used his authority to lure conscripts out of their hiding-places so that he could hand them over to the military (66). Another, in the Morbihan, so impressed his congregation with his sermon on the moral perils of *insoumission* that one of his parishioners approached him at the door of the church to turn in his son (67). Such behavior endeared itself immediately both to Portalis and to the Emperor himself. In the diocese of Vannes, the Minister told Napoleon with obvious pride, "les curés et desservants étaient en usage de se réunir alternativement, les uns chez les autres, pour y prêcher l'amour du gouvernement, la soumission aux lois, et les devoirs religieux" (68). One does not have to be deeply devout to find the order of priority of these goals rather interesting.

Antoine-Xavier Pancemont, the bishop of Vannes between 1802 and his death in 1807, committed his clergy so wholeheartedly to the cause of the First Empire that he could with some justice be described as a government agent in the troubled West of France. One of the first bishops to be appointed after the Concordat, he was very clearly a political nominee, in his minister's words, "éclairé et vertueux et plein d'admiration pour le Premier Consul" (69). This meant that he combined his episcopal duties with a policing role in the West directed equally against deserters and refractories, *chouans* and the supporters of the *Petite Eglise*, a role that gained him such notoriety among some at least of his flock that he was kidnapped and held for ransom by *chouans* in the summer of 1806. Significantly, one of the demands of the kidnappers was that the bishop's ring and the *croix de la Légion d'Honneur* which the Emperor had bestowed on him should be surrendered to them, a gesture indicative of their contempt for both his spiritual and his temporal activities in his diocese (70). When his work on behalf of the government is examined, their contempt becomes easy to understand. For the bishop was systematically supplying to Portalis, and through him to the government, detailed information about the political activities of local communities. Suspects were identified by name in his pastoral reports, and conversations overheard in bars and markets were reproduced verbatim for the minister to read and act on (71). The haunts of deserters and counterrevolutionaries were indicated to the Minister, with a recommendation that they be visited or even demolished; demolition, he implies, would be a final solution to the problem of lawlessness that they constituted and a lesson to others in the neighborhood (72). In particular, Pancemont saw it as his role to educate his people in their civic duty as regards conscription. Indeed, such was his enthusiasm for the Imperial armies that his "excellent" pastoral letter on the subject was published in full in the *Moniteur.* "Est-ce blesser la loi de Dieu de se soustraire à la conscription militaire?" asked the bishop rhetorically; "la réponse est 'oui' catégorique" (73). He was quite aware of the value of the information he supplied, and seems to have attached no conditions to his service. On one occasion he went so far as to offer advice on the most promising policing tactics that might be adopted, sharing with his minister not only his intelligence about deserters' whereabouts but also his specialist knowledge of the difficult terrain of the rural Morbihan. Fully conscious of the fact that his reports on supposedly spiritual matters were being passed directly from the *Ministre des Cultes* to his colleague at *Police générale,* Pancemont offered counsel on improvements of technique that would greatly strengthen policing in these isolated village communities along the south Breton coast. Existing practice, he explained, was just too obvious, and suspects were able to read the *gendarmes'* intentions far too readily. For

> on arrive dans une commune le soir, et on ne fait les visites que le lendemain. On ne visite pas avec assez de soin l'intérieur des maisons isolées. On met trop de régularité dans des recherches qui devraient être faites, coup-sur-coup, et au moment où on y pense le moins. On n'a pas la précaution de faire déguiser ceux qui font ces recherches. (74)

It is not an exaggeration to describe part, at least, of the function of this bishop as that of a police spy, working through his contacts and confidences on behalf of the Imperial regime. He was particularly assiduous in matters of conscription, and in several instances seemed intent on turning his *curés* into *gendarmes* in the pursuit of refractories. In fact, he had a number of spectacular successes: the *curé* of Le Faouët encouraged thirteen conscripts to submit, the *curé* of Pontivy a further sixteen, and, most triumphantly of all, the *curé* of Grandchamp, in the notoriously recalcitrant *landes* of the Morbihan, persuaded twenty-one young conscripts to give themselves up and accept the necessity of army service (75). Of course Pancemont was in no sense typical of the Napoleonic episcopacy, though others, like the bishop of Saint-Brieuc, also deemed it their duty to keep the government intimately informed of the activities of local *chouans* (76). But Pancemont's career does indicate how very valuable the restored church could be in the policing of conscription and the supply of privileged information.

The use of spies and agents in this way might pinpoint the whereabouts of deserters or demonstrate the existence of particularly troublesome communes. Rarely, however, could it effect arrests or eliminate refractories. For that purpose the state needed to have at its disposal an efficient and well-drilled police force to act on information received and provide an element of repressive force. In the eighteenth century the capture of deserters had been one of the principal tasks allotted to the *maréchaussée,* the uniformed force that assured such policing as there was in rural areas of the country. In terms of Choiseul's instruction of 1767, the top priority of the *cavaliers* was to patrol main roads and ensure safe communication between different parts of the kingdom. Such patrols had three main functions: to ensure the safety of travelers and the transport of tax receipts, but, first and foremost, to capture deserters (77). Equally, as they were a military force subject to the control of the Minister of War, they were liable to be called on to perform purely military functions, from running the military postal service to disarming the civilian population in times of emergency (78). This is not to say that they executed these tasks efficiently. The archives of the Ancien Regime are well stocked with complaints from the provinces about the inadequacy of the *maréchaussée,* the effects of its venality, and the glaring contrast between what it was expected to do and what its meager resources allowed it to achieve. In contrast to the city of Paris, widely believed to be the best-policed city in the eighteenth century, country areas were sadly neglected (79). The strength of the total force from the *ordonnance* of 1720 until the Revolution was seldom more than 3,500 men. Pay and conditions were just about enough to place the average *cavalier* above subsistence level, and morale was generally very low. From 1778 entry into the force was restricted to those who had already served for at least sixteen years in the army, which had the result of excluding many good recruits and turning the force into a sort of reward for loyal and active service with the military (80). When the revolutionary government abolished the *maréchaussée* in 1790 and offered to replace it with the *gendarmerie nationale,* there were few tears or remonstrances. For many people it seemed as if the problems of an undermanned and disspirited police force were finally to be put to rest.

How far were these hopes realized? The numbers of *gendarmes* were certainly greatly increased, but so were the numbers of missions on which they were sent, with the result that the problem of undermanning did not instantly disappear. Like their predecessors, the *gendarmes* were divided into small units of five or six men, *brigades* generally under the command of a *brigadier,* to maintain order along highways and at markets and fairs. But the work they were expected to cover, especially once war had been declared, multiplied out of all proportion to their numbers. It was the *gendarmes* who in most cases were expected to hunt down deserters and break up brigand bands aside from their normal policing duties. It was a heavy load of responsibility, spelled out carefully by the Minister of the Interior to the departments of France in Year VI. He described the "attributions de la gendarmerie" as

"la répression du vagabondage et de la mendicité, la visite des passeports, la surveillance des routes et des campagnes, l'escorte des deniers publics et des courriers, la translation et conduite des prisonniers, l'assistance aux foires et marchés et autres lieux de rassemblement, la recherche et arrestation des prêtres et autres individus dans le cas de déportation, celle des émigrés, des déserteurs et réquisitionnaires, celle des voleurs, des assassins et brigands . . ." (81).

To make matters worse, since *gendarmes* were still technically military personnel, they could be ordered into action when the needs of the armies demanded it, and local forces found themselves denuded of men in deference to the demands of the battalions on the Rhine or in the Pyrénées. In Year II, the district of Saint-Girons, a corner of France where lawlessness always threatened, found that its entire brigade of *gendarmes* had been despatched to fight the Spaniards, leaving them with no police cover whatever and no alternative but to try to raise an equal number of supplementary National Guardsmen to maintain order (82). Similarly on the eastern frontier in 1792, Remiremont was stripped of its *gendarmes* to help with the war effort, and it was left to eight citizens of the town to volunteer their services as a sort of unofficial vigilante squad (83). It is true that the most dramatic instances of such interference with the workings of the police occurred in the early years of the war, before the administration became more established and proficient, but throughout the 1790s there were continued complaints that the *gendarmerie* was being sacrificed when military needs seemed pressing. By the end of the decade the department of the Cantal was attempting to police its difficult terrain with only forty *gendarmes* (84); and reduced policing levels meant that parts of the Morbihan, despite the *chouan* menace, had had to be virtually abandoned (85). In the Nord the number of brigades had been reduced from twenty-eight to twenty-one, with the result that they were far too dispersed to achieve efficient policing. The prefect, protesting about the reductions that he had had to accept, noted that half the city of Lille was now unpoliced because of manpower shortages, that each brigade in rural areas had an area of three or four cantons to cover, and that, in consequence, "les brigades ne font de service régulier que dans les villes et les chefs-lieux de leur résidence," appearing in rural communes no more than once every ten days. It was a recipe for the breakdown of law and order (86). In the process the policing of desertion could not but suffer, since many *commissaires de police* did not have the men to tackle the problem with any degree of seriousness. The terms governing the choice of *gendarmes* were openly flouted in the Ariège in Year VII, because otherwise there would be no means of chasing refractory conscripts (87). In the Seine-et-Oise cuts in the strength of foot patrols resulted in cavalry being deployed against deserters, even "sur des points montueux et boisés où l'emploi de brigades à pied serait plus convenable" (88). But the problems there pale into insignificance compared with those of the Southeast, where manpower cuts left towns like Crest undefended and presented a golden opportunity to deserters and brigands alike (89). With commendable honesty the local authorities explained that despite national priorities, they faced far too serious threats to order on their immediate doorstep to permit them to release *gendarmes* for the pursuit of conscripts.

The effectiveness of the *gendarmerie* depended, of course, not only on their numbers but also on their quality and their standing in the communities they served. They too often lacked the support they needed from local people, and their morale suffered accordingly. The Gironde was only one department among many where supplies and pay failed to filter through to the local brigades and where the *gendarmes* resented the fact that their services were taken for granted. "La gendarmerie," it was noted in Year IV, "ferait son service avec exactitude si elle était sur un pied plus régulier. Beaucoup de gendarmes revenus des armées n'ont pas de chevaux, la modique solde qu'ils retirent n'est pas suffisante pour les faire exister, et dans la plupart des résidences du département, le commissaire ordonnateur n'a pu encore lui faire délivrer les vivres et fourrages des magasins de la république" (90). Their anger was compounded by the feeling that their work was not appreciated by the local community, a feeling substantiated by the flood of criticism that was showered on them. In the Haute-Garonne their image was undermined by constant attacks: "on lui reproche généralement d'être composée d'hommes qui se sont mal conduits pendant les différents chocs de la Révolution, et de donner chaque jour des preuves de la partialité la plus nuisible" (91). This criticism was more difficult to bear because of the lack of cooperation between the *gendarmes* and many local councils, who saw them as a form of intrusion by the state and who resented their interference in what they regarded as matters for the local community alone. At times the lack of communication amounted almost to complicity in the crimes of that community. In Year VI, for example, the *gendarmes* in the Drôme felt aggrieved that neither the municipal administration nor the *commissaire* of the Directory offered any support after seven of their number had been murdered by an *attroupement armé* in the hamlet of Guisan (92). They were, it seemed, callously abandoned to whatever fate might befall them. Yet the same administrators would insist that they be consulted and informed before any police action was launched in their area. Even a routine search for deserters had to be agreed to by the prefecture before it could legitimately go ahead (93). It is hardly surprising that the *gendarmerie* sometimes felt that they were caught between the twin pincers of the military and civilian administrations, a plaything in the political game that was being played between the different rival authorities and in the course of which the maintenance of order was too lightly sacrificed. Unloved and unpaid, the *gendarmes* could be driven to cynicism and even to disloyalty, and the result, as in the Pas-de-Calais in Year VI, could involve the draining of any sense of public duty:

Sans solde depuis plus d'une année (lors de la dépréciation du papier-monnaie) les gendarmes, soit par besoin pour alimenter leurs familles indigentes, soit par propension à la séduction, ont fait un commerce infame de leur état. Les prêtres, les déserteurs, les réquisitionnaires obtenaient leur tranquillité à prix d'argent; quand une aussi forte atteinte a été portée à la moralité, il est difficile de faire cesser le mal sur le champ. Autrefois on recevait des dons ou des gratifications, y étant contraint par la misére; aujourd'hui on reçoit encore par habitude. (94)

Though resentment of public indifference remained an important source of demoralization, the efficacy of the *gendarmerie* did improve markedly over the period of the Revolution and Empire through better administration and clearer lines of demarcation. In the 1790s the force had suffered from certain inbuilt ambiguities inherited from the *maréchaussée*. In particular, there was a damaging ambivalence about the authority on which they carried out interrogations and effected arrests, for though they were themselves answerable to the Minister of War, they were continually being called on to act in support of the civil authorities. It was an ambivalence that caused endless conflict and embarrassment (95). Only after the *thermidorian coup* in Year III was the position clarified, with the creation of a separate Ministry of Police générale and the institution of a more streamlined administration for the *gendarmes*. The long period of Fouché's ministry, and the reorganization of the force in Year VIII, gave added assurance to a body of men who required fixed and clearly understood lines of authority if it was to operate effectively, especially in matters like conscription which impinged on both military and civil responsibilities. Local policing was also reorganized during the period, following the example of the capital in having *commissaires de police* in charge of every town of 5,000 or more inhabitants. These men, elected during the Revolution, came to be appointed officials under the Empire, answerable to the prefect of the department (96). But how efficient were they? Some, we know, were dismissed for dereliction of duty, and the impression is easily created that *commissaires* were lazy and prone to corruption. Daniel, from Mirecourt, for instance, was removed when it was demonstrated that he never bothered to investigate allegations of fraud while he, as a merchant, had accumulated unpaid debts (97). Loeuilliet-Rousseau, at Douai, was forced to resign when it was pointed out that his position as *commissaire* was incompatible with his trading interest as a brewer in the town (98). Dutour, at Montélimar, was dismissed when the Minister learned that he had simply abandoned his post and left policing in a very sensitive district of the Drôme to the men under his command (99). There are clear examples of poor appointments. Equally, there were parts of France, like the Ariège, where it proved enormously difficult to find men of any caliber to fill the post in the first place, since the number of candidates with any knowledge of the law was negligible (100). But it must be said that most of the men chosen survived in their jobs without being denounced, at least until 1815 when the criterion for remaining in post was more a political one than one of legal competence. The men chosen tended to combine social standing in the community with at least a modicum of legal experience; they were most commonly landowners and government administrators, lawyers and army officers (101). And some at least of the denunciations may have reflected on local rivalries as much as on the worth of the *commissaires* themselves. At Bordeaux in Year XIII both their immediate superior, the *commissaire général de police* in the city, and the prefect of the Gironde had occasion to comment on the qualities possessed by their *commissaires de police*. The result is most interesting. In only two instances did the two men agree. Jean-Baptiste Boyer was to his superiors "probe, zélé, et propre aux fonctions qui lui sont attribuées"; but the prefect commented acidly that "on le dit très ignorant, incapable de dresser un procès-verbal; on le taxe de favoriser les maisons de prostitution." Jean-Baptiste Lamoissonnière, to the *commissaire-général,* was "extrêment probe, plein de zèle et justement estimé"; the prefect found him "fort cupide et brutal." And whereas the *commissaire-général* praised Jean-Baptiste Marie Jogan for being "probe et très zélé, même avec dévouement," the prefect ignored his present qualities to concentrate on his past career, noting with evident disfavor that "on dit qu'il a joué un rôle très actif dans les temps de la Terreur. On cite plusieurs personnages importants qu'il a dénoncés et qui ont péri. On le dit brutal, insolent . . ." (102). The evidence would seem to suggest that even highly competent *commissaires de police* were vulnerable to denunciation and to personal malice.

What emerges from an examination of the selection of *commissaires de police* is the weight attached to the personal circumstances of each candidate, to probity measured by personal sacrifice and family commitments. Of Mazois, a candidate for the post at Bordeaux in Year XIII, it was claimed that he was a "père de famille très estimable," that he had lost his fortune in the Revolution— he was, predictably, a *négociant* on the Bordeaux waterfront—"par une suite des malheurs de la guerre maritime et des désastres des colonies," and that he had in his care "la veuve et des enfants d'un frère qui a péri à Saint-Domingue" (103). He was, in short, a very worthy man, though these attributes did not nec- essarily ensure his suitability for the post. The same general criticism can be made of the selection process for *gendarmes*. To be eligible, a man had to have served in the armies for a fixed number of years, to be older than twenty-five years of age, and to have a basic literacy. The government stressed the military requirement, just as had been the practice with the old *maréchaussée*, in order that the police should not come to be seen as a valid escape route for those wishing to avoid the attentions of the recruiting-sergeant (104). In the revolu- tionary years eight years' service was a normal requirement, and applications for placement stressed the ardor and number of each candidate's campaigns. Suffering seemed to provide its own justification: "Il ne lui reste qu'une année à faire pour avoir seize ans de service et son congé . . . dans toutes ces occasions son régiment a été très maltraité, au point que de trois cents hommes il n'en est revenu que trente . . ." (105). Applicants presented themselves as though the *gendarmerie* was there to provide outdoor relief for veterans, to allow men who had worn themselves out in the national cause to be honorably employed in their home village or close to their relatives. Sébastien Reynaud from Valence justified his selection on just such grounds, that because "ayant fait contre les ennemis toutes les campagnes d'Egypte et d'Italie, s'étant comporté toujours comme un brave et loyal soldat," he merited a place in the force (106). More poignantly still, Charlemagne Dalle, a *brigadier* with the Sixth Regiment of the Nord, had found that when he retired from the army he had neither the possi- bility of employment nor any source of income to feed his family. He wrote as a professional soldier who had completed sixteen campaigns, who had subse- quently commanded the *garde nationale* at Le Quesnoy, and who knew no other life than that of the barracks. His appeal came close to simple begging. Now that he could no longer fight, he explained, "il se voit maintenant dans l'impossibilité de pourvoir à la subsistance de ses enfants et de leur procurer les choses même de première nécessité si le gouvernement ne vient à son secours" (107). His case was given sympathetic consideration because his were the qualities that the *gen- darmerie* was looking for. Under the Empire, indeed, the principal source of recommendations for placement in the *gendarmerie* was the army itself. After some years of service, soldiers were being specifically proposed for transfer to the *gendarmerie* by their officers, and recruits were selected directly from each regiment of infantry or cavalry, from the hussars and dragoons. The selection, once again, was made on the grounds of merit, defined in terms of years of service, number of campaigns, morality and *civisme* (108). Discipline and age were the principal virtues; literacy, although a contributory factor, would not seem to have been indispensible, since men were recommended whose "bonne conduite et bonnes moeurs" were deemed to outweigh the fact that they could neither read nor write (109).

These were not necessarily the optimal criteria for recruiting an active and intelligent police force. Long years of war service could wear out men who were long past their prime when they returned to their *pays* to become *gendarmes.* The introduction of a jury system under the Directory to select from among the available candidates and to grant *réformes* to those too ill or too unsuited to serve did have the effect of forcing some retirements and improving the overall quality of force. Their findings were scarcely reassuring. In the Nord those retired in Year VI included some whose useful service lay far in the past: a *maréchal des logis* from Lille who at the age of sixty-six years was "dans un état de décrépitude"; another, aged seventy-five years from Douai who had been seriously injured in a fall from his horse; a *gendarme* of sixty-one years from Cassel who had been wounded both in his right leg and his left arm and who suffered from deafness; or a *gendarme* of fifty years, again from Douai, who was "frappé d'un coup de sabre sur la tête et atteint de douleurs rhumatismales suite de fatigues de la guerre" (110). The list reads like the entry book to a military hospital. Others were weeded out for disciplinary reasons, which again suggest that for some at least of the former soldiers who joined the *gendarmerie,* policing seemed more like retirement than hard work. The shortcomings listed by the jury speak for themselves: "cabaleur, insubordonné, sans tenue, sans intelligence"; "ivrogne incorrigible"; "non seulement insubordonné, mais encore immoral" to cite just a few of the observations on the men dismissed from the service in the reorganization of Year X in the Seine-et-Oise. Some took their pay as *gendarmes* but devoted themselves to a totally different trade. One *gendarme* at Ecouen spent his time at "son ancienne profession de faiseur de bas"; another, at Montgeron, passed his days in town making shoes (111). Furthermore, the average age of *gendarmes* was necessarily rather high, since it was effectively a force of army veterans. In the Seine-et-Oise at the time of that reorganization, there was not a single man younger than twenty-five years of age in the department; of 189 *gendarmes,* the highest concentration was in the thirty-five to forty-four age range (75 men), though 25 were fifty- to fifty-four-years old, 11 fifty-five to fifty-nine, and 6 older than sixty years old (112). During the Empire especially, much was done to improve the professionalism of the *gendarmerie,* and they were much more capable than the *maréchaussée* had been. But one is entitled to ask whether their recruitment procedures produced the most appropriate force for the pursuit of young conscripts across the French countryside.

At various moments during the period other officers were co-opted by the authorities for the policing of refractories to complement the hard-pressed *gendarmes.* Customsmen, who already encountered hostility from the local community because of their much hated role in the prevention of smuggling, were one group who found themselves ordered to join the hunt for deserters, especially in frontier regions where their knowledge of the mountain tracks used by smugglers and shepherds made them especially valuable to the *gendarmerie.* In the marshy coastal region around Queyrac in the Gironde, where it was known that deserters sought refuge, the use of *gendarmes* and of mounted soldiers had produced only minimal results, and the *capitaine de gendarmerie* argued in 1809 that the ideal weapon would be a unit of *douaniers* whose local *connaissance* was unrivalled (113). By the end of the Napoleonic wars they were even, in some areas, being used as part of the garrisons imposed on refractory villages (114). Such steps were highly controversial, as they exposed the customsmen to the possibility of reprisals and made their routine duties all the more difficult to fulfill. But the policing of conscription was unquestionably the higher priority, and the *douaniers* were merely following in the footsteps of others who, as *gardes-champêtres* or *gardes-forestiers,* had been incorporated into the government's assault on refractories. Again, the normal duties of the *gardes* in protecting woodland and detecting poaching offenses had acquainted them with likely hiding-places and sharpened their ears to unexplained sounds in woods and copses—qualities that could be of evident service in hunting down deserters, especially as the young men were known to seek shelter in communal woods and forests. One commune in the Nord, Steenvoorde, specifically asked that the brief of the *gardes* be widened so that they could operate beyond the communal boundaries and become, in effect, rural *gendarmes* with powers of surveillance and arrest (115). There were numerous instances where prefects ordered the *gardes* to join with the *gendarmerie* in hunting down such deserters as surfaced on the territory of their municipalities, a provision made possible by an Imperial decree of 1806 (116).

The *gardes,* in short, found their powers extended and their concerns widened from *braconnage* to *insoumission.* It was not an enviable position, especially because many of those they encountered were young men from their own and surrounding villages. More serious still was the fact that the *gardes* seldom enjoyed much respect or status in the communities they served, since they were poorly paid and badly educated, the objects of pity rather than regard, and since the laws on poaching were only intermittently obeyed. In the Haute-Garonne the prefect noted that even their arrests were often ignored, since "la plupart des juges de paix ne tenaient aucun compte des procès-verbaux qui leur étaient remis" (117). Moreover, the process of making an arrest had become so cumbersome that *gardes* were reluctant to take any action against wrongdoers. Their inability to read and write meant that they had to make their report to a *greffier* so that the *procès-verbal* could be drawn up, which in turn involved the *garde* in a long journey and often the cost of the *greffe*. Was it any wonder, asked the canton of Remiremont in Year IV, "que les gardes-forestiers, la plus grande partie pères de famille et sans fortune, ne recevant plus depuis longtemps aucun salaire, se bornent à faire quelques rapports contre des citoyens peu aisés, tandis qu'ils favorisent les citoyens riches à commettre des délits pour en retirer du grain ou autres subsistances" (118). Given their low status and the lack of support from the rest of the community, it was impossible to replace them or to find better qualified candidates. In the former royal forests of the Paris Basin, around Versailles and Marly, Meudon and Saint-Cloud, they were better respected than most. Here they received under the Empire salaries of 500 francs per year (though there were some *gardes* in these areas who survived on much less), in contrast to many village *gardes* in the South who were dependent on the local peasantry for any remuneration and were often reduced to near starvation. They came from poor families, either from families of *gardes,* from military families, or, in some cases, from careers as woodworkers, gardeners, or unskilled laborers (119). Often they were sick or suffering from wounds received in the army. The majority of the *gardes* at Rambouillet, for example, seem to have been either suffering from rheumatic attacks or pulmonary complaints or bearing the wounds of their military past (120). Nor could their poverty necessarily be equated with honesty. Reports on the quality and morality of *gardes* in the Drôme during the Empire demonstrated the range of misdemeanors to which they turned to supplement their meager pay. Several retained "un goût prononcé pour la chasse" or were "braconniers par goût et par spéculation," even though this conflicted with their central purpose as *gardes.* Maillet, at Allan, was known to be "le protecteur des braconniers qu'il rassemblait au nombre de six et de huit et avec lesquels il chassait en tout temps et en tout lieu." Charrière, at Saint-Laurent, went even further, making private deals with wood merchants so that wood cut in the communal forest passed freely by the cartload on its way to the riverside. The *garde* at La Roche-sur-le-Buis, Jussian, devoted himself to keeping his *cabaret* well-stocked and to maintaining his popularity with the locals, with the result that "il avait sciemment laissé voler la majeure partie des bois de la forêt de réserve." His colleague in the Imperial forest at Mantaille was denounced for using his office to gain favors of another kind, the mayor reporting that "j'ai reçu une déclaration de grossesse d'après laquelle, s'il faut ajouter foi à la déclaration, il lui fit un enfant sous la promesse de ne pas verbaliser contr'elle pour vol de fagots dans Mantaille" (121). Such cases lend some weight to the caustic judgment of the *conseil-général* of the department in Year X that the institution of the *gardes* had generally proved more harmful than useful in matters of rural policing, since "ces gardes sont pour la plupart des fainéants qui n'embrassent cette profession que parce qu'ils ne sont propres à aucune autre" (122).

As the scale of resistance grew, so the state extended its arsenal of repression. Prefects became increasingly concerned at the failure of the *gendarmerie* to achieve the substantial success rate that was expected of them. There were instances where details of police actions were leaked in advance to the conscripts they were hunting (123); others where months of supposedly thorough policing failed to result in a single arrest (124). In consequence, by Year VII prefects were themselves taking dramatic initiatives to try to reverse a pattern of failure, without waiting for the government to pass decrees or to grant them authority. In particular, they turned to the use of *garnisaires* as a means of putting pressure on refractories by punishing their parents, in the hope that the cost and inconvenience of having soldiers garrisoned on their property would drive a wedge between peasant families and their recalcitrant sons and force the fugitives back into the armies. From Year VII (around the time of the first conscriptions) this became a common tactic in villages where recruitment had consistently proved difficult, used first against the parents of *insoumis* believed to be concealed in the community and therefore at their parents' beck and call, but later extended to all parents whose sons had been convicted of desertion or *insoumission.* Only in 1807 and 1808 were these measures legalized by the *Conseil d'Etat* (125). The troops serving in the garrisons had to be paid a daily allowance and their food and bedding had to be provided by the families on whom they were billeted, either the families of deserters or frequently the richest families in the community, a device by which the authorities thought to create divisions of interest and force the conscripts' own parents to give up their resistance to the law. By the last years of the Empire the use of garrisoning had become standard throughout France, and in 1811 prefects were reminded of the circumstances when they were obliged to resort to it: when communes were known to be giving shelter to refractories, when previous conscriptions had ended in tumult and riot, and above all, when the proportion of *retardataires* in a town or village exceeded one in eight of those called (126). The same ministerial instruction drew their attention to the various forces whom they could incorporate into garrisons: the *gendarmerie,* of course, but also the reserve company of the department, units stationed on the territory of the department, veterans and former soldiers who were judged capable of the duties involved.

In consequence *garnisaires* came to be imposed on a very wide scale and at high cost to the local community. In December 1808 one prefect shocked the Minister of the Interior when he revealed that in his department there were 146 communes where garrisons could profitably be used. Rather more cautiously, the Minister advised that their use be restricted to the 23 most disobedient instances, in the belief that other communities might be inspired by their example to carry out the letter of the law (127). He was unrealistically optimistic in his expectations. In 1809 *garnisaires* had to be used in every canton of the department, at a total cost to the inhabitants of nearly 85,000 francs (128). There *were* local success stories to report. When a garrison was sent in to the village of Rochefort in the Gard to punish the villagers for sheltering a deserter who had escaped from police custody, the village almost immediately gave up its *protégé* and the deserter was taken off to the citadel at Nîmes (129). But the imposition of *garnisaires* was not the panacea for which the government had been hoping. Administrative and judicial confusion arose that both impeded the work of the troops and led to court decisions in favor of the plaintiffs (130). In many parts of France the wealthy had already bought themselves out of service or had found a substitute. *Insoumission* was increasingly a problem of the poor, and they could not hope to pay either the heavy fines imposed by the courts or the costs of maintaining garrisons in their homes. Conscripts whose families could pay were well aware of the risks, as the prefect of the Loire astutely recognized,

> en sorte que le conscrit pourra calculer d'avance les sacrifices qu'il a à faire pour échapper à la loi; ces sacrifices, y compris l'amende, sont loin d'équivaloir à ceux que lui nécessiterait son remplacement; n'est-il pas à craindre, alors, que celui-là même qui jusqu'ici a cédé à la considération de la fortune ne prenne l'idée de spéculer sur sa désobéissance? (131)

Thus the operation was being increasingly conducted against impoverished families who had little or nothing to lose, with the result that the fines imposed on them were not a real threat to their livelihood. Of 150 refractories condemned at Aurillac between Year XI and 1806, 49 were equipped with a *certificat d'indigence* from their mayor, and in only 36 cases did the authorities have reason to think that they might recover part of the money owed (132). In poor communes, indeed, the use of garrisons was often regarded as counterproductive, since the sums raised for the government were small and the long-term effects of the garrison could be quite ruinous. The people of Gentioux in the Creuse went so far as to petition the government in Year VIII, complaining that "on n'épargne ni meubles, ni gerbes, ni fourrage, ni bestiaux, même ceux destinés à l'agriculture, en un mot on a totalement dévasté et ruiné ses maisons," with the result that tax payments throughout the commune were seriously delayed (133). In such cases where the majority of the people involved were impoverished, it was the whole community that was obliged to pay, since the garrisons were almost always billeted at the inn at communal expense (134). As for the conscripts, they had little reason to give themselves up, since their parents were beyond the reach of the state through the fact of their poverty. Often the garrison received a less than hospitable welcome from its enforced hosts. In the Tarn it was noted that most of the parents refused to pay the soldiers or to provide them with food, while in the more isolated hamlets the men found themselves threatened and maltreated by friends and relatives (135). More extreme still was the uncompromising response of parents in the Bouches-du-Rhône in Year VIII, where the arrival of the *garnisaires* was prompting a secondary desertion. At Aubagne one conscript's father followed his son into hiding "emportant avec lui le peu de meubles qui y étaient," and elsewhere it was quite common for those threatened with garrisons to empty their houses and store their furniture with relatives until the danger had passed (136). Local administrators were not always keen to encourage the imposition of garrisons, for they knew what their arrival could mean in terms of public morale. In the sober words of the prefect of the Loire-Inférieure, "l'administration qui a été forcée de l'employer dans le cours de 1809 sait quels murmures elle a occasionnés, combien elle avait exaspéré et froisseé l'opinion publique" (137).

Where the costs of the garrison were imposed on the wealthiest landowners in the commune, the government's intention was clear—to turn the richer farmers against the poor and thus to secure the denunciations which they required. In this way, it was felt, the solidarity of rural communities in the face of conscription could effectively be ended. The reality, again, was more clouded. Where conscripts were pressured into giving themselves up, the cost in social tensions within the village could be high, and the richer farmers ran a real risk of retaliatory measures against themselves or their property. Even the legality of punishing the *notables* for the sins of their fellow villagers was highly dubious, as the *sous-préfet* at Cambrai tellingly pointed out in 1813. It was often uncertain which of the landowners were liable to be taxed in this way. Was the payment to be levied on the villager who owned the land or on the land itself? For if it were the land, then a large number of outsiders would be involved, despite the fact that they did not live in the village and took no hand in the crimes committed by the village. Could they be charged? Many of them, he added, were themselves doing their military service, or had sons in the armies. Could they be included in the *contribution?* There was, claimed the *sous-préfet,* no evidence in his area that the parents of refractories were moved by the sight of their neighbors paying fines on their behalf, and no sign of the clutch of denunciations that the government assumed would follow. And why? Because in small communes the element of fear was far stronger than the distaste engendered by an enforced payment toward the costs of the garrison. In the *campagnes* around Cambrai, and doubtless in many other parts of rural France, "les riches payent de peur d'être brûlés. On arme contr'eux l'intérêt de la multitude qui rit de les voir contribuer pour elle. Il n'y a pas un seul exemple d'une dénonciation" (138).

The use of *garnisaires* was part of a larger trend in the policing of conscription. For increasingly, that job was being given to soldiers. Troops who had resisted the temptation to desert were set in pursuit of those who had not. In the 1790s there were attempts to mobilize the local units of the *garde nationale* against deserters and *insoumis,* but the fact that this involved the arrest of neighbors and friends meant that results were often negligible and that the *gardes* were accused of conspiring with the fugitives. The town of Nyons was one which turned to the *garde* in Year III, ordering them to join the local *gendarmes* in a joint operation. They never turned up, even when it became a question of putting down an armed mutiny of local conscripts (139). The sympathies of the local guardsmen were, not surprisingly, divided, even the most patriotic among them hesitating to use force against their childhood friends. Their use against refractories proved dangerous and unpredictable, with the constant fear that they might lend their support to the enemies of public order. In the Gironde it was noted that the insistence that guardsmen operate against refractories resulted in a cooling of their ardor for service (140). At Rabastens in the Hautes-Pyrénées it was even suggested that they had deliberately freed prisoners left in their care (141). Slowly but surely the authorities learned the basic lesson that it was inadvisable to use local troops in the search for local refractories, that the impersonal element that crept into policing when it was being carried out on someone else's territory was indispensable to efficiency and the maintenance of military discipline. By the same token they appreciated the value of a force of soldiers drawn from outside the area whose task was to interrogate and arrest all young men discovered in their path, all who could not justify their presence in their villages by the production of a *congé* or *réforme.*

From this the notion of the *colonne mobile* was born. This was a military unit that would sweep from village to village, searching out refractories and deserters in the fields and barns and outhouses, and spreading fear and respect for the law by means of blanket policing. Permission to establish a special force for the policing of recruitment was given under a law of *floréal* Year IV that allowed for "la création dans chaque canton de la République d'un détachement sédentaire de garde nationale qui devrait prendre le nom de colonne mobile et qui aurait pour but de se tenir constamment prêt à voler partout où la tranquillité publique semblerait compromise" (142). But this law was not widely implemented, largely because of the vociferous opposition that greeted it. In the Corrèze we learn that local opinion deemed it too severe and feared that its implementation would simply antagonize the community (143). The first mention of widespread use of *colonnes* was in Years VII and VIII, when they seemed to have fairly casual forces made up of whatever troops happened to be available in the area at the time (144). Essentially a prefect would call in such a unit for a short, temporary campaign against deserters when he became convinced that there was a crisis in his area that went beyond the capacities of the local *gendarmerie*. It was for this reason that the prefect of the Vosges, not normally a problem department from the point of view of conscription, resorted to a *colonne mobile* at the very end of Year VIII in a determined effort to stamp out what he saw as an incipient threat (145). These early experiments, almost always to police the first conscriptions, were hardly unqualified successes for the authorities. In the Drôme *colonnes* of local men were drawn up but they refused to move against their compatriots (146). In Bordeaux, where again a force was assembled, they had no rifles and had to be disbanded before they even saw action (147). And in the villages of the Nord the *colonne* was being cold-shouldered and treated with contempt by the villagers, who ignored its questions and refused to find food for the soldiers while they were on patrol (148). With the less stringent demands for conscripts in the years that followed, no further use was made of *colonnes* until the later years of the Empire, when the draining campaigns to the East and in the Peninsula were forcing an increase in conscription. The *grandes opérations* of these columns were launched from 1810 onward, with the greatest successes achieved in the difficult conditions of 1810 and 1811. Four columns were at work between July 1810 and February 1811, resulting in a wave of nearly 14,000 arrests. From February a further eleven columns were brought into action and their activity was extended to ninety-nine departments of France and the *pays réunis*. By the time they were disbanded in February 1812 some 63,000 deserters and refractories had been arrested and the problem of public order was seemingly ended (149). In particular, draft evasion no longer seemed an attractive option in villages where the *colonnes* threatened to descend at any moment. In 1811 there were only 6,600 new cases of *insoumission* recorded by the Ministry of War compared with nearly 54,000 new desertions (150).

These figures provided their own justification as delighted prefects reported during 1811 and 1812 that the *colonnes* had virtually wiped out refractory behavior in their areas of jurisdiction. Where there were complaints they were seldom about the effectiveness of the policing, except occasionally in areas of difficult terrain where the soldiers lacked the local *connaissances* needed to master the conditions they faced. At Carbon-Blanc, a notorious hiding-place for *insoumis* and for criminals of all kinds, the *colonne mobile* was hampered by problems of communication and lost its prey. As the prefect of the Gironde expressed it, "le mauvais état des chemins et la situation topographique d'un pays coupé par des ruisseaux qui empêchent les communications avaient considérablement retardé la marche de la colonne mobile et avaient donné le temps aux insoumis de se soustraire aux recherches" (151). More often local people protested about the brutality of the troops sent into their communities, or about the wrongful arrests that resulted from their visits (152). Or again, the arrival of a military force that had to cooperate with the civil authorities in the towns through which it passed gave rise to inevitable squabbles about authority, as the local councils resisted any possible encroachment on their powers and sometimes tried to defend their *administrés* against outside force. In 1813 when on the Emperor's instructions *colonnes* were again prepared to root out refractories in key departments, the Minister of War drew attention to this problem of authority, to the ambiguity that necessarily existed between their military and civilian function. Soldiers for the columns should be taken, he insisted, from the *légion d'élite* and senior officers should be placed in command, so that the force could hope to command respect from locally elected officials and to impose its will on prefects and senior administrators (153). These difficulties should not be exaggerated, however. By this time the power of the *colonnes* was appreciated throughout France, and they were recognized for what they were, the most feared and most effective element in the armory of police measures against desertion and *insoumission.*

The *colonnes mobiles,* like the *gendarmes* and the *garnisaires,* achieved their goals by spreading terror and by making life for refractories and their families too unpleasant to bear with equanimity. They forced men out of hiding; they were certainly not in the business of winning hearts or of persuading them of the virtues of military life. The major part of the policing of conscription during the Revolution and Empire followed that pattern. It was repressive rather than persuasive, and if the battalions were duly filled it was with reluctant and often resentful recruits. But repression was tempered, as it had traditionally been during the Ancien Regime, with mercy and moderation, at such moments as the government judged appropriate to the overriding goal of getting men back into uniform. The use of amnesties was a case in point. In the seventeenth and eighteenth centuries periodic amnesties had been offered to deserters, interspersed with periods of severe repression, in an attempt to lure waverers back to their units. So in the revolutionary wars governments turned again to this traditional weapon against those who had escaped the clutches of the army, playing on their fears, on the discomfort of their lives on the run, and on the promise of a free pardon if they gave themselves up. Those who had passed a certain age could even hope to return to their farms and workshops as free men, without either the stigma of having deserted or the constant fear of being discovered and arrested. The amnesty law of March 1810 spelled out the terms on offer: those men who had deserted before 1 January 1806 were free to return to their homes in safety, whereas for those who had left their regiments since that date meant only that they could return to their units without fear of retribution. The amnesty lasted for only two months, and those who continued to defy the law knew very well that after it expired, they would be less numerous than before, more vulnerable to arrest, and pursued with greater vigor than before (154). The amnesty, too, was a measure of state police, however much disguised in a gloved hand.

Amnesties were a familiar feature of the military landscape. As early as 23 *thermidor* II, a fortnight after the overthrow of Robespierre, those condemned by the *Tribunal Criminel* for simple desertion within the territory of France became eligible for amnesty if they accepted to return to their units (155). The device was tried again in Year VIII and Year X, after the victory at Friedland in 1807, and, most munificently of all, to celebrate the Emperor's marriage with Marie-Louise in 1810. Opinions varied on their effectiveness as a measure of police. Certainly they did lead to considerable numbers of men returning to their villages to live within the law, which itself reduced the pressures on the *gendarmerie* and facilitated the policing process. According to official statistics, which may be taken as an approximate guide only, the amnesty of 1810 allowed more than 49,000 men to return to civilian life free from penalty or prosecution; but of the 35,500 deserters and *insoumis* from the *classes* of 1806 to 1810, those who would have had to rejoin to enjoy the benefit of the amnesty, only 6,000 came forward (156). The comments offered by prefects in 1810 throw interesting light on both the strengths and weaknesses of amnesties as a means of overcoming the problem of disobedience. In the Cantal the benefits were emphasized, but they were benefits less for the army than for agricultural life in the department, to which hundreds of fugitives were usefully returned. Generally local administrators were reserved in their praise and conservative in their expectations. In both the Tarn and Tarn-et-Garonne there was a suspicion that the news of an *amnistie absolue* would undermine the *amnistie conditionnelle,* with the result that very few soldiers would reappear in their regiments. In the Landes rumor further destroyed the possible military advantage, since the belief had spread from village to village that men of the last five *classes* would also be granted complete immunity in celebration of the birth of an heir to the throne (157). All seemed agreed that when a possible amnesty was mooted, the result was highly damaging for the conscription effort, as men held back from committing themselves lest legislation provide them with a means of escape. Uncertainty was willfully created, and this made the administration's task more difficult to achieve (158).

It was the blatant inconsistency of a policy that condemned deserters to long years of hard labor at one moment and granted them a total reprieve the next which made amnesties so controversial. Many felt that the government would do better to pursue a single-minded and intelligible campaign against refractories rather than confuse local communities with apparently contradictory decrees. Was desertion or *insoumission* a serious crime to be treated with appropriate severity, or was it a minor peccadillo that could be excused come the next Imperial amnesty? The prefect of Taro in northern Italy expressed the frustrations of many of his colleagues in 1810 when he commented that "l'amnistie, en suspendant les mesures de rigueur qui s'exerçaient contre les familles, va retarder nos succès." For, he explained, "les habitants réclament la jouissance de ce bienfait dans toute sa plénitude. Nous n'avons rien à leur opposer" (159). It was not just administrative tidiness that motivated those who objected to the government's seeming vaccillation. They genuinely feared for public order if young men were given the impression that they could avoid service with impunity, if only they could remain in hiding for a sufficiently long period. It was a challenge to their powers of resilience. In Douai the prefect was quite scathing:

En effet, les conscrits appellés ont journellement sous les yeux le tableau des communes rurales où sont en foule des conscrits désignés des classes amnistiées, qui ne doivent leur liberté qu'à l'opiniâtreté de leurs efforts pour demeurer récalcitrans et s'être soustrait aux poursuites des autorités judiciaires, civiles et militaires. (160)

Not only was the policy visibly counterproductive in the view of the authorities in the Nord, it also gave rise to blatant unfairness. Many of the men of the *classes* covered by the amnesties were still serving in the regiments and were being refused *congés* by their superior officers. In other words, the privilege of an amnesty was being granted only to those too recalcitrant or too cowardly to serve, while the men who had been incorporated were condemned to sacrifice still more years of their lives to the army (161). Again everything seemed weighted against those who obediently performed their civic duty, and many officials saw this as yet another obstacle to persuading refractories that it was in their interest to submit. Fortunately, perhaps, the policy seemed to confuse the fugitives as much as it frustrated the authorities. The extent of rumor and whisper was such that priests and mayors found themselves in positions of great influence as interpreters of the government's intention. The result was often doubt and deliberate obfuscation. In the Ardèche and Aveyron, for example, it was widely believed in outlying hamlets that the amnesty of Year X should be treated with the greatest caution since it was "un piège tendu à leur bonne foi" (162).

A further "mesure de douceur" was employed in those frontier areas where recruitment proved particularly recalcitrant, and again it was a traditional remedy with a long and honorable pedigree. Where men refused in large numbers to accept incorporation, but where there was every evidence that they would willingly accept to fight for hearth and home, the government was tempted by the idea of creating *bataillons auxiliaires* for purposes of purely local defense. The idea was tried in March 1793 with the formation of eleven companies of *chasseurs basques,* small units of 150 men each, who were used after the outbreak of war with Spain for the defense of French *avant-postes* along the Pyrenean frontier. Because they were fighting to protect their own communities, they performed creditably against the Spaniards, and throughout the 1790s the companies were allowed to retain their separate status and were specifically exempted from the *amalgame.* In Year VIII when their incorporation into the armies was being actively discussed, the officers of the Second Battalion of Chasseurs Basques wrote a spirited defense of their special statute and demanded that it be retained. The men of the Basque mountains would serve loyally, they claimed, if they were allowed to fight in their own way under their own officers, men "qui connaissent conséquemment leur langage et leurs habitudes"; the alternative would bring chaos and mass refusal (163). Their *nostalgie* was deemed to play a much more fundamental role than did simple *mal du pays* elsewhere, and opinion among their officers was unanimous that Napoleon would be ill-advised to go ahead with any plans for incorporation (164). He did, however, creating out of the *chasseurs* two *demi-brigades* of light infantry in *pluviôse* IX, a move that met with the predicted protests and indiscipline on the part of the Basques. There was similar resistance to incorporation among other groups of *chasseurs,* from the *chasseurs de la Vendée* in the West to the *barbets* in northern Italy, a sort of private army in the pay of the King of Sardinia (165). In the eyes of the regular battalions these *bataillons auxiliaires* could seem an unnecessary nuisance that ought to be swept away. General Cervoni, commander of the Eighth Division Militaire in Marseille, pointed out in Year X that they obstructed rather than helped army maneuvers and that along the Italian frontier prefects were tending to use the *barbets* as an unofficial private army, a rival to the military (166).

In 1808, however, the government resumed the idea of auxiliary battalions in the Southwest specifically for the purpose of defending the Spanish frontier now that war in the Peninsula was being pursued in earnest. The decree of 6 August 1808 established thirty-four companies of *miquelets* for this purpose, eight in each of four departments (the Ariège, Basses-Pyrénées, Hautes-Pyrénées, and Pyrénées-Orientales) and two in the neighboring Haute-Garonne. Those eligible to join were defined as refractories from these five departments, of any age between the last conscription and forty years old; and they were bribed by the specific promise that their service would be of limited duration, until the end of the troubles with Spain. The prefect of the Ariège recommended it to his *administrés* as an instance of the Emperor's generosity, since "il n'exige de vous qu'un service momentané sur vos frontières, pour prix de votre grâce et votre congé" (167). The recruitment was a huge success, the companies oversubscribed several times over. The *sous-préfet* of Saint-Girons, the most troublesome part of the Ariège, went in person to the most remote and recalcitrant communities to advertise the terms offered, and was delighted by the response he encountered. With cautious optimism he reported that much could be expected of these men if they were handled carefully by officers from their own villages who understood their strengths and their limitations:

> J'ose croire que ce seront de bons miquelets. L'avantage de n'être employé que sur la frontière d'Espagne les a généralement décidés, il serait peut-être impolitique de donner, du moins encore, une autre destination à l'excédant du bataillon demandé. Mais lorsqu'ils seront aguerris, exercés, accoutumés à être ensemble, je suis persuadé que les généraux pourront en disposer utilement. (168)

This optimism did not long survive the recruitment of the *miquelets,* for the new service was to prove a hornet's nest for the authorities. The attractive terms resulted in a new form of conscription fraud, as men who were not eligible for the *miquelets,* including youngsters who had not yet reached conscription age, forged documents to be admitted (169). The problem, indeed, was not one of finding men for these companies, but rather of finding officers of sufficient caliber to provide a modicum of leadership. In the Ariège the eight original companies of *miquelets* had, said the prefect, "épuisé la plus grande partie de ceux capables de faire la guerre" (170). And then there were the subsequent problems of persuading them to obey orders and of forging them into fighting units. The fact that the overwhelming majority of the soldiers were men with an established track record of disobedience made them impervious to military discipline. Of the ordinary soldiers in the eight companies of the Haute-Garonne, for example, only 15 were drawn from other units or had voluntarily enrolled; 732 were *conscrits réfractaires*. In the Ariège, with much larger numbers, the pattern was similar. In December 1809, of 1,200 *miquelets* in the First Battalion, 50 were listed as *gardes nationaux* and 8 as volunteers; the rest were all *réfractaires* (171). Their knowledge of the difficult terrain of the frontier might make them seem valuable to the war effort; but this was offset by their indiscipline, their reputation for theft and violence, and their tendency to drift from soldiering into the realm of smuggling and *brigandage* (172). In the mountains above Auzat their haul was symptomatic—"1400 moutons, 30 vaches, quelques chevaux et mulets"—and demonstrated why the *chasseurs* could seem a mixed blessing to the frontier communities they were ordered to protect (173).

In any case, these battalions did not provide a solution to the most fundamental problem of all, the problem that had justified their original formation. If they signed on with unbounded enthusiasm, so they deserted with equal commitment. Often their period of service could be counted in months or even weeks. In the Ariège each of the new companies raised in April and May of 1808 could boast its list of deserters by the beginning of July—seventy-one men of the Second company, sixty-six from the Fifth, and so on. All had taken advantage of the army's generous provision of arms and cartridges. Often they had been recruited in groups from the same village, had served together, and then deserted together to return home. Of the sixty-six men who deserted from the Fifth company, sixteen came from the frontier village of Massat; all had been recruited on 17 May and all chose the same day to desert, 27 June. There was no shame attached to their action, and there was little that the army could do to prevent it (174). Nor did amnesties serve any useful purpose, since at best the *chasseurs* merely accepted the government's generosity and rejoined to desert yet again (175). Whenever they were sent away from their home valleys to patrol another part of the frontier, the desertion figures mounted ominously, and by 1809 the government was forced to raise another 1,000 *miquelets* in the Southwest to replace men who had slipped off home. On this occasion they extended the geographic spread of recruitment, in the hope that they could tap reserves of good will elsewhere, and the new recruits came from the more lowland areas of the region: the Landes, Gironde, and Basses-Pyrénées. But still the result was meager, the crumbling away of a force of 1,000 over a few months, until in August 1810 only 466 remained (176). Their utility was further limited by the fact that they believed they were only obliged to serve on French territory, with the implication that it was not their responsibility to chase Spanish troops across the frontier into Spain (177). As the fortunes of the war fluctuated, so the desertion rate ebbed and flowed, but it was clear that the *miquelets* could never be molded into a fighting unit capable of playing a major part in the Peninsular campaign. Disillusioned by the entire experiment, the Minister of War reported to the Emperor in November 1810 that there was little point in maintaining the *chasseurs* on the Pyrenean front, that further recruitment should be abandoned, and that those who remained should be *dépaysés* and transferred to serve in Corsica. The source of their desertion and indiscipline, he concluded, lay not in the army, which had successively tried tactics of severity and gentleness to win over the former *insoumis,* but in the character of these mountain people themselves. Further repression would serve little purpose, since "pousser plus loin la rigueur, ce serait donner le spectacle affligeant d'une population presqu'entièrement envoyée aux fers, sans qu'il en résultât aucun avantage" (178). The *bataillons* were written off as an interesting failure.

From this point on the government would rely on repressive power to
destroy the remaining kernels of resistance to its recruitment policy. *Douceur*
was exposed as a failure; the palpable successes of 1811 and 1812 would redound
to the credit of the *colonnes mobiles* and would seem to justify the abandonment
of persuasion and inducement. In general terms, of course, it had been armed
strength that had been the mainstay of policing deserters and refractories
throughout the period. In the last years of the Empire the reliance on the army
and the *gendarmerie* was simply more naked than previously, and the vast
majority of conscripts were for the first time cowed into submission. But it
should be emphasized that the use of repression was strictly controlled throughout the Consulate and Empire, with prefects and military commanders regularly
reminded of their obligation to remain within the law. Administrators might
cajole and hector, they might make an example of those arrested by making
them "marcher les premiers" at the next conscription, they could make full use
of the propaganda machine that was provided for them. They were not, however, encouraged to go beyond the law. The prefect of the Pas-de-Calais received
no support from central government when he proposed parading the first thirty
or forty deserters or *retardataires* through the streets of their towns and villages
to be publicly humiliated, "pour être employés, sous les yeux de leurs concitoyens, à balayer les rues, à traîner des tombereaux, à nettoyer les égouts, en un mot
aux travaux les plus vils et les plus dégoûtants" (179). His colleague in the Lozère was angrily reprimanded when he informed the Minister that he had taken
steps on his own initiative to humiliate those conscripts who had mutilated
themselves to avoid service. "Je les ai fait tous arrêter et conduire, la chaîne au
col, aux dépôts des régiments de sapeurs," he boasted; "j'espère que cette mesure
dégoûtera de se mutiler ainsi" (180). The principal disgust it caused was in Paris,
where it was seen as a dangerous example of an official taking the law into his
own hands and exceeding his legal authority, when his main task was to persuade the local community to respect and obey that very law. Whatever else it
achieved, the government's recruitment policy brought the people of villages
and *bourgs* face to face with the law as never before. It brought the enforcers of
the law into every hamlet in the land. It was, par excellence, the area of government activity that brought the police and the people into direct contact, and
often into confrontation, over a period of nearly a quarter of a century.

10

Desertion, the State, and the People

GOVERNMENT MINISTERS saw little that was exceptionable in their commitment to mass conscription. In their eyes it was no more than a requirement of civic duty, like the payment of taxes or respect for the laws; it was an essential part of the sublimation of the individual's self-interest in deference to the more important interest of the nation. Viewed from the village square, however, it was a demand that was widely contested, especially since it could be seen to present an affront to local custom and tradition. The popular image of the state itself risked being tarnished, with the role of the recruiting-sergeant overshadowing the more bountiful image of the law-giver or the fount of justice. Recruitment, more than any other single issue, alienated community from government in those parts of France where central control was still eyed with confused suspicion. In Isser Woloch's phrase, conscription became "the touchstone of the relationship between the state and civil society," replacing tax collection as the most bitter bone of contention between government and governed. With Napoleon, says Woloch, "conscription became the battleground, the ultimate contest of wills between individuals and local communities on the one hand and a distant impersonal state on the other" (1). By 1814 there is no doubt that Napoleon had succeeded in implanting habits of obedience that would have seemed inconceivable even twenty years before. The war effort and the enforced sacrifices imposed by war had in their own way contributed greatly to the added authority of the state (2). Yet these changes were not wrought without considerable resistance, particularly at village level where the smooth running of the state machine was often thwarted by a lack of popular understanding or cooperation. The extent of such resistance could not fail to undermine in its turn the moral and political authority of central government.

In its most basic form this popular resistance could be measured in terms of cold indifference, a stubborn withdrawal of cooperation from the agents of the state, and a calculated lack of interest in the tasks that they had come to perform. Government *commissaires,* recruiting officers, *gendarmes,* the men of the *colonnes mobiles,* all might seek to work closely with the local communities where they were assigned, but there was no guarantee that they would be able to elicit a positive response. Mayors and municipal officers often showed their loyalty to their villagers by a tightly guarded silence and pretense at ignorance which their *administrés* had few qualms about emulating. Whole communities could erect a conspiratorial wall of innocence that frustrated and angered the authorities but that they were helpless to combat. Again and again the state found itself thwarted by the reticence of its own citizens. Mayors were denounced for the "vil intérêt" that they displayed (3); for their limited education and even more limited horizons (4); and they were accused of sabotaging the good police work of the *gendarmerie* through "indifférence" and "faiblesse" (5). The occasional frauds that came to light and that resulted in mayors being arraigned before the courts were, it was implied, just the tip of a huge iceberg. Municipal indifference and village jealousy were so deeply engrained in the mentalities of rural Frenchmen that the decrees of central government were being treated with ill-disguised contempt. The conscription issue was simply the area where these forces became most public and the conflicting interest of state and locality came into the sharpest focus.

Faced with local hostility and suspicious of the men with whom they had to deal, the *gendarmerie* and the military found it all too easy to place the blame for their own failures on civil authorities. They pointed out incessantly that they were dependent on the good will of municipal officials to an unreasonable degree, since the law forbade them from entering private property even during hours of daylight unless they were accompanied by the appropriate *officier municipal.* As a result, they believed that their task was being impeded by local complicity. In the Lozère, for instance, they noted that "l'appel d'un maire ou de son adjoint entraînait des délais: que souvent même leur éloignement ou leur absence ferait échouer les poursuites; que cette mesure pourrait donner l'éveil à une commune, faire attrouper les jeunes gens, amener des mouvements séditieux et une rébellion armée" (6). To protect civilian consciences the whole exercise of policing deserters was being frustrated. This in turn encouraged soldiers and *gendarmes* to lash out wildly at those who stood in their path, and relations between officials who should have been cooperating closely with one another often deteriorated into mutual recrimination. In Year XII mayors in the Pas-de-Calais were being accused not only of being weak and sentimental toward draft dodgers, but of being enemies of the state who offered protection to deserters for political ends. They were, claimed the *général de brigade* in Arras, closet Jacobins, "des brigands de 93 qui promettent amnistie, qui défendent, protègent, recèlent tout déserteur, qui . . . ne cessent de conspirer contre le gouvernement" (7). Mayors did not always do much to help their own cause. They could be infuriatingly slow in executing government decrees, standing on their municipal dignity and insisting on their petty privileges while the *gendarmes* could only stand by, fuming with impotent rage. In one extreme case, at Morizécourt (Vosges) in Year V, bureaucratic delay was such that the fugitive was effectively presented with a head start of some six to eight months before the authorities could give chase (8). In another, in the Gironde, a recalcitrant mayor insisted on a literal interpretation of the law on the imposition of garrisons to such a degree that no garrison could ever be billeted on his area (9). The Minister of War, impatient at the lack of progress in bringing recalcitrant soldiers to book, preferred to look no further than the local town halls and tried to pass the responsibility to the prefects and his colleague at the Interior. But mayors also felt aggrieved by the disputes that raged over conscription and they insisted that the blame did not rest entirely with the civil authority.

According to the civil arm of government, the army ought to share in the general recrimination that resulted from recruitment policy. Where there were serious breakdowns in communication between different branches of officialdom, the military were hardly blameless. Indeed, there would seem to have been general crises of cooperation at every level which raised questions about the efficacy of the new administrations and their overlapping responsibilities. In areas near to borders and military zones the civil authorities were especially outspoken in their criticism of the army for its surveillance of its own men. At Hazebrouck the government *commissaire* remarked somewhat tartly that civil responsibility ended when refractories were arrested and handed over to the military. It was strange that the army was unable to keep them under effective guard, and infuriating for the police to have to hunt down the same deserters three and four times (10). Bordeaux was another town where the civil authority refused to accept the army's accusations against mayors and municipalities. Why was it, asked the prefect in Year XI, that when his men tried to imprison the deserters they captured, they found that the army at once ordered their release (11)? There was anger and incomprehension in Year XI when police control was finally taken away from the prefectures and vested in the *généraux de division*, a decision which was roundly denounced by civil administrators in the Nord, who went so far as to criticize the Emperor himself. Dismissing the new initiatives as "des mesures vexatoires," Desmouliers, a *conseiller de préfecture* at Douai, wrote that the measure "prouve que Bonaparte ne soit pas sans faiblesse, car il a dans cette circonstance caressé le bras par préférence à la tête" (12). These were rash words; however, they indicate the degree of animus that the control and policing of desertion had created between the civil administration and the military, an animus reflected in mutual criticism and allegations of imcompetence.

Often the germ of the dispute lay elsewhere, and the conscription issue merely caused old rivalries and sensibilities to flare into open conflict. At Nyons relations between the mayor and the *maréchal des logis* charged with the policing of the town had never been cordial. They had staged a public altercation over the siting of the *bal public* to celebrate French victories in Year XIV sufficiently bitter to recall Gabriel Chevallier's Clochemerle. They had countermanded each other's instructions when the *maréchal* refused to remove his dungheap in accordance with the mayor's new public health bylaw, drawing his sword on the municipal employees who came to sweep it away and claiming total sovereignty over the police building and its courtyard. Therein, of course, lay the root of the problem—the total refusal of stubborn officials to make any concessions when they felt that their autonomy and dignity were being challenged (13). The implementation of recruitment laws, the policing of the *départ*, above all the questioning of suspected refractories and the arrest of young men seeking shelter in a village were all areas of police activity that accentuated the clash of authority between mayor and *gendarme,* community and state. What help, for instance, was a mayor obliged to provide for *gendarmes* from a neighboring town who came on to his territory to arrest one of their conscripts who had taken flight? The mayor of Commines in the Nord interpreted his obligations very literally when faced by this quandary in Year XI, refusing to accept *gendarmes* from Armentières in his commune, reminding them of past provocations between the men of the two towns, and insisting that the *gardes-champêtres* were the only force he required to keep good order in Commines. The fugitive was not included in his communal list of refractories and deserters; and the mayor saw his responsibility ending there (14). Lack of cooperation of this kind was not, of course, confined to mayors. The involvement of the *gendarmerie* was resented by local authorities who felt that their legitimate interests were being transgressed. Public wrangles over jurisdictions were embarrassingly common. The *sous-préfet* and mayor of Die were just two of many officials who allowed their rivalry to spill over into public denunciation, and the prefect felt obliged to send a *commissaire* to the town to prevent the breakdown of public confidence (15). So persistent were the demands made by Paris on the filling of conscription lists that no level of officialdom was immune from reproach. Even prefects felt threatened by the issue, and their anxieties could on occasion affect their judgment and their ability to cooperate with their colleagues in other departments. In Year XIV, goaded by a rebuke from his minister, the prefect of the Gironde tried to pass on the blame for his failures to his counterpart in the neighboring Dordogne. For, he alleged, those from his department who left their units while under escort rarely did so before passing into the Dordogne, and he pointed an accusatory finger at the town of Périgueux as "le lieu où ils abandonnent leurs conducteurs; jamais ceux qui n'ont nulle envie de joindre leurs corps ne dépassent cette ville. Ils y trouvent sans doute des facilités qui ne leur sont point offertes ailleurs" (16). It was a vague and poorly substantiated taunt which the prefect of the Dordogne angrily rebuffed. But, like the divisions between prefects and the military, it did nothing to consolidate the authority of the new administrative structure on which both the Revolution and the Empire so deeply relied.

If the day-to-day implementation of the recruitment law placed strains on the loyalties of officials, moments of crisis could undermine them entirely. When the police or a unit of the military descended on a community in search of refractory conscripts, or when they received a ministerial order to hand over all fugitives hiding on local farms, administrators found themselves in a dreadful quandary. Should they obey the state at the inevitable cost of alienating local opinion? Were their loyalties as *citoyens* more binding than their simple, age-old loyalties to family and community? Mayors were especially vulnerable to divided loyalties of this kind, which ran far deeper than any threats of retaliation or bribes of favors from their fellow villagers. Those who were denounced or dragged before the courts were generally guilty of something more tangible than weakness or indecision. They were men who sought to turn their delicate position to their own advantage, who interfered with the documentation with which they were entrusted, and who bought and sold men's lives through frauds and forgeries (17). Much more prevalent, however, and ultimately just as serious a threat to the functioning of the state, was the reluctance of many village mayors to play their part with the vigor and energy that the law demanded. In drawing up lists of refractories they demonstrated an understandable "timidité" (18), or they typified the attitude of those around them by showing favor to family and friends (19). One mayor at Rothau in the Vosges threatened to resign on the spot if the authorities did not agree to grant a *congé absolu* for his sick son who was of requisition age and had just been incorporated in a regiment of hussars (20). Local officials, and here perhaps is the root of the problem, simply did not share the government's perception of recruitment as a problem of the first importance. Seen from village France, it paled into insignificance when compared to the more urgent demands of the agricultural year, to sowing and harvesting, or the regulation of common lands. In the Nord, as in other parts of the country, what deterred mayors and their *adjoints* from initiating proceedings against suspected deserters and *insoumis* was less the risk of public outcry than the certainty of long and troublesome routine. The prefect explained in Year X that their reluctance should be understood rather than simply condemned, especially that shown by the *adjoints* "qui sont chargés de la poursuite des délits de police par-devant les juges de paix ... Ce qui paralyse surtout le zèle et l'action des adjoints, c'est qu'ils sont obligés de faire des voyages au chef-lieu de canton pour exercer leurs poursuites ... et qu'ils ne reçoivent ni salaires ni indemnité pour ces voyages qui les exposent à des dépenses" (21). Mayors and their *adjoints* were often simple *cultivateurs* like the majority of the community. They did not have the leisure or the financial security needed to take time off to devote to such time-consuming bureaucratic rituals. In the Southwest it was not realistic to expect local officials to concentrate on the policing of desertion when they had more pressing matters, like the *vendange,* on their minds. In consequence, little was ever done in August and September, when mayors and their *adjoints* were fully occupied in harvesting the grapes and preparing the new season's wine (22).

Mayors were not, of course, full-time officials; and to the annoyance of central government they did not act with the instincts or the single-mindedness of men whose devotion to government policy was determined by their place on the government's payroll. Rather they were village notables, proud of the honorary role that had been bestowed on them by their fellows in the balmy days of 1790, but unwilling and sometimes unable to carry out the increasingly burdensome duties that the state was demanding of them. It was one thing to ask that they officiate at local *fêtes* and republican ceremonies, chair council meetings, and review the local detachment of the National Guard. These were purely honorific functions that cost little in either time or social position; and many of the village mayors of the early months of the Revolution clearly basked in the reflected admiration of their constituents. But increasingly the tasks imposed on them became onerous and even invidious, earning the animosity of other villagers and the opprobrium of those who placed traditional village freedoms above the new found pretensions of the state. The issue of military recruitment lay at the very heart of this new role. Maintaining the *état civil* in good order, with the names listed in neat columns, might be no more than a formal task, reflecting the new civic consciousness of the secular authorities. But making use of that document to send one's sons and neighbors to serve in the regiments went far beyond the purely honorific. It was an aspect of state policing, not of municipal dignity. Furthermore, it placed unforseen pressures on mayors who had become involved in municipal affairs in 1790 for reasons that had nothing to do with politics. The nature of the job had changed, and disillusion frequently set in. In the Vosges, for instance, levels of enthusiasm ebbed quickly as the new nature of municipal responsibilities became clear. In Year VII it was recognized that few of the department's mayors, *adjoints,* or *agents municipaux* had much stomach for the highly *dirigiste* role that they were being expected to play:

> La plupart des agents municipaux ne regardent leurs fonctions que comme un lourd fardeau dont ils désirent vivement de se décharger. S'ils font quelqu'usage de l'autorité dont ils sont revêtus, ils craignent toujours que ceux qu'elle frappe ne deviennent autant d'ennemis personnels et dangereux, et cette considération les rend malheureusement très faibles et négligents dans l'exercice de leurs fonctions. (23)

As time passed, and as the mayor's role became increasingly that of exercising regular surveillance on all the young men resident in their area of administrative competence, so the joys of titular leadership in communal affairs became visibly diminished. (24)

Disillusionment was frequently translated into resignation. Of course public officials seldom hinted at differences of opinion or disagreements with state policy; they hid behind reasons of health or business pressures. Many offered a bluntly materialist explanation, claiming that the costs involved in carrying out municipal duties had become too onerous and that they must therefore tender their resignation. An *agent municipal* at Valence excused himself from office in Year IV on the grounds that "la modicité de mon traitement et les circonstances malheureuses où nous nous trouvons m'ont enfin contraint d'abandonner mes fonctions pour aller chercher du pain ailleurs" (25). Another, at Rambervillers, pleaded business engagements that conflicted with the demands of his office: "L'exposant est marchand, ce sont les jours de foire et de marchés où son commerce le retient dans sa boutique, ce sont cependant ces jours-là où les fonctions d'adjoint l'appelleront de toute nécessité et sans interruption" (26). The submission could assume a more humanitarian guise. Tournaire *aîné,* the government's *commissaire* at Châteauneuf-de-Mazène (Drôme), offered a whole list of excuses to justify his resignation, as though he believed, perhaps rightly, that no one reason would carry sufficient weight with his political masters:

> . . . que j'ai mon épouse malade, n'étant pas sortie de ma maison depuis plus d'une année; j'ai une fille aveugle, un frère estropié d'un rhumatisme, il y a quatre ans qu'il n'est pas sorty de sa chambre, son état exigeant des soins pénibles. Je suis eloigné de deux grands lieux de Châteauneuf, chef-lieu de canton, des chemins mauvais, y ayant la rivière des Sabron à passer sans aucun pont, ce qu'il rend surtout en temps d'hiver la communication presque impossible. (27)

What these men and hundreds of others like them had in common after several years of the Republic was a conviction that they wanted quite desperately to be relieved of their public office and of responsibilities that they found increasingly intolerable for themselves and their families.

The government was well aware of the serious implications of such discontent for the smooth running of the governmental machine. Good men with the sort of skills that were required to guarantee efficiency were less and less likely to offer their services, and the image of mayoral office became tarnished in the eyes of the general public. The prefect of the Loire admitted in his report for 1807 that the conscription laws had played a major part in creating public demoralization and loss of confidence in local government, "en éloignant les hommes qui y conviendraient le mieux" (28). This in turn helped to create a climate in which the government had little trust in the abilities of its local officials. In some rural departments it was a serious problem to find men of even the most basic literacy to fill communal offices, however explicitly the law might define literacy as a basic requirement for mayors. In the Cantal mayors were often incapable of reading or interpreting tax laws, which made tax collection difficult, if not impossible. One of the men appointed as *percepteurs des contributions* for the department was dismissed in Year XI after being acquitted in a fraud case in which he pleaded not guilty on grounds of total illiteracy (29). In the Pyrénées illiterate mayors posed problems of comprehension and communication. The mayor of Loubières (Ariège) was finally dismissed in Year XIII for his illiteracy, or, more accurately, for his total failure to answer administrative correspondence, a direct result of his lack of reading skills (30). And in the neighboring Roussillon it was noted that village mayors who could not read or write were prone to hold back several young men from the annual conscription to help them with their administration—a habit that was harmful to public morale but was very common "dans des pays où les citoyens propres à dresser les rolles des contributions, en sachant bien lire, sont très rares" (31). Although it is true that many of the more dismissive remarks about the quality of village mayors betray the sense of urban superiority of prefects and their staff, the respect in which they were held was often quite minimal. In some villages there were no candidates for office who could demonstrate the most basic understanding of the workings of local government, which makes their subsequent apathy and dilatoriness of conduct all the easier to understand. At Groix in the Morbihan the only candidate who could be found "qui soit capable de gérer cette place dignement" was the parish priest, an eventuality forbidden by law (32). Elsewhere they were frequently village *cultivateurs* more motivated by self-interest than by concern for the public good. The *sous-préfet* in Dunkerque, an area where cooperation between the *gendarmerie* and local mayors had never been strong, replied to criticism of his administration by pointing to the limited outlook and literacy of the men who accepted mayoral office in the countryside:

Les seuls renseignements qu'il me soit possible de donner, c'est qu'en général les maires manquent de nerf et de zèle, et beaucoup de l'intelligence nécessaire pour remplir leurs devoirs; mais ce mal est sans remède. Les campagnes ne sont habiteés que par des cultivateurs, et on n'y trouve point de propriétaires qui, par leur éducation, offriraient plus de moyens de faire marcher les choses comme il conviendrait. (33)

This rather bleak view was confirmed by the Directory's *commissaire* in Maubeuge in Year VII, who noted that local government was already being undermined by the refusal of men of property, "les gens aisés," to have any part in it, with the result that public office was left increasingly to the poor, peasants with little land of their own, and day laborers (34).

The decline in the status of mayors and their *adjoints* and the refusal of suitable candidates to present themselves for election further constrained the government's freedom of political maneuver. For Paris had no means of forcing local men to serve. In a surprisingly frank statement the prefect of the Gironde warned the *conseiller d'état* in Year XII of the frustration and impotence that he felt when faced with public apathy and noncooperation. Mayoralties, he said, were no longer sought after, with the result that the government had no choice but to accept patently inadequate candidates:

> Il ne faut pas oublier, M. le Conseiller d'État, qu'on est libre de les accepter ou de les refuser; qu'elles sont purement gratuites; qu'elles font perdre leur temps à ceux qui les occupent; que même elles constituent un frais. Il n'y a qu'un avantage qui contrebalance ces inconvénients, c'est la considération qu'elles font rejaillir dans une commune sur l'homme qui les remplit, mais cette espèce de talisman n'a pas de puissances sur toutes les âmes. (35)

In such an unreceptive climate the government's clear interest was to hold on to the mayors it had for as long as it could; replacing or dismissing them made little sense when candidates were so rare and public good will so lacking. If officials were local men of limited horizons, faithful representatives of local society, any attempt to discipline them for errors or for omissions could only serve to stir up opposition in the community at large. Hence prefects and ministers were left in something of a quandary. Did they take action against mayors who cheated or defrauded in matters of recruitment and risk alienating local opinion still further, or did they continue to recognize the powers of the mayors who were implicated and risk appearing to condone their offenses? Often they were only too glad to accept a face-saving compromise. When the mayor of Massy (Seine-et-Oise) was suspected of providing certificates to a known and convicted deserter in 1810, the Minister not surprisingly insisted on his dismissal from office; however, the prefect was so concerned that he would be unable to find a replacement that he intervened and offered evidence in his defense (36). Concern that the public humiliation of a country mayor would stir up sympathy against the government was a strong argument in favor of adopting a conciliatory approach. This was especially true, of course, in parts of the country where royalism and counterrevolution were rampant, where terrorization effectively ensured that loyal republican candidates for public office rarely stepped forward. At Pierrelatte in the Drôme not a single replacement could be found when the municipal council was dismissed in Year V. One by one the men designated as replacements offered their apologies and declined to serve. Yet all had given excellent service to the community in the past and were men of known and trusted opinions. Fear clearly lay at the root of their new found intransigence, fear for their property and the welfare of their families. As the government *commissaire* in Pierrelatte warned, "tant que les prêtres réfractaires seront protégés, qu'ils trouvent dans le corps législatif de chaleureux défenseurs, que les déserteurs pourront se montrer impunément, les bons citoyens, les véritables soutiens du gouvernement, n'oseront accepter les places dans la crainte d'être les victimes du fanatisme, et, disons-le, du royalisme" (37). Intimidation could so easily bring whole communities to the verge of ungovernability. When the mayor of Saint-Urcize in the Cantal helped to arrest a conscript in the village inn, public anger forced him to resign through fear of violent reprisals. More significantly, perhaps, no one else would agree to replace him, and all those who were proposed for the office threatened to leave the town rather than agree to work with the *gendarmerie* (38).

It can, of course, be argued that with more than 37,000 communes and local government entrusted to the new *classe politique* created in 1790, isolated instances of resistance or indifference were only to be expected. New habits and customs could not be created overnight, and the revolutionary and Napoleonic institutions were bound to suffer teething problems, especially at village level. But in many parts of the country the malaise that set in over the issue of military recruitment ran much deeper, with the result that in wide areas of France (the rural Gironde as well as the frontier regions of the Ariege) it became increasingly difficult to find local men of any stature willing to serve as village mayors. This posed problems of credibility as well as of simple authority for the government. Paris needed mayors and elected *conseils municipaux* if they were to retain the sense of local involvement on which their effective rule was dependent. The mayor, decked out in his *tricolor* sash and resplendent in his municipal insignia, was a symbol of the new order of representative government, and was particularly vital to the success of unpopular policies like the annual *tirage* for the armies (39). Without his symbolic involvement the intrusion of outside force was exposed much more brutally as a naked aggression against local custom, and all sense of government by consensus risked being lost. In the last resort, of course, the government had alternatives, but it was loathe to make use of them. It could depend more widely on the advice of appointed *commissaires,* trusting their judgment over that of its elected officials, though this policy was not without its perils. *Commissaires* themselves could be subjected to local pressures or become the victims of violence (40). The unpopularity of *commissaires* under the Directory could lead to the post being left vacant for months and even years, as happened at Auray—a particularly delicate posting in *chouan* country—in Year V (41). There were even instances where a *commissaire,* after being dismissed for his over-sympathetic attitude to local conscripts, had to be reinstated after a decent interval because no other candidates were available (42). Nor was there any guarantee that the men appointed by the government would actually carry out their duties with the required degree of efficiency. They were, after all, no less open to corruption than elected officials, and the temptations of their office were substantial. At Saales in the Vosges the *commissaire du Directoire* in Year VI was denounced for taking bribes from the relatives of conscripts and for granting illegal exemptions that were more commonly associated with village mayors. From one *réquisitionnaire* he received "deux livres de lin et une somme de trois livres", from another "une livre de lin," and from a third "une livre de lin et un boisseau de froment (43). His price, it seems, was endearingly cheap. But the real disadvantage to Paris of trying to rule extensively through appointed officials lay in the adverse effect that this had on public opinion. Their lack of local responsibility left them and the government that relied on them vulnerable to public criticism. They were too often depicted as self-important busybodies, reveling in the power that their office bestowed, throwing their weight around needlessly and disturbing the quiet tenor of municipal councils that were working smoothly and undemonstratively (44). Like the other authoritarian solutions to local intransigence—the sending in of the military or the forcible amalgamation of two adjacent communes (45)—the reliance on *commissaires* could not substitute for the demise of elected local government.

The anger of local people was directed not only at the process of recruitment that brought the state into their lives, but also at the methods of policing that were adopted. The *gendarmes* might complain about the lack of cooperation that they received from local communities, but for local people it was the abuse of power by the *gendarmes* that caused most outcry; and the gendarmes were the visible, tangible representation of the state itself. The build-up of a police presence in areas of provincial France which had been accustomed only to the rather patchy surveillance of the *maréchaussée* was almost bound to occasion conflict, especially with the new municipal authorities who guarded their local liberties jealously against real and imagined slights. The fact that deserters and refractories sought shelter in practically all the communes of France at one time or another opened everyone to the possibility of a visit from the *gendarmerie*. And the behavior of the *gendarmes,* especially when they felt thwarted by a lack of immediate help and cooperation, could itself contribute to inflaming relations with the local population. *Gendarmes* could be rough and insolent and could use their status and their uniform to badger and bully countrymen suspected of shielding fugitives. A report from the Twenty-seventh Division Militaire in Turin admitted as much in Year XI:

La gendarmerie n'est pas aussi bien composée qu'on pourrait le désirer pour la tranquillité de ce pays; elle abuse souvent des pouvoirs qui lui sont confiés et aliène d'elle par cette conduite l'esprit des habitants; il y a peu de gendarmes qui mettent d'abord en usage les moyens de douceur; leur fierté mal placeé dégénère souvent en brutalité, et c'est là l'une des grandes causes des révoltes qu'elle se plaint d'exciter partout où elle poursuit les méchants . . . (46)

As time passed it became increasingly obvious that it was the *gendarmerie* rather than the recruitment process which was the principal target for popular venom; and where violence broke out local councils were prone to defend their *concitoyens* and turn their anger against the police (47). Familiarity with the new policing conventions did nothing to win public trust or understanding.

If opinion in a village favored the refractory conscript against the demands of the state, there was little that the police could do to win hearts in support of their operation. They would be regarded with fear and suspicion from the first moment of their approach, and the arrival of a *peloton* of *gendarmes* was viewed as a gross intrusion and abuse of state power. This was a traditional response in many towns and villages, the one they had reserved for the *maréchaussée* when they had come to police desertion in the Ancien Regime. What was new was the scale and ambition of policing, which multiplied that traditional distrust of out-siders a hundred fold. The use of *garnisaires* was deeply hated by local com-munities. The resort to ambushes and dawn raids elicited the deepest loathing, and the imposition of severe fines on individuals and on whole communities aroused new levels of collective anger. The sight of *colonnes mobiles* swarming across the countryside like locusts, rounding up every young man unfortunate enough to fall into their clutches, left an indelible impression on many a peas-ant's mind. In areas of the country where the search for deserters overlapped with the search for counterrevolutionary insurgents, the Hostage Law of Year VII, implemented in a cluster of the most intransigent communities, so inflamed public opinion against the authorities that it served only to harden resistance and to gain new recruits for the *brigands* (48). When the state chose to make an example of a town or village by ordering the disarming of its entire population (49), by reducing its civil status (50), or by laying siege to it militarily (51)—as happened when the patience of the Minister of War finally snapped—the response of the local inhabitants could be unforgiving. Savage policing of recruitment might succeed in forcing more men into uniform. It might even impress peasant society with a demonstration of state power. But it was not an effective instrument for winning friends or inspiring admiration.

Public hostility to the *gendarmerie* was increased in those instances where subterfuge and deceit were used to track down deserters and *insoumis*. Villagers were quick to reject measures that used cheating and duplicity, or the use of tactics that violated popular conceptions of fair play. In the Nord knives were drawn on *gendarmes* founding stalking deserters in plain clothes, and the Min-ister of Justice felt dutybound to warn his men that they should even on the most delicate operations be sure to carry some mark of their identity (52). Yet undercover work was a necessary part of policing, and accounts of operations against deserters and their protectors in villages along the Belgian frontier make it clear that the Minister's instruction was routinely ignored. In sensitive frontier regions where deserters hung out in considerable numbers and where local peo-ple were tempted to offer them assistance, stealth and subterfuge were essential if the *gendarmes* were to make any significant inroads into the problem (53). Entry into private houses at night was not permitted by law; thus the police had to move with some alacrity if they were to make mass arrests in areas where deserters were known to be hiding. In Bordeaux in Year VII, for instance, the *gendarmes* had a list of safe houses for those on the run that they intended to raid. Their orders were suitably terse and explicit, that the move must be coor-dinated and that "il est important que cette arrestation se fasse à six heures du soir ou du matin, au même moment dans toutes les maisons désignées" (54). Elsewhere police activity against deserters was marked by its cunning and inven-tiveness. In the Yonne in Year VII two gendarmes, heavily disguised, went into the woods where conscripts had been reported to gather, making notes of their observations and providing intelligence for the night raid that was to follow (55). At Saint-Girons in 1808 the authorities made use of "trois gendarmes de Foix, travestis"; at Rivèrenert, less sensationally, they were disguised as "chasseurs sur la montagne" (56). Knowing that conscripts could not resist the attractions of fairs and markets, the *commissaire-général de police* in Bordeaux arranged a special welcoming party for them at the October *foire* in the city in 1808. He constructed a *baraque* on the fairground where men could drink and gamble, in the belief that this would ensnare deserters and criminals attracted by the pleasures of cards and the lure of financial gain. He was not disappointed. His haul of thirty-four prisoners included ten army and six navy deserters (57). At times the methods of underground policing deployed came close to encouraging crime, so keen were the authorities to inform themselves of the networks that protected deserters. The fruits of such policing could be rich indeed. In Year VI a number of soldiers disguised themselves as Dutch troops from Berg-op-Zoom across the frontier, claimed to have deserted their units, and invited talk from the local people they encountered in bars and inns. The result was a very impressive piece of military espionage against deserters and the rings of civilians who organized their passage. In their own words,

> Nous nous sommes déguisés en soldats déserteurs, puis transportés sur les huit heures du soir dans un cabaret sur la route de Bréda, où nous nous sommes annoncés comme déserteurs: en cette qualité nous avons demandé à la femme dudit cabaret les renseignements propres à favoriser notre évasion; elle s'y est très volontairement prêtée. Dans le cours de la conversation, elle a raconté que deux jours auparavant un complot de désertion de vingt-deux hommes s'était formé dans sa maison, d'où ils étaient partis pour la France; qu'il s'organisait dans ladite France une armeé royale de cent mille hommes ... Elle nous donna ensuite son fils ou domestique pour nous conduire par chemins détournés sur la route d'Anvers. (58)

The collection of intelligence of this kind made a favorable impression on the men's military commanders. For the population at large, however, such exploits seemed underhanded and dishonest, particularly when they themselves were the objects of police surveillance.

Their sense of outrage was maximized in those cases in which the *gendarmes* not only invaded the space of the local community and resorted to trickery or low cunning, but also insulted their deeply held religious faith. In Catholic areas the police were strongly tempted to take advantage of religious festivals and key dates in the Christian calendar when they knew from experience that Catholic families made every effort to be together and that refractories and deserters customarily came out of hiding. Perennially short of manpower and under orders to make the arrest of conscripts a high priority, the *lieutenants de gendarmerie* would have had to be singularly saintly not to take advantage of such an opportunity for a successful cull. In their eyes it was merely a question of tactical advantage; there was no inherent moral ambiguity to be considered. In the Nord policing was concentrated on "les jours des ci-devant dédicaces des communes," the days when religious festivals were held in Flemish villages to celebrate the dedication of their churches. A circular to *commissaires* in Year VII made it clear that it was government policy fully supported by the authorities in Douai to take advantage of these simple ceremonies to arrest the local boys defying the requisition. "Quand vous savez qu'une dédicace doit avoir lieu," they were instructed, "prévenez-en à l'avance le lieutenant de gendarmerie de votre arrondissement, et invitez-le à réunir plusieurs brigades pour les envoyer vers le soir dans la commune où la fête devra se célébrer et y arrêter les déserteurs" (59). Such operations always carried an element of risk, since public reaction could be angry and violent. Above all, military or police action was bound to center on the church building itself, at the very moment when mass was being celebrated, which could assume the guise of an act of blasphemy as well as constituting an underhanded tactic against the villagers. The inner sanctum of the collective life of the village was being brutally violated. Moreover, some of the police actions were very ruthless. At Saint-Laurent in the Médoc the *gendarmes* surrounded the village church during the morning mass one Sunday in 1809. Without waiting for the service to end, they entered the church, cleared the building of women and children, and took more than fifty young men away to Bordeaux, the majority of them completely innocent of any recruitment offense. (60). The interruption of the mass by the entry of armed men caused fear and outrage, and it was perhaps a disproportionate price to pay for seven recruitment convictions.

Two instances of police action against the congregations of village churches in the Ariège illustrate graphically the tension and disorders that they could cause. At Ségura in 1806 the *gendarmerie* mounted a siege of the village church after the mayors of local communes had refused any assistance in tracking down refractories. They suspected strongly that the young men of the area had come down from the hills to attend midnight mass, and consequently surrounded the church to catch those coming out after the service. It was a clinically mounted military operation against the building, "à minuit un quart . . . nous avons été nous embusquer dans un petit bois à trois cents pas à peu près de l'église . . . afin de pouvoir y arrêter quelqu'un des conscrits réfractaires à la sortie de la messe." After the mass was over, they had the mayor accompany them inside the church building, but were met with a startled refusal and by an angry denunciation from the *curé,* who proclaimed from the pulpit that the *gendarmes* had defiled the building and that his church had been reduced to "un rassemblement de voleurs." In the confusion that followed the *gendarmes* were engulfed by an angry mob of some 200 worshippers, and the men they had arrested were set free (61). Even more provocative was the presence of the *gendarmes* at the midnight mass on Christmas Eve in the village church at Lacourt in Year XIII. According to the mayor, a joint service was being held by the inhabitants of several surrounding villages, candles were lit and mass was being said, when "un grand tumulte" broke out inside the church among members of the congregation. The police had entered the building during the service and had infiltrated the rows of worshippers, ready to swoop on the young and robust as soon as the mass was complete. But panic broke out when it was observed that the *gendarmes* guarding the door had drawn their guns and swords. In the tumult that followed shots were fired and the candles extinguished, plunging the church into darkness and replacing the serenity of the *office* with screams and agitation (62). In his report, François Dubois, the *lieutenant de gendarmerie* in charge of the operation, made it clear that it was a routine police search following fruitless enquiries in the village and surrounding fields. For the villagers of Lacourt, however, it was a deeply shocking incident that threw into sharp relief the deep gulf that separated them and their community from the agents of the state.

There can be little doubt that relations between the police and the people suffered grievous damage during this period because of the part played by the *gendarmes* in searching for draft dodgers. Villagers had never been ecstatic about being policed and supervised. Policing was too modern a concept, and the role of the centralized state too little understood, for it to be welcomed as a natural safeguard against crime and abuse. There were few instances where mayors would turn voluntarily to the *gendarmerie* to assist with purely local problems. But their reaction was often one of mild hostility or bland indifference until the conscription issue heightened the police presence in local communities and aroused latent village animosities against the state and its pretensions. It was conscription that turned rural communities into *foyers* of hatred for the *gendarmes* and that drove them to the use of force, lashing out often blindly against men perceived as oppressors. In many parts of the countryside violence and popular disturbance reached unprecedented levels in these years as a direct result of recruitment policy, and it was turned increasingly against the government and its agents. That is not to say that it was political in any counterrevolutionary sense; however, it was political to the extent that it was used in defense of local rights and customs against the imposition of unwelcome innovation from outside the community. The *commissaire* of the Directory in the Aude, commenting on the levels of violence he had to contend with and the air of menace that seemed to hang over many of the communities under his administration, attributed popular animosity to custom and tradition and a dislike of change, to inflexible attitudes "telles que l'ignorance du peuple qui le rend inaccessible aux nouveautés, les vieilles habitudes et les préjugés de l'enfance qui dirigent la plupart des individus, enfin le fanatisme religieux, foyer éternel de dépravation" (63). In other words, he was admitting that government action in this sphere ran counter to the most basic political instincts of the rural community.

The violence stimulated by recruitment and conscription fell into several clear categories. At the moment of the *tirage* there was always a strong possibility of violent resistance, either on the part of the men designated, their families, or the young men of the community acting out a collective peer group role. When the government passed a law ordering an augmented level of service or an exceptional levy, the agents entrusted with the decree might suffer violent handling by an angry community. Or the day designated for the *départ* of the young men of the locality might attract to the town hall a murmuring crowd of malcontents, hurling abuse at the municipal officials and those *gendarmes* sent to escort the new conscripts to their units. Sometimes, as at Elven in the Morbihan in 1809, public hostility was so evident that the *gendarmerie* mounted special policing operations in a bid to prevent rioting and disorder. In this case there was a well-accredited rumor in the department that open insurrection might ensue (64). Over time it seemed that the targets of popular anger underwent a subtle but significant change. Whereas in the early years of revolutionary recruitment most of the violence was directed against the recruiting-sergeant and the selection process, by 1800 it was the agents and representatives of the state who found themselves under fire. The conscription process increasingly, as has been demonstrated, passed without serious incident, but those who represented the government or who symbolized the authority of the state came more and more to have that authority called into question. The *gendarmerie* were particularly regarded with suspicion and open hostility when they carried out their duties in the village community, especially when those duties involved the search for conscripts or the arrest of young men hiding in the fields and outhouses. When they made a capture or began to lead their prisoners back to the nearby town, popular fury often bore down on them, and violence, even murder, could easily ensue.

What is especially significant about this violence is the general support that it evoked across large sectors of rural society. Even when the deserters themselves attacked the *gendarmerie* to secure their own release, it is clear that they did so with the absolution of their families and friends (65). The arrival of *gendarmes* to carry out a *rafle* in houses and outbuildings was nearly always met with sullen opposition, at times interrupted by jeers and catcalls. And it took very little for that opposition to be inflamed into physical assault. The very sight of uniformed officers in villages that had offered their protection to deserters could suffice to heighten tension and spark off violence. A dawn raid on a hamlet in the Pas-de-Calais where the mayor was known to favor refractories was greeted with threats and abuse, the suspect succeeding in attracting a small army of villagers to his defense, armed with pitchforks and scythes. The *gendarmes* could only parry the blows aimed at them and withdraw empty-handed (66). In several other villages in the north of France the police were stoned by angry villagers infuriated by their presence and by the purpose of their visit. At Ognies where seventy-six men had deserted in an act of mass disobedience a few weeks previously, *gendarmes* were greeted by a hail of stones and forced to abandon their mission (67). It was this generalized collusion in violence against the police that proved most frustrating and disspiriting for members of the force. When they were attacked, injured, on occasion killed during these campaigns against desertion, no one in the local community seemed to care. At Loubens (Ariège) two officers were subjected to a barrage of abuse in the village bar while they prepared to take their captive, a deserter from the Ninety-third Line Regiment, back to prison. Even when the prisoner grabbed a bottle full of wine and smashed it in the face of one of his tormentors, no one could be found to testify against him. The court subsequently reduced the charge on the grounds that a bottle should be seen less as an offensive weapon than as an everyday object in a cabaret (68). In a separate incident a few miles away, several young men attacked and disarmed the *gendarmes* who had arrested one of their number for draft evasion. They were noisy and rowdy, firing pistol shots and threatening the police, yet again not a soul in the village came forward with evidence (69). The *gendarmes* were too familiar with hostility and with their best-laid plans being betrayed by local people for any illusions to remain. In many parts of the *hexagone* they knew that anti-police violence enjoyed popular support in the local community. They knew too that there could be no stigma attached to such violence as long as their presence was resented as an intrusion from the outside world.

This view is strongly supported by the evidence of those involved in attacks on the *gendarmerie,* the different kinds of people who might at one time or another throw themselves into riotous assembly. The formula would seem to have been almost infinitely variable. *Maires* and village notables, already implicated in the eyes of the state to the extent that they were responsible for *esprit public* within their communities, often did nothing to oppose the overwhelming sentiment of the villagers and took a leading part in riots to free deserters (70). The immediate family of those at risk were equally likely to figure among the rioters. In a violent incident at Le Taillan near Bordeaux the *gendarmes* arresting a local man for avoiding conscription found themselves suddenly assailed by "son père, deux de ses frères, sa soeur et plusieurs autres habitants armés de haches," a formidable demonstration of family unity, even if in this case it failed to secure the young man's release (71). Women as well as men and the old as well as the young threw themselves into such attacks, and at times it was their particular contribution that freed sons, husbands, and nephews. When a conscript was arrested by a *garde-champêtre* near Charpey in the Drôme in 1806, it was his illegitimate daughter and two other village women who attacked the *garde* and threatened him with a rich variety of weapons, from a knife to an axe to an armory of stones and rocks (72). Village women were every bit as fierce as their men in defending their families against arrest or forcible removal to the armies, and their sheer, single-minded devotion to the freedom of their sons and husbands could leave the *gendarmes* powerless. An incident in the village of Courlon in the Yonne provides a good example. The two *gendarmes* sent to arrest a local deserter had seized and bound him when the whole village seemed to explode around them. Even allowing for the natural exaggeration of two very frightened officers, their description conjures up graphic images of family solidarity:

> Ils avaient effectué cette arrestation, mais qu'immédiatement étaient survenus François Verrien, frère du deserteur, Anne Verrien, femme Bernard Leroux, la citoyenne Cheinot et la veuve Verrien, mère du déserteur, qui s'étaient tous armés de pierres et de bâtons, avaient frappé les gendarmes sur les bras et sur la tête et avaient lâché sur eux un gros chien qui déchira leurs vêtements; que cette scène s'est passée devant un rassemblement de soixante personnes, tant hommes que femmes, parmi lesquels plusiers criaient, 'Tuez ces coquins-là!'' (73)

In this as in so many other instances, the officers had little choice but to release their prey. Or again, it might be the young men of the community, the friends of the victim and those who, like him, knew what it was to undergo the *supplice* of the ballot for the armies, who confronted the *gendarmes* and secured their companion's freedom. In one spectacular attack, a young cowherd from the Cantal was freed from captivity by some thirty of his friends, who abandoned their beasts on the mountainside to ambush the police as they escorted their captives along the main road between Aurillac and Tulle (74). Bonds of friendship among the young men of the village community, like family bonds, could be turned to the assistance of those on the run and could thwart the ambitions of *gendarmes* and government alike.

From this it was but a short step to full-scale antigovernment rioting, sparked off by the arrival of the *gendarmes* in a village or by rumors of an impending raid to arrest draft dodgers. So many different interests were antagonized by a police presence that the reaction against them could include the entire community. If country families were prepared to attack the police in defense of their sons and brothers, so, too, they would risk their lives and their liberty to free their neighbors' children, their farmservants, or those who had thrown themselves on their mercy. In the battle to defend conscripts against the authorities a sense of loyalty and of belonging quickly developed. The *gendarmes* who entered their village to seize their children or the young men who depended on their protection had, as a matter of honor, to be repulsed; their purpose dictated that they should be cast as the enemy of the entire community. In 1806 when officers from Foix entered the village of Merens to arrest deserters, they encountered the armed opposition of the majority of the villagers in a *bagarre* of considerable violence. Not only was the raid foiled, but in the struggle the symbols of the *gendarmes'* authority were sought as trophies, tangible evidence of a famous collective victory. The villagers noisily proclaimed their anger at the violation of their community, tore free the unfortunate conscript who had been arrested, and, in the mayor's words, "on est parvenu . . . à arracher le baudrier ainsi que le fourreau de sabre" of one of the gendarmes (75). Parents sometimes took a leading part in such mêlées and their anger acted as a catalyst to others. There were even instances where determined fathers lost their lives in clashes with the *gendarmes* (76). But the conflict was usually extended far beyond the family context, since the honor of the entire village was felt to be at stake. A refractory conscript or a deserter had to be given some protection. He was in their custody, and the act of handing him over to outsiders would be a gross act of personal betrayal. The "honnêteté" of the village, in the sense defined by Yves Castan, was impugned by the demands made by the state (77). Even when the fugitive was sought for serious criminal offenses elsewhere—as in the case of one deserter near Mirecourt who was suspected of murder—any attempt by the *gendarmerie* to remove him from the custody of the villagers was violently resisted (78). In cases like this the police might feel perplexed as well as aggrieved; however, it was the deserter who was closer to the pulse of the local community, who understood the villagers' sense of what was right and wrong. Faced with the *gendarmerie,* men on the run from authority knew very well that they could with some assurance throw themselves on the mercy of their fellows and take a gamble that village opinion would not allow them to be sacrificed.

Rioting was an extreme response, a rejection by the local community of the state and the law that it was trying to impose. But in much of rural France, and occasionally in larger towns and cities (79), the issue of recruitment ensured that hostility to this conception of law remained deeply embedded in the popular consciousness. The sight of *gendarmes* and other state officials systematically persecuting the young for a cause that enjoyed little popular support merely served to spread disaffection (80). There was little sympathy for the police in their task, and, in a society that accepted a high level of everyday violence, few qualms about causing them wounds or injuries. *Gendarmes* entering villages on unpopular missions were habitually jeered and humiliated by local people, or greeted with the roars of derision that accompanied the traditional village *charivari* from time immemorial. At Lucenay in the Rhône, for example, two *gendarmes* arrived to arrest a deserter whom they knew to be at work threshing corn with other lads from the village community. They went up to groups of harvesters and exchanged pleasantries with them, only to be greeted with sullen hostility. For "les batteurs ne reconnaissant point, ou feignant de ne point reconnaître les gendarmes, s'emparent d'un de ces derniers, lui demandent le pourboire qu'on exige aux étrangers qui entrent dans l'aire sans permission, et, sur son refus de donner ce pourboire, font subir à ce gendarme une punition corporelle très humiliante" (81). The message was clear. Not only were they unwelcome in the community, but on that territory it was local custom that should prevail. In other villages the welcome reserved for the agents of the law could be even more unpleasant, involving physical injury or even death. The thirty-four members of the *colonne mobile* from nearby Preches who arrived in the village of Felleries (Nord) in Year VII to hunt for deserters at first faced little more than abuse from the local population. But as the night wore on and everyone became the worse for drink, so tempers rose and general brawling took over. Members of the force were attacked, local people were heard to urge that they be put to death, punches were exchanged, and one of the *gendarmes* was knocked out with a *pelle à feu* (82). The hatred and lack of respect for the troops and the job they were sent to perform were clear to everyone. But the violence in Felleries was as Boulevard comedy compared to what occurred in other parts of France. When a *gendarme* was murdered in the village of Saignes (Cantal) in 1808, only the rural bourgeoisie offered the authorities any assistance. The rest of the community, particularly *bouviers* and those living in the outlying hamlets, actively protected the men who had committed the outrage, and the majority of local people showed neither sympathy for the victim nor any desire to see the killers brought to justice (83). Similarly in the Pyrenean village of Rivèrenert where a *gendarme* was killed in the course of a riot over the arrest of deserters, his death caused little sorrow or compunction among the villagers (84). At times, indeed, there was something wholly gratuitous, even joyous, about the violence used against those seeking to enforce unpopular laws. At Clazay (Deux-Sèvres) in 1806 three *gendarmes* who were leading captured deserters back to their base were attacked with carefree brutality. Two of them were killed by gunshots— "ils essuyèrent une décharge de quarante à cinquante coups de fusils"—while the third, lying seriously wounded, was callously finished off by one of the rioters who smashed his riflebutt across the officer's head (85).

Attacks on state officials occurred more frequently over conscription than over any other single question. Neither taxation nor food supply was the occasion for such sustained rejection of the pretensions of central government or such persistent attacks on the agents and symbols of the state. At Hazebrouck in 1813—a riot that was savagely repressed with the imposition of four death sentences—conscription provided the backcloth for a mass insurrection involving some 1,200 to 1,500 people, in which the *sous-préfet*, the government's representative, was "outragé, maltraité et frappé" and forced to flee for his life (86). The choice of target was no accident. To local people the *sous-préfet* symbolized the very essence of state power and personified Napoleonic centralism. In its pursuit of deserters the government had intruded as never before into people's everyday lives, with troops and *gendarmes* dismantling hayricks and bursting into bedrooms. Louis Bergeron has remarked that "the consular and imperial power was a power that defended itself by attacking," a judgment fully sustained by a study of recruitment policy. He adds that it was established so rapidly because its active opponents were minorities who could be easily isolated and who failed to mobilize popular support (87). In large tracts of France those who were opposed to one significant aspect of government policy, that of recruitment for the armies, were far more numerous, and the intrusion of national politics into village affairs risked turning their resentment into a vocal and violent opposition to the government itself. Much of village France clung to its customs and traditions and remained stubbornly archaic in its structure for decades after the Emperor's abdication. It was not fertile ground for Napoleon's wholesale administrative and judicial reforms or for a committed role in the creation of a modern nation-state. In the long term annual conscription was to play an important part in modernizing the French countryside, in making peasants into Frenchmen. But in the short term the enervating recruitment policy pursued in the revolutionary and Napoleonic years did little to persuade the inhabitants of the Causses or of the Auvergne that the brave new world had much to offer them. It served rather to revive their village archaisms and to jeopardize the new civic order that was Napoleon's greatest and most enduring achievement.

Notes

PREFACE

1. Woloch, I., "Napoleonic conscription: state power and civil society," *Past and Present* 111 (1986), pp. 111–12.

CHAPTER 1

1. Archives Nationales (A.N.), F^{1c}III Var 11, report from Cuers (Var) on the incidence of resistance to conscription, 18 *pluviôse* VII.
2. A.N., F^{1c}III Basses-Pyrénées 7, report from *commissaire du Directoire exécutif* in Pau to Minister of Police générale, 20 *pluviôse* IV.
3. Auvray, M., *Objecteurs, insoumis, déserteurs,* p. 158.
4. Ibid., pp. 9–10.
5. Scott, S. F., *The response of the Royal Army to the French Revolution,* p. 36.
6. Gillet, D., "Etude de la désertion dans les armées royales à l'époque de Louis XIV," pp. 46–50, 73.
7. Léonard, E.-G., *L'armée et ses problèmes au dix-huitième siècle,* pp. 229–30.
8. Corvisier, A., *L'armée française de la fin du dix-septième siècle au ministère de Choiseul: le soldat,* p. 137.
9. Chagniot, J., "Quelques aspects originaux du recrutement parisien au milieu du dix-huitième siècle," *Recrutement, mentalités, sociétés: colloque international d'histoire militaire,* pp. 112–13.
10. Bernos, C.-E., "Souvenirs de campagne d'un soldat du régiment du Limousin, 1741–1748," *Carnet de la Sabretache* (1902), p. 672.
11. Bertaud, J. P., *La Révolution armée,* p. 38.
12. Scott, op. cit., p. 37.
13. Corvisier, op. cit., p. 228.
14. A.N., F^{1c}III Lot-et-Garonne 7, report from *commissaire du Directoire exécutif* in Agen, 1 *ventôse* VII.
15. Corvisier, op. cit., p. 711.
16. Kennett, L., *The French armies in the Seven Years' War,* p. 85.

239

17. Cameron, I., *Crime and repression in the Auvergne and the Guyenne, 1720–1790,* especially p. 73.
18. Kennett, op. cit., p. 76.
19. Corvisier, op. cit., p. 155.
20. Ibid., p. 65.
21. Ibid., p. 176.
22. Ibid., pp. 179–80.
23. Achard, C., "Le recrutement de la milice royale à Pézenas de 1689 à 1788," *Recrutement, mentalités, sociétés,* p. 45.
24. Laporte, P., "La milice d'Auvergne, 1688–1791," *Revue d'Auvergne,* p. 24.
25. Carrot, G., "Garde nationale et recrutement de l'armée à Grasse," *Annales du Midi* 89 (1977), p. 45.
26. Dessat, L.-A., and de l'Estoile, C. J., *Origine des armées révolutionnaires et impériales d'après les archives départementales de l'Ariège,* p. 2.
27. Corvisier, op. cit., p. 204.
28. Achard, op. cit., p. 47.
29. Serrant, H., *Le service de recrutement de 1789 à nos jours,* p. 2.
30. Achard, op. cit., p. 47.
31. Marion, M., *Dictionnaire des institutions de la France aux 17e et 18e siècles,* p. 377.
32. Achard, op. cit., p. 48.
33. Corvisier, op. cit., p. 204.
34. Ibid., p. 65.
35. Serrant, op. cit., p. 4.
36. Corvisier, op. cit., p. 114.
37. Ibid., p. 109.
38. Serrant, op. cit., p. 1.
39. Fourastié, V. (ed.), *Cahiers de doléances de la sénéchaussée de Cahors pour les Etats-Généraux de 1789,* pp. 316–19.
40. Giraud, M., *Levées d'hommes et acheteurs de biens nationaux dans la Sarthe en 1793,* pp. 75–6.
41. Goubert, P., and Denis, M. (ed.), *1789: Les Francais ont la parole,* pp. 207–8.
42. Dalby, J. R., "The French Revolution in a rural environment: the example of the Department of the Cantal, 1789–1794," p. 243.
43. Goubert and Denis, op. cit., p. 209.
44. Giraud, op. cit., p. 88.
45. Goubert and Denis, op. cit., p. 207.
46. Achard, op. cit., p. 48.
47. Corvisier, op. cit., p. 124.
48. On the localism and particularism of southern communities, see Jones, P. M., "Parish, seigneurie and the community of inhabitants in southern central France during the eighteenth and nineteenth centuries," *Past and Present* 91 (1981), pp. 74–108.
49. Braudel, F., *The Mediterranean and the Mediterranean world in the age of Philip II* 1, pp. 39–40.
50. Corvisier, op. cit., p. 742.
51. chevalier des Pommelles, *Observations sur le recrutement et l'emplacement de l'armèe active par cantons et par départements,* p. 4.
52. Ibid., pp. 6–7.
53. Statistics drawn from Corvisier, op. cit., pp. 415–18.
54. Ibid., pp. 6–7.
55. chevalier des Pommelles, *Tableau de la population de toutes les provinces de France et mémoire sur les milices,* pp. 12–13.

56. Scott, op. cit., p. 110.
57. Bertaud, op. cit., p. 42.
58. Scott, op. cit., p. 78.
59. Bertaud, op. cit., p. 47.
60. Archives Départementales (A.D.) Meurthe-et-Moselle, L211, extrait des délibérations du *Directoire du département,* 1790.
61. Scott, op. cit., p. 95.
62. Ibid., pp. 155ff.
63. Ibid., p. 157.
64. Soboul, A., *L'armèe nationale sous la Révolution, 1789–1794,* p. 71.
65. Bertaud, op. cit., p. 194.
66. Scott, op. cit. p. 190–202.
67. Meynier, A., "L'armée en France sous la Révolution et le Premier Empire," *Revue d'études militaires,* p. 17.
68. Woloch, I., *Jacobin Legacy,* p. 163.
69. Tulard, J., *Napoléon ou le Mythe du sauveur,* p. 360.
70. Morvan, J., *Le soldat impérial, 1800–1814* 1, p. 37.
71. Dupâquier, J., "Problèmes démographiques de la France napoléonienne," *Revue d'histoire moderne et contemporaine,* p. 346.

CHAPTER 2

1. Castel, J.-A., "L'application de la loi Jourdan dans l'Hérault: les levées directoriales de l'an VII," pp. 5–6.
2. Houdaille, J., "Pertes de l'armée de terre sous le premier Empire, d'après les registres matricules," *Population* 27, pp. 49–50; see also Bois, J.-P., "Conscrits du Maine-et-Loire sous l'Empire: le poids de la conscription, 1806–14," *Annales de Bretagne et des pays de l'Ouest* 83, p. 467n.
3. Déprez, E., *Les volontaires nationaux, 1791–1793,* p. 10.
4. Soboul, A., *Les soldats de l'an II,* pp. 69–71.
5. Bertaud, J.-P. *La Révolution armée,* p. 77.
6. Girault, P.-R., *Mes campagnes sous la Révolution et l'Empire,* p. 13.
7. Bertaud, op. cit., p. 68.
8. Archives de la Guerre (A.G.) Vincennes, X^{w}16, list of *volontaires* in the canton of Aurillac, 1791.
9. Bertaud, op. cit., pp. 66–7.
10. Crépin, A., "Armée de Révolution, armée nouvelle? L'exemple de la Seine-et-Marne," pp. 66–74.
11. A.G. Vincennes, X^{w}17, procès-verbal of the district of Aurillac, 14 March 1792.
12. Soboul, op. cit., p. 72.
13. A.G. Vincennes, X^{w}95, district of Versailles, *enrôlements de volontaires* for 1792. The men involved came from a total of forty-six departments.
14. Archives Départementales (A.D.) Cantal, L202, reports from Lascelles and Laroquevieille (district of Aurillac); L203, reports from Salers, Saignes, Apchon, and Les Arbres (district of Mauriac).
15. Dalby, J. R., "The French Revolution in a rural environment: the example of the Department of the Cantal, 1789–1794," p. 245.
16. A.D. Cantal, L202, letter from mayor of Monsalvy to the *procureur-syndic* of the district of Aurillac, 8 July 1792.
17. Bertaud, op. cit., pp. 82–3.

18. A.G. Vincennes, X^w18, list of *volontaires* from the commune of Cayrols (Cantal), 22 January 1793.
19. Archives Nationales (A.N.), F⁹160, fixed *primes* for *volontaires* in 1792 (imprimé, Paris, 1792); minute of the department of the Aude, 18 February 1792.
20. Bertaud, op. cit., p. 81.
21. A.D. Cantal, L207, petition from Chazal from Saint-Flour, 1 June 1792.
22. A.D. Cantal, L207, petition from Antoine Offroy from Mauriac, 6 July 1792.
23. Dalby, op. cit., p. 248.
24. Ibid., p. 247.
25. *Le Moniteur*, vol. 14, p. 248.
26. Bertaud, op. cit., p. 93.
27. A.D. Cantal, L205, letter from district of Saint-Flour to department of Cantal, 23 August 1792.
28. A.G. Vincennes, X^w70, letter from commune of Ploërmel, 26 October 1792.
29. A.G. Vincennes, X^W95, statistics for voluntary engagement, district of Versailles, 1792–1798.
30. A.D. Seine-et-Oise, 2LR113, petition from Jean Constant, 27 March 1792.
31. A.D. Seine-et-Oise, 2LR26, petition from the mayor and municipal council of Courgent, 27 April 1793.
32. A.G. Vincennes, X^w94, letter from the president of the canton of Arpajon (Seine-et-Oise), 4 *pluviôse* V.
33. A.N., F⁹225, minute of department of Nièvre, 29 *floréal* VII.
34. A.N., AF^IV1122, *états des enrôlés volontaires* for Year XI. The sixteen departments that did not provide a single volunteer were the Allier, Alpes-Maritimes, Aveyron, Gers, Golo, Landes, Liamone, Loir-et-Cher, Haute-Loire, Lozère, Puy-de-Dôme, Hautes-Pyrénées, Haute-Saône, Tarn, Haute-Vienne, and Yonne.
35. Bertaud, op. cit., p. 99.
36. A.G. Vincennes, X^w73, letter from district of Cambrai in response to decree of 24 February, 16 March 1793.
37. A.G. Vincennes, X^w73, letter from district of Lille to department of Nord, 18 August 1792.
38. A.D. Gironde, 5L46, letter from department of Gironde to district of Bazas, 11 October 1792.
39. A.D. Gironde, 8L46, petition from district of La Réole, 11 July 1792.
40. Giraud, M., *Levées d'hommes et acheteurs de biens nationaux dans la Sarthe en 1793*, p. 81.
41. A.D. Cantal, L253, letter from Ruat in Saint-Flour to district of Saint-Flour, 7 May 1793.
42. Giraud, op. cit., pp. 98–9.
43. A.D. Morbihan, L572, report from *municipalité* of Ploërmel on recruitment riots, 13 March 1793.
44. Sangnier, G., *La désertion dans le Pas-de-Calais de 1792 à 1802*, p. 47.
45. A.D. Cantal, L248, report on recruitment in Marcolès, 13 March 1793.
46. For a fuller discussion of the kinds of suspicion and unfairness that could result see Forrest, A., *The French Revolution and the poor*, pp. 140–48.
47. A.D. Drôme, L347, minute of *municipalité* of Bollène, 20 March 1793.
48. A.G. Vincennes, X^w18, petition from volunteers from the commune of Saint-Mamet, 2 April 1793.
49. A.G. Vincennes, X^w18, report of *commissaires* to the village of Thiézac, March 1793.
50. A.N., AF^III 182, letter from a member of the division du Contrat Social in Paris to the *commission militaire* of the *Conseil des Cinq-Cents*, 8 *ventôse* VI.

51. Arch. Comm. Oust (Ariège), *registre communal* for 14 March 1793 (A.D. Ariège, 132Esup.5).
52. A.D. Morbihan, L572, report from commune of Tréal, October 1793.
53. A.D. Morbihan, L572, letter from commune of Ploërmel, 9 October 1793.
54. A.G. Vincennes, Xʷ18, report from district of Saint-Flour on recruitment at Chaudesaigues, 4 April 1793.
55. A.G. Vincennes, Xʷ73, letter from *conseil militaire* to district of Le Quesnoy, 9 October 1792.
56. A.G. Vincennes, Xʷ73, report from district of Douai, 2 February 1793.
57. A.G. Vincennes, Xʷ7, communal reports from the Ariège on the *levée des 300,000,* February and March 1793.
58. A.G. Vincennes, Xʷ5, report on recruitment meeting at La Bastide-de-Besplas, 24 February 1793.
59. A.D. Nord, L6103, letter from Landschoote, *garçon majeur* in Coudequerque, to district of Bergues, 9 May 1793.
60. A.D. Cantal, L253, petition from ten citizens of Junhac, 31 March 1793.
61. A.D. Cantal, L253, petition from commune of La Besserette, 31 March 1793.
62. A.D. Cantal, L248, letter from commune of Marcolès, 17 March 1793.
63. A.G. Vincennes, Xʷ73, letter from district of Cambrai to department of Nord, 22 September 1792.
64. A.G. Vincennes, Xʷ18, letter from department of Cantal to commune of Laroquebrou, 17 June 1793.
65. A.D. Drôme, L347, *levée des 300,000,* recruitment list for district of Romans, 1793.
66. A.G. Vincennes, Xʷ107, report on *levée des 300,000* in department of Vosges, 1793.
67. A.D. Drôme, L347, letter from district of Crest to department of Drôme, 10 March 1793.
68. A.G. Vincennes, Xʷ30, letter from Kellermann to Minister of War, 1 March 1793.
69. Decree of 23 August 1793, quoted in Bertaud, op. cit., p. 115.
70. Bertaud, op. cit., p. 111.
71. Aulard, *CSP* 7, p. 7.
72. A.D. Morbihan, L572, *état général nominatif* of *première réquisition,* department of Morbihan, September 1793.
73. Bertaud, op. cit., p. 114.
74. A.G. Vincennes, Xʷ5, response of commune of La Bastide-de-Besplas to *commissaire du district,* 11 *pluviôse* II.
75. Crépin, op. cit., p. 267.
76. A.G. Vincennes, Xʷ9, letters from *procureur-général-syndic* in Carcassonne to Committee of Public Safety, 19 July and 12 August 1793.
77. A.N., BB¹⁸912, letter from *directeur du jury d'accusation* in Epinal (Vosges), 25 *ventôse* IV.
78. Vallée, G., *La conscription dans le département de la Charente,* p. 15.
79. A.G. Vincennes, Xʷ6, report from district of Saint-Girons to department of Ariège on the *levée* of Year III, 12 *thermidor* III.
80. A.N., AFᴵᴵᴵ145ᴬ, letter from Vernier to *Directoire exécutif* from Quimper, 28 *pluviôse* IV.
81. Vallée, op. cit., pp. 10–11.
82. Moody, W.S., *The introduction of military conscription in Napoleonic Europe, 1798–1812,* p. 31.
83. Quoted by Bergès, L., *Le civil et l'armée au début du dix-neuvième siècle,* p. 58.
84. Castel, J.-A. *L'application de la loi Jourdan dans l'Hérault,* p. 7.
85. Bergès, op. cit., p. 67.

86. Much of the detail that follows, drawn from the *Bulletin des lois,* is summarized in Louis Bergès' thesis, pp. 48ff.

87. A.D. Ariège, 5L21, list of the five *classes* of Year VII, canton of Belesta.

88. A.N., F⁹241, letter from prefect of the Rhône to Minister of Interior, 14 *brumaire* XIV.

89. A.N., F¹ᶜIII Pas-de-Calais 8, letter from prefect of the Pas-de-Calais to Minister of Interior, 17 *prairial* XII.

90. Bergès, *op. cit.,* p. 118. (Bergès puts great stress throughout on Napoleon's readiness to break the law to secure the soldiers he required.)

91. Darquenne, R., "La conscription dans le Département de Jammapes, 1798–1813," *Ann du Cercle Archéologique de Mons,* 67 (1968–1970).

92. A.N., AFᴵᴵᴵ149, report from *commissaire du Directoire exécutif* at Lons-le-Saunier (Jura), 30 *brumaire* VII.

93. A.D. Gironde, 11L290, letter from *commissaire du Directoire exécutif* at Quinsac to *commissaire du Directoire exécutif* in the department of Gironde, 21 *fructidor* VII.

94. A.N., AFᴵᴵᴵ149, report from department of Haute-Garonne, 2 *brumaire* VII.

95. Castel, *op. cit.,* p. 11.

96. A.D. Cantal, 1R164, *tableau* of conscription for the canton of Salers, *classe* of 1806.

97. A.N., F¹ᶜᴵᴵᴵLot-et-Garonne 8, prefect's report for the *trimestre de juillet,* 1807.

98. A.N., F⁹239, report from department of Bas-Rhin on conscription problems, 28 *floréal* VII.

99. A.D. Vosges, L536, letter from *commissaire du Directoire exécutif* at Rambervillers, 19 *thermidor* VII; A.D. Nord, 1R230, letter from maire of Bousbecque to *sous-préfet* of Lille, 16 May 1812.

100. A.D. Nord, 1R230, letter from *sous-préfet* of Lille to prefect of Nord, 9 June 1812.

101. A.D. Gironde, 3L267, letter from *commissaire du Directoire exécutif* in Bordeaux to all cantons in the Gironde, 6 *pluviôse* IV.

102. A.D. Seine-et-Oise, série R (*non-classée*), carton D, gendarmerie report from Dourdan, 1er *brumaire* XIV.

103. Such misunderstandings are reported, for example, in the Pas-de-Calais and the Seine-et-Oise in Year VIII (A.N., F⁹232 and 250).

104. A.N., AFᴵᴵᴵ158, letter from Bernard Coton, 13 *messidor* VII.

105. A.D. Nord, L2404, report from *commissaire du Directoire exécutif* sent to Avesnes to activate the conscription law, 18 *floréal* VII.

106. A.N., F⁹306, report on riot in the Toulousain, 17 *vendémiaire* VII.

107. A.D. Seine-et-Oise, 16L36, letter from *maire* of Gif to canton of Jouy-en-Josas, 9 *germinal* VIII.

108. A.N., AFᴵⱽ1121, circular letter from Minister of War, 3 *messidor* VIII.

109. A.N., F⁷3603, letter from prefect of Morbihan to Minister of Interior, forwarding deliberation of the *conseil-général* of his department, 5 *floréal* XIII.

110. A.N., F⁹189, letters from the prefect of the Gironde to Minister of Interior, 7 *ventôse* XII and 27 *frimaire* XII.

111. A.N., AFᴵⱽ1123, dossier of Hargenvilliers dated 1808, entitled "Compte général sur la conscription depuis son établissement."

112. A.N., AFᴵⱽ1123, correspondence of Lacuée, especially letter to the *Conseil d'Etat,* 21 January 1807.

113. Bois, J.-P., "Conscrits du Maine-et-Loire sous l'Empire," pp. 482–85.

114. A.N., F⁹158, letter from *Directeur-général de la conscription* to prefect of the Ariège, 19 September 1813.

115. A.N., F⁹158, letter from the prefect of the Ariège to the *Directeur-général de la conscription,* 19 September 1813.

116. Germain-Charpentier, M., "La levée des gardes d'honneur de 1813—l'exemple de Béziers," *Recrutement, mentalités, sociétés: colloque international d'histoire militaire,* p. 215.
117. A.N., AF^{IV}1158, report of troubles in the department of the Landes, 12 January 1814; A.N., BB^{18}54, reports of troubles at Avesnes and Hazebrouck (Nord), 21 November and 22 September 1813.
118. A.N., F^{1c}III Cantal 6, reports dated 18 October 1811, 18 January 1812, 17 April 1812, 14 October 1812, 8 January 1813, and 15 July 1813.

CHAPTER 3

1. Archives Nationales (A.N.), F^{9}179, printed address by the *commissaire du Directoire exécutif* in Valence to the people of the Drôme, 26 *floréal* VII.
2. A.N., F^{1c}III Gironde 5, "Observations par le substitut du commissaire du pouvoir exécutif," *thermidor* and *fructidor* VI.
3. A.N., F^{1c}III Vosges 7, letter from canton of Martigny to Minister of Interior, 17 *pluviôse* IV.
4. Bergès, L., *Le civil et l'armée au début du dix-neuvième siècle,* p. 118.
5. Aron, J.-P., Dumont, P., and Le Roy Ladurie, E., *Anthropologie du conscrit français,* pp. 170–71.
6. A.N., F^{9}199, letter from prefect of Landes to Minister of Interior, 13 *brumaire* XI.
7. A.N., F^{7}3615, letter from prefect of Vosges to *deuxième arrondissement* of Police générale, 27 April 1808.
8. A.N., F^{9}257, letter from prefect of Vendée to Minister of Interior, 29 May 1807.
9. A.N., F^{7}6466, letter from prefect of Aisne to Grand Juge, 3 April 1808.
10. A.N., F^{1c}III Seine-et-Oise 8, "Compte moral et politique du département de Seine-et-Oise pour les six premiers mois de 1812" from prefect of Seine-et-Oise in Versailles.
11. A.N., F^{9}229, report from prefect of Oise to Minister of Interior, 6 *germinal* XIII.
12. Archives Départementales (A.D.) Cantal, L280, procès-verbal of the conseil de révision at Vic-sur-Cère, 17 *frimaire* VII.
13. A.N., AF^{IV}1123, Hargenvilliers, "Etat général des hommes réformés depuis l'an VII jusques et y compris l'an XIII."
14. A.N., F^{9}247, "Lettre confidentielle sur la conscription de 1813" from prefect of Seine-Inférieure, 5 November 1812.
15. A.N., AF^{IV}1125, report from Minister of War to *secrétairerie d'Etat,* 27 April 1811.
16. Quoted in Bertaud, J.-P., "Voies nouvelles pour l'histoire de la Révolution," p. 80 note.
17. A.D. Gironde, 2R287, letter from *général de division* to prefect of Gironde, 17 June 1813.
18. A.N., F^{7}3605, letter from prefect of Nord to Minister of Police générale, 2 *floréal* XIII.
19. A.N., F^{1c}III Lot-et-Garonne 7, letter from *commissaire du Directoire exécutif* in Agen to Minister of Interior, 11 *germinal* VI.
20. A.N., F^{9}156, decree setting up the departmental jury in the Ardèche, 4 *fructidor* VIII.
21. A.N. F^{9}250, circular from prefect of Seine-et-Oise, 12 *vendémiaire* XIV.
22. A.D. Cantal, L267, minute-book of the *conseil de révision* of the canton of Massiac, 7 *frimaire* VII.

23. A.D. Gironde, 11L23, report of the *conseil de révision* of the canton of Bordeaux-Nord, 27 *messidor* VII.
24. A.N., F⁹189, decree of prefect of Gironde, 11 July 1809.
25. A.N., F⁹189, letter from prefect of Gironde to Minister of Interior, 16 October 1806.
26. A.N., F⁷6466, letter from prefect of Somme to mayors in his department, 29 August 1806.
27. A.N., BB¹⁸15, letter from *procureur-général* in Riom to Minister of Justice, 31 July 1811.
28. A.D. Seine-et-Oise, série R (non classée), carton A, minutes of *conseil de recrutement*, 1812–1814.
29. A.N., F⁹158, letter from prefect of Ariège to Minister of Interior, 3 May 1815.
30. Legrand, R., *Le recrutement des armées et les désertions, 1791–1815*, p. 54.
31. Viard, P., "La désignation des conscrits appelés à marcher de 1800 à 1813 dans le département du Nord," p. 291.
32. A.N., F⁹288, letter from Minister of Interior to department of Rhône, 17 *nivôse* VII.
33. A.N., F⁹189, letter from prefect of Gironde to Minister of Interior, 28 *fructidor* IX.
34. A.N., F⁹286, letter from prefect of Basses-Pyrénées to Minister of Interior, 8 *pluviôse* VIII.
35. A.N., BB¹⁸75, cases notified to Minister of Justice by the *maire* of Mézy (Seine-et-Oise), 13 February 1813.
36. A.D. Gironde, 2R285, letter from Minister of Interior to prefect of Gironde, 14 April 1808.
37. Legrand, op. cit., pp. 53ff.
38. A.D. Drôme, 1R6, petition from Jean Delhomme to prefect of Drôme, n.d., 1813.
39. A.D. Drôme, 1R6, letter from *maire* of Erôme to prefect of Drôme, 14 May 1813.
40. A.D. Drôme, 1R6, letter from *sous-préfet* of Nyons to prefect of Drôme, 21 May 1813.
41. Viard, op. cit., p. 290.
42. A.N., F⁷3583, letter from prefect of Aisne to Minister of Police générale, 30 January 1813.
43. A.N., F⁷3583, letter from prefect of Calvados to Minister of police générale, 6 January 1813.
44. Legrand, op. cit., p. 54.
45. A.N., BB¹⁸54, denunciation of Petit by *procureur* in Douai, 6 February 1811.
46. A.N., F⁷3583, op. cit.
47. A.N., F⁹288, letter from *municipalité* of Gorze (Moselle) to Minister of Interior, 4 *ventôse* VII.
48. A.D. Mayenne, 1J409, letter from Louis Goddos to his parents in Larchamp, November 1813.
49. Archives de la Guerre (A.G.) Vincennes, Xʷ94, report from *conseil municipal* of Mantes, 5 March 1793.
50. A.N., AFᴵⱽ1124, report from Minister of War to Emperor, 19 July 1809.
51. Viard, op. cit., p. 292.
52. A.N., F⁷3583, letter from prefect of Loir-et-Cher to Minister of Police générale, 1 July 1813.
53. Darquenne, R., "La conscription dans le Département de Jemmapes, 1798–1813," p. 216.
54. Vallée, G. "Population et conscription de 1798 à 1814," pp. 220–24.
55. A.D. Rhône, 1L769, decrees of the Convention promulgated on 14 March and 2 April 1793.
56. Legrand, op. cit., p. 15.

57. See petitions from *notaires* in Pamiers (A.N., BB¹⁸142), Blaye (A.N.,BB¹⁸361), and Valenciennes (A.N., BB¹⁸598). Such petitions continued to be sent throughout the Empire.

58. A.N., F⁹239, petition from J.-J. Oberlin, librarian in Strasbourg, 14 *brumaire* VII.

59. A.N., AFᴵᴵᴵ149, letter from Minister of War about Papin, *professeur d'histoire* at the *école centrale* of the department of Maine-et-Loire in Angers, 15 *thermidor* VI.

60. A.D. Morbihan, L571, petition from Marie Horau, *veuve,* from Ploërmel, 1793.

61. A.D. Morbihan, L571, petition from Mathurin Morice, *laboureur,* from Taupon, 1793.

62. A.N., AFᴵᴵᴵ145ᴬ, list of men exempted in the canton of Hellimer (Moselle), 2 *nivôse* IV.

63. A.D. Cantal, L257, list of men exempted in the commune of Pleaux, 9 *ventôse* VI.

64. A.D. Cantal, L257, list on men exempted in the commune of Pierrefort, 21 *pluviôse* VI.

65. A.N., AFᴵᴵᴵ146, letter from *député* Pflieger to Minister of War, 15 *pluviôse* IV.

66. A.N., F⁷8363, letter from the *chef de bureau* of the *premier arrondissement* of Police générale on the apparent exemption of Jews in Sembach, n.d.

67. A.N., F⁹288, intercession by the department of Indre-et-Loire, 9 *ventôse* IV.

68. A.N., AFᴵᴵᴵ145ᴬ, letter from *commissaire du Directoire exécutif* in Volmunsther (Moselle) to Minister of War, 7 *nivôse* IV.

69. A.N., F⁹288, letter from department of Meurthe to Minister of War, 17 *nivôse* VI.

70. A.N., AFᴵᴵᴵ145ᴬ, requests from Vaillant, *commissaire-ordonnateur* in Brest, and Bourrassaud, in the naval administration, 22 *frimaire* IV and 27 *frimaire* IV; A.N., AFᴵᴵᴵ147, report of Minister of War, 5 *ventôse* IV.

71. A.N., F⁹225, minute of department of Nièvre, 12 September 1792.

72. A.G. Vincennes, Xʷ6, minute of commune of Sabarat (Ariège), 12 *thermidor* III.

73. A.N., AFᴵᴵᴵ182, letter from "des républicains de Dijon" to *Conseil des Cinq-Cents,* 9 *thermidor* VII.

74. A.D. Morbihan, L554, "Loi sur les classes des gens de mer," 7 January 1791.

75. A.N., AFᴵⱽ1209, report to Emperor on naval recruitment in the "départements littoraux," 3 February 1813.

76. A.N., F⁷3595, letter from prefect of Gironde to Minister of Police générale, 5 *fructidor* XIII.

77. A.N., F⁹222, letter from *conseil municipal* of Lorient to Minister of Interior, 28 *brumaire* XI.

78. A.D. Nord, 7R8, letters from *sous-préfet* in Dunkerque to prefect of Nord, 17 March and 15 May 1812.

79. A.D. Nord, 7R4, petition from *agent-général* of the *mines d'Anzin, ventôse* XII.

80. A.N., F⁹222, letter from Minister of Navy to Minister of Interior, 26 *frimaire* XI.

81. A.D. Nord, L3502, scribbled note from prefect of Nord to *commissaire* in Dunkerque, Year VI.

82. A.N., AFᴵⱽ1209, letter from Minister of Navy to Emperor, 29 *germinal* XII.

83. A.N., F⁹312, letter from prefect of Pyrénées-Orientales to Minister of Interior, 12 *brumaire* XII.

84. A.N., F⁹199, letter from prefect of Landes to Minister of Interior, 27 *fructidor* XII. A.N., BB¹⁸50, letter from *Directeur-général de la conscription* to Minister of War, 12 March 1814.

86. Schnapper, B., *Le remplacement militaire en France,* p. 17.

87. For a lucid discussion of the difference between *remplacement* and *substitution,* see Isser Woloch's paper on "Napoleonic conscription: state power and civil society," *Past and Present,* pp. 111–18.

88. Schnapper, op. cit., p. 23.
89. Maureau, A., "Le remplacement militaire de l'an VIII à 1814 d'après les registres de notaires d'Avignon—aspect juridique et social," p. 121.
90. Ibid., p. 127.
91. Vidalenc, J., "Les conséquences sociales de la conscription en France, 1798–1848," p. 301.
92. Maureau, op. cit., p. 131.
93. Ibid., p. 139.
94. A.D. Drôme, L364, petition by Claudine Fiard, 5 *prairial* VII.
95. Vidalenc, op. cit., p. 305.
96. A.N., F⁹232, *contrôles nominatifs* of soldiers from the Pas-de-Calais, *germinal* and *thermidor* VIII.
97. A.N., AF^IV1121, letter from *sous-préfet* of Saint-Jean-d'Angély to Minister of War, n.d.
98. A.D. Drôme, L369, excerpt from register of deliberations of district of Crest, 29 *fructidor* III.
99. A.D. Vosges, 8R1, register of *actes de remplacement* for 1813–1815.
100. A.D. Cantal, 1R186, register of "actes passés entre le conscrit désigné par le sort et son remplaçant" at the *sous-préfecture* of Aurillac, 18 October 1813–March 1814.
101. A.N., AF^III182, letter from *municipalité* of Fontaine-au-Bois (Nord) to Minister of War, n.d.
102. Sangnier, G., *La désertion dans le Pas-de-Calais de 1792 à 1802,* p. 89.
103. Bergès, op. cit., p. 293.
104. A.N., AF^IV1123, Hargenvilliers, *Etat général des déserteurs,* in report to Minister of War in 1806.
105. A.D. Cantal, 2R365, letter from Minister of War to prefect of Cantal, 6 May 1809.
106. A.N., F⁹303, printed list of *conscrits réfractaires* in the Charente-Inférieure, 7 *frimaire* XIV.
107. A.N., F⁷3611, letter from prefect of Seine-et-Oise to the Police générale, *premier arrondissement, 28, prairial* XIII.
108. A.D. Drome, L350, reports of Year VII on the *levée des 200,000* from cantons of Valdrome and Saint-Nazaire-le-Désert.
109. A.D. Gironde, 2R294, "Nouveau contrôle des réfractaires à poursuivre pour le paiement de l'amende, classe de 1806."
110. A.N., F⁹316, letter from Minister of War to Minister of Interior, 23 *nivôse* IV.
111. A.D. Drôme, L370, report from *commissaire du Directoire exécutif* in L'Unité-sur-Isère (Bourg-de-Péage) to *commissaire* of department of Drôme in Valence, 20 *brumaire* V.
112. A.N., AF^IV1121, report from prefect of Nord to Minister of Interior, 29 *nivôse* IX.
113. A.N., F⁹241, report from prefect of Rhône to Minister of Interior, 14 *brumaire* XIV.
114. A.N. F⁷6466, report from prefect of Arno to Minister of Interior, 27 April 1811.
115. A.D. Gironde, 11L299, report of the arrest of two deserters of Saint-André-de-Cubzac, 22 April 1793.
116. A.N., F⁷3611, report from prefect of Seine-et-Oise to Minister of Police générale, 21 August 1807.
117. A.N., F^IcIII Drôme 7, prefect's "compte de la situation morale et politique" for the department, 1810.
118. A.G. Vincennes, X^w70, letter from *Armée des Côtes de Brest* to department of Morbihan, 14 *ventôse* II.
119. A.G. Vincennes, X^w16, letter from district of Maurs, 8 *germinal* III.
120. A.N., F⁹316, letter from department of Tarn to Minister of Interior, 11 *prairial* VII.

121. A.N., F⁹316, letter from *commissaire du Directoire exécutif* in Amiens (Somme), 21 *floréal* VII.

122. A.D. Rhône, 1L738, letter from *procureur-syndic* of district of Roanne, 22 February 1792.

123. A.D. Cantal, L255, arrest of François Vergnes, 21 May 1793.

124. A.D. Rhône, 1L738, letter from district of Lyon-Campagnes, 5 March 1792.

125. A.N., F⁷8540, arrest of Joseph Boussard, 13 November 1810.

126. A.D. Nord, L2636, letter from district of Valenciennes, 22 *floréal* III.

127. A.D. Drôme, L394, letter from *commissaire du Directoire exécutif* in Valence to the district authorities in the Drôme, 1er *ventôse* IV.

128. A.D. Drôme, L394, letter from Minister of War to department of Drôme, 11 *fructidor* VI.

129. A.G. Vincennes, Xʷ59, "Compte-rendu des ex-administrateurs de la Lozère de leur gestion depuis le 3 brumaire an VI au 13 germinal an VIII," on the impracticality of the system of *feuilles de route.*

130. A.D. Gironde, 11L357, letter from *commissaire provisoire* in Sauveterre to *commissaire du Directoire exécutif* in Bordeaux, 28 *nivose* IV.

131. A.D. Ariège, 5L21, letter from department of Ariège to commune of Bélesta, 23 *pluviôse* VII.

132. A.N., AFᴵᴵᴵ145ᴬ, letter from Lavalette, *officier de santé,* to the Directory, received 5 *pluviôse* IV.

133. A.N., F⁹304, *arrêté* of prefect of Dordogne summarizing the state of legislation on deserters, 9 *pluviôse* XII.

134. A.D. Bouches-du-Rhône, L862, letters from district of Aix, 7 January and 20 June 1792.

135. A.N., F⁹222, letter stating destinations of soldiers from Morbihan in *classe* of 1809, 29 October 1808.

136. A.D. Drôme, L395, "Registre des militaires voyageant isolément: bordereau des mandats délivrés pour le payement de 15 centimes par lieue," for Years IX and X.

137. A.N., F⁹302, register of department of Calvados, 15 October 1792.

138. A.D. Gironde, 10L79, decree of Convention of 18 *messidor* III.

139. A.D. Gironde, 4L231, letter from Paganel to district of Bordeaux, 1er *floréal* III.

140. A.D. Drome, L364, circular letter from Minister of War, 8 *vendémiaire* V.

141. A.D. Gironde, 4L231, *permission* of Pierre Guillemot, 14 *fructidor* III.

142. A.D. Drôme, L364, letter from *commissaire du Directoire exécutif* in Valence to *commissaires* with cantonal authorities in the department, 18 *ventôse* VI.

143. A.D. Gironde, 8L46, "Bataillon de La Réole, état des volontaires," Year III.

144. A.D. Gironde, 10L79, letter from General Michaud to district of Libourne, 25 *pluviôse* II.

145. A.D. Drôme, L674, letter from *quartier-général* at Chambéry to district of Crest, 22 *germinal* III.

146. A.N., AFᴵᴵᴵ145ᴮ, letter from Clément to the Directory, 8 *pluviôse* IV.

147. A.G. Vincennes, Xʷ94, letter from Minister of War to department of Seine-et-Oise, 11 *vendémiaire* VII.

148. A.D. Nord, L2405, list of *militaires* still in their homes in the commune of La Bassée, 2e *jour complémentaire* VI.

149. A.N., F¹ᶜIII Drôme 6, report from *commissaire du Directoire exécutif* in the Drôme, *thermidor* VII.

150. A.N., F¹ᶜIII Lot-et-Garonne 7, report from *commissaire du Directoire exécutif* in the Lot-et-Garonne, 1er *ventôse* VII.

151. A.N., F⁹308, letter from prefect of Landes to Minister of Interior, 3 *vendémiaire* X.

152. A.N., AF^{IV}1123, Hargenvilliers, "Compte général sur la conscription depuis son établissement," 1808.
153. A.N., AF^{IV}1121, report of Minister of War to Consuls on the working of the amnesty of 24 *floréal* X, 13 *pluviôse* XI.
154. A.N., AF^{IV}1147, report of January 1813 on refractories and deserters, by department.
155. A.N. F^{7}3582, "Police générale, *deuxième arrondissement:* situation relative à la conscription des années 1806 à 1810."
156. Bois, J.-P., "Conscrits du Maine-et-Loire sous l'Empire: le poids de la conscription, 1806–1814," p. 491.
157. A.N., AF^{IV}1123, Hargenvilliers, "Compte-général sur la conscription depuis son établissement," 1808.
158. A.N., AF^{IV}1126, "Situation des départements sur les déserteurs."
159. A.N., AF^{IV}1147, report of Minister of War to Emperor, January 1813.
160. Waquet, J., "Réflexions sur les émotions populaires et le recrutement militaire de 1799 à 1831," *Actes du 9le Congrès national des Sociétés savantes,* p. 57.
161. A.N., F^{7}8724, Police générale, *deuxième arrondissement,* reports on conscription from prefects of the Ardennes, Aube, Côte d'Or, Doubs, and Haute-Saône in Year XII.
162. A.N., F^{9}260, report of *commissaire du Directoire exécutif* in the Vosges to Minister of Interior, 9 *prairial* VII.
163. A.N., F^{9}260, letter from prefect of Vosges to Minister of Interior, 19 June 1807.
164. A.N., AF^{IV}1123, Hargenvilliers, op. cit.
165. A.N., F^{Ic}III Drôme 6, report of *commissaire de Directoire exécutif* in the Drôme to Minister of Interior, *thermidor* VII.
166. A.G. Vincennes, X^{w}18, letter from commune of Tournemire to department of Cantal, 1 April 1793.
167. A.G. Vincennes, X^{w}16, cantonal lists of "jeunes gens de la première réquisition qui n'ont jamais servi ni appartenu à aucun corps," by commune, Year VI.
168. A.N., F^{9}312, "Première liste des conscrits de la première classe qui ont lâchement déserté en se rendant au poste," for the Puy-de-Dôme, 18 *ventôse* VII.

CHAPTER 4

1. Archives Nationales (A.N.), F^{9}302, printed circular from department of Calvados, 5 *fructidor* VII.
2. A.N., F^{9}303, letter from department of Cher to Minister of Interior, 4 *messidor* VII.
3. Archives de la Guerre (A.G.) Vincennes, X^{w}59, report from the *commissaires* sent to the Lozère in 1793 n.d.
4. A.N., F^{Ic}III Vosges 7, letter from *commissaire du Directoire exécutif* in Epinal to Minister of Interior, 18 *frimaire* VIII.
5. A.N., F^{9}207, circular letter from prefect of Lot to the recruits of his department, 22 *floréal* VIII.
6. A.G. Vincennes, X^{w}74, letter from district of Cambrai to department of Nord, 9 May 1793.
7. A.N., F^{9}190, letter from prefect of Hérault to Minister of Interior, 11 *thermidor* VIII.
8. A.G. Vincennes, X^{w}9, report to department of Pyrénées-Orientales, 30 August 1793.
9. Archives Départementales (A.D.) Nord, L2637, letter from *commissaire du Directoire exécutif* in Douai to department of Nord, 12 *vendémiaire* V.

10. A.N., F¹ᶜIII Haute-Garonne 9, report from prefect of Haute-Garonne to Minister of Interior, 8 March 1814.
11. Corvisier, A., *L'armée française de la fin du dix-septième siècle au ministère de Choiseul,* pp. 113–15.
12. Lefebvre, G., *Les paysans du Nord,* p. 580.
13. A.N., F⁹209, prefect of Lozère, "Mémoire sur la conscription militaire dans le Département de la Lozère," 1806.
14. A.N., F⁹301, letter from prefect of Ardèche to Minister of Interior, 8 *nivôse* IX.
15. A.N., F¹ᶜIII Haute-Garonne 9, report from prefect of Haute-Garonne to Minister of Interior, 8 March 1814.
16. A.N., F⁹303, letter from prefect of Liamone to Minister of Interior, 10 *pluviôse* XII.
17. A.N., F⁹163, report from prefect of Bouches-du-Rhône to Minister of Interior, 6 *pluviôse* XI.
18. A.N., F¹ᶜIII Var 11, report from the commune of Cuers (Var) on resistance to conscription, 18 *pluviôse* VII.
19. Bertaud, J.-P, contribution to *débat,* in Viallaneix, P. and Ehrard, J.(ed.), *La bataille, l'armée, la gloire, 1745–1871,* vol. 1, p. 195.
20. Waquet, J., "La société civile devant l'insoumission et la désertion à l'époque de la conscription militaire," *Bibliothèque de l'Ecole des Chartes,* p. 191.
21. A.N., F⁷3592, report from *sous-préfet* of Die to prefect of Drôme, 8 *germinal* XIII.
22. A.N., F⁹165, letter from prefect of Cantal to Minister of Interior, 1er *pluviôse* XI.
23. A.N., F⁹165, letter from prefect of Cantal to Minister of Interior, 4 *fructidor* XIII.
24. A.N., F⁹239, letter from prefect of Bas-Rhin to Minister of Interior, 17 *brumaire* XIV.
25. A.N., F⁹260, report from *commissaire du Directoire exécutif* in Epinal, 9 *prairial* VII.
26. A.N. F⁷3592, report from prefect of Drôme on contrasting responses to conscription in his department, Year XIII.
27. A.N., F⁹250, report from prefect of Seine-et-Oise to Minister of Interior, 5 *thermidor* VIII.
28. A.N., F¹ᶜIII Pas-de-Calais 8, report from *commissaire du Directoire exécutif* in Arras to Minister of Interior, 2 *pluviôse* VI.
29. A.D. Vosges, L535, report on the *levée en masse* in district of Rambervillers, 28 July 1792.
30. A.D. Morbihan, L557, complaint from municipality of Le Faouët, 18 June 1793.
31. A.G. Vincennes, Xʷ18, letter from municipality of Laroquebrou, 13 March 1793.
32. A.N., F¹ᶜIII Nord 7, reports of *commissaire du Directoire exécutif* in Douai for *nivôse* VI and *fructidor* VI.
33. A.D. Cantal, L256, letter from Grasset, *agent secondaire* for raising the Deuxième Réquisition, to department of Cantal, 2 *messidor* III.
34. A.N., F⁹301, letter from *commissaire du Directoire exécutif* in Charleville-Mézières to Minister of Police générale, 27 *frimaire* V.
35. A.D. Bas-Rhin, 1L1435, minute of *conseil municipal* of Strasbourg, 6 *pluviôse* IV.
36. A.N., F⁹310, letter from *commissaire du Directoire exécutif* in Armentières to Minister of Interior, 6 *pluviôse* IV.
37. A.N., F⁷3581, list of conscripts arrested in Paris on the orders of the prefect of police, 2 May 1806.
38. A.N., F⁹189, letter from prefect of Gironde to the "autorités administratives et militaires de Bordeaux," 8 *floréal* XI.
39. A.N., F⁹189, letter from prefect of Gironde to *conseiller d'Etat,* 31 August 1806.
40. A.D. Gironde, 4L231, letter from Voidet, *commissaire des guerres* at Blaye, to *procureur-général* of district of Bordeaux, 24 *prairial* III.
41. A.D. Gironde, 3L267, minute of department of Gironde, 27 April 1793.

42. A.D. Gironde, 11L23, letter from *commissaire du Directoire exécutif* in Bordeaux to his counterpart in canton of Bordeaux-Sud, 9 *germinal* VII.

43. A.N., F⁹217, 250 and 312, prefects' reports to Minister of Interior, on the topography of the departments of Mayenne, Seine-et-Oise, Puy-de-Dôme, and Hautes-Pyrénées.

44. A.N., F⁹308, letter from prefect of Landes to Minister of Interior, 3 *vendémiaire* X.

45. A.D. Drôme, L370, report from *commissaire du Directoire exécutif* in Condorcet, 24 *nivôse* VII; A.N., BB¹⁸280, reports on stagecoach robberies in the southern Drôme, Years X and XI.

46. A.N., F⁹225, letters from prefect of Nièvre to Minister of Interior, 15 *messidor* VIII and 9 *thermidor* VIII.

47. A.D. Gironde, 2R287, denunciation of Antoine Bonneau *fils*, conscript of 1809.

48. A.D. Gironde, 2R284, report from prefect of Gironde to Minister of Interior, 15 November 1809.

49. A.N., F⁹158, report from prefect of Ariège to Minister of Interior, 11 *thermidor* VIII.

50. A.N., F⁷3586, letter from *sous-préfet* of Saint-Girons to prefect of Ariège, 26 April 1807.

51. A.N., F⁷3589, letter from prefect of Cantal to Minister of police générale, 4 *fructidor* XIII.

52. A.N., BB¹⁸54, letter from *procureur-général* in Douai to Minister of Justice, 4 October 1808; A.N., F⁹310, letter from *commissaire du Directoire exécutif* in Armentières to Minister of Interior, 6 *pluviôse* IV.

53. A.D. Nord, L2404, report from *commissaire* in Dunkerque to department of Nord, 16 *floréal* VII.

54. A.N., F⁹156, letter from prefect of Ardèche to Minister of Interior, 30 *nivôse* XI.

55. A.N., F¹ᶜIII Ain 5, report from prefect of Ain to Minister of Interior, 28 July 1812.

56. A.N., F⁹209, prefect of Lozère, "Mémoire sur la conscription militaire dans le département de la Lozère," 1806.

57. A.N., F¹ᶜIII Haute-Garonne 8, report from department of Haute-Garonne to Minister of Interior, 6 *frimaire* VII.

58. A.N., F⁹158, letter from prefect of Haute-Garonne to Minister of War, 6 *vendémiaire* XIV.

59. A.N., AFᴵᴵᴵ151ᴮ, letter from Governor of Val d'Aran to general in command of the 10e Division militaire, 23 August 1799 *(sic)*.

60. A.N., F¹ᶜIII Basses-Pyrénées 7, letter from *commissaire du Directoire exécutif* in Saint-Jean-de-Luz to Minister of Police générale, 29 *ventôse* IV.

61. Archives de la Guerre (A.G.) Vincennes, Xʷ73, letter from *général de division* in Lille to *commissaire du Directoire exécutif* in Douai, 15 *fructidor* VI.

62. A.N., AFᴵⱽ1156, report from *gendarmerie* in the departments of Haute-Saône, Doubs, Jura, and Léman, 19 November 1806.

63. A.D. Nord, 1R68, letter from prefect of Nord to his *sous-préfets,* n.d. (1807).

64. A.N., BB¹⁸585, letter from *chef de brigade* of a unit from the Lys to the department of the Lys, 4 *thermidor* VII.

65. A.N., F⁹317, letter from prefect of Taro to Minister of Interior, 23 September 1808.

66. Hufton, O., *The poor of eighteenth-century France, 1750–1789,* pp. 69–70.

67. A.N., F²⁰434, report from prefect of Cantal on migration, 27 April 1812.

68. Quoted in Béteille, R., "Les migrations saisonnières en France sous le premier Empire: essai de synthèse," p. 428.

69. A.N., F²⁰434–435, prefectoral returns on migration into and out of their departments, 1807–1813.

70. Chatelain, A., "Valeur et faiblesses d'une source classique—l'enquête des préfets sur les migrations périodiques, 1807–1813: l'exemple du département de la Seine-et-Marne," pp. 153–61.

71. Béteille, op. cit., pp. 427, 431–36.
72. Goron, L., "Les migrations saisonnières dans les départements pyrénéens au début du dix-neuvième siècle," pp. 249–60.
73. A.N., F^{20}434, prefect's report on migration in the Ariège, 23 May 1810.
74. A.N., D^{III}20^A, judicial correspondence on the case of three *émigrés* from Seix (Ariège), 26 *frimaire* II.
75. A.N., F^{1c}III Basses-Pyrénées 7, report from *commissaire du Directoire exécutif* in Saint-Jean-de-Luz to Minister of Police générale, 29 *ventôse* IV.
76. A.N., F^{20}434, prefect's report on migration in the Cantal, 27 April 1812.
77. A.D. Cantal, L276, *tableau des conscrits* from district of Saint-Flour, Year VII.
78. A.D. Cantal, L266, list of those absent from commune of Lugarde during Year VII, 8 *germinal* VII.
79. A.D. Cantal, L265, *tableau des conscrits* from district of Chaudesaigues, Year VII.
80. A.D. Cantal, 1R164, lists of those absent from the *classes* of Year XIII and 1806 in commune of Pleaux.
81. A.D. Cantal, L277, *tableaux* of Year VII for district of Saint-Flour extra-muros: communes where everyone was absent include Andelat, Talizat, and Vieillespesse.
82. A.N., F^{9}165, letter from prefect of Cantal to Minister of Interior, 18 *germinal* XI.
83. A.N., F^{9}165, letter from Minister of War to Minister of Interior, 27 August 1807.
84. Béteille, op. cit., p. 426.
85. A.N., F^{20}434, prefect's report on migration in the Cantal, 27 April 1812.
86. A.N., F^{9}165, letter from *procureur-général-syndic* of Cantal to Minister of Interior, 27 August 1792; and report from prefect of Cantal, 9 August 1820.
87. A.N., F^{7}8418, letter from prefect of Cantal to Minister of Police générale, 7 July 1806.
88. Chatelain, A., "Résistance à la conscription et migrations temporaires sous le premier Empire," p. 608.
89. A.G. Vincennes, X^{w}18, letter from district of Saint-Flour to department of Cantal, 24 March 1793.
90. A.D. Cantal, L253, petition from Prunet *frères,* from Thiézac (Cantal), May 1793.
91. A.D. Cantal, L250, petition to district of Murat from commune of Saint-Bonnet (Cantal), 23 March 1793.
92. A.D. Cantal, L252, judgments of district of Saint-Flour in cases arising from the *levée des 300,000,* 1793.
93. A.G. Vincennes, X^{w}18, case of Pierre Devèze and Jacques Pradel from Saint-Martin-de-Valois, March 1793.
94. A.N., BB^{18}139, case of Alibert *père* from Mirepoix (Ariège), *frimaire* XII.
95. A.D. Vosges, 39R2, letter from prefect of Charente to prefect of Vosges, 30 September 1806.
96. A.G. Vincennes, X^{w}30, report from district of Nyons (Drôme), 14 May 1793.
97. A.N., BB^{18}139, report of *rixe* at the *foire* at Foix (Ariège), 27 *nivôse* XI.
98. A.N., F^{1c}III Ain 5, report from *commissaire du directoire exécutif* in Bourg-en-Bresse to Minister of Interior, 7 *thermidor* VII.
99. A.N., F^{1c}III Aude 5, *rapport décadaire* of *agent national* in Narbonne, Year III.
100. A. G. Vincennes, X^{w}6, petition from commune of Saint-Ybars (Ariège), 25 *fructidor* II.
101. A.N., F^{9}312, letter from prefect of Basses-Pyrénées to Minister of Interior, 21 *germinal* IX.
102. A.G. Vincennes, X^{w}73, report from department of Nord to Minister of Interior, 12 *brumaire* II.
103. A.N., F^{7}8504, prefect's report on state of policing in Vosges, 29 October 1806.
104. Bergès, L., "Le civil et l'armée au début du dix-neuvième siècle," p. 254.

105. A.D. Seine-et-Oise, series R (non classée), *contrôle* of *sous-officiers* and *soldats* who abandoned their regiments in 1814, district of Rambouillet.

106. A.G. Vincennes, X^w17, petition from Jean Pléchaud of Chavagnac (Cantal), 6 September 1792.

107. See Chapter 9.

108. A.G. Vincennes, X^w70, report from department of Morbihan, 30 *germinal* II.

109. Reports on the poverty of deserters' families are especially common in the southern Massif; see, for instance, dossiers in A.D. Cantal, 2R368, 2R370, 2R372.

110. A.N., F^9232, report from *sous-préfet* of Béthune to prefect of Pas-de-Calais, 3 January 1806.

111. A.N., F^73605, letter from prefect of Nord to Minister of Police générale, 22 October 1811.

112. On social and welfare measures taken by the governments of the revolutionary period, see Forrest, A., *The French Revolution and the poor,* pp. 148–152.

113. A.G. Vincennes, X^w70, report from district of La Roche-Sauveur to department of Morbihan, ler *messidor* III.

114. A.N., F^9306, report of department of Gard to Minister of Interior, 26 *germinal* VII.

115. A.N., F^9184, report of department of Finistère to Minister of Interior, 8 July 1807.

116. A.D. Ariège, 5L *(sans cote),* letter from canton of Saint-Lizier to *chef du dépôt des chevaux,* 23 *nivose* IV.

117. A.N., AF^III151^A, report of Minister of War, *brumaire* VIII.

118. A.G. Vincennes, X^w5, letter from *municipalité* of Foix to department of Ariège, 16 *thermidor* III.

119. A.D. Vosges, L539, report of Clément, *chef du 37e escadron de gendarmes,* 14 *fructidor* VII.

120. Lewis, G., *Life in Revolutionary France,* p. 154.

121. A.G. Vincennes, X^w73, report of *commissaire* to Armée de la Moselle, 10 December 1792.

122. A.G. Vincennes, X^w30, letter from Niderbaum of the *5e bataillon de la Drôme,* 29 *frimaire* II.

123. A.D. Bouches-du-Rhône, L2010, letter from Joseph Capellin, 5 June 1793.

124. A.N., F^1cIII Var 11, report from commune of Cuers, 19 *pluviôse* VIII.

125. A.N., F^9301, letter from department of Basses-Alpes to Minister of Interior, 9 *fructidor* VII.

126. A.G. Vincennes, X^w95, petition from wives of *défenseurs de la patrie* in the Seine-et-Oise, Year II.

127. A.N., AF^III144^B, anonymous petition, signed "les défenseurs," registered 29 *fructidor* IV.

128. A.N., AF^III145^A series of petitions against military suppliers.

129. A.N., BB^18585, letter from *chef de brigade* of conscripts from the Lys to department of Lys, 4 *thermidor* VII.

130. For a discussion of the proposed remedies to the problem, see Chapter 3.

131. Reinhard, M., "Nostalgie et service militaire pendant la Révolution," *Annales historiques de la Révolution française* 30 (1958), passim.

132. Ibid., p. 6.

133. Ibid., p. 1.

134. A.D. Drôme, L371, *états de déserteurs,* 1793–Year IV.

135. A.N., BB^18840, register of *conseil militaire* at Versailles, 2e *jour complémentaire* III.

136. A.D. Vosges, 39R1, letter from Minister of War to department of Vosges, 25 *floréal* IX.

137. A.N., F^9318, report from *agent national* at Soullans (Vendée), 20 *thermidor* IV.

138. A. D. Drôme, L1213, letter from commander of *4e régiment d'artillerie* in Grenoble to the town of Romans, 27 *germinal* III.

139. A.D. Morbihan, L592, interrogation of Jean Valos and François Soval, 15 June 1793.

CHAPTER 5

1. Erckmann, E. and Chatrian, L., *The history of a conscript of 1813,* pp. 36–51.

2. Ibid., p. 34.

3. Ibid., pp. 43–4.

4. Archives Nationales (A.N.), F⁹307, report from prefect of Hérault to Minister of Interior, 13 March 1808.

5. A.N., F⁹208, report from prefect of Lot-et-Garonne to Minister of Interior, 14 *pluviôse* XII.

6. A.N., F⁹309, "état nominatif des conscrits déserteurs arrêtés dans le département du Lot-et-Garonne," 11 *pluviôse* XI–5 March 1814.

7. A.N., F⁹307, "état nominatif des conscrits déserteurs et marins du département de l'Hérault," 8 *brumaire* XIII–13 January 1814.

8. A.N., F⁹305, list of those arrested for desertion in the department of the Doubs, Year XII–1813.

9. A.N., F⁹319, list of those arrested for desertion in the department of the Vosges, Year XIII–1813.

10. Bergès, L., "Le civil et l'armée au début du dix-neuvième siècle," pp. 396ff.

11. A.N., F¹ᶜIII Rhône 5, report from district of Villefranche, 3e *décade* of *messidor* III.

12. A.N., F⁹312, letter from prefect of Puy-de-Dôme to Minister of Interior, 16 March 1808.

13. A.N., F⁷8429, letter from subprefect of Nyons to prefect of Drôme, 11 *brumaire* XIII.

14. Archives Départementales (A.D.) Nord, 1R230, letter from mayor of Saint-Amand to prefect of Nord, 3 March 1812.

15. A.N., BB¹⁸359, report to Minister of Justice on a murder at La Blancheterie (Gironde), 24 *messidor* XI.

16. A.N. AF^IV1045, letter from Minister of Cultes to Emperor, 27 October 1806.

17. A.D. Drôme, L674, letter from regimental commander to district of Crest, 4 October 1793.

18. A.D. Nord, L2633, report from municipal council of Dunkerque to department of Nord, 6 July 1792.

19. A.N., F⁷8363, interrogation of Jean-Joseph Bataille, 20 November 1808.

20. Archives de la Guerre (A.G.) Vincennes, X^W30, letter from district of Montélimar to Minister of War, 4 *nivôse* III.

21. For a discussion of policing and repressive legislation, see Chapter 9.

22. A.N., F⁹309, letter on the troubles at Puymirol (Lot-et-Garonne) to Minister of Interior, 21 *pluviôse* V.

23. A.N. F¹ᶜIII Ariège 6, letter from *commissaire du Directoire exécutif* in Foix to Minister of Interior, 29 *nivôse* VIII.

24. A.D. Cantal, 2R365, letter from prefect of Cantal to Minister of War, 22 April 1811.

25. A.D. Nord, L2632, letter from department of Somme to department of Nord, 4 *frimaire* II.

26. A.N., F¹ᶜIII Lozère 5, letter from prefect of Lozère to Minister of Interior, 14 *floréal* VIII.

27. A.N., F⁹199, letter from prefect of Landes to Minister of Interior, 29 *frimaire* XII.

28. A.N., F⁹241, letter from prefect of Rhône to Minister of Interior, 1er *prairial* VIII.
29. A.N., BB¹⁸15, report from prefect of Cantal on *attroupement* at Saint-Urcize, 8 *nivôse* XII.
30. A.N., F¹ᶜIII Ariège 6, letter from *commissaire du Directoire exécutif* in Foix to Minister of Interior, 26 *frimaire* VI; A.N., F⁹310, letter from *commissaire du Directoire exécutif* to Minister of Interior, 29 *prairial* VII.
31. Bergès, op. cit., p. 379.
32. The evidence for this degree of dependence on hand-outs from parents is overwhelming: see the letters sent to their parents by conscripts serving in the armies throughout the war period (for example, A.D. Drôme, 6R3-3, 20R1-2).
33. A.D. Cantal, 2R370, "Bureau d'Aurillac: amendes de désertion antérieures à l'arrêté du 19 vendémiaire XII."
34. A.D. Nord, 1R228, *états de situation* for the collection on fines imposed on deserters and their parents, bureau of Le Cateau (Nord), 15 July 1809.
35. Letter from *sous-préfet* of Saint-Girons (Ariège) to Minister of Interior, quoted by Bergès, op. cit., p. 376.
36. A.D. Ariège, 86K1, letter from *arrondissement* of Pamiers to prefect of Ariège, 3 August 1808.
37. A.G. Vincennes, Xᵂ70, letter from district of Pontivy to department of Morbihan, 5ᵗʰ day of the 2ⁿᵈ decade of Year II.
38. A.N., BB¹⁸20, case against a *battelier* from La Roche-sur-Glun (Drôme), 22 December 1808.
39. A.D. Drôme, L370, letter from *commissaire du Directoire exécutif* at Loriol to department of Drôme, 2 *brumaire* VI.
40. A.D. Nord, L6103, letter from *municipalité* of Dunkerque to canton of Dunkerque, 11 *messidor* VII.
41. A.D. Gironde, 11L67, list of conscripts from Bazas who were officially listed as *réfractaires,* 1er *thermidor* IV.
42. A.N., BB¹⁸7, petition from Joseph Pothevin of Saint-Ybars (Ariège), 10 June 1806.
43. A.N., F⁹316, report from department of Tarn to Minister of Interior, for Year VII.
44. A.D. Nord, 1R213, letter from Minister of War to prefect of Nord, 4 July 1811.
45. This is, once again, sustained by almost any sample of soldiers' letters of the period (cf. note 32).
46. A.N., F⁹227, letter from *commissaire du Directoire exécutif* in Merville (Nord) to Minister of Interior, 15 *vendémiaire* V. On the policing of inns and bars, see Chapter 9.
47. A.D. Nord, L6103, *gendarmerie* report of the arrest of deserters at Craywick (Nord), 7 *germinal* II.
48. A.N., F⁹8516, police reports on three *aubergistes* in the Ariège, dated 4 July, 3 August, and 18 September 1809.
49. A.D. Gironde, 2R285, letter from prefect of Gironde to Mazois, *commissaire de police,* 11 February 1809.
50. A.N., BB¹⁸75, report on *rixe* at Le Roussay (Seine-et-Oise), 19 October 1807.
51. A.N., F⁹301, letter from Minister of Police to Minister of Interior, 24 *brumaire* V.
52. A.N., F¹ᶜIII Lot-et-Garonne 9, police report for first *trimestre* of 1811.
53. A.N., F⁷8531, police report on death of Pierre Carnelle, 28 September 1810.
54. A.N., BB¹⁸216, report from *inspecteur-général of gendarmerie* to Minister of Justice, 27 *brumaire* XI.
55. Cobb, R. C., "The Bande d'Orgères," *Reactions to the French Revolution,* pp. 181–211.
56. A.N., F¹ᶜIII Lot-et-Garonne 9, police report on Jeanne Manset, 5 February 1811.

57. A.N., F⁷8539, police report on François Eynard, 10 June 1809.
58. A.D. Gironde, 11L67, list of conscripts from Bazas officially designated as *réfractaires,* 1er *thermidor* IV.
59. A.D. Ariège, 2R97, "observations" on individuals denounced as refractories, district of Saint-Girons, 12 October 1810.
60. A.N., BB¹⁸50, case of Yves Calvèz from Kergos (Morbihan), 23 January 1808.
61. A.D. Cantal, 2R372, case of Antoine Felgine and Pierre Nuc from Marcolès (Cantal), 6 August 1806.
62. A.N., BB¹⁸54, case of Pierre Lamblin from Marchiennes (Nord), 15 September 1809.
63. A.N., F⁹189, letter from prefect of Gironde to *conseiller d'état,* 31, August 1806.
64. A.N., F⁷8539, case of two *bergers réfractaires* at Creyers (Drôme), 6 August 1808; and of Jean-Pierre Champon, from Allex (Drôme), 8 December 1808.
65. A.N., F⁹314, letter from *commissaire du Directoire exécutif* in Saône-et-Loire to Minister of Interior, 5e j.c. VI.
66. A.N., F⁹319, letter from *maire* of Coulours (Yonne) to Minister of Interior, 6 *fructidor* IX.
67. A.N., F⁷3611, letter from Minister of Police to department of Seine-et-Oise, 4 December 1813.
68. A.G. Vincennes, Xʷ7, letter from *municipalité* of Le Bosc (Ariège) to Minister of War, 25 *floréal* III; A.D. Vosges, L533, report to department of Vosges on the *forges* at Liffol-le-Grand, 27 *messidor* VII.
69. A.N., F⁹314, letter from department of Saône-et-Loire to Minister of Interior, 3 *nivôse* VII.
70. A.N., F⁹225, letter from prefect of Nièvre to Minister of Interior, 15 *messidor* VIII.
71. A.N., F⁹227, letter from canton of Quesnoy-lès-Lille to Minister of Interior, 7 *nivôse* VIII.
72. A.D. Nord, L2635, letter from *commissaire du Directoire exécutif* in canton of Lewarde to department of Nord, 12 floréal VII.
73. A.N., BB¹⁸139, case of Alibert *père* and *fils* from Mirepoix (Ariège), *frimaire* XII.
74. A.D. Gironde, 3L325, reports from prefect of Gironde to *commissaire principal de la marine* on the employment of *marins déserteurs* in the Gironde, Year V.
75. A.N., F⁹302, letter from prefect of Calvados to Minister of Interior, 24 *vendémiaire* XII.
76. A.D. Drôme, L369, case of Henry Reynier from Aouste (Drôme), 2 *thermidor* IV.
77. A.N., BB¹⁸839, case of Etienne Robilliard from Aulnay (Seine-et-Oise), 16 March 1808.
78. A.N., BB¹⁸913, letter from *commissaire du Directoire exécutif* in department of Vosges to Minister of Justice, 13 *nivôse* V.
79. A.G. Vincennes, Xʷ6, letter from *municipalité* of Pamiers to Jouardet, *chef de bataillon,* 27 *pluviôse* III.
80. A.D. Drôme, L674, extract from minutes of *conseil municipal* of Crest, 27 November 1792.
81. A.G. Vincennes, Xʷ5, letter from *agent municipal* in Foix to *commissaire du Directoire exécutif* in Ariège, 5 *prairial* IV.
82. A.N., F⁷3611, letter from Minister of Police to department of Seine-et-Oise, 4 December 1813.
83. A.N., BB¹⁸8, dossier on Vincent Viguerie, *maire* of Génat (Ariège), 14 December 1809.
84. A.N., BB¹⁸31, denunciation of *procureur* at Lesparre by Faure, *instituteur,* September 1809.
85. A.N., F⁹310, case of Moreau *père,* from Norroy-le-Sec (Meurthe), 20 *frimaire* XIV.

86. A.D. Cantal, L255, letter from district of Aurillac to department of Cantal, 18 August 1793.
87. A.N., F⁹314, pronouncement by *commissaire du Directoire exécutif* in Haut-Rhin, 29 *frimaire* V.
88. A.D. Vosges, L533, letter signed by "plusieurs voluntaires de la commune de Saule (Vosges)," from the armies of the Rhin, Nord, and Sambre-et-Moselle, to *commissaire du Directoire exécutif* in the Vosges, 8 *pluviôse* VI.
89. A.D. Gironde, 2R287, denunciation of Antoine Lambaut by men of the *classe* of 1814 from Lesparre, 15 April 1814.
90. A.N., F⁹315, denunciation of Magloire Verrobbier from Paris, 8 *nivôse* IV.
91. A.N., BB¹⁸8, denunciation of Cathala and others from Saint-Quintin (Ariège), 15 September 1809.
92. A.D. Gironde, 2R287, letter from *général de division* to prefect of Gironde, 17 June 1813.
93. A.N., F⁹312, report of *police générale* at Hesdin (Pas-de-Calais), 14 *frimaire* VII.
94. See Chapter 9.
95. A.N., F⁹302, denunciation of Guy Fleuriot in the Calvados, 5 *thermidor* VII.

CHAPTER 6

1. Much of the evidence used in this chapter is drawn from my previous article, "Conscription and crime in rural France during the Directory and Consulate," in Lewis, G., and Lucas, C. (ed.), *Beyond the Terror: essays in French regional and social history,* pp. 92–120.
2. Archives Nationales (A.N.), BB¹⁸277, dossier on Brochier presented to the *tribunal correctionnel* of Valence (Drôme), Year V.
3. A.N., F⁹309, letter from *commissaire provisoire du Directoire exécutif* in the Lot-et-Garonne to Minister of Interior, 2 *prairial* VII.
4. A.N., F⁹315, printed notice from department of Sarthe to its citizens, 18 *nivôse* V.
5. A.N., BB¹⁸587, letter from *directeur du jury* of the *arrondissement* of Dunkerque to Minister of Justice, 13 *frimaire* VIII.
6. A.N., AF^IV1147, report of *police générale,* 11 May 1813.
7. A.N., F¹ᶜIII Vosges 7, report from canton of Martigny to Minister of Interior, 17 *pluviôse* IV.
8. Archives de la Guerre (A.G.) Vincennes, X^w5, report from commune of Lagarde to department of Ariège, 3 *fructidor* III.
9. A.N., BB¹⁸831, complaint by Minister of Finance about judgment of *juge de paix* at Saint-Germain-en-Laye (Seine-et-Oise), 13 *ventôse* IV.
10. A.N., F⁷8514, case of Pierre Amilhat and his two sons from Seix (Ariège), 29 January 1808.
11. A.N., F¹ᶜIII Haute-Garonne 8, report from district of Mont-Unité, *brumaire* III.
12. A.N., F⁷8516, report of prefect of Ariège on "rébellions pour fait de contrebande" in Suc and Lavelanet, 8 October 1810.
13. A.N., F⁷8516, police report on band of smugglers at Sorgeat (Ariège), 4 July 1810.
14. A.N., AF^III147, letter from Minister of Finance on *chasseurs basques,* 25 *messidor* IV; A.N., AF^III150^A, letter from a merchant in Livia to Crampagna, *capitaine des chasseurs-éclaireurs* at Montlibre, 1 *brumaire* VII.
15. A.N., F⁹317, "Résultat des mesures de rigueur exécutées pendant les premiers mois de 1810 et situation du département du Taro au 11 mai 1810," *rapports des maires* for Monchio, Margasso, and Carpaneto.

16. A.N., F⁷8516, report from prefect of Ariège on smuggling in Andorra valley, 12 October 1810.
17. A.N., AF^{IV}1042, "Tableau des crimes qui ont donné lieu à des poursuites devant les cours de justice de l'année 1810" (ministère de la Justice); A.N., BB¹⁸361, list of crimes committed in department of Gironde in 1805–1806, 3 February 1807; A.N., F⁹308, list of arrests in the Landes, *vendémiaire–thermidor* IX.
18. A.N., BB¹⁸587, letter from *directeur du jury* of *arrondissement* of Dunkerque, 13 *frimaire* VIII.
19. A.N., F⁷8446, letter from prefect of Gironde to *conseiller d'état, troisième arrondissement*, 24 April 1806.
20. A.N., F⁷8555, letter from *maire* of Arsac to prefect of Gironde, 9 August 1809.
21. Archives Départementales (A.D.) Nord, 1R213, case of Charles Buffin, from Valenciennes, 1 April 1811.
22. A.N., BB¹⁸591, report of *inspection-générale* in Dunkerque to Minister of Justice, 19 *floréal* XII.
23. A.N., BB¹⁸594, report of *procureur-général* in Douai (Nord) to Minister of Justice, 26 *thermidor* XIII.
24. A.N., F⁷8539, reports on activities of band of deserters at Châtillon (Drôme), 19 August and 13 September 1808.
25. A.G. Vincennes, B¹³36, letter from Simon to district of Bourganeuf (Creuse), 27 *messidor* III.
26. A.N., BB¹⁸358, letter from *commissaire du gouvernement* in Gironde to Minister of Justice, 11 *messidor* X.
27. A.N., BB¹⁸358, letter from *commissaire du gouvernement* in Gironde to Minister of Justice, 7 *frimaire* IX.
28. A.N., BB¹⁸582, *dossier* Salembier.
29. A.N., BB¹⁸582, report of *accusateur public* of *Tribunal criminel* of department of Lys on the *bande de Salembier*, 18 *pluviôse* V.
30. A.N., AF^{IV}1157, report of Minister of War on activities of conscripts in the Sarthe, 19 February 1809.
31. A.D. Nord, L2637, letter from department of Jemmapes to department of Nord, 12 *prairial* VII.
32. A.N., F⁹301, letter from *commissaire du gouvernement* in Ardèche to Minister of Interior, 30 *ventôse* VIII.
33. A.N., F⁷8428, *dossier* on brigands arrested in the Drôme, interrogations dated Year IX.
34. A.N., F⁹310, report of prefect of Mayenne to Minister of Interior, 15 May 1809.
35. A.N., F⁷8428, report from *sous-préfet* of Nyons (Drôme), 3 *pluviôse* X.
36. For a discussion of the links between desertion and counterrevolution, see Chapter 7.
37. A.N., BB¹⁸552, report to Minister of Justice on *assassinat* at Camors (Morbihan), 17 *brumaire* VII.
38. A.N., F⁷8430, report of prefect of Drôme to Minister of Police, 16 *fructidor* XIII.
39. A.N., F⁷8538, account of *"attroupement nocturne"* at Bourg-lès-Valence (Drôme), 30 January 1808.
40. A.N., F^{1b}II Drôme 15, letter from *commissaire du Directoire exécutif* in Valence, 8 *pluviôse* V.
41. A.N., BB¹⁸588, report of robbery committed on a *négociant* from Neuchâtel, 23 *brumaire* IX.
42. A.G. Vincennes, B¹³35, minute of department of Aisne, 21 *prairial* III.
43. A.N., F⁷8418, report of *juge de paix* at Chaudesaigues (Cantal), 5 March 1805.

44. A.N., F¹ᶜIII Lot-et-Garonne 7, report of prefect of Lot-et-Garonne to Minister of Interior, 23 *fructidor* VIII.
45. A.N., F⁷8628, report of *inspection-générale* in Epinal to Minister of Justice, 2 June 1810.
46. Ibid., 5 May 1810.
47. Gutton, J.-P., *La sociabilité villageoise dans l'ancienne France*, p. 52.
48. A.N., BB¹⁸216, report from *sous-préfet* in Murat (Cantal), 8 *prairial* XI.
49. A.N., BB¹⁸599, report of *procureur* at Douai (Nord) to Minister of Justice, 25 March 1813.
50. A.N., BB¹⁸31, report of trial of André Boussaye at Libourne (Gironde), 3 May 1808.
51. A.N., F⁷8531, letter from *sous-préfet* in Mauriac to prefect of Cantal, 28 July 1809.
52. A.N., BB¹⁸280, report of trial of the two murderers at Valence (Drôme), 21 *vendémiaire* XI.
53. A.N., BB¹⁸594, report of confession of Pierre-François Fautrel, 14 April 1806.
54. A.N., F⁷8627, report of prefect of Vosges to Minister of Justice, 5 January 1808.
55. A.N., BB¹⁸75, report on trial of David Pouge, 3 August 1808.
56. A.N., AFᴵᴵᴵ144ᴮ, extract from registers of city of Marseille, *arrondissement du Midi*, 29 *thermidor* VII.
57. A.N., BB¹⁸915, report on murder at Autreville (Vosges), 30 December 1807.
58. A.N., F⁹307, report of *maire* of Poujols (Hérault) to Minister of Interior, 4 *prairial* VII.
59. A.N., BB¹⁸363, report of *procureur-général* in Bordeaux to Minister of Justice, 11 July 1811.
60. A.N., BB¹⁸355, report of *juge de paix* in canton of Cadillac (Gironde) to Minister of Justice, 6 *floréal* VIII.
61. Kaplan, S. L., *Provisioning Paris: merchants and millers in the grain and flour trade during the eighteenth century*, pp. 283–90.
62. A.N., BB¹⁸594, report of Minister of Justice on fire at a *moulin* at Ennevelin (Nord), 13 *fructidor* XIII.
63. A.N., BB¹⁸591, report to Minister of Justice on fire at Haverskerque (Nord), ler *thermidor* XII.
64. A.N., BB¹⁸580, report of *commissaire du Directoire exécutif* in Avesnes (Nord) to Minister of Justice, 16 *messidor* IV.
65. A.N., BB¹⁸598, report of *procureur* in Douai (Nord) to Minister of Justice, 28 April 1812.
66. A.N., BB¹⁸580, report of *commissaire du Directoire Exécutif* in Avesnes (Nord) to Minister of Justice, 16 *messidor* IV.
67. A.N., F¹ᶜIII Nord 7, report of *commissaire du Directoire exécutif* to Minister of Interior, 2e decade of *frimaire* VI.
68. A.N., F⁹156, F⁹176, and F⁷3589, reports on the *esprit* of local mayors over question of conscription.
69. A.N., AFᴵⱽ1156, report on attack on the *gendarmerie* at Clazay (Deux-Sèvres), 3 February 1806.
70. A.N., F⁷8418, report on attack on the *gendarmerie* at Saint-Rémy (Cantal), 22 *fructidor* XIII.
71. A.N., F⁹312, report of Police générale to Minister of Interior, 27 *messidor* VII.
72. A.N., AFᴵⱽ1156, *gendarmes'* report on escape of prisoners under escort near Cannes, 9 June 1806.
73. A.N., F¹ᶜIII Lozère 5, report of *commissaire du Directoire exécutif* in Mende to Minister of Interior, ler *nivôse* VI.
74. A.N., BB¹⁸913, report of Grosjean *aîné* from Remiremont (Vosges) to Minister of Justice, 25 *frimaire* V.

75. A.N., BB¹⁸15, report on *attroupement* at Saint-Urcize (Cantal), 8 *nivôse* XII.
76. A.N., F⁷8418, report of *sous-préfet* of Murat (Cantal), 15 *brumaire* XIII.
77. A.D. Ariège, 5L, canton of Saint-Girons, *cahiers de correspondance,* reports on effects of fire of 5/6 *nivôse* VII.
78. A.N., BB¹⁸139, letter from Minister of Justice to *commissaire* in department of Ariège, 6 *brumaire* XII.
79. A.D. Ariège, 5L34, canton of Daumazan, minute of 4 *frimaire* VII.
80. A.D. Ariège, 2R94, dossier on conscription offenses in Quérigut, 19 March 1807.
81. A.N., F⁷8405, letter from prefect of Ariège on consequences of fire at prefecture in Foix, 29 *frimaire* XIV.
82. A.N., BB¹⁸31, case of Jean Pauly *aîné* from Bourdelle (Gironde), 26 October 1809.
83. A.N., BB¹⁸914, case of Talotte from near Charmes (Vosges), 14 *brumaire* VII.
84. A.N., BB¹⁸75, letter from prefect of Seine-et-Oise to Minister of Justice, 23 August 1806; A.N., BB¹⁸54, letter from *procureur* of Valenciennes to Minister of Justice, 5 January 1811.
85. See law of 13 *prairial* XII in the Gironde (A.N., BB¹⁸31).
86. A.N., BB¹⁸50, case of Guillemette Boulo, *fermière* from Béganne (Morbihan), 18 June 1807.
87. A.N., BB¹⁸54, letter from *procureur* in Lille to Minister of Justice, 5 October 1809.
88. A.N., F⁷3605, case of Meunier, *maire* of Anor (Nord), 25 May 1811.
89. A.N., BB¹⁸913, letter from *commissaire du Directoire exécutif* in Epinal to Minister of Justice, 13 *nivôse* V.
90. See Chapter 5.
91. A.N., AF¹¹¹149, report from Minister of War to Directory, 5 *brumaire* VII.
92. A.N., F⁹176, report of prefect of Dordogne to Minister of Interior, 3 May 1809.
93. A.N., F⁹286, letter of *commissaire du Directoire exécutif* in Mâcon to Minister of Interior, 11 *prairial* VII.
94. A.N., AF¹¹¹158, letter from commune of Simorre (Gers) to Minister of War, 20 *frimaire* VII.
95. A.D. Ariège, 2R94, report from commune of Vicdessos, 10 October 1807.
96. A.N., F⁹199, minute of department of Landes, 29 *prairial* VII.
97. A.N., F⁹189, report from prefect of Gironde to Minister of Interior, 8 June 1807.
98. A.N., F⁹315, letter from two deputies from the Creuse to Minister of Interior, 18 *nivôse* IV.
99. A.N., F⁹247, letter of prefect of Seine-Inférieure to Minister of Interior, 11 November 1812.
100. A.N., F⁷8531, report from *sous-préfet* of Murat (Cantal) to Minister of Police générale, 25 March 1807.
101. A.D. Gironde, 2R287, denunciation of Jacques Biralleau from Saint-Antoine, canton of Saint-André-de-Cubzac, conscript of 1811.
102. A.N., BB¹⁸15, case of Pierre Rolland from Clavières (Cantal), conscript of 1807.
103. A.N., F⁹316, report from *commissaire du Directoire exécutif* in Amiens to Minister of Interior, 21 *floréal* VII.
104. A.N., F⁷6466, letter from prefect of Vienne to Minister of Police générale, 12 October 1806.
105. A.N., F⁹189, letter from prefect of Gironde to *conseiller d'Etat,* 31 August 1806.
106. A.N., BB¹⁸75, letter from Denis Filleau, *chirurgien en chef* at Etampes (Seine-et-Oise), to Minister of Justice, 9 *fructidor* XI.
107. A.N., BB¹⁸591, report from the *administration de la guerre* in Lille, 25 *ventôse* XII.
108. A.N., BB¹⁸54, case against Huard from Englefontaine (Nord), 4 April 1808.
109. A.N., F⁷3605, letter of prefect of Nord to *Directeur-général de la conscription,* 24 January 1807.

110. A.D. Vosges, L533, case of Nicolas Georgel from Vomécourt, near Rambervillers, 29 *germinal* VII.
111. A.N., BB¹⁸31, case of Pierre Girardin from Bordeaux, 21 July 1811.
112. A.N., F⁹286, denunciation of juries in the Loire-Inférieure, 6 *nivôse* IX.
113. A.N., F⁹286 contains a cross-section of case studies of the various kinds of fraud involved.
114. A.N., BB¹⁸50, case against Saint-Pierre, *syndic des marins* at Locmariaquer (Morbihan), 9 January 1807.
115. A.D. Ariège, 2R95, report of an incident at La Bastide-de-Bouzignac (Ariège), 18 *prairial* XIII.
116. A.D. Cantal, 2R372, case against Jean-Baptiste Chavaribeyre, *gendarme* at Laroquebrou (Cantal), 28 February 1811.
117. A.N., BB¹⁸15, ruling of the *cour d'appel* at Saint-Flour on the "affaire du Cantal," 17 November 1812.
118. A.N., F¹ᶜIII Rhône 5, report of prefect of Rhône to Minister of Interior, *2e trimestre* of 1812.
119. A.D. Cantal, L202, case of Comby, *maire* of Saint-Etienne-de-Maurs (Cantal), 1792.
120. A.N., F⁹286, case studies of frauds by *maires:* individual dossiers.
121. A.N., BB¹⁸7, case of Piquemol, *maire* of Bethmale (Ariège), 18 March 1807.
122. A.N., F⁷3581, report from prefect of Puy-de-Dôme to Minister of Police générale, March 1807.
123. A.N., BB¹⁸54, case against Ribeaucourt, *maire* of Bréaugis (Nord), 11 December 1812.
124. A.N., BB¹⁸20, report from Colombier-le-Vieux by *commissaire du gouvernement* in the Ardèche, 11 *frimaire* XII.
125. A.N., F¹ᵇII Cantal 8, case of Brioude, *maire* of Deux-Verges (Cantal), extract from minutes of *secrétaire d'État,* 2 July 1807.
126. A.N., F¹ᵇII Ariège 13, case of former *maire* and *adjoint* of Larbont (Ariège), 9 May 1808.
127. A.N., BB¹⁸31, case of *sous-préfet* of Bazas (Gironde), *ventôse* XII.
128. A.D. Nord, 1R231, letter from Minister of War to prefect of Nord, 1 October 1812.
129. A.N., F⁷8514, 8515, 8516, enumeration of cases brought against *maires* and municipal officers in the Ariège.
130. A.N., F⁷8743, *mémoire* on conscription frauds by *juge* Darmaing, 5 October 1806; and report from prefect of Ariège to Minister of Justice concerning the *mémoire,* 11 April 1807.
131. A.N., BB¹⁸20, case of Louis Bourguignon, arrested in the Drôme, 13 December 1808.
132. A.D. Gironde, 2R285, case of Duroux, 25 July 1807.
133. A.N., BB¹⁸54, letter from *procureur-général* of Nord to Minister of Justice, 10 September 1808.
134. A.N., F⁷8504, case of Nicolas Joannesse from Plainfaing (Vosges), 30 April 1806.
135. A.N., F⁷3605, interrogation of Georges Allin at Lille, 8 June 1807.
136. A.N., BB¹⁸15, letter from *substitut du procureur* in Aurillac to *procureur* in Riom, 14 June 1811.
137. A.D. Gironde, 2R285, report of *procureur* in Bordeaux, 5 December 1808.
138. A.N., F⁷3611, case of Charles Douchin at Versailles, 30 May 1811.
139. A.N., BB¹⁸20, case of Devienne and Caillet at Valence, 22 August 1807.
140. A.N., F⁷8540, arrest of Jean Lavigne at Saint-Jean-en-Royans (Drôme), 17 September 1810.
141. A.N., BB¹⁸75, case of Nicolas Lecomte from Asnières-sur-Oise (Seine-et-Oise), 5 April 1809.

142. A.N., BB[18]54, case of Yves Joseph Vauban from Saint-Amand (Nord), 3 March 1808.
143. A.N., F[7]8442, *dossier* on *escroquerie* in rural areas of the Gironde, Year XIII–1808.

CHAPTER 7

1. Scott, S. F., *The response of the Royal Army to the French Revolution,* pp. 67–9.
2. Ibid., p. 106.
3. See Cobb, R., "The White Terror," *A second identity,* pp. 92–104.
4. Gendron, F., *La jeunesse dorée,* p. 83.
5. Ibid., pp. 110ff.
6. Rural counterrevolution is discussed by Godechot, J., *La contre-révolution, 1789–1804,* which places it in its more general context; and by numerous analytical monographs, notably Lewis, G., *The second Vendée* (Oxford, 1978); Hutt, M., *Chouannerie and counterrevolution* (Cambridge, 1983); Sutherland, D., *The Chouans* (Oxford, 1982); Bois, P., *Les paysans de l'Ouest* (Paris, 1962); Tilly, C., *The Vendée* (London, 1964); and Lacouture, J., *Le mouvement royaliste dans le Sud-Ouest, 1797–1800* (Hossegor, 1932).
7. Lacouture, J., *Le mouvement royaliste dans le Sud-Ouest,* p. 4.
8. Lucas, C., "The problem of the Midi in the French Revolution", p. 2.
9. Le Goff, T.J.A., *Vannes and its region,* pp. 364–65.
10. Jones, P., "Common rights and agrarian individualism in the southern Massif Central, 1750–1880", in Lewis G., and Lucas C., (ed.), *Beyond the Terror,* p. 122.
11. Tilly, op. cit. and Bois, op. cit.
12. See D. Sutherland, *The Chouans,* p. 220.
13. Le Goff, T.J.A., and Sutherland, D., "The social origins of counterrevolution in western France", *Past and Present* 99 (1983), p. 65.
14. Arch. mun. Bordeaux, D174, 175, 176, correspondence of the *bureau de police* of the *Bureau central,* Year IV–VIII.
15. Lewis, G., *The second Vendée,* pp. 113–15.
16. Lucas, C., "Themes of southern violence after 9 thermidor", in Lewis G., and Lucas C. (ed.), *Beyond the Terror,* p. 169.
17. On the importance of the role played by local *chefs* in the Midi, see Lewis, G., *The second Vendée,* p. 113.
18. Maltby, R., "Crime and the local community in France; the department of the Drôme, 1770–1820" (D. Phil. thesis, Oxford University, 1981), p. 320.
19. Hutt, M., *Chouannerie and counterrevolution,* p. 146.
20. Sutherland, D., *The Chouans,* p. 261.
21. Lewis, G., "Political brigandage and popular disaffection in the South-east of France, 1795–1804", in Lewis, G., and Lucas C., (ed.), *Beyond the Terror,* p. 196.
22. Sutherland, op. cit., p. 29.
23. Archives Nationales (A.N.), F[1c]III Rhône 5, report from the *commissaire du Directoire exécutif* in the district of Villefranche, for the *troisième décade* of messidor, Year III.
24. A.N., F[9]222, report from the *commissaire du Directoire exécutif* in the department of Morbihan, 6 *fructidor* V.
25. A.N., F[1b]II Morbihan 14, suspension of the mayor of Pénestin, 6 *brumaire* X.
26. A.N., F[1b]Cantal 10, dismissal of the *adjoint municipal* of Narnhac, 7 *fructidor* VI.
27. A.N., F[1b]II Ariège 13, report from commune of Lavelanet, 14 *frimaire* IV.
28. A.N., F[1b]II Drôme 12, report from commune of Moras, 19 *nivôse* V.

29. A.N., BB¹⁸214, report from the *commissaire du pouvoir exécutif* in Cantal on *esprit public* in Chaudesaigues, 10 *floréal* IV.
30. Lewis, op. cit., pp. 219–21.
31. Sutherland, op. cit., p. 220.
32. Lewis, op. cit., pp. 219–21.
33. Archives Départementales (A.D.) Ariège, 2R96, interrogation of Fossat, priest at Aulus, 22 October 1808; A.N., F⁹317, report on *esprit public* in various communes of the department of Taro, May 1810; A.N., BB¹⁸358, letter from *commissaire du pouvoir exécutif* in Bordeaux to Minister of Justice, 2 *messidor* IX.
34. A.D. Ariège, 2R94, letter from archbishop of Toulouse to prefect of Ariège, 24 *brumaire* XIV.
35. A.N., BB¹⁸138, appeal by Jean-Pierre Souquet from Aulus (Ariège), 21 *nivôse* VIII.
36. A.N., F¹ᶜIII Nord 7, report from *juge de paix* of La Bassée, 15 *thermidor* III.
37. A.N., F¹ᶜIII Pas-de-Calais 8, report of *commissaire du Directoire exécutif* in Arras to Minister of Interior for the *premier trimestre* of Year VI.
38. Lacouture, J., *Le mouvement royaliste dans le Sud-Ouest*, p. 131.
39. Hutt, M., *Chouannerie and counterrevolution*, pp. 60–1.
40. Lewis, op. cit., pp. 195–204.
41. Dalby, J., "The French Revolution in a rural environment: the example of the Cantal, 1789–1794" (Ph.D. thesis, Manchester University, 1981) p. 284.
42. Jones, P., "Common rights and agrarian individualism in the southern Massif Central, 1750–1880", in Lewis G., and Lucas C. (ed.), *Beyond the Terror*, p. 124.
43. Gauthier, F., *La voie paysanne dans la Révolution française*, p. 206.
44. Lewis, op. cit., p. 225.
45. Ibid., pp. 221–22.
46. A.D. Drôme, L207, report from General Merck in Saint-Paul-Trois-Châteaux, 20 *prairial* VI.
47. A.D. Drôme, M1322, report on *brigandage* from the *sous-préfet* of Montélimar, 10 *prairial* VIII.
48. Sutherland, op. cit., pp. 36–7.
49. A.N., F⁹319, report from department of Yonne to Minister of Interior, 4 *vendémiaire* VIII.
50. A.N., F¹ᵇII Drôme 9, report from department of Drôme to Minister of Interior, 15 *vendémiaire* VI.
51. A.N., F¹ᵇII Cantal 9, register of department of Cantal relating to the dismissal of several members of the commune of Mauriac, 28 *brumaire* VI.
52. A.N., F¹ᵇII Drôme 12, letter from department of Drôme to Minister of Interior, 27 *messidor* IV.
53. A.D. Haute-Garonne, L274, report from *commissaire du gouvernement* in Léguevin, 18 *pluviôse* VIII.
54. A.D. Ariège, 5L (non classée), report of events at a conscription meeting in the commune of Moulis, 28 *floréal* VII.
55. A.N., BB¹⁸353, case against Pierre-Guillaume Capdeville and Louis Cavazza, 12 *ventôse* VI.
56. A.N., BB¹⁸830, case against Julien Quentin of Saint-Cloud (Seine-et-Oise), 9 *pluviôse* IV.
57. A.D. Nord, L6103, report of attempted subversion of troops at Nogent, 17 *messidor* VII.
58. A.D. Drôme, L426, letter from Minister of Police to General Chateauneuf Randon, circularized 30 *ventôse* IV.
59. A.N., F⁹309, letter from *commissaire du Directoire exécutif* in Puymirol (Lot-et-Garonne) to Minister of Interior, 24 *ventôse* V.

60. A.N., BB^{18}830, letter from *juge de paix* at Rambouillet (Seine-et-Oise) to Minister of Justice, 19 *brumaire* IV.
61. A.D. Haute-Garonne, L2272, "Tableau des individus qui ont figuré dans la conspiration royale du mois de thermidor an VII," canton of Aurignac.
62. The examples here are drawn from documents in A.N., F^{9}305 (Doubs); A. G. Vincennes, X^{w}5 (Ariège); A.N., BB^{18}277 (Drôme); and A.N., F^{7}8386 (Morbihan).
63. A.N., BB^{18}596, dossier on Félix Lamy and his fellow *embaucheurs,* 22 October 1808.
64. A.N., F^{1c}III Morbihan 6, letter from *commissaire du Directoire exécutif* in Vannes to Minister of Interior, 30 *frimaire* V.
65. Hutt, M., *Chouannerie and counterrevolution,* illustrates the flimsiness of Puisaye's organization in the West, the poor communications that existed between the various *chefs de chouans,* and the petty jealousies that rent their organization and undermined their effectiveness.
66. A.D. Haute-Garonne, L2270, "Tableau des insurgés royalistes (an VIII–an VII)," canton of Carbonne.
67. A.D. Haute-Garonne, L2272, "Tableau des insurgés royalistes (an VII–an VIII)," canton of Saint-Martory.
68. A.D. Haute-Garonne, 267U4, case of Jean Grimaud from Saint-Martin, 15 *vendémiaire* VII.
69. A.D. Haute-Garonne, L2272, "Tableau des insurgés royalistes (an VII–an VIII)," canton of Aurignac.
70. Ibid.
71. A.N., AF^{III}146, report from Minister of Interior to Directory, 2 *pluviôse* IV.
72. A.D. Morbihan, L593, report from the *commandant de la place* in Pontivy, 5 *prairial* IV.
73. A.D. Morbihan, L592, interrogations of *réfractaires,* Years II and III.
74. A.N., F^{1c}III Morbihan 6, letter from *commissaire du Directoire exécutif* to Minister of Interior, 30 *vendémiaire* VIII.
75. A.D. Morbihan, L566, report on a *fouille* in the area around Josselin, *1er jour complémentaire* II.
76. A.N., AF^{III}151^A, report from Minister of War to Directory, 16 *brumaire* VIII.
77. A.N., BB^{18}136, dossier on Guillaume Sibra and Etienne Duran from Mirepoix (Ariège), Years V and VI.
78. A.D. Morbihan, L^{z}842, *tribunal du district d'Auray,* dossier on René Maho.
79. For cases of dismissal over the ringing of church bells, see dossiers in series A.N., F^{1b}II. In particular, from the departments under special scrutiny here, see dossiers in A.N., F^{1b}II Cantal 7; F^{1b}II Drôme 12; and F^{1b} Seine-et-Oise 11.
80. A.D. Ariège, 5L (non classée), report of incident in the commune of Moulis, 28 *floréal* VII.
81. A.D. Morbihan, L^{dj}108, interrogation of Jean Penyres about the royalist *rassemblement* at Bignan, 1er *germinal* II.
82. A.D. Haute-Garonne, 267U4, dossier on Joseph and Jean-Baptiste Daigny.
83. A.D. Haute-Garonne, 267U4, interrogation of Jean Raimond from Miramont, 15 *fructidor* VII.
84. A.D. Haute-Garonne, 267U4, interrogation of Arnaud Latour from Miramont, 15 *fructidor* VII.
85. A.N., BB^{18}135, confession of Louis Maury at Foix, 7 *frimaire* VI.
86. A.D. Vaucluse, 7L86, testimony of Dumaine *père,* 6 *brumaire* VI, quoted in Maltby, op. cit., p. 329.
87. Archives de la Guerre (A.G.) Vincennes, B^{13}35, report from deputies on mission to the Lozère, from Mende, 3 *messidor* III.

88. A.G. Vincennes, B¹³36, report from Bonnet, deputy on mission to the departments of Loire, Haute-Loire and Ardèche, from Saint-Etienne, 16 *thermidor* III.
89. A.D. Haute-Garonne, L2269, "Tableau des insurgés royalistes (an VII–an VIII)," canton of Léguevin.
90. Ibid.

CHAPTER 8

1. Vallée, G., *La conscription dans le département de la Charente, 1798–1807,* pp. 50ff.
2. Bertaud, J.-P., *La vie quotidienne des soldats de la Révolution, 1789–99,* p. 265.
3. Houdaille, J., "Le problème des pertes de la guerre," pp. 420–22.
4. Vidalenc, J., "La désertion dans le département du Calvados sous le premier Empire," p. 62.
5. Vermale, F., "La désertion dans l'Armée des Alpes après le 9 thermidor," p. 512.
6. Archives Départementales (A.D.) Nord, L3502, reports from the *commissaire du Directoire exécutif* in department of Nord, 6 *ventôse* VI and 24 *fructidor* VI.
7. A.D. Cantal, L255, letter from *vice-procureur-syndic* in Saint-Flour to municipal council in Aurillac, 16 August 1793.
8. Archives de la Guerre (A.G.) Vincennes, Xʷ30, report of mutiny in the Compagnie Borel, Year II.
9. Archives Nationales (A.N.), F⁹174, *tableau* of conscripts of the Creuse, by commune, for Year VIII, 22 *vendémiaire* IX.
10. A.N., F⁹308, report on desertion in the Haute-Loire, 23 *nivôse* VIII.
11. A.N., F⁹199, report on conscription in the Landes, Year VII.
12. A.N., F⁹156, report from prefect of Ardèche to Minister of Interior, 10 *thermidor* VIII.
13. Meynier, A., "L'armée en France sous La Révolution et le Premier Empire," pp. 23–30.
14. A.N., F⁹303, circular letter from prefect of Cantal to *sous-préfets* in his department, 20 March 1816.
15. A.N. F¹ᶜIII Seine-et-Oise 8, report of the prefect on his tournée of the department in Year VIII, 12 *frimaire* IX.
16. A.D. Drôme, L369, report from district of Nyons, 28 February 1793.
17. A.D. Morbihan, L572, *état nominatif* of recruits of the première Réquisition of 1793.
18. Mignot, M., "La conscription dans le département de la Meuse sous le Directoire," p. 147.
19. A.N., BB¹⁸53, report from canton of Douai (Nord), 7 May 1807.
20. See A.N., AF¹¹¹158, petition from canton of Saint-Martin-Boulogne (Pas-de-Calais), 11 *prairial* VII.
21. Bertaud, J.-P., *La Révolution armée,* p. 240.
22. Ibid., p. 241.
23. Gross, J.-P., *Saint-Just: sa politique, ses missions,* p. 30.
24. A.G. Vincennes, Xʷ9, decree of Soubrany and Milhaud, 20 *pluviôse* II.
25. A.D. Cantal, 2R365, letter from Minister of War to prefect of Cantal, 29 *prairial* VIII.
26. A.G. Vincennes, Xᵏ36, *arrêté* on desertion and its punishment, 19 *vendémiaire* XII.
27. A.N., BB¹⁸50, case of Pierre-Noël Blanche, 13 October 1808.
28. A.D. Gironde, 3L267, minute of department of Gironde, 27 April 1793.
29. A.N., F⁷8386, report from prefect of Morbihan to Minister of Police générale, 29 July 1806.
30. A.N., BB¹⁸830, case of Pierre Lamy, 22 *nivôse* IV.
31. A.D. Nord, L6103, interrogation of Mathieu Leys, from Spycker, 14 May 1793.

32. A.D. Nord, L5704, letter from department of Nord to district of Avesnes, 22 May 1793.
33. A.D. Nord, L5704, report of arrest in the commune of Trélon, 29 *germinal* II.
34. A.N., F⁹304, *arrêté* of prefect of Dordogne, 9 *pluviôse* XII.
35. A.N., BB¹⁸836, letter from prefect of Seine-et-Oise to Minister of Justice, ler *pluviôse* X.
36. A.N., BB¹⁸599, letter from *procureur-général* in Douai to Minister of Justice, 25 November 1814.
37. A.G. Vincennes, B¹³36, report to Convention from Vicquy, deputy on mission at Vernon (Eure), 17 *messidor* III.
38. A.N., BB¹⁸599, op. cit., 25 November 1814.
39. See the bundles of letters from soldiers to their parents in the Oise, in A.D. Oise, series R *(non classée)*.
40. A.D. Drôme, 20R1-2, letter from Jean Chuilon from Padua, 10 May 1813.
41. A.D. Drôme, 20R1-2, letter from Louis Berton from Genoa, 5 February 1813.
42. A.D. Oise, series R *(non classée)*, letter from François Crosnier, in Lunébourg, to his parents in Saint-Martin-le-Neuf (Oise), 4 November 1811.
43. Petitfrère, C., *Le général Dupuy et sa correspondance*, p. 49.
44. Legrand, R., *Le recrutement des armées et les désertions, 1791–1815*, p. 28.
45. Sangnier, G., *La désertion dans le Pas-de-Calais de 1792 à 1802*, p. 107.
46. Vachin, H., "Les Lozériens dans la Grande Armée", p. 19.
47. Bertaud, op. cit., pp. 194ff.
48. Gross, op cit., p. 25.
49. Herlaut, A., *Le colonel Bouchotte, ministre de la Guerre en l'an II*, p. 243.
50. A.N., F¹ᶜIII Drôme 6, *compte décadaire* of *agent national* in Valence, *thermidor* VII.
51. A.G. Vincennes, Xʷ6, letter from municipal council of Saint-Girons (Ariège) to *général de brigade* Mué, 17 July 1793.
52. A.N., F⁷8553, letter from prefect of Gironde to Minister of Police générale, 1 March 1808.
53. A.N., BB¹⁸54, letter from *procureur* in Dunkerque to *procureur-général* in Paris, 21 August 1813.
54. A.N., F¹ᶜIII Gironde 5, report from prefect of Gironde to Minister of Interior, 2e *trimestre* 1811.
55. A.N., F¹ᶜIII Drôme 6, report from *agent national* in district of Montélimar, 21 *prairial* II.
56. A.N., F¹ᶜIII Drôme 7, report from prefect of Drôme to Minister of Interior, *trimestre de juillet* 1811.
57. A.G. Vincennes, Xʷ73, letter from Minister of War to department of Nord, 14 November 1792.
58. A.N., AF^IV1091, report from 21e Division militaire (Bourges), 29 *vendémiaire* XI.
59. A.N., BB¹⁸839, reports on *excès* and *délits militaires* at Versailles, sent to Minister of Justice, 9 August 1806.
60. A.N., F¹ᶜIII Rhône 5, report from *commissaire du Directoire exécutif* in Lyon, 5 *messidor* VI.
61. A.N., BB¹⁸139, letter concerning *rixe* at Tarascon, 13 *nivôse* XII.
62. A.N., AF^IV1091, report from 16e Division militaire (Lille), 29 *vendémiaire* XI.
63. A.N., F⁷8393, letter from prefect of Seine-et-Oise to *premier arrondissement*, Police générale, 30 September 1812.
64. A.N., F⁷8540, report on *rixe* at Pierrelatte, 27 November 1809.
65. A.N., F¹ᶜIII Haute-Garonne 8, report from *administration centrale* of the department of Haute-Garonne to Minister of Interior, 8 *germinal* VII.

66. A.N., F⁷8430, *dossier* on *rixe* at Montélimar, 31 January 1806.
67. A.D. Seine-et-Oise, 36L39, letter from president of *administration centrale* of department of Seine-et-Oise to municipal council of Sèvres, 29 *thermidor* VI.
68. A.N., BB¹⁸216, letter from *procureur* in Aurillac to Minister of Justice, 29 January 1807.
69. A.N., BB¹⁸839, letter from *procureur* in Versailles to Minister of Justice, 2 May 1809.
70. A.N., AFᴵᴵᴵ146, letter from municipal council of Nantes to Minister of War, 5 *fructidor* IV.
71. A.N., BB¹⁸840, report from *procureur* in Rambouillet to Minister of Justice, 4 June 1813.
72. Pétigny, X. de, *Un bataillon de volontaires: le troisième bataillon de Maine-et-Loire, 1792–1796*, p. 65.
73. Girault, P.-R., *Mes campagnes sous la Révolution et l'Empire*, p. 31.
74. A.N., F⁷8556, report from prefect of Gironde, 27 January 1810.
75. A.G. Vincennes, Xʷ6, report of troubles among men of the 4e Bataillon de l'Ariège at Ustou, 20 July 1793; A.D. Ariège, 5L *(non classée)*, report of the theft of pigs by garrison at Saint-Lizier, 24 *brumaire* VIII.
76. A.D. Drôme, L198, letter from conseil d'administration of the 4e Bataillon de la Drôme, 17 April 1792.
77. A.G. Vincennes, Xʷ94, series of petitions from department of Seine-et-Oise, Year VI–VII.
78. A.N., AFᴵⱽ1091, year report from 18e Division militaire (Dijon), 14 *vendémiaire* XI.
79. A.N., BB¹⁸142, report on incident at Ercé (Ariège), 28 February 1811.
80. A.D. Drôme, L398, letter from municipal council of Pierrelatte to department of Drôme, 29 January 1791.
81. A.N., BB¹⁸912, petition from Claude Chalabre, *apothicaire* at Rambervillers (Vosges), to Minister of Justice, 11 *fructidor* IV.
82. A.G. Vincennes, Xʷ105, petition from commune of Challans (Vendée), 18 *nivôse* II.
83. A.D. Gironde, 11L227, complaint from commune of Pauillac, 29 *nivôse* VIII.
84. A.N., F⁹307, letter from commander of 9e Division militaire (Montpellier) to Minister of Interior, 25 *vendémiaire* IX.
85. A.N., F⁹184, letter from *commissaire du Directoire exécutif* in the Finistère to *commissaires* in the cantons of his department, 11 *fructidor* VII.
86. A.N., F⁹317, letter from prefect of Var to Minister of Interior, 2 *prairial* VIII.
87. A.N., F⁹308, letter from Minister of War to Minister of Interior, 6 *germinal* XIII.
88. A.N., BB¹⁸363, letter from *Secrétaire d'Etat to Chancelier*, 26 October 1814.
89. A.G. Vincennes, Xʷ30, letter from General Perrin in Avignon to department of Drôme, 18 *fructidor* III.
90. A.G. Vincennes, Xʷ6, letter from municipal council of Pamiers (Ariège), 6 *messidor* III.
91. Delmas, J., "La patrie en danger: les volontaires nationaux du Cantal," p. 192.

CHAPTER 9

1. Gross, J.-P., *Saint-Just: sa politique et ses missions*, p. 166.
2. Meynier, A., "L'armée en France sous la Révolution et le premier Empire," p. 20.
3. Ibid., p. 21.
4. Ibid.
5. Archives de la Guerre (A.G.) Vincennes, Xᵏ36, decree of 19 *vendémiaire* XII.
6. Bergès, L., "Le civil et l'armée au début du dix-neuvième siècle", pp. 494–96.

7. Archives Nationales (A.N.), AF^{IV}1154, letter from Minister of War to the Consuls, 7 *messidor* IX.
8. A.N., BB¹⁸31, letter from *procureur-général* in Bordeaux to Minister of Justice, 5 *vendémiaire* XIII.
9. A.N., BB¹⁸551, letter from President of the *tribunal correctionnel* in Vannes to Minister of Justice, 6 *nivôse* IV.
10. A.N., F^{1b}II Drôme 12, letter from *commissaire du Directoire exécutif* in Pierrelatte to Minister of Interior, 4 *frimaire* V.
11. A.N., BB¹⁸140, dossier on the murder of Jean Jau, 25 August 1806; BB¹⁸142, denunciation of the *procureur* at Saint-Girons (Ariège), 17 May 1813.
12. A.N., F⁹306, report from deputy on mission at Evreux to Minister of Interior, 29 *frimaire* VIII.
13. A.N., F⁹165, letter from prefect of Cantal to Minister of Interior, 30 January 1811.
14. A.N., F^{1b}II Drôme 8, letter from prefect of Drôme to Minister of Interior, 8 December 1812.
15. A.N., BB¹⁸594, letter from *procureur-général* in Douai to Minister of Justice, 28 *germinal* XIII.
16. Archives Départementales (A.D.) Morbihan, R540, *jugements* of the *tribunal de première instance* of the Morbihan, 31 October 1806.
17. A.D. Morbihan, R541, cases of deserters and refractories heard in the four districts of the Morbihan during January 1806.
18. A.N., F^{1b}II Ariège 20, letter from *sous-préfet* of Saint-Girons to prefect of Ariège, 29 *prairial* X.
19. A.N., BB¹⁸552, letter from *accusateur public* at *tribunal criminel* of the Morbihan to Minister of Justice, 4 *frimaire* VI.
20. A.N., F⁹307, letter from *commissaire du Directoire exécutif* in the Hérault to Minister of Interior, 19 *germinal* IV.
21. A.N., BB¹⁸585, case against Cornez, *juge de paix* at Fenain (Nord), 6 *prairial* VII.
22. A.N., BB¹⁸913, letter from Grosjean *aîné* to Minister of Interior on *brigandages* in the district of Remiremont (Vosges), 25 *frimaire* V.
23. A.N., BB¹⁸836, letter from prefect of Seine-et-Oise to Minister of Justice, 11 *pluviôse* IX.
24. A.N., F⁷8743, BB¹⁸54, papers relating to the *Cour de Justice Criminelle et Spéciale de l'Ariège,* 1806–1807, and to the *Tribunal Spécial* in the Nord, 1813–1814.
25. A.D. Ariège, 2R97, dossier of sentences handed down by the *Cour de Justice Criminelle et Spéciale de l'Ariège,* 1806–1807.
26. A.N., BB¹⁸352, letter from Minister of Justice to Renauldon, *capitaine de grenadiers* in the Gironde, 18 *floréal* IV.
27. A.N., BB¹⁸553, letter from André, *capitaine rapporteur* of the Premier Conseil de Guerre of the Morbihan to the Minister of Justice, 18 *frimaire* VII.
28. A.D. Cantal, 2R373, 374, *jugements* of deserters by the individual *conseils de guerre* in the Cantal, Year VII–1813.
29. A.N., F⁹260, letter from prefect of Vosges to Minister of Interior, 6 *brumaire* IX.
30. A.D. Gironde, 11L67, letter from *commissaire du Directoire exécutif* in Bazas to commune of Bazas, 21 *germinal* IV.
31. A.D. Gironde, 11L67, letter from *commissaire du Directoire exécutif* in Bazas to the *commissaire-général* for the department of the Gironde, 8 *floréal* IV.
32. See Chapter 2.
33. Bergès, op. cit., pp. 48ff.
34. Prefects dismissed included those of the Gironde (Year XI) and of the Cantal, following the "affaire du Cantal" in 1810.

35. Tulard, J., *Napoléon ou le Mythe du sauveur,* p. 225.
36. See Chapter 3.
37. *Bulletin des lois,* loi du 10 *vendémiaire* IV.
38. A.N., F⁷8514, police report on incident at Serres (Ariège), 9 March 1808.
39. A.D. Seine-et-Oise, 2LR26, report of the *juge de paix* of the canton of Argenteuil to district of Mantes, 15 *fructidor* VII.
40. A.N., F¹ᶜIII Drôme 6, report of prefect of Drôme to Minister of Interior, *trimestre de juillet* 1811.
41. Cobb, R., *The police and the people,* pp. 21–2.
42. A.N., F⁹303, decree of Riou, prefect of Cantal, 15 July 1808.
43. A.D. Cantal, 2R373, interrogation of Jean Laroussinie, *aubergiste* at Arpajon, 27 February 1809.
44. A.N., F¹ᶜIII Nord 7, report of *commissaire du Directoire exécutif* at Douai, for the *troisième décade* of *brumaire* VI.
45. Cobb, op cit., p. 19.
46. A.N., F⁷3605, letter from prefect of Nord to Minister of Police générale, 24 *fructidor* XIII.
47. A.N., F⁷3605, ibid.
48. A.N., F⁹310, report by prefect of Mayenne to Minister of Interior, 15 May 1809.
49. A.D. Cantal, 2R365, letter from *sous-préfet* of Murat to *général de brigade* Saint-Martin, 10 *prairial* XII.
50. A.D. Nord, 1R238, letter from *sous-préfet* of Cassel to prefect of Nord, 21 July 1814.
51. A.D. Seine-et-Oise, R *(non classée),* carton D, letter from "agent ambulant du canton d'Ablis" to *sous-préfet* of Etampes, 11 *prairial* XIII.
52. A.N., F⁷8515, letter from prefect of Ariège to Minister of Police générale, asking for 200 francs to pay for the occasional expenses incurred in such espionage, 6 July 1812.
53. A.N., F⁹309, letter from prefect of Lot-et-Garonne to Minister of Interior, 26 August 1806.
54. A.D. Nord, 1R212, letter from prefect of Nord to Minister of State concerned with conscription, 4 July 1808.
55. A.D. Drôme, L369, letter from *général de division* in control of police in the Drôme to the department of the Drôme, 9 *floréal* IV; other information on Gély's activities can be found in A.D. Drôme L370 and in A.N., F¹ᵇII Drôme 12.
56. *Bulletin des lois,* decree of 12 March 1806.
57. A.N., F⁹165, pastoral letter from bishop of Saint-Flour to the *curés* of his diocese, 3 *floréal* XI.
58. A.N., AFᴵⱽ1046, report of *ministre des Cultes* to the Emperor, 7 February 1807.
59. A.N., F⁹178, pastoral letter from bishop of Besançon to the *curés* of his diocese, *s.d.*
60. A.N., F⁹209, letter from prefect of Lozère to Minister of Interior, 27 July 1813.
61. A.N., F⁹209, letter from Minister of War to prefect of Lozère, 13 July 1813.
62. A.N., F¹ᶜIII Drôme, report from prefect of Drôme to the First Consul, 20 *nivôse* X.
63. A.N., AFᴵⱽ1046, report of *ministre des Cultes* to the Emperor, 13 January 1807.
64. Ibid., 21 May 1807.
65. Ibid., 29 April 1807.
66. Ibid., 5 May 1807.
67. Ibid., 7 February 1807.
68. Ibid., 29 April 1807.
69. Langlois, C., *Le diocèse de Vannes au dix-neuvième siècle,* p. 136.
70. Langlois, C., "Complots, propagandes et répression policière sous l'Empire, 1806–1807", p. 370.
71. A.N., AFᴵⱽ1045, letter from bishop of Vannes to *ministre des Cultes,* 3 October 1806.

72. Ibid., 12 October 1806.
73. Langlois, C., *Le diocèse de Vannes,* p. 195.
74. A.N., AF^{IV}1045, letter from *ministre des Cultes* to the Emperor, 17 November 1806.
75. Langlois, C., *Le diocèse de Vannes,* p. 212.
76. A.N., AF^{IV}1045, op. cit., 14 October 1806.
77. Cameron, I., *Crime and repression in the Auvergne and the Guyenne,* p. 73.
78. Ibid., pp. 79–80.
79. Emsley, C., *Policing and its context, 1750–1870,* pp. 1–9; see also Williams, A., *The police of Paris, 1718–1789,* pp. 5–16.
80. Emsley, op. cit., p. 15.
81. A.D. Vosges, L539, circular from Minister of Interior to departments, 26 *nivôse* VI.
82. A.G. Vincennes, X^{w}6, report from commune of Saint-Girons (Ariège), 28 *prairial* II.
83. A.D. Vosges, L539, letter from commune of Remiremont to department of Vosges, 30 September 1792.
84. A.N., F^{9}165, letter from prefect of Cantal to Minister of Interior, 8 *thermidor* VIII.
85. A.N., F^{1c}III Morbihan 6, letter from *commissaire du Directoire exécutif* in Vannes to Minister of Interior, 9 *messidor* VII.
86. A.D. Nord, 5R4, letter from prefect of Nord to Minister of Police générale, 17 *germinal* IX.
87. A.G. Vincennes, X^{f}68, letter from members of the *jury départemental* of the Ariège to Minister of War, 4 *nivôse* VII.
88. A.D. Seine-et-Oise, R *(non classée),* letter from Minister of War to department of Seine-et-Oise, 8 *vendémiaire* IX.
89. A.D. Drôme, L207, plea for the retention of *gendarmes* by commune of Crest, 6 *floréal* IV.
90. A.N., F^{1c}III Gironde 5, report from Department of Gironde to Minister of Interior, 6 *frimaire* IV.
91. A.N., F^{1c}III Haute-Garonne 8, report from prefect of Haute-Garonne to Minister of Interior, 15 *frimaire* IX.
92. A.N., F^{9}323, letter from Minister of Justice to Minister of Interior, 14 *nivôse* VI.
93. A.D. Nord, 5R33, letter from Jouvancourt, *chef d'escadron* of the *gendarmerie* in Lille, to prefect of Nord, 2 *ventôse* XIII.
94. A.N., F^{1c}III Pas-de-Calais 8, letter from *commissaire du Directoire exécutif* in Arras to Minister of Interior, 2 *pluviôse* VI.
95. Emsley, op. cit., pp. 32–52.
96. *Bulletin des lois,* loi du 28 *pluviôse* VIII.
97. A.N., F^{7}9874, denunciation of Georges-Joseph Daniel, *commissaire de police* at Mirecourt (Vosges), 9 February 1809.
98. A.N., F^{7}9860, denunciation of Loeuilliet-Rousseau, *commissaire de police* at Douai (Nord), 14 June 1810.
99. A.N., F^{7}9846, denunciation of Dutour, *commissaire de police* at Montélimar (Drôme), 7 February 1810.
100. A.N., F^{7}9841, report of prefect of Ariège to *conseiller d'Etat, troisième arrondissement* of Police générale, 17 *brumaire* XIII.
101. Emsley, op. cit., pp. 43–4; evidence corroborated from cases in A.N., F^{7}9841 (Ariège), F^{7}9846 (Drôme), F^{7}9860 (Nord) and F^{7}9874 (Vosges).
102. A.N., F^{7}9851, "Etat des commissaires de police du département de la Gironde," 28 *brumaire* XIII.
103. A.N., F^{7}9851, letter from *sénateur* Pierre Sers to Minister of Police générale, 19 *pluviôse* XIII.
104. A.D. Nord, 5R1, circular letter from Minister of War to prefects, 7 *messidor* X.

105. A.D. Seine-et-Oise, 1LR643, petition from Adrien Belly of Montdidier, *n.d.*

106. A.N., F⁹323, letter from Sébastien Reynaud, *cordonnier,* of Valence (Drôme), 29 December 1809.

107. A.D. Nord, 5R22, letter from Charlemagne Dalle to *sous-préfet* of Lille, Year X.

108. A.G. Vincennes, Xᶠ246, "dossiers de militaires désignés pour concourir au recrutement de la gendarmerie," Year XI–1806.

109. A.G. Vincennes, Xᶠ246, list of *militaires désignés* from the 7e Régiment de Ligne, 19 *brumaire* XIV.

110. A.G. Vincennes, Xᶠ75, "Etat des gendarmes non conservés," department of Nord, 27 *frimaire* VI.

111. A.D. Seine-et-Oise, R *(non classée),* carton 6, comments on the reorganization of the *gendarmerie* in Year X.

112. A.D. Seine-et-Oise, R *(non classée),* carton 6, *contrôle* of *gendarmes* in the Seine-et-Oise, Year X.

113. A.D. Gironde, 2R284, letter from *capitaine de gendarmerie* in Queyrac to prefect of Gironde, n.d.

114. A.D. Nord, 1R238, letter from prefect of Nord to *directeurs des douanes* at Dunkerque and Valenciennes, 13 June 1815.

115. A.D. Nord, L2635, letter from commune of Steenvorde to prefect of Nord, 18 *nivôse* IV.

116. A.D. Cantal, 2R368, order by prefect of Riou to involve *gardes-forestiers* and *gardes-champêtres,* 16 July 1810.

117. A.N., FˡᶜIII Haute-Garonne 8, report from prefect of Haute-Garonne to Minister of Interior, 15 *frimaire* IX.

118. A.N., BB¹⁸912, complaint by canton of Remiremont (Vosges) about breakdown in the policing of *délits ruraux,* 8 *nivôse* IV.

119. A.D. Seine-et-Oise, IVM1³, "Renseignements statistiques sur la Seine-et-Oise: mission du conseiller d'Etat Lacuée," Year IX.

120. A.D. Seine-et-Oise, R *(non classée),* "Etat nominatif et par commune des gardes-champêtres de l'arrondissement de Rambouillet," addressed to the prefect of Seine-et-Oise, 26 March 1814.

121. A.D. Drôme, 1PM3, "Gardes forestiers: notes sur leur moralité, leur capacité, et leur service," *dossiers individuels* submitted by cantons to the prefect of Drôme during 1810. Some of the examples quoted are drawn from Richard Maltby's thesis, "Crime and the local community in France: the department of the Drôme, 1770–1820," pp. 221–22, which also makes use of this rare source. Equivalent lists do not exist in the archives of the other departments visited.

122. A.N., F⁷8428, extract from minutes of the Conseil général of the department of the Drôme, Year X.

123. A.N., F⁹309, letter from *commissaire du Directoire exécutif* in the Lot-et-Garonne to Minister of Interior, 21 *pluviôse* V.

124. A.D. Ariège, 5L *(non classée),* report from canton of Saint-Girons to department of Ariège, 24 *floréal* VII.

125. On the state of the law on *garnisaires,* see Bergès, op. cit., pp. 527–41.

126. A.D. Nord, 1R67, circular letter to prefects on the use to be made of *garnisaires,* 16 April 1811.

127. A.D. Cantal, 2R368, letter from Minister of Interior to prefect of Cantal, 15 December 1808.

128. A.D. Cantal, 2R366, announcement of the employment of *garnisaires* in the department, 3 January 1809; A.D. Cantal, 2R368, report of prefect for 1809, listing the cost of using *garnisaires.*

129. A.N., F⁹316, letter from prefect of Gard to Minister of Interior, 11 *fructidor* XI.
130. A.D. Nord, 1R236, letter from mayor of Etroeungt to *sous-préfet* of Avesnes, 15 *messidor* IX.
131. A.N., F⁷6466, letter from prefect of Loire to *Directeur-général des revues,* 8 September 1807.
132. A.D. Cantal, 2R370, dossier entitled "Bureau d'Aurillac: amendes des conscrits," Year XI–1806.
133. A.N., F⁹174, petition from individuals in the canton of Gentioux (Creuse), 27 *frimaire* VIII.
134. A.N., F⁹318, letter from prefect of Haute-Vienne to Minister of Interior, 11 *thermidor* XI.
135. A.N., F⁹316, decree on the placement of *garnisaires* in the homes of conscripts by the prefect of Tarn, 21 *prairial* VII.
136. A.N., F⁹163, bulletin on the state of recruitment in the Bouches-du-Rhône, 15 *thermidor* VIII; A.N., BB¹⁸139, case of Antoine Blazy from Saurat (Ariège), 3 *messidor* XI.
137. A.N., F⁹308, letter from prefect of Loire-Inférieure to *Directeur-général des revues,* 18 July 1811.
138. A.D. Nord, 1R236, letter from *sous-préfet* of Cambrai to prefect of Nord, 28 September 1813.
139. A.D. Drôme, L794, letter from *lieutenant de gendarmerie* in district of Nyons to the district administration, 15 *messidor* III.
140. A.N., FˡᶜIII Gironde 5, letter from department of Gironde to Minister of Interior, 6 *frimaire* IV.
141. A.N., F⁹312, letter from Minister of War to Minister of Interior on indiscipline among the *garde nationale* at Rabastens (Hautes-Pyrénées), 17 *nivôse* X.
142. Bastide, L., *Lois militaires sous la Révolution: leur application dans la Corrèze,* p. 22.
143. Ibid., pp. 29–30.
144. Bergès, op. cit., p. 577.
145. A.N., F⁹260, letter from prefect of Vosges to Minister of Interior, 2e *jour complementaire* VIII.
146. A.N., FˡᶜIII Drôme 6, report from *commissaire du gouvernement* in Valence to Minister of Interior, 9 *nivôse* VII.
147. A.D. Gironde, 11L227, scribbled *brouillon* from *commissaire du gouvernement* in Bordeaux to commune of Lesparre, 29 *vendémiaire* VIII.
148. A.D. Nord, L2404, report from "commissaire civil envoyé pour activer la conscription" from Walincourt to department of Nord, 18 *floréal* VII.
149. A.N., AFᴵⱽ1126, report from Minister of War to *secrétairie d'Etat,* 25 April 1812.
150. A.N., AFᴵⱽ1126, "Situation des départements sur les déserteurs et sur les réfractaires des années 1806, 1807, 1808, 1809, 1810 et 1811" (two reports), 1812.
151. A.N., F⁷3595, report from prefect of Gironde to Minister of Police générale, 29 April 1811.
152. A.D. Gironde, 2R289, protests from mayors about conduct of the *colonne mobile,* 1813–14; A.D. Gironde, 2R291, complaints from mayors about the costs of the *colonnes,* January 1814.
153. A.G. Vincennes, C¹⁰136, report from Minister of War to the Emperor, 5 August 1813.
154. A.N., F⁷6126, Imperial decree of 25 March 1810.
155. A.N., AFᴵᴵᴵ184, appeals by Henry Scheideker and Georges Steiger from Cayenne, *prairial* II.

156. A.N., F⁷3582, "Amnistie de 1810—statistique départementale."
157. A.N., F⁷3582, comments on the working of the Amnesty of 1810 from the prefects of Cantal, Landes, Tarn, and Tarn-et-Garonne.
158. A.N., F¹79, letter from prefect of Drôme to Minister of Interior, 15 February 1807.
159. A.N., F⁹137, letter from prefect of Taro to Minister of Interior, 7 April 1810.
160. A.N., F⁷3605, letter from prefect of Nord to Minister of Police générale, 9 *frimaire* XII.
161. A.D. Nord, L2636, letter from *commissaire du Directoire exécutif* in Douai to Minister of War, 24 *pluviôse* VI.
162. A.N., AF^IV1091, report from the 9e Division militaire to the First Consul, from Montpellier, 14 *vendémiaire* XI.
163. A.G. Vincennes, X^k11, "Mémoire adressé au Général Dufour par les officiers du 2e Bataillon des Chasseurs Basques," 3 *floréal* VIII.
164. A.G. Vincennes, X^k11, letter from Harriet, chef du Premier Bataillon des Chasseurs basques, to the First Consul, received 24 *messidor* VIII.
165. A.N., AF^III147, letter from Minister of War to Directory, 14 *prairial* IV; A.N., AF^III149, letter from General Garnier to Minister of War, from Nice, 5 *brumaire* VII.
166. A.N., AF^IV1092, letter from General Cervoni, commander of the 8e Division militaire (Marseille) to the First Consul, 20 *frimaire* X.
167. A.D. Ariège, 4R21, decree of 6 August 1808 and comments of the prefect of Ariège of his *conseil-général du Département.*
168. A.N., F⁹745, letter from prefect of Ariège to Minister of Interior, 15 September 1808.
169. A.G. Vincennes, X^k12, letter from commander of Premier Bataillon des Chasseurs de la Montagne de l'Ariège to Minister of War, 10 January 1810.
170. A.G. Vincennes, X^k12, letter from prefect of Ariège to Minister of War, 20 October 1808.
171. A.D., Ariège, 4R21, *état* of Premier Bataillon de l'Ariège, 1 December 1809; A.G. Vincennes, X^k12, *état* of Premier Bataillon de la Haute-Garonne, 16 September 1810.
172. A.G. Vincennes, X^k13, report to Minister of War on the state of *miquelets* recruited in the Basses-Pyrénées and Pyrénées-Orientales, 26 February 1810.
173. A.N., AF^IV1066, letter from prefect of Ariège to Minister of Interior, 14 October 1810.
174. A.D. Ariège, 2R92, lists of deserters from the companies of *miquelets* in the Ariège, 10 July 1808.
175. A.N., F⁹306, letter from prefect of Haute-Garonne to Minister of Interior, June 1809.
176. Bergès, op. cit., pp. 640–41.
177. A.G. Vincennes, X^k13, report of Minister of War to the Emperor, 2 February 1809.
178. Ibid., 28 November 1810.
179. A.N., F⁹232, letter from prefect of Pas-de-Calais to Minister of Interior, 5 *floréal* XII.
180. A.N., F⁹209, letter from prefect of Lozère to *Directeur-général des revues,* 7 June 1813; reply from Minister of War to prefect, 13 July 1813.

CHAPTER 10

1. Woloch, I., "Napoleonic conscription: state power and civil society," p. 111.
2. See Emsley, C., "The impact of war and military participation on Britain and France, 1792–1815", in Emsley, C., and Walvin, J. (ed.), *Artisans, peasants, and proletarians, 1760–1860: essays presented to Gwyn A. Williams,* pp. 57–80.

3. Archives Nationales (A.N.), F⁷6466, letter from prefect of Lot-et-Garonne to his mayors, 10 March 1808.

4. A.N., F⁹241, letter from prefect of Rhône to Minister of Interior, Year XI.

5. A.N., AF^IV1154, report from Minister of War to the Consuls, 7 *messidor* IX.

6. A.N., F⁹209, report of General Moucey, *inspecteur-général de la gendarmerie,* for the Lozère, 8 *prairial* XI.

7. A.N., F⁹232, letter from *général de brigade* in Arras to Minister of Interior, 2 *brumaire* XII.

8. Archives Départementales (A.D.) Vosges, L536, letter from *chef d'escadron* to commune of Lamarche (Vosges), 14 *thermidor* V.

9. A.N., F⁹189, letter from mayor of Bordeaux-Nord to prefect of Gironde, 8 *floréal* XI.

10. A.D. Nord, L2635, letter from *commissaire du Directoire exécutif* in Hazebrouck to department of Nord, 28 *fructidor* VII.

11. A.N., F⁹189, letter from prefect of Gironde to Minister of War, 5 *prairial* XI.

12. A.D. Nord, 1R64, letter from *conseiller de préfecture* Desmouliers to prefect of Nord, 4 *fructidor* XI.

13. A.N., F⁷8429, report on dispute between mayor of Nyons and *maréchal des logis, vendémiaire* XIV.

14. A.N., BB¹⁸590, reports from *inspection-générale de la gendarmerie,* 23 *ventôse* XI, and from the mayor of Commines (Nord), 28 *ventôse* XI.

15. A.N., F¹ᵇII Drôme 9, letter from prefect of Drôme to Minister of Interior, 12 *frimaire* XIII.

16. A.N., F⁷8445, letters from prefects of Gironde and Dordogne, 9, 11, and 23 *frimaire* XIV.

17. See Chapter 6.

18. A.N., F⁹222, letter from prefect of Morbihan to Minister of Interior, 30 *messidor* XI.

19. A.N., BB¹⁸31, denunciation of Romegoux, *maire* of Belliet (Gironde), October 1807.

20. A.N., F¹ᵇII Vosges 18, letter from *commissaire du Directoire exécutif* at Rothau to Minister of Interior, 20 *floréal* V.

21. A.N., F¹ᶜIII Nord 8, "compte de tournée" of prefect of Nord for Year X, 2 *thermidor* X.

22. A.D. Gironde, 11L51, report from *commissaire du Directoire exécutif* in Bordeaux extra-muros, 25 *vendémiaire* VII.

23. A.N., F¹ᶜIII Vosges 7, report of *commissaire du Directoire exécutif* in Epinal, 9 *frimaire* VII.

24. A.N., F⁹303, letter from prefect of Cantal to Minister of Interior, 30 *vendémiaire* XIV.

25. A.N., F¹ᵇII Drôme 8, letter of resignation from Natte, *agent municipal* at Valence, 17 *messidor* IV.

26. A.N., F¹ᵇII Vosges 17, letter of resignation from Jaquiné, *adjoint* at Rambervillers, 18 *brumaire* IV.

27. A.N., F¹ᵇII Drôme 8, letter of resignation from Tournaire aîné, *commissaire* at Châteauneuf, 29 *thermidor* IV.

28. A.N., F⁷6466, letter from prefect of Loire to Minister of Police générale, 12 March 1808.

29. A.N., BB¹⁸216, *dossier* on Michel Cantuel, 2 *germinal* XI.

30. A.N., F¹ᵇII Ariège 13, decree ordering the dismissal of the mayor of Loubières, 20 *thermidor* XIII.

31. A.N., F¹ᵇII Pyrénées-Orientales 1, letter from *commissaire du Directoire exécutif* in Perpignan to Minister of Interior, 4 *ventôse* IV.

32. A.N., F¹ᵇII Morbihan 10, letter from commune of Groix to Minister of Interior, 13 *thermidor* XI.

33. A.D. Nord, 1R214, letter from *sous-préfet* of Dunkerque to prefect of Nord, 6 March 1815.

34. A.D. Nord, L2635, report from *commissaire du Directoire exécutif* in Maubeuge, 25 *fructidor* VII.

35. A.N., F⁷8440, letter from prefect of Gironde to *conseiller d'Etat*, 26 *fructidor* XII.

36. A.N., F¹ᵇII Seine-et-Oise 17, letter from prefect of Seine-et-Oise to Minister of Interior, 9 January 1810.

37. A.N., F¹ᵇII Drôme 12, letter from *commissaire du Directoire exécutif* in Pierrelatte to Minister of Interior, 4 *frimaire* V.

38. A.N., BB¹⁸15, report of *attroupement* at Saint-Urcize (Cantal), 8 *nivôse* XII.

39. A.N., F⁹150, letter from prefect of Ain to Minister of Interior, 31 December 1820.

40. A.N., F¹ᶜIII Nord 7, police report from Berlaimont, 2e *décade* VI.

41. A.N., F¹ᵇII Morbihan 8, letter from *commissaire du Directoire exécutif* in Vannes to Minister of Interior, 5 *frimaire* V.

42. A.N., F¹ᵇII Seine-et-Oise 11, letter from *commissaire du gouvernement* in Versailles to Minister of Interior, 8 *nivôse* VIII.

43. A.N., F¹ᵇII Vosges 19, letter from *commissaire du Directoire exécutif* in Epinal to Minister of Interior, 24 *fructidor* VI.

44. A.N., F¹ᶜIII Basses-Pyrénées 7, letter from *commissaire du Directoire exécutif* in Pau to his colleagues in the communes of his department, ler *frimaire* V.

45. A.N., F¹ᵇII Ariège 13, letter from prefect of Ariège to Minister of Interior, 17 May 1806.

46. A.N., AF^IV1091, report to First Consul from *27e Division militaire* in Turin, 19 *brumaire* XI.

47. See, for instance, Chevillot, M., "Rixe à Wassy," passim.

48. Maltby, R., "Crime and the local community in France: the department of the Drôme, 1770–1820", p. 201.

49. A.N., AF^IV1156, punishment of a canton in the Tarn following an assault on the *gendarmerie,* 6 January 1806.

50. A.N., F⁹227, punishment of town of Hazebrouck by revoking its status as a *sous-préfecture,* 8 July 1814.

51. A.N., AF^III150ᴬ, punishment of canton of Gourin (Morbihan) after nonpayment of fine for assault on a *garde-champêtre,* 6 *frimaire* VII.

52. A.N., BB¹⁸54, letter from Minister of Justice to prefect of Nord, 13 January 1808.

53. A.N., F⁹316, letter from Minister of Interior to *commissaire du Directoire exécutif* in Rouen, 17 *fructidor* VII.

54. A.D. Gironde, 3L269, instruction to *lieutenant de gendarmerie* in Bordeaux, 16 *nivôse* VII.

55. A.N., F⁹319, report of police action in canton of Quarré (Yonne), 16 *prairial* VII.

56. A.N., F⁷8743, reports to *procureur* in Foix from Saint-Girons and Rivèrenert (Ariège), 7 October and 19 October 1808.

57. A.N., F⁷8439, letter from *commissaire général de police* in Bordeaux to Minister of Justice, 14 *brumaire* XII.

58. A.N., AF^III149, report to Minister of War on military espionage in Holland, 6 *germinal* VI.

59. A.D. Nord, L2635, circular letter to *commissaires* in the Nord, 29 *fructidor* VII.

60. A.N., F⁷8555, report from *lieutenant de la résidence* in Bordeaux, 31 July 1809.

61. A.N., BB¹⁸7, report to Minister of Justice of *attroupement* at Ségura (Ariège), 12 March 1806.

62. A.N., BB¹⁸140, report from mayor of Lacourt on *attroupement* in village church, 4 *nivôse* XIII.

63. A.N., F¹ᶜIII Aude 5, report of *commissaire du Directoire exécutif* in Carcassonne to Minister of Interior, 21 *germinal* VII.

64. A.N., F⁷3603, letter from *inspecteur-général de la gendarmerie* to Minister of Police générale, 2 March 1809.

65. A.N., AFᴵⱽ1156, reports from Minister of War to *secrétairerie d'Etat* between 1806 and 1808.

66. A.N., F⁹312, letter from prefect of Pas-de-Calais to Minister of Interior, 23 *thermidor* XII.

67. A.N., F⁹310, letter from Minister of War to Minister of Interior, 10 *fructidor* VIII.

68. A.N., BB¹⁸7, *dossier* on Pierre Vergé, 7 July 1808.

69. A.N., BB¹⁸138, report on attack on *gendarmes* at Castelnau-Durban (Ariège), ler *frimaire* X.

70. A.D. Ariège, 2R98-104, details of accusations brought against mayors in the Ariège.

71. A.N., F⁷8446, report on attack on *gendarmes* at La Taillan (Gironde), 20 February 1806.

72. A.N., F⁷8430, report on attack on a *garde-forestier* at Charpey (Drôme), 16 July 1806.

73. A.N., F⁹319, report on an *attroupement* at Courlon (Yonne), 10 *ventôse* VII.

74. A.N., F⁷8531, report from prefect of Cantal to Minister of Police générale, 30 December 1808.

75. A.D. Ariège, 2R94, letter from *capitaine de gendarmerie* in Foix to prefect of Ariège, 5 January 1806.

76. A.N., BB¹⁸7, report from *procureur-général* in Foix to Minister of Justice, 13 May 1807.

77. Castan, Y., *Honnêteté et relations sociales en Languedoc, 1715–1780,* passim.

78. A.N., BB¹⁸84, report from prefect of Vosges on an "acte de rébellion" against the *gendarmes* at Attigny, 29 *nivôse* XII.

79. For instance, in the very heart of Bordeaux (A.N., BB¹⁸355, report to Minister of Justice, 14 *fructidor* VIII).

80. A.N., BB¹⁸595, report to Minister of Justice on an incident near Ounain (Nord), 3 May 1806.

81. A.N., F¹ᶜIII Rhône 5, report on *esprit public* in the Rhône for the *troisième trimestre* of 1812.

82. A.D. Nord, L2638, report of the *colonne mobile* from Preches to department of Nord, 2 *ventôse* VII.

83. A.N., F⁷8531, report from prefect of Cantal to Minister of Police générale, 4 January 1808.

84. A.N., F⁷8516, examples of "rébellion contre la gendarmerie" in various communes of the Ariège, 1809–1810.

85. A.N., AFᴵⱽ1156, report to Minister of War on an attack on *gendarmes* at Clazay (Deux-Sèvres), 3 February 1806.

86. A.N., BB¹⁸54, report from *procureur-général* in Lille to Minister of Justice, 22 September 1813.

87. Bergeron, L., *France under Napoleon,* p. 22.

Bibliography

PRIMARY SOURCES

Archives Nationales

Série D - Comités des Assemblées

D^{III}20^A Comité de Législation, correspondance administrative et judiciaire, 1793–an III, département de l'Ariège

Série F^{1b}II - Personnel administratif

Série départementale: F^{1b}II Ariège 10–20, Cantal 6–10, Drôme 8–15, Morbihan 8–15, Nord 14–23, Pyrénées-Orientales 1, Seine-et-Oise 11–17, Vosges 15–22

Série F^{1c}III - Esprit public et élections

Série départementale: F^{1c}III Ain 5, Ariège 6, Aude 5, Cantal 6, Drôme 6–7, Haute-Garonne 8–9, Gironde 5–6, Lot-et-Garonne 7–9, Lozère 5, Morbihan 6–7, Nord 7–8, Pas-de-Calais 8, Basses-Pyrénées 7, Rhône 5, Seine-et-Oise 8, Var 11, Vosges 7

Série F^7 - Police générale

The following files of reports and correspondence were valuable for the study of recruitment offenses and recruitment-related crime. Parts of the series are arranged by department:

F^7 3581, 3582, 3583, 3586, 3589, 3592, 3595, 3603, 3605, 3611, 3615, 6126, 6466, 8363, 8386, 8393, 8405, 8418, 8428, 8429, 8430, 8439, 8440, 8442, 8445, 8446, 8504, 8514, 8515, 8516, 8531, 8538, 8539, 8540, 8553, 8555, 8556, 8627, 8628, 8724, 8743

The series also contains dossiers on the operations of *commissaires de police:*

F^7 9841, 9846, 9851, 9859, 9860, 9870, 9874

279

Série F⁹ - Affaires militaires

F⁹ 150–261   Recrutement, correspondance générale (série départementale)
286–288   Recrutement, fraudes et dispenses
301–319   Désertion—série départementale
744–745   Armée de réserve, colonnes mobiles

Série F²⁰ - Statistique

F²⁰ 434–435   Migration, série départementale

Série AF^{III} - Directoire exécutif

Reports, correspondence, petitions and other papers from the Ministry of War between Year IV and Year VIII are contained in the following dossiers:
AF^{III} 144–151^B, 158, 182, 184

Série AF^{IV} - Secrétairerie d'Etat impérial

The reports and correspondence of several ministries proved valuable for the study of desertion and its civilian repercussions:

AF^{IV} 1042   Ministre de la Justice
1043   Ministre de la Police
1045–1046   Ministre des Cultes
1066   Ministre de l'Intérieur
1090–1092   Rapports des généraux commandant les divisions militaires
1121–1126   Ministre de la Guerre
1147   Ministre de la Guerre (1813–1814)
1154–1158   Ministre de la Guerre: gendarmerie et police militaire
1209   Ministre de la Guerre: matelots, conscrits

Série BB^{18} - Ministère de la Justice, Division criminelle

The correspondence was used for a sample of *départements,* both for offenses relating directly to recruitment and for general criminality:

Conscription: BB^{18} 7–8, 15, 20, 31, 50, 53–54, 75, 84
Crime: BB^{18} 135–142, 214–217, 277–281, 352–363, 551–554, 579–599, 830–840, 912–915

Archives de la Guerre (Vincennes)

Série B - Correspondance militaire générale
B^{13} 35–36   Correspondance des armées, June–July 1795

Série C
C^{10} 136   Formation des colonnes mobiles, 1813–1814

Série X^f - Gendarmerie

X^f 68–75   Gendarmerie, organisation définitive, an V–VI (série départementale)
246   Gendarmerie, recrutement: dossiers de militaires désignés pour concourir au recrutement de la gendarmerie, an XI–180

Série X^k - Troupes spéciales

X^k 11–13   Bataillons de chasseurs des montagnes et des miquelets
36   Dépôts des conscrits réfractaires, an XII–1814
37   Bataillones de déserteurs français rentrés, 1802–1814

Série X^w - Volontaires nationaux

This series is organized by department and consists of documents relating to army recruitment copied from the holdings of departmental archives. The following *cartons* proved especially useful:

X^w 5, 6, 7, 9, 16, 17, 18, 30, 48, 59, 70, 73, 74, 94, 95, 104, 105, 107

Archives Départementales

Most of the relevant material for this study is to be found in either Series L (Période révolutionnaire) or Series R (Affaires militaires). Other series more occasionally quoted include K (Laws and ordinances), M (General administration), P (Finance), and U (Justice). Documents classed J have come to the Archives by means other than the normal administrative channels. Those marked E sup are documents transferred to the Departmental Archive from the individual communes.

1. ARIEGE

5L 21, 32, 34, 49,   Correspondance des cantons
  also 5L *non classée*
86K 1   Finances: déserteurs et réfractaires
132E sup 5   Registre des délibérations de la commune d'Oust
2R 92–96   Conscription: mesures de haute police
2R 97   Liste de gens arrétées pour falsification de l'état civil
2R 98–104   Dossiers des affaires intéressant les maires et adjoints
4R21   Miquelets, chasseurs des montagnes de l'Ariège

2. BOUCHES-DU-RHONE

L 735, 736, 737   Recrutement
L 862, 2010   Mendicité et assistance

3. CANTAL

L 200–207, 216, 226   Volontaires nationaux (1792–1793)
L 248–255   Levée des 300,000

3. CANTAL (*Continued*)

L 256–257	Première réquisition
L 263–280	Conscription: série cantonale
1R 55, 65	Conscription: tableaux nominatifs
1R 161, 164	Conscription: procès-verbaux cantonaux
1I 186	Conscription: actes de remplacement
2R 365–374	Justice militaire: instructions, correspondance, dossiers

4. DROME

L 198	Troubles: insurrection à Nyons
L 207	Statistique des cantons, an IV–VII
L 347	Levée des 300,000: correspondance avec les districts
L 350	Levée des 200,000 de l'an VII
L 364	Remplacements, an VII
L 368–371	Déserteurs: états et correspondance
L 394–395	Militaires voyageant isolément
L 398	Conduite des militaires: comptes-rendus des communes
L 426	Lettres des généraux de l'Armée d'Italie et des Alpes
L 674, 794, 996	Désertion: correspondance des districts
L 1213, 1247	Désertion: correspondance des cantons
M 1322	Police générale: rapports des sous-préfets, an VIII
1 PM 3	Gardes-forestiers: notes sur leur moralité et capacité
6R 3–3, 20R 1–2	Lettres de soldats

5. HAUTE-GARONNE

L 274	Police générale des cantons: réfractaires et déserteurs
L 2269–2272	Tableaux des insurgés royalistes, an VII–VIII
267 U 4, 268 U 2	Répression de l'insurrection royaliste: procédures

6. GIRONDE

3L 260	Recrutement, volontaires, an IV–VIII
3L 267–269	Déserteurs, insoumis
3L 325	Marins déserteurs
4L231	Déserteurs et insoumis: district de Bordeaux
5L46, 8L 46, 10L 79	Affaires militaires: districts of Bazas, La Réole, Libourne
11L 23, 51, 67, 227, 290, 299, 357	Affaires militaires: cantons, an IV–VIII
2R 284–287	Déserteurs et insoumis: délits et abus
2R 289, 291	Colonne mobile: correspondance, frais des garnisaires

Archives municipales de Bordeaux

D 174, 175, 176   Correspondance du bureau de police de Bordeaux, an IV–VIII

7. MAYENNE

1J 409   Lettres de conscrits de la Mayenne

8. MORBIHAN

L 554, 557, 562, 566, 568, 571, 572	Recrutement, réquisitions, 1790–an II
L 592–594	Déserteurs et réfractaires, 1790–an VIII
Lz 842, 847, 849	Troubles de mars 1793: tribunaux des districts
Ldj 104	Chouannerie, district de Josselin: interrogatoires, an II
Ldj 108	Rassemblement de Bignan: interrogatoires, an II
R 540, 541, 542	Réfractaires, insoumis, volontaires qui se sont mutilés

9. NORD

L 2404, 2405	Rapports des commissaires civils envoyés pour activer la conscription dans le Nord, an VII
L 2632	Correspondance des représentants en mission sur la désertion
L 2633–2637	Déserteurs et réfractaires, 1792–an VII
L 2638	Colonne mobile
L 3502	Marine: recrutement, an II–VIII
L 5704	Désertion, district d'Avesnes
L 6103	Désertion, district de Bergues
L 6165	Marine, correspondance, district de Bergues
1R 64, 67, 68	Mesures pour faire rejoindre les conscrits
1R 211–214	Réfractaires et déserteurs: instructions, correspondance
1R 223, 227, 228	Jugements: fraudes, recels des conscrits
1R 230	Contrôles, extraits mortuaires
1R 231	Faux en matière de conscription
1R 236	Garnisaires: correspondance
1R 238	Colonne mobile: correspondance
5R 1, 4	Gendarmerie: organisation, augmentation des brigades
5R 22	Gendarmerie: demandes d'admission
5R 33	Gendarmerie: rapports au préfet et aux sous-préfets
7R 3, 4	Inscription maritime

10. OISE

(non classée)	Lettres de soldats de l'Empire à leurs familles

11. BAS-RHIN

1L 1415–1417	Déserteurs: dossiers collectifs et individuels
1L 1435	Déserteurs: Strasbourg, 1792–an VII

12. RHONE

1L 216, 217	Première réquisition: levée, désertions
1L 738	Volontaires: correspondance relative aux enrôlements
1L 769	Exemptions de la réquisition

13. SEINE-ET-OISE

1 LR 643	Gendarmerie: dossiers individuels
2 LR 26	District de Mantes: recrutement, 1792–an VIII

13. SEINE-ET-OISE (*Continued*)

2 LR 111–113	District de Versailles: recrutement, 1792–an IV
16L 26	Conscription, désertion: canton de Jouy-en-Josas
36L 39	Conscription, désertion: canton de Sèvres
40L 36	Conscription, désertion: canton de Versailles
IV M 1–3	Renseignements statistiques sur la Seine-et-Oise, an IX
R (non classée)	Affaires militaires: désertion

14. VOSGES

L 533	Affaires militaires: recrutement
L 535	Recrutement: levée en masse
L 536	Déserteurs, réfractaires
L 539	Gendarmerie, Garde nationale
4R 4	Listes de tirages par arrondissement, 1813
8R 1	Actes de remplacements, 1813–1815
39R 1, 2	Affaires militaires: correspondance générale, an IV–1806

Printed Collections

Aulard, F.-A., *Recueil des actes du Comité de Salut Public avec la correspondance officielle des représentants en mission* (Paris, 1889–1895).

Bulletin des lois, for the period of the Revolution and Empire.

Des Pommelles, chevalier, *Observations sur le recrutement et l'emplacement de l'armée active, par cantons ou par départements* (Paris, 1789).

——— *Tableau de la population de toutes les provinces de France* et *Mémoire sur les milices* (Paris, 1789).

Fourastié, V. (ed.), *Cahiers de doléances de la sénéchaussée de Cahors pour les Etats Généraux de 1789* (Cahors, 1908).

Goubert, P. and Denis, M. (eds.). *1789: Les Français ont la parole* (Paris, 1964).

Réimpression de l'Ancien "Moniteur" (Paris, 1840–1845).

SECONDARY SOURCES

Arnold, E. A. jr., "Some observations on the French opposition to Napoleonic conscription, 1804–1806," *French Historical Studies* 4 (1966).

Aron, J.-P., Dumont, P., and Le Roy-Ladurie, E., *Anthropologie du conscrit français d'après les comptes numériques et sommaires du recrutement de l'armée, 1819–1826* (Paris, 1972).

Auvray, M., *Objecteurs, insoumis, déserteurs: histoire des réfractaires en France* (Paris, 1983).

Bastide, L., *Lois militaires sous la Révolution: leur application dans la Corrèze* (Tulle, 1903).

Bergeron, L., *France under Napoleon* (Princeton, 1981).

Bergès, L., "Le civil et l'armée au début du dix-neuvième siècle: la résistance à la conscription dans les départements aquitains, 1798–1814" (*thèse de l'Ecole des Chartes,* 1980).

Bernet, J., "Les troubles sociaux causés par les réquisitions d'hommes dans le District de Compiègne, mars–septembre 1793," *Annales historiques compiègnoises modernes et contemporaines* 2 (1978).

Bernos, C.-E., "Souvenirs de campagne d'un soldat du régiment du Limousin, 1741–1748", *Carnet de la Sabretache* (1902).

Bertaud, J.-P., "Aperçus sur l'insoumission et la désertion à l'époque révolutionnaire," *Bulletin d'histoire économique et sociale de la Révolution Française* (1969).

———— "L'armée française de 1789 à l'an VI—étude sociale" (*thèse de doctorat*, Université de Paris-I).

———— *La Révolution armée: les soldats-citoyens de la Révolution française* (Paris, 1979).

———— *La vie quotidienne des soldats de la Révolution, 1789–1799* (Paris, 1985).

———— "Voies nouvelles pour l'histoire de la Révolution—histoire militaire", *Annales historiques de la Révolution française* 47 (1975).

Best, G., *War and society in Revolutionary Europe, 1770–1870* (London, 1982).

Béteille, R., "Les migrations saisonnières en France sous le premier Empire: essai de synthèse," *Revue d'histoire moderne et contemporaine* 17 (1970).

Bois, J.-P., "Anthropologie du conscrit angevin sous l'Empire," *Annales de Bretagne et des Pays de l'Ouest* 84 (1977).

———— "Conscrits du Maine-et-Loire sous l'Empire: le poids de la conscription, 1806–1814," *Annales de Bretagne et des Pays de l'Ouest* 83 (1976).

Bois, P., *Les paysans de l'Ouest* (Paris, 1962).

Boissonnade, P., *Histoire des volontaires de la Charente, 1791–1794* (Angoulême, 1890).

Braudel, F., *The Mediterranean and the Mediterranean world in the age of Philip II* (London, 1972).

Broers, M. "The restoration of order in Napoleonic Piedmont 1797–1814" (*D. Phil. thesis*, University of Oxford, 1986).

Cameron, I., *Crime and repression in the Auvergne and the Guyenne, 1720–1790* (Cambridge, 1981).

Cardénal, L. de, *Recrutement de l'armée en Périgord pendant la période révolutionnaire, 1789–1800* (Périgueux, 1911).

Carrot, G., "Garde nationale et recrutement de l'armée à Grasse," *Annales du Midi* 89 (1977).

———— 'Le recrutement militaire à Grasse de la fin de l'Ancien Régime à 1814," *Actes du 101ᵉ Congrès des Sociétés savantes* (Lille, 1976).

Castan, N., *Justice et répression en Languedoc à l'époque des Lumières* (Paris, 1980).

Castan, Y., *Honnêteté et relations sociales en Languedoc, 1715–1780* (Paris, 1974).

Castel, J.-A., "L'application de la loi Jourdan dans l'Hérault: les levées directoriales de l'an VII" (*thèse de maîtrise*, Université de Montpellier, 1970).

Centre d'histoire militaire et d'études de défense nationale à Montpellier, *Recrutement, mentalités, société: colloque international d'histoire militaire* (Montpellier, 1974).

Chatelain, A., *Les migrants temporaires en France de 1800 à 1914* (Lille, 1977).

———— "Résistance à la conscription et migrations temporaires sous le premier Empire", *Annales historiques de la Révolution française* 44 (1972).

———— "Valeur et faiblesses d'une source classique—l'enquête des préfets sur les migrations périodiques, 1807–1813—l'exemple du département de la Seine-et-Marne", *Bulletin d'histoire économique et sociale de la Révolution française* (1970).

Chaulanges, M., *Les mauvais numéros* (Paris, 1971).

Chevillot, M., "Rixe à Wassy," *Les cahiers haut-marnais* 140 (1980).

Choury, M., *Les grognards et Napoléon* (Paris, 1968).

Cobb, R. C. *Les armées révolutionnaires* (Paris, 1961–1963).

———— *The police and the people: French popular protest, 1789–1820* (Oxford, 1970).

———— *Reactions to the French Revolution* (Oxford, 1972).

———— *A second identity* (Oxford, 1969).

Corvisier, A., *Armies and societies in Europe, 1494–1789* (Bloomington, Ind., 1979).

———— *L'armée française de la fin du dix-septième siècle au ministère de Choiseul: le soldat* (2 vol. Paris, 1964).

Crépin, A., "Armée de Révolution, armée nouvelle? L'exemple de la Seine-et-Marne" (*thèse de troisième cycle*, Université de Paris-I).

Dalby, J. R., "The French Revolution in a rural environment: the example of the Department of the Cantal, 1789–1794" (*Ph.D. thesis*, University of Manchester, 1981).

Darquenne, R., "La conscription dans le Département de Jemmapes, 1798–1813", *Annales du Cercle Archéologique de Mons* 67 (1968–1970).

Delmas, J., "La patrie en danger: les volontaires nationaux du Cantal", *Revue de la Haute-Auvergne* (1901–1902).

Déprez, E., *Les volontaires nationaux, 1791–1793* (Paris, 1908).

Désert, G., "Le remplacement dans le Calvados sous l'Empire et les monarchies censitaires", *Revue d'histoire économique et sociale* 43 (1965).

Dessat, L.-A. and de l'Estoile, C.-J., *Origine des armées révolutionnaires et impériales d'après les archives départementales de l'Ariège* (Paris, 1906).

Dupâquier, J., "Problèmes démographiques de la France napoléonienne," *Revue d'histoire moderne et contemporaine* 17 (1970).

Emsley, C., "The impact of war and military participation on Britain and France, 1792–1815," in Emsley C., and Walvin J. (ed.), *Artisans, peasants, and proletarians 1760–1860: essays presented to Gwyn A. Williams* (London, 1985).

———— "La marechaussée à la fin de l'Ancien Régime: note sur la composition du corps", *Revue d'histoire moderne et contemporaine* 33 (1986).

———— *Policing and its context, 1750–1870* (London, 1983).

Erckmann, E., and Chatrian, L., *The history of a conscript of 1813* (London, 1909).

Forrest, A., *The French Revolution and the poor* (Oxford, 1981).

———— "Military recruitment and the popular classes in Revolutionary France", in Butel P. (ed.), *Sociétés et groupes sociaux en Aquitaine et en Angleterre* (Bordeaux, 1979).

Gallaher, J. G., "Recruitment in the District of Poitiers, 1793," *French Historical Studies* 3 (1963–1964).

Gendron, F., *La jeunesse dorée* (Quebec, 1979).

Gillet, D., "Etude de la désertion dans les armées royales à l'époque de Louis XIV" (*mémoire de maîtrise*, Université de Paris-I, 1973).

Giraud, M., *Levées d'hommes et acheteurs de biens nationaux dans la Sarthe en 1793* (Le Mans, 1920).

Girault, P.-R., *Mes campagnes sous la Révolution et l'Empire* (Paris, 1983).

Goron, L., "Les migrations saisonnières dans les départements pyrénéens au début du dix-neuvième siècle," *Revue géographique des Pyrénées et du Sud-Ouest* 4 (1933).

Gross, J.-P., *Saint-Just: sa politique et ses missions* (Paris, 1976).

Gutton, J.-P., *La sociabilité villageoise dans l'ancienne France: solidarités et voisinages du seizième au dix-huitième siècle* (Paris, 1979).

Hauteclocque, G. de, "Le Pas-de-Calais sous l'administration préfectorale du Baron de la Chaise," *Mémoires de l'Académie des Sciences, Lettres, et Arts d'Arras*, 2e série, 25 (1894).

Herlaut, A., *Le colonel Bouchotte, ministre de la Guerre en l'an II* (Paris, 1946).

Higgs, D., *Ultraroyalism in Toulouse from its origins to the Revolution of 1830* (Baltimore, 1973).

Houdaille, J., "Pertes de l'armée de terre sous le premier Empire, d'après les registres matricules," *Population* 27 (1972).

———— "Le problème des pertes de la guerre," *Revue d'histoire moderne et contemporaine* 17 (1970).

Hufton, O., *The poor of eighteenth-century France, 1750–1789* (Oxford, 1974).

Hutt, M., *Chouannerie and counterrevolution: Puisaye, the princes, and the British government in the 1790s* (Cambridge, 1983).

Jacquot, P., 'Les bataillons de volontaires en Haute-Marne, 1791–1799" (*thèse d'Université*, Université de Dijon).

Jones, P. M., "Parish, seigneurie and the community of inhabitants in southern central France during the eighteenth and nineteenth centuries," *Past and Present* 91 (1981).

———— *Politics and rural society—the southern Massif central, c. 1750–1880* (Cambridge, 1985).

Kaplan, S. L., *Provisioning Paris: merchants and millers in the grain and flour trade during the eighteenth century* (Ithaca, 1984).

Kennett, L., *The French armies in the Seven Years' War* (Durham, N.C., 1967).

Lacouture, J., *Le mouvement royaliste dans le Sud-Ouest, 1797–1800* (Hossegor, 1932).

Langlois, C., "Complots, propagandes et répression policière en Bretagne sous l'Empire, 1806–1807," *Annales de Bretagne* 78 (1971).

———— *Le diocèse de Vannes au dix-neuvième siècle, 1800–1830* (Paris, 1974).

Laporte, P., "La milice d'Auvergne, 1688–1791," *Revue d'Auvergne* 71 (1957).

Lefebvre, G., *Les paysans du Nord* (Paris, 1924).

Le Goff, T.J.A., *Vannes and its region: a study of town and country in eighteenth-century France* (Oxford, 1981).

———— and Sutherland, D., "The social origins of counterrevolution in western France," *Past and Present* 99 (1983).

Legrand, R., "A propos des désertions sous la Révolution et l'Empire," *Revue du Nord* 46 (1964).

———— *Le recrutement des armées et les désertions, 1791–1815* (Abbéville, 1957).

———— *Vie et société en Picardie maritime, 1780–1820* (Paris, 1986).

Léonard, E.-G., *L'armée et ses problèmes au dix-huitième siècle* (Paris, 1958).

Lévy, J.-M., "L'effort de guerre dans le département du Rhône et dans les départements voisins au cours des dix premières années de la Révolution," *Cahiers d'histoire* (1965).

Lewis, G., *Life in Revolutionary France* (London, 1972).

———— *The second Vendée: the continuity of counter-revolution in the department of the Gard, 1789–1815* (Oxford, 1978).

———— and Lucas, C. (ed.), *Beyond the Terror: essays in French regional and social history, 1794–1815* (Cambridge, 1983).

Lucas, C., "The problem of the Midi in the French Revolution," *Transactions of the Royal Historical Society* 28 (1978).

Lynn, J. A., *The bayonets of the Republic: motivation and tactics in the army of Revolutionary France, 1791–1794* (Urbana, Ill., 1984).

Lyons, M., "Politics and patois—the linguistic policy of the French Revolution", *Australian Journal of French Studies* 18 (1981).

Lytle, S., "Robespierre, Danton, and the *levée en masse*," *Journal of Modern History* 30 (1958).

Maltby, R., "Le brigandage dans la Drôme, 1795–1803," *Bulletin d'archéologie et de statistique de la Drôme* 79 (1973).

———— "Crime and the local community in France: the department of the Drôme, 1770–1820" (*D.Phil. thesis,* University of Oxford, 1981).

Manry, A. G., "Réfractaires et déserteurs dans le Puy-de-Dôme sous le Directoire, le Consulat et l'Empire," *Revue d'Auvergne* 72 (1958).

Marcoux, H., "Déserteurs et réfractaires dans l'Yonne au temps de Napoléon," *L'Echo d'Auxerre* (1968).

Marion, M., *Dictionnaire des institutions de la France aux 17e et 18e siècles* (Paris, 1923).

Maureau, A., "Le remplacement militaire de l'an VIII à 1814 d'après les registres de notables d'Avignon—aspect juridique et social," *Revue de l'Institut Napoléon* 131 (1975).

Mazauric, C., "Quelques réflexions sur les relations entre occupants et occupés dans les pays vendéen et chouan pendant la Révolution française," *Occupants, occupés, 1792–1815* (Brussels, 1969).

Meynier, A., "L'armée en France sous la Révolution et le Premier Empire," *Revue d'études militaires* (1932).

Mignot, M., "La conscription dans le département de la Meuse sous le Directoire," *Annales de l'Est* 6 (1955).

Moody, W. S., "The introduction of military conscription in Napoleonic Europe, 1798–1812" (*Ph.D. thesis,* Duke University, 1971).

Morvan, J., *Le soldat impérial, 1800–1814* (2 vol. Paris, 1904).

Mouillard, B., *Le recrutement de l'armée révolutionnaire dans le Puy-de-Dôme* (Paris, 1926).

Nicolas, J. (ed.), *Mouvements populaires et conscience sociale, XVIᵉ–XIXᵉ siècles* (Paris, 1985).

Ogès, L., "La conscription et l'esprit public dans le Finistère sous le Consulat et l'Empire," *Mémoires de la Société d'histoire et d'archéologie de Bretagne* (1962).

Perrot, J.-C., "La population du Département de Calvados sous la Révolution et l'Empire," *Contributions à l'histoire démographique de la Révolution française,* 2e series (1965).

Pétigny, X. de, *Un bataillon de volontaires: le troisième bataillon de Maine-et-Loire, 1792–1796* (Angers, 1908).

Petitfrère, C., *Le Général Dupuy et sa correspondance* (Paris, 1962).

———— *Les Vendéens d'Anjou* (Paris, 1981).

Pillorget, R., *Les mouvements insurrectionnels de Provence entre 1596 et 1715* (Paris, 1975).

Reinhard, M., "Nostalgie et service militaire pendant la Révolution," *Annales historiques de la Révolution française* 30 (1958).

Richard, J., "La levée des 300,000 hommes et les troubles de mars 1793 en Bourgogne", *Annales de Bourgogne* 132 (1961).

Rousseau, F., "La désobéissance militaire au dix-neuvième siècle: déserteurs et insoumis héraultais" (*thèse de doctorat,* Université de Montpellier-III, 1985).

Sangnier, G., *Le brigandage dans le Pas-de-Calais de 1789 à 1815* (Blangermont, 1962).

———— *La désertion dans le Pas-de-Calais de 1792 à 1802* (Blangermont, 1972).

Schnapper, B., *Le remplacement militaire en France* (Paris, 1968).

Scott, S. F., "The regeneration of the line army during the French Revolution," *Journal of Modern History* 42 (1970).

———— *The response of the Royal Army to the French Revolution: the role and development of the line army, 1787–93* (Oxford, 1978).

————— "Les soldats de l'armée de ligne en 1793," *Annales historiques de la Révolution française* 44 (1972).

Serrant, H., *Le service du recrutement de 1789 à nos jours* (Paris, 1935).

Soboul, A., *L'armée nationale sous la Révolution, 1789-1794* (Paris, 1945).

Sutherland, D., *The Chouans: the social origins of popular counter-revolution in Upper Brittany, 1770-96* (Oxford, 1982).

————— *France, 1789-1815: revolution and counter-revolution* (London, 1985).

Tilly, C., *The Vendée* (London, 1964).

Tulard, J., *Napoléon ou le Mythe du sauveur* (Paris, 1977).

Vachin, H., "Les Lozériens dans la Grande Armée," *Revue du Gévaudan* (1973).

Vallée, G., *La conscription dans le département de la Charente, 1798-1807* (Paris, 1936).

————— "Population et conscription de 1798 à 1814," *Revue de l'Institut Napoléon* (1938).

————— "Le remplacement militaire en Charente sous le régime de la conscription," *Révolution française* 80 (1927).

Vermale, F., "La désertion dans l'Armée des Alpes aprés le 9 thermidor," *Annales révolutionnaires* 6 (1913).

Viallaneix, P., and Ehrard, J. (eds.), *La bataille, l'armée, la gloire, 1745-1871* (Clermont-Ferrand, 1985).

Viard, P., "La désignation des conscrits appelés à marcher de 1800 à 1813 dans le département du Nord," *Revue du Nord* (1924-1926).

Vidalenc, J., "La conscription dans la Seine-inférieure en 1830," *Revue d'histoire moderne et contemporaine* 20 (1973).

————— "Les conséquences sociales de la conscription en France, 1798-1848," *Cahiers internationaux d'histoire économique et sociale* 5 (1975).

————— "La désertion dans le départment du Calvados sous le premier Empire," *Revue d'histoire moderne et contemporaine* 6 (1959).

Waquet, J., "L'insoumission et la désertion sous le Consulat et le premier Empire vues à travers les états d'arrestations," *Actes du 93e Congrès des Sociétés savantes* (Tours, 1968).

————— "Réflexions sur les émotions populaires et le recrutement militaire de 1799 à 1831", *Actes du 91e Congrès national des Sociétés savantes* (Rennes, 1966).

————— "La société civile devant l'insoumission et la désertion à l'époque de la conscription militaire (1798-1814), d'après la correspondance du Ministre de l'Intérieur", *Bibliothèque de l'Ecole des Chartes* 126 (1968).

Williams, A., *The police of Paris, 1718-1789* (Baton Rouge, 1979).

Woloch, I., *The French veteran from the Revolution to the Restoration* (Chapel Hill, 1979).

—————, *Jacobin legacy: The Democratic movement under the Directory* (Princeton, 1970).

————— 3 "Napoleonic conscription: state power and civil society," *Past and Present* 111 (1986).

Index